MIDLOTHIAN PUBLIC LIBRARY

D1129458

Midlothian
Public Library
14701 S. Kenton Ave.
Midlothian, IL 60445

BALANCING ACT

ALSO BY MARTIN GOTTFRIED

A Theater Divided

Opening Nights

Broadway Musicals

Jed Harris: The Curse of Genius

Live and in Person: The Great Entertainers

All His Jazz: The Life and Death of Bob Fosse

More Broadway Musicals

Sondheim

Nobody's Fool: The Lives of Danny Kaye

George Burns and the Hundred-Year Dash

BALANCING ACT

THE AUTHORIZED BIOGRAPHY OF ANGELA LANSBURY

MARTIN GOTTFRIED

LITTLE, BROWN AND COMPANY
BOSTON NEW YORK LONDON

First Edition

Library of Congress Cataloging-in-Publication Data
Gottfried, Martin.
Balancing act : the authorized biography of Angela Lansbury / Martin Gottfried. — 1st ed.
p. cm.
Includes index.
ISBN 0-316-32225-3
1. Lansbury, Angela, 1925– . 2. Actors — United States — Biography. I. Title.
PN2287.L2845G68 1998
792'.028'092 — dc21
[b] 98-38751

10 9 8 7 6 5 4 3 2 1

MV-NY

Book design by Barbara Werden Design

Printed in the United States of America

For my darling and magical Margo, who has given me inspiration, serenity, and a happiness that I never believed possible.

CONTENTS

PREFACE

I CHOSE Angela Lansbury as the subject of a biography because she was an exceptional actor, one whose career could well represent the courage and vulnerability, the survivalism and grandeur, the total commitment of all actors at their best. As a professional drama critic, I wanted to pay tribute to the players who had given me a lifetime of unexpected magic. I also chose Angela Lansbury because she had become an American icon, and so her life had taken on a unique resonance. I chose her, too, because, having known her personally for some twenty years, I was aware that she was a fascinating and admirable woman — not just gifted but intelligent, articulate, and adult.

She was interested in collaborating on a book about her life as an actor, but the production schedule of her popular television series, *Murder, She Wrote,* was exhausting, and during its summer breaks, she wanted only to rest at her second home in Ireland. When the series finally came to an end in the spring of 1996, she wrote to say, "I think it's time for our book."

An as-told-to autobiography was fleetingly considered, but I did not relish writing in her voice, and she wanted no part of the exposure that such books require. This conservatism of character, I would soon learn, reflected a profound sense of privacy, which ran deeper than mere reserve. Nevertheless, she did want to share her fifty years of thoughts about and experiences with acting; she wanted to honor the legacy inherited from her grandfather, the British statesman George Lansbury; and she had a philosophy to express about the importance of balance in her life. In fact, the title "Balancing Act" came at her suggestion.

It is not related to her birth sign of Libra. While she is curious about astrology, her own balancing act, she feels, is a conscious commitment to maintaining values and perspective, "the balancing of the real life with the artificial aspects of fame and success."

An "authorized biography" was the form we settled upon, and as our interviews began, her memory proved formidable. A single question could prompt a half-hour reply that was all but formally composed in complete paragraphs. In addition, she encouraged her husband, family, friends, and colleagues to speak with me freely and at length. She gave me access to her files, papers, and correspondence. She not only assured me of freedom to be critical of her work, she positively relished it. While there was no discussion of approval, I promised to show her the manuscript before publication. "If I say it," she anticipated, "you are going to write it. But if it is totally out of line and wrong, I'm going to tell you."

A man who is writing the story of a woman's life must seek to understand and even capture the female sensibility. It is a formidable challenge, not dissimilar from that confronting a novelist or playwright who is trying to create a character of the opposite sex. The proposition is to leap the gender gap, a subject in which Angela was particularly interested. On several occasions, she had expressed disappointment that Jessica Fletcher, her virtual alter ego in *Murder, She Wrote,* thought "like a man." The male writers of the show, she felt, "just [didn't] get it." During one of our interviews, in fact, she glanced up, raised a quizzical eyebrow in my direction, and added, "I'm not so sure that you get it either. I see that mystified look on your face."

As a biographical subject, Angela posed other challenges. Her public image was practically saintly while, in my experience, the best subjects were not only dead males but mean and nasty ones. Interesting men and women — powerful, successful, or accomplished ones — usually develop aggressive egos. Smart people tend to be opinionated or impatient, even downright unlikable — but they are fascinating, while nice people can be so bland. Lansbury gave the lie to that. She is as intelligent and decent, as warm, honest, and mature as she seems on television, but she is also tough, sharp-witted, and funny. And complicated. In short, she is a layered person who reveals herself carefully and only when she has fully prepared the entrance. It is small wonder that she is a character actress.

Here, then, is a woman who has not only kept her personal life from being overbalanced by a very public life; she has also kept a specific set of personal values in balance with a profound commitment to acting. That commitment is based on a shining talent which she believes was simply given her by the gods. It is a talent that she considers her emotional foundation, "a rock of stability at the center," and she feels the presence of this talent the same way that we might know we are right- or left-handed. She describes it matter-of-factly as "a repeating ability to produce a result which kept me always in the forefront artistically if I was doing something that was meaningful and had substance." And so she is neither falsely modest, which would insult the talent, nor does she take it for granted, which would abuse it.

"Having that rock at the center," she told me, "has been my salvation, because even though, to outward appearances, mine has been a life filled with success and happiness and joy and laughter and attainment, what was going on behind the apparent joys and happiness was turmoil in my private life. The only way I could deal with it was by having this rock which represented stability. The one thing I knew that was right and true and possible."

As might be expected, she is a tough judge of her own work. Although she has had an immensely productive career, she frets that she might have done more, particularly on the stage, which is the medium she takes most seriously. And she plans to do still more there. She also continues to crave a great leading role in a movie — something she feels she has never had. It is as if she is still hurting from those early years in Hollywood, when she was routinely relegated to playing secondary roles. As for the vast body of her movies and television films, I have dealt with only those which, from my point of view, were most relevant to her work or life. This is a biography, not a résumé. A full listing of her stage, film, and television work can be found at the end of the book.

Angela Lansbury has had a career of astonishing and perhaps unparalleled success in three media, each at a climactic time in its history. She was a movie actress for two decades in the glory days of the Hollywood studio system. She was a Broadway leading lady in the last decade of glamorous musical comedy. She was a television star in the final era of network dominance, when an audience of many millions could still be held in thrall in a nationwide living room. It was, of course, in the television series *Murder, She Wrote* that she became one of the best-loved and most-admired women in America — indeed, in the world — and yet, she has remained her own person.

She told me at the outset, "I want it to be believable, and not a whitewash. I've got my problems and I know that. I'm not the easiest person to live with." When she read the manuscript, she certainly did tell me where she thought it was "wrong" or simply too invasive of her family's privacy, but never, not once, did that relate to herself, personally or professionally, nor did she ever complain about how she was being characterized. It was the privacy of her husband, her children, and her grandchildren that concerned her. As for herself, she has a personal aversion to flattery. After one particularly draining back-and-forth, I half-joked that I'd send her two dozen roses in the morning.

"Don't give me that bullshit," she snapped. "You're dealing with a seventy-four-year-old battle-ax."

If she and I had to do battle at times, we did battle, but when the dust cleared, we were all the closer for it, and closer, I believe, to the truth as well. When she first agreed to participate in the book, she said, "It's a journey, you know. It should make an interesting read."

I hope so.

Martin Gottfried
New York City
August 1998

BALANCING ACT

CHAPTER 1

GL'S GRANDDAUGHTER

AS the stage manager taps on her dressing room door backstage at the Winter Garden Theatre, Angela Lansbury puts the final touches to her makeup. Through the tinny backstage loudspeakers, she can hear the orchestra tuning up. With one final glance in the mirror, she pushes away from the table, rises, and walks out of that door for the last time, heading down the metal spiral stairs that lead to the stage level.

For two years, this theater has been at the center of her life. The notion of a last performance in *Mame* had always seemed remote, but then so had being a glamorous Broadway star. Yet Mame Dennis has become her identity, or at least one of her identities.

The centerpiece of *Mame* is its title song, a huge production number performed as a toast to the title character. It begins with a hush, yet also a promise of big things to come as a banjo strums the catchy Jerry Herman melody. All is still on the stage, although it is filled to bursting with a big plantation house setting and an ensemble of singers and dancers. Their clothes are ravishingly absurd. The girls wear the costumes of a plantation operetta, with rainbow-colored hoopskirts, bonnets, and parasols. The boys (all Broadway chorus people are called boys and girls) are dressed for riding to the foxes, in scarlet jackets with swallowtails, white riding breeches, high black boots, and top hats. As intended by the designers, they look like no reality that ever was, but rather, the characters in a Hollywood movie of the 1930s.

The song "Mame" is a celebration, ostensibly of the heroine herself, but that is only an excuse, for it is really an homage to all musical comedy divas, as personified by the actress who is playing Mame. Even though she does not sing one note of this song in her honor, she is at its center and she has to have earned the adulation or else the number will not work.

The ensemble sings the opening lines with an easy hush, moving only their arms, swinging them gently.

You coax the blues right out of the horn, Mame,
You charm the husk right off of the corn, Mame,

Tomorrow, Angela Lansbury will be going home to Los Angeles. Tonight, May 31, 1968, she is before an audience of fifteen hundred people, their faces shining in the reflected glow of the stage light that bathes her in luxurious blues and pinks. They absorb the massed colors and the energy of the spectacle. Now, as the ensemble is singing, all attention is focused on Angela.

You've got the banjoes strummin'
And plunkin' out a tune to beat the band,

She takes a stroll past her handsome male dancers and, one fellow at a time, they drop to a knee and sweep off their hats in salute. Each of them looks at her adoringly. The number is held in check for tension's sake. The dancers still take only small steps, and use their arms sparingly. Their only motion is a rocking from one side to the other. It is the audience that is stirring, in response to being prodded for excitement.

You've brought the cakewalk back into style, Mame,
You make the weepin' willow tree smile, Mame,

The music rises a half step with each chorus, and with each ascension the dance movement grows more pronounced with bolder steps. The chorus struts and kicks in tight movements, their precision and uniformity magnetic in the light and color.

In her long movie career, Angela has never before played a leading role, nor has she ever been given the star part in a stage play. With *Mame* she has been playing not only the lead role, but the *title* role in a big Broadway musical. She has become everything that the strange word "star" means to a performer — outstanding, glorified, admired, and spotlit at the center of an evening's universe.

It has made her feel, for the first time in her life, beautiful and sexy. Gone is the dowdy, overweight British girl she has always thought she was. In that girl's place is the toast of Broadway, a woman in the best condition of her life, slim, sinewy, and muscled, with a new hairstyle to show for it, a boyish cut long enough to let her gold hair flash in the light as she flies on the arms of her escort dancers.

Mame has had a liberating effect on her personality. She has become a star offstage, too, glamorous wherever she goes, and she feels comfortable in the role, comfortable exposed, and now she is dancing to prove it.

As the number builds, she leaps into the arms of her supporting boys and, carried aloft, kicks her legs and opens her arms wide, taking in the cheers, and the ovation.

You came, you saw, you conquered
And absolutely nothing is the same.
Your special fascination'll
Prove to be inspirational,
We think you're just sensational, Mame.

These triple rhymes, set on musical phrases that rise half tones, do double stage work, the rhymes setting a rhythm and the rise stimulating a tingle. A wave of spinal shivers sweeps through the theater. It is an effect that has been cannily achieved. Angela can now ride upon the exhilaration.

You've made me feel alive again,
You've given us the drive again,
To make the South revive again,

The number has burst into a full dance, a simulated fox hunt as the men "gallop" in a big circle, with Angela at its center, and when it comes to an end at last, the coda is unique, a marvelous series of cascading, modulating chords.

Mame, Mame, Mame, Mame, Mame.

At the curtain call, Angela appears at the top of a staircase. When the director first told her that she was going to have to walk down those stairs, she knew that he wasn't just talking about the stairs. He was talking about taking command of the entire show. She knew what he meant but she did not know how to do it. For how does a reserved and private person who has developed imitation into the high art of character acting become an exhibitionist who can exploit her self in a public performance? That was what walking down a staircase was really about. Angela Lansbury, who keeps herself to herself, was going to have to exude charisma and create excitement. In theater parlance, she was going to have to *take stage,* as the star of a Broadway musical had to do. If Lansbury was ever going to fulfill her lifelong dream of being a star, this self-effacing woman was going to have to glorify herself; this introverted woman was going to have to explode.

She came through, even if she had to find her own way to do that. *Mame* was a big hit, and to a great extent it was because of her. She imbued its show business flash with a warmth and a humanity rare in the callow world of musical comedy. In return, the show gave her the flamboyance, the glamour, and the sexuality she never knew she had for the first forty years of her life. And because of what the show released in her as well as the reputation it created for her, she would know how to — and would be — a star for the rest of her life.

So, naturally, when she stood at the top of that staircase for the last time, it was as a vastly different woman than the one who had first taken an apprehensive glance down the flight of stairs toward the abyss below.

With her appearance at the top now, the audience roars its congratulations. She is wearing a spectacular fur-trimmed white dress that was designed expressly for this moment. She pauses in the spotlight, so that the applause can be released. Then, with the orchestra in full fanfare, she strides down the stairs in radiant command.

This audience knows it is watching Angela Lansbury's last performance at the Winter Garden as Mame. It gives her an ovation that threatens to lift the roof right off the top of the theater. She takes her bow at center stage, her fellow players arrayed behind her. The cheering resounds through the theater as the audience rises to its feet. The musical director reaches up from the orchestra pit and hands her a bouquet of roses. She would remember imagining that the air is filled with flowers. Her eyes are moistening and sparkling.

There are performers who live only in the show world. Lansbury is comfortable on that side of the footlights. On the other side of them is the front of the house, the rest of the world, and she has a life there, as well. That is the equation of her life.

As tears stream down her cheeks in farewell to her beloved company of players and to this transcending experience, some of the actors look to her instead of at the audience. It is a performers' moment, and when, after all the curtain calls are over, and after the applause has faded away, she says good-bye to them, she tells them, "Happiness is being your 'Mame,'" and wishes that it could only be that simple.

Angela Brigid Lansbury was the first child of Edgar and Moyna Lansbury. The couple lived in a ground-floor garden flat on Hamilton Terrace in central London's Regents Park. From there, Edgar drove to work every day in the Ford he had bought to replace his old Essex. But the office took a second place to his family, which included Moyna, her daughter Isolde, and now Brigid. That was the name by which Angela would be called for the first seventeen years of her life.

Edgar was smitten with his wife, and had been ever since he'd met her. At the time, he was a thirty-eight-year-old bachelor businessman and she a twenty-six-year-old Irish beauty with a three-year-old daughter and a husband named Reginald Denham. Unfortunately for Reginald, he was in Ireland when his wife ran into Edgar in London, and ironically, their affair began just as Denham's own career was blossoming at long last. But luck just wasn't on his side. His work only separated them the more.

When his wife announced that she was leaving, he was hurt but remained a gentleman to the core. As he described it,

> Somewhere around March 1923, Moyna asked me for a divorce; she had fallen in love with someone else. When the actual moment of the break came, it was a bitter shock; we had been through so many ups and downs together. But nevertheless, I felt that it was only right for us to call it a day if she so wished it. One can't cling to something that doesn't exist just for the sake of clinging. Sometime in October, Moyna left and took Isolde with her.

Adultery was the common basis for divorce in England at the time. In his suit, Reginald named Edgar as co-respondent, but he was neither nasty then nor bitter later. Even after the decree was granted the following year, he would remain helpful to his ex-wife and positively amiable toward her new husband. Perhaps more important, at least to Moyna the actress, Reginald Denham would insist ever after that she was "the best Desdemona I have ever seen."

Moyna and Edgar were married in 1924, one year after the divorce.

Moyna Macgill had been born Charlotte Lillian McIldowie in Belfast, Northern Ireland, on December 10, 1895. Her mother was the former Elizabeth ("Cissy") Mageean, and her father, Willie McIldowie, was a well-to-do solicitor and a director of the Belfast Opera. That position, apparently, was the source of the daughter's interest in theatrics.

She was still in her teens when George Pearson, a director of silent pictures, discovered her on London's underground subway. After appearing in several of his films, she turned to the stage, getting the role of an understudy in James Barrie's *Dear Brutus.* Then, in 1918, when she was twenty-three, she made her professional stage debut at the Globe Theatre in a minor play called *Love in a Cottage.*

The role inaugurated a first-class acting career. Moyna would never be a star, but she did become a leading actress of her day, a serious one and a busy professional. Appearing in boulevard comedies, melodramas, and the occasional high drama, she played opposite such considerable actors as Godfrey Terle, Herbert Marshall, and Philip Merivale. She was in Eugene O'Neill's *The Great God Brown* with John Gielgud. In one of the plays she did (*Interference*), the leading man, Gerald Du Maurier, suggested she take the professional name Moyna Macgill, which would invariably be misspelled as "MacGill" or "McGill." Her Desdemona, so impressive to Reginald Denham, was played opposite the Othello of Basil Rathbone. In short, she was an actor of unassailably professional standing, and a familiar face on the London stage.

Meanwhile, work for Edgar was running the Stratford Veneer Mills, which was his mother's family business. Her maiden name was Elizabeth Jane Brine, and the mill had been founded by her father, Isaac Brine. But when she was married in 1880, her husband, George Lansbury, declined to work for his father-in-law. George had other interests and higher, or at least different, values, and Elizabeth supported him in that. She was a wife whose first concern was her husband, and George called the marriage, "the most blessed and fortunate thing that ever happened to me."

George Lansbury was special from the very start. Born in 1859, the son of a railway worker, he grew up in the interracial and interdenominational East End of London, which is still one of the city's poorest areas. His first job was as a manual laborer, unloading coal trucks onto barges. At twenty-one, after marrying Elizabeth, he took a job managing a coffee bar. Even when the couple was struggling to care for the three daughters who had been born in rapid succession, he refused to go to work in her father's considerable business. Instead, he migrated with his family to Queensland, Australia.

His career choices were no better there, and after struggling through a year as a common laborer, he had little choice but to bring his brood back to London and bow to the inevitable. He accepted a position at Stratford Veneer Mills, which continued to prosper under his management despite his apparent disinclination toward capitalistic enterprise. Not that he was an incompetent executive; rather, his sympathies and identification were with the working class.

George and Elizabeth found a tiny, four-room house in the borough of Bow, deep in the East End of London. This was in the heart of Cockney country, and it was at Bow's church that the Lansburys worshipped. According to legend, anyone could say he was a Cockney if he'd been "born within the sound of Bow bells." It happened that those chimes could be heard from five miles away but as George Lansbury said, "Any Londoner worth his salt would want to call himself a Cockney."

If two adults and three children in four rooms made for cramped quarters, Elizabeth's fertility threatened to burst the little house apart. She ultimately presented George with five more daughters and four sons, for a total of twelve children. Of these, Edgar Lansbury was born near the middle. (For the record, the girls were Annie, Constance, Doreen, Dorothy, Nellie, Daisy, Bessie, and Violet, and the other boys were Bill, George, Jr., who died young, and Eric.)

Despite his responsibility for this considerable family, George found time to be elected to the Borough Council of Poplar in 1892 at the age of thirty-three. Poplar was in the wharf and warehouse district of his home base in Bow, and although the position of councilman was not a full-time or paying office, it became his passion. He might have been a businessman by necessity, but by choice he was in the public service, with a commitment to improving the life and lot of the working man.

Within a decade he became a crusader for his constituents' rights and, when his principles were challenged, a firebrand. He was jailed in 1913 for urging women to, if necessary, "burn and destroy" for the right to vote. He was briefly imprisoned again in 1919 (this time along with his son Edgar, now an activist, too), for urging constituents not to pay property taxes, which he considered excessive. Finally, he was roundly criticized — but not jailed — for wearing his hat in the presence of Queen Mary (outdoors notwithstanding).

George Lansbury served on the Poplar Borough Council for thirty-two years while his children were growing up and was eventually elected the borough's mayor. Given his constituency, he devoted himself particularly to labor problems, developing work-relief programs and ways of improving conditions in the workhouses. Retiring from the lumber business in 1924, he decided at the advanced age of sixty-five to run for Parliament, and represent Poplar in the House of Commons. His victory began a political career that by 1931 would make George Lansbury the head of the Labour Party and, ultimately, an eminent man in Great Britain.

When his father-in-law died, the management of Stratford Veneer Mills had succeeded to George. Now it went to his sons, and the business continued to thrive. One of their proudest achievements was supplying the handsome wood veneers for the new luxury liner the *Queen Mary*. The Lansbury boys — Bill, Eric, and Edgar — seemed to be sailing along too, right up until the moment that the stock markets crashed in New York and throughout Europe. But this was one instance where a class system was useful. An Englishman might be ruined financially but nothing could change his class. Whatever the Lansburys lost, it was not their dignity.

Edgar was a big man, five feet eleven inches and broad through the shoulders. Moyna was smaller, not only in height (she was five feet six inches) but in her bone structure, although she would always battle a weight problem. Worse, and to her everlasting grief, she was cursed with heavy thighs. Even so, Angela would think "her face was always so beautiful that it didn't really matter." Much of that had to do with her style and flair. "She just had a look about her."

This vision of her mother was one of the earliest memories for Angela Brigid Lansbury, who was born on October 16, 1925. Angela would later become convinced that Moyna preferred calling her by her middle name, "Brigid," because it was more Irish; besides, "Angel" was Edgar's pet name for Moyna. Ultimately, Angela would value both of her ancestries. "The Irish in me is where I got my sense of comedy and whimsy," she'd say. "As for the English half, that's my reserved side. . . . But put me on a stage and the Irish comes out. The combination makes for a good mix."

Even "Brigid" didn't always stick. Apparently Moyna was brought up to believe that no woman should be without a pet name. As she herself had been "Chattie" (pronounced "Shattie") to her family and "Tats" to her father, so she became "Moe" to her children. Angela was called "Bids" or "Bidsie," and Isolde was "Zil."

Isolde was an understandably unhappy child, wrenched as she'd been from her home and her father. Expressing her resentment by being selfish and argumentative, the little girl became even more difficult after Angela was born. Meanwhile, Moyna Macgill continued to act on the London stage until she again became pregnant. Then she quit for the duration and on January 12, 1930, gave birth to twin boys, Edgar, Jr., and Bruce. She briefly resumed her acting career, but then decided to retire temporarily from the theater and tend to her young family.

Angela, who would come to think of her childhood as a frequently depressing time, vividly remembers the first appearance of her twin brothers, because they "took the attention away, *big.*" She was, as she says, a timid little girl, one who "always hid behind my mother's skirt when meeting strangers." Now she even lost her nanny — Amy Wallis — who had taken care of her since she was six months old. "Amy-Nan" found caring for the newborn boys too much of an added burden, and so a new woman was hired, a trained children's nanny named Pauline Humphries. Angela found her "very large and jolly, but it was an enormous adjustment to lose my Amy-Nan." That feeling was reciprocated, for Amy Wallis continued to send presents to Angela and Isolde — chocolate bars and their favorite sweets, licorice Allsorts and Wine Gums, for which Angela would have a weakness all her life.

As for Isolde's problems, by the time the twins were born, she was ten years old and more secure. She went by her father's name, as Isolde Denham, but she also accepted her half sister. In fact, whenever that term was used, both she and Angela would insist that they were not half sisters, but "complete sisters." Isolde even shared her deepest dream with Angela — to become an actress like their mother, and a dancer, too.

Dance and music were constant presences in the Lansbury home. A friend who was an expert dancer came to the house to give Edgar and Moyna tango lessons and to teach the two little girls how to tap-dance. They fixed themselves up in satin shorts and red tap shoes, rolled up the carpets in the foyer, and had a class. As for music, Angela would be enchanted when her mother sat down at the Broadmoor piano to struggle her way through a piece called "The Butterfly." Perhaps there were lots of wrong notes, but the manner was grand. Edgar was musical, too, and especially enjoyed the recordings of the violinist Fritz Kreisler. He also loved opera, and would play records of Grace Moore, Caruso, and Gigli on the living room gramophone.

Finally, Angela worked up the nerve to try the piano, and even taught herself how to play simple melodies by ear. "My first success," she remembers proudly, "was the ability to play the *Coppelia* waltz on the black keys. And with both hands!"

Formal piano lessons followed, and soon she was able to read music and play from it on the good piano in the drawing room — the Bechstein upright that Moyna's mother had given them. "As my piano playing improved I was allowed to practice on that piano. I adored playing, and practicing was no problem for me. I wanted to learn the music so desperately! My parents were very encouraging."

She was a sensitive child and found that music had a profound emotional effect on her, although not always for the good. "Some music I found depressing and made me cry. I simply couldn't bear Beethoven and Brahms. There was a funereal sound that depressed me beyond words."

She cheered up by listening to the family collection of popular recordings, "discs by the great British musical comedy star Jessie Matthews and Bing Crosby." Crosby's theme song, which began, "When the blue of the night/Meets the gold of the day," became a favorite of hers and Isolde's. They would perform it at the family's "home entertainments," with Isolde inventing the choreography and the two girls dressing up as butterflies, with wings of gauze and dresses of crepe paper. Then they would proceed to sing the song with the misheard lyrics "When the cool of the night/Meets the dawn of the day," as children so often do.

These home entertainments were popular at festive times like Christmas and Easter, and when the twin boys were old enough, they, too, were recruited into the shows that Moyna put on for the uncles, aunts, and cousins who were seldom seen except on such holiday occasions. Angela remembers that "the family would all sit down and watch and absolutely scream their heads off even though we were really quite inept."

She recalls one of the skits with a particular fondness, a piece that had been inspired by her own gift for improvisation. "That was something that I did as a child and even though I was younger than Isolde, she recognized that it worked, and used it."

The idea was this: Moyna was attracted to the spirit world, which encouraged the girls to work Angela's improvisations into a comedy routine about a medium who was able to contact the dead. Isolde played the spiritualist, while Angela did the voices of the people who were contacted.

"Me," Angela chuckles, "a seven-year-old medium!"

But that incongruity was doubtless what made their little skit a success. "We just went to town with it. I thought it would bring my grandmother to her knees with laughter. It was very early improvisation, something that I did all my young life, constantly improvising, playing roles, talking to somebody in a voice, taking an attitude with somebody else. I copied everything that I ever saw, but Isolde fed this in me. She just recognized it, in a way.

"I acted my way through childhood."

With the twins' arrival, Edgar and Moyna looked for a bigger house, and found it at number seven Weymouth Avenue, in suburban Mill Hill. It was a large place with four bedrooms and a maid's room. There were good-sized gardens there, back and front, and a circular driveway, called an "in and out" in England.

With the move they became an island unto themselves, Edgar, Moyna, and the children, a tight little unit, which was an arrangement Angela would grow up to duplicate in her own family. Their insularity may also have been a result of feeling like outsiders in suburban Mill Hill, for motherhood had not affected Moyna's unconventionality nor had the temporary retirement from the stage altered her style. She was still a woman of the theater. To that she now added the role of *home star,* turning the Mill Hill house into a salon for actors, writers, directors, musicians, and artists.

"I can't say we had an ordinary childhood," Angela recalls, "because my mother was keenly artistic." It was not unusual for the girls to come home from school and walk in on a small audience attending a vocal recital, or find an artist with an easel and canvas, painting a picture of a woman stretched out naked on the living room sofa. As a five-year-old, Angela would creep into Moyna's room to watch her preparations for an evening of theater or for dinner at an elegant restaurant or a private home. Exquisitely costumed at last, Moyna would confide to her pint-sized handmaiden that "I'm going to cut a bit of a dash." Then, Angela remembers, she would "go out in a flurry of powder and perfume."

By the time Angela was eight and Isolde thirteen, they were being given household responsibilities. Although there was plenty of help — two maids, a cook, and a parlor maid — Moyna believed in the ideal of housekeeping and Angela was learning to appreciate it, too. "The kitchen was where I loved to spend time, watching the cook, getting underfoot in the scullery, and always ready to lick the bowl. Being allowed to 'help.' Putting spinach through the sieve for the twins' lunch. Feeding the dog, Rory, an Irish terrier and a fierce fellow. My father was forever buying new trousers for the postman."

It was Moyna's magic that transformed homely chores into enriching experiences. To Edgar, there was always a glow around his wife, a glow enhanced for the girls by his open adoration of their mother. He would surprise her with lavish gifts and let the children be there to watch, so that they might share his love. One evening, Angela looked on blissfully as her father handed a tiny velvet box to her mother. Opening it very slowly, with a dramatic gravity to befit the occasion, and finally peeking within, Moyna gasped. To the shrieks and squeals of the children, she slowly and theatrically withdrew a platinum ring with a dazzling, square-cut ruby surrounded by diamonds.

Another time, on the occasion of their ninth wedding anniversary, Edgar summoned the whole family outside (everyone, at least, except Isolde, who had gone off to boarding school). Angela clung to her mother's waist as Moyna stepped through the front door on that frosty fall evening. Out front was parked a glorious brand-new, shiny maroon, four-door Chrysler.

Angela was thrilled, as was Moyna, who loved cars. The enormous new Chrysler was kept in a second garage that was built especially for it, replacing a little rock garden where Isolde and Angela used to squat and smoke Moyna's discarded cigarette butts.

When Moyna took her place behind the wheel, she *drove.* Angela considered her mother very modern, "very go-ahead," and thought that her driving style reflected all of that go-aheadness. She would shift gears rapidly as she wove through traffic, stopping and lurching so abruptly that the little girl would later claim she had scars all over her forehead from hitting the dashboard.

Just as the London traffic did not intimidate Moyna, neither did traffic regulations. Parking tickets were her daily diet, and as for moving violations, it seemed to Angela that her mother was ticketed so often that she got to know most of London's bobbies. "But she was so beautiful," Angela says, "that they always kind of saluted her and let her get by. And," she adds, "in those days, the policemen in London were some of the tallest [by requirement, at least six feet], most attractive men around. Oh God, yes. In the 1930s, the policemen in London were *absolute knockouts.* Moyna always had an eye for that."

The little girl's reaction to policemen was curiously different when her father was driving. One day when Edgar was taking her to school, he was pulled over for a minor traffic infraction. As the officer approached, the child sat in the front seat and trembled, clasping her hands tightly in her lap. Then, glancing at the approaching bobby, she stared straight through the windshield. For the rest of her life she would remember "wee-weeing in my pants, I was so frightened, so terrified that my father was going to be thrown in jail."

Thinking about it many years later, she realized, "I was very afraid of men when I was a little girl; terrified of men. I was afraid of my father's friends; I was afraid of my girlfriends' fathers. It was a very curious thing, and I've never been able to figure out why."

The family took the Chrysler, as well as the old Austin Seven, when they went to the summer house that Edgar rented in the tiny village of Berrick-Salome in Oxfordshire, close by the Thames River. Every one of the children seemed to remember that as an idyllic place in an idyllic time. Although they rented the house, Moyna added personal touches, like shiny chintzes in the room that Angela shared with Isolde, "chintzes," Angela remembers, "in delicately pale colors." The three-hundred-year-old farmhouse itself was sprawling enough to function like a two-family house with a common kitchen, and the Lansburys shared it with a family friend, the humorist Stephen Potter, and his wife, the artist Mary Potter. The two families hired a local woman to cook, an old lady who would arrive in a long black skirt, her hair done up in a bun. Even as the children were waking, they could already smell the bacon frying, the toast toasting.

Sharing a room, Bruce and little Edgar were now toddlers, inseparable as pals and indistinguishable in their appearance, except for the fact that they were "mirror" twins, one left-handed and the other right-handed. Even their hair grew in opposite directions. They were often dressed alike. It was inevitable with twins at the time, but then Moyna loved any excuse for dressing up, and she included the boys with the rest of the family in any kind of costume party or parade. Angela was invariably done up as a colleen in a little apron and a green skirt, because Moyna just would never let her forget her Irish blood.

It was during those summer afternoons in the country — when the twins chased each other around the garden; when the girls went swimming or fishing in the river and snapped photos of their father diving from a stanchion; when they watched him ride off on horseback with Moyna or went for long, slow walks through the woods — in those summers, and in such surroundings, it is hardly surprising that Angela developed a lifelong appreciation of birds, and of her own family's joy in nesting.

By all appearances the Lansburys were well off, but that was beginning to be more of a memory and an illusion than a reality. The Depression had seriously hurt Stratford Veneer Mills, and the family budget was being stretched to the limit. Even so, throughout London, people in their class seemed unable to live any other way. As Angela puts it, "You did all that — the cars, the summer place — on a shoestring. You did it with friends, and nothing cost very much. Even in a Depression, you might have had no money, but food didn't cost that much, and if you were in the moderate 'haves,' you could have a bank overdraft, so you could have a maid, you could have a car, insurance, and all those things."

Moyna and Edgar continued to fill their evenings with dinner and dancing, and did not cut back on their theatergoing, as the company managers remembered her and gave them free seats. They still went to the fashionable restaurants like the Café de Paris, or the Café Royal. Angela would beg for the privilege of ironing her father's silk handkerchief and white silk scarf. And on Saturday afternoons, after he had played golf at his club, he would drive her and the twins to the countryside, where they would play with a soccer ball. On the way home, he would buy them all little boxes of Parkinson's English Toffees and then, while he drove, he would serenade them with songs from his childhood in the East End of London; songs like the "Fire Brigade" song that ended,

When we get there, the fire is out
Or there isn't a fire at all!

Being older, the girls were sometimes invited to go along to a glamorous event. Because their grandfather was George Lansbury ("GL" to the family) and First Commissioner of Works, they were once taken to the mayor of London's fancy dress ball. That did not mean formal dress, but costumes, and Moyna took the girls to Berman's, the theatrical costumer, where Angela chose to become Madame Pompadour, complete with a draped brocade hoopskirt, a white wig piled high with curls, and, of course, a beauty spot.

Through it all, Edgar and Moyna were living ever more beyond their means, Angela would remember. "Yes, there would come a day of reckoning and where would you get the money? You got it from an uncle or an aunt who left you a small legacy and you paid off a few bills. It was a very curious time."

Even with the dwindling resources, the children's clothes were top grade, but they were chosen carefully. Isolde and Angela each had three summer dresses. In the fall, they wore school uniforms. Moyna engaged a dressmaker to run up one new winter dress apiece, in matching styles but different colors. Angela remembers "one wool dress I had probably at seven or eight, and it seems to me I wore it every day. Of course when we were playing we wore pinafores over our clothes to keep them clean."

In the spring, they were each given another new outfit, and for the summer, Angela remembers, "Our cottons arrived in a huge box on approbation from John Lewis's department store, and Moyna let us choose one or two. They usually had matching bloomers.

"We were on our uppers," she says, "just managing to hang on with a lot of help from my grandmother." That was Moyna's mother, "Grannie McIldowie," a woman Angela remembers as "rather Victorian by our family's standards, but she did let me light her cigarettes and do needlepoint." She also taught little Angela how to make her first cake, "a chocolate sandwich cake — every ingredient is the weight of three eggs!"

Their other grandmother, George Lansbury's beloved Bessie, no longer had such financial resources, but she earned her own place in the little girl's memory, and not just for preparing unusual teas and serving cakes with violets in them. Emulating GL's liberalism and progressiveness, Elizabeth Brine Lansbury raised her five daughters to be more than just housewives, and Angela would remember those aunts as "an extraordinary group of women . . . extremely intelligent, independent, forceful women who might have only gone to the London School of Economics, and not schools like Oxford and Cambridge — but they made something of their lives. Dorothy became a judge, Daisy became GL's secretary, and Violet became a Communist and went and lived in Moscow."

Granny Lansbury died in 1933, breaking GL's heart and plunging him even more deeply into his political work. The unrelenting Depression had only intensified his commitment to the underclasses, and from Poplar to Birmingham, whenever he could find a platform, he spoke out against economic inequity. He had been appointed First Commissioner of Public Works by Prime Minister Ramsay MacDonald two years earlier, when the Labour Party came into power. After that, he no longer had to look for platforms. He traveled abroad to champion the cause of pacifism and later went on a speaking tour across the United States with Eleanor Roosevelt.

Angela remembers him "speaking to enormous crowds at the Albert Hall," and describes him as a mesmerizing public speaker, whether his audience numbered in the thousands or was a small gathering in Hyde Park. Being a part of the crackling forum among the other protestors, agitators, and vendors of assorted causes only stimulated him. On such occasions he would bring along his eight-year-old granddaughter, and Angela would actually hang on to his coattails with one hand while cradling his big black cat in the other arm, trying to keep up with the long legs of her rangy grandfather. He had tremendous physical energy, and she thrilled to the strides of this huge (to her, though not in actuality) and "enveloping," ruddy-faced man with muttonchop whiskers and "an incredible beard" that brushed her face when he kissed her. She remembers even the smell of him, "soap and linen."

This awe-inspiring grandfather would also, on occasion, invite the family along to the House of Commons, where they might watch part of a session, go to lunch, and then have tea with him on the terrace. And when he brought his political friends to her parents' home for dinner, Angela would sit silently, staring through her big, slate blue eyes and listening raptly. These men seemed to be conducting momentous conversations, making great proclamations of duty and avowals of public responsibility. Because of them, Angela Lansbury's first remembered ambition, unlike Isolde's, was not to be an actress like her mother, but a politician like her grandfather.

He had time for his grandsons, too, although whenever this devout pacifist came to see them, Moyna had to hide the twins' war toys, their tin soldiers, swords, and pistols. One day, he stopped by at their kindergarten, "Miss Lloyd's," setting Eddie and Bruce to giggling with embarrassment and pride as he greeted their little classmates. Then he took them along on his annual Empire Day tour of the neighborhood. And several Christmastimes, Grandfather George brought his pair of little boys around to a local orphanage so that Bruce and Eddie might know that there were children less fortunate than they. He hoisted one of them and then the other high over his head so that all the orphans could see them and afterward, gave each of the twins a half crown. "Put it in your pocket, boys," he said, "and you'll never go hungry."

That was a fair amount of money, more than twice the shilling that Angela got for her weekly allowance. She had barely enough to buy a water ice (one pence), or a chocolate ice (thruppence) from the Wall's ice cream man, who came down the street in his striped navy blue jacket and peaked military cap, ringing the bell of his bicycle cart.

So this grandfather was a vivid personality, a famous and charismatic man who was actually on speaking terms with Queen Mary and King George V. GL was described in the *New Statesman and Nation* as having the only name "that is known in every town and village in Great Britain."

Such a man might well have awed even the most secure of sons, but Edgar Lansbury, in the memories of his children, was himself a considerable fellow. In his daughter's adoring eyes — and Angela describes herself as a "daddy's girl" — he certainly worshipped but "was never intimidated by GL. He was politically sophisticated and became an enormous help to his father, but he had to remain a businessman and run the Stratford Veneer Mills to support his family."

Perhaps even more important to all of the children, their father was a gentle fellow. His own son, little Eddie, remembers being confused by a word, "S'pose," that was completely new to him. His father had used it while showing him the function of a screwdriver. "Now," Edgar had said to his son, "S'pose you want to drive this screw into this piece of wood."

"What," Eddie asked, "does that mean — 's'pose?'" The memory of his father's explanation stayed with him all his life. "I was only four years old, and that was a difficult word to understand, an abstract concept to grasp." His father could hardly have begun with a discussion of hypothetical notions. Instead, he demonstrated, showing the boy the screwdriver, the screw, and the wood, and then explaining the point of the job.

"It was from those little sessions," Edgar, Jr. said, "that I remembered what that word, 'suppose,' meant. I've never forgotten that, and he was very good about teaching like that — using a tool kit and teaching you the meaning of a word like 's'pose.'"

So it came as a bewildering development when this gentle and patient father — who had stopped playing golf at his club, "Potter's Bar," and started spending a lot of time in bed — became so sick that he had to go to the hospital.

CHAPTER 2

THE DEPUTY

WHILE Edgar was in the hospital, Moyna had a dream which was so curious and which she took so seriously that her children would remember it all of their lives.

She placed a great deal of faith in dreams and believed that they related to a higher consciousness. But they were only one of her supernatural interests. Moyna was also fascinated with notions of previous lives, life after death, communication with the dead, and touch healing. She lent such energy to her psychic beliefs that anytime she went into one of these modes, the youngsters were enthralled. And sometimes she demonstrated what seemed to be actual, unexplainable magical powers.

As far as Moyna was concerned, then, a dream was not, as psychiatrists would have it, a message from the subconscious. Rather, she viewed it as privileged information from a higher place. In this particular dream, she said, "somebody" — she herself did not know who — came to her and told her, "Angela will be Edgar's deputy."

In her opinion, there were two parts to this message. First, it implied that Edgar was going to die. Secondly, Moyna found it significant that her daughter was referred to as "Angela" in the dream, because everyone called her "Angela," especially Moyna, *and she was the one doing the dreaming.* That was proof, if proof was needed, that her body had been only the medium for a missive from beyond the mortal world.

But the ultimate meaning was bewildering. That word, "deputy," was such an odd one to crop up in a dream, and again, it was not a word that she herself would have chosen. In one respect, however, the dream was clear: When Edgar was finally opened up in the operating room, his stomach was found to be riddled with inoperable cancer. Since there was nothing to be done for him, he was sent home to wither away. The house soon began to resemble a hospital, and because there was an urgent need for quiet, and no reason for the twins to watch their father completely and finally deteriorate, Moyna sent Bruce and Eddie away to the country, to stay in Devon with their Uncle Eric and Aunt Emily.

The girls were given no medical details. Angela learned about the situation only through Isolde, who at fourteen was old enough to grasp the fact that whatever was ailing her stepfather was going to kill him.

When Angela was taken in to see him for the last time, he was in a near-coma, skeleton-thin. His arms lay flat and motionless on either side of his body, resting on top of the bedsheet. His mouth was open, but he could not speak, and his eyes were closed. It was 1934 and he was forty-eight. His nine-year-old daughter stood at the bedside, holding her mother's hand. She never saw her father again.

On the day of the cremation, Moyna arranged for Angela to have lunch with the family who lived across the street, on Weymouth Avenue. A few days later, she was allowed to come and look at the flowers that had been sent.

"To this day," she said, sixty-four years later, "I hate the smell of lilies."

Moyna drove to Devon, fetched the boys, and brought them home. When she pulled into the garage, Bruce looked out of the window of the mini-Austin, expecting to see his father greeting them.

"Where's Daddy?" he asked.

"Daddy," she said, "has gone to heaven."

"Well," Eddie asked without missing a beat, "where are our toys?"

He would long wonder why his and Bruce's reactions were not any more pronounced. For Eddie, all memory of his father was tied up in being taught the meaning of "s'pose." He thought, "It's a funny sort of memory to have, but it's all I've got."

Perhaps Moyna had something to do with their particular calm. "Maybe it was the way she told us," Eddie wondered, because he didn't think their father's death left Angela with any psychological scars either. He was wrong about that. She felt it intensely, but could not express it, and would not be able to for many years. However, she took her father's diaries when he died, and saved them ever since.

Moyna acted to cushion the jolt of Edgar's death, not just for the children's sake but also for her own, for she, too, was in a state of shock. Her husband was dead after only eleven years of a good marriage; she was on her own with four dependent children, and in a precarious financial condition.

She was herself a child in many ways, and seemed to look for help *from* her children. Isolde might have been in the best position to provide it, being not only the eldest but a stepdaughter. But it was Angela who was her insensitive choice, and if Moyna had been more perceptive, she would have realized that the girl was too young and too hurt to immediately assume the responsibility of being her father's "deputy." Indeed, Angela recalls feeling "a need for a tremendous amount of support from my mother.

"But she leaned on me at that very young age," and being a good, dutiful girl came first. "Moyna depended on me. Being very psychically oriented, she didn't have the underpinnings to deal with my father's death."

Both the McIldowies and the Lansburys rushed to comfort widow and children, inviting them for one country weekend after another. Moyna's sister Marjory ("Mars") took Moyna, Angela, and the twins to Positano, the gorgeous beach town south of Salerno on the west coast of Italy. They found rooms in an inexpensive pensione, and Angela embraced the trip as a heady escape. "I had my first taste of Italian café latte. I walked the beaches and swam in the deep waters off the rocks. I slathered myself with olive oil, to prevent sunburn, but of course, it only made my skin cook, especially in that fierce Mediterranean sun in June."

She romped with the twins, climbing the fig trees that were everywhere, and they all gorged themselves on that rich fruit. She discovered pizza at "Festas," the local cafe, and went for rides in a *carozza* — a wagon that was pulled by a horse with a hat on its head to protect it from the sun — on the winding roads that led up from the beach and along the steep hillside.

"It was such a strain for that horse to pull the whole family up that hill," she would remember with a chuckle. "He just kept letting out these huge farts."

So therapeutic was the trip to beautiful Positano that, as soon as they were back in London, Moyna whisked the family off again, this time to her beloved Ireland. It was supposed to be a retreat and a journey of recovery, but coming so soon after Positano, it seemed more like flight.

Even so, "We had an incredible trip," Angela remembers. The family crowded into the little Austin, "and we took the car on the boat, over to Ireland, and then drove across to Achill [as in "tackle"] Island, which is in County Mayo, on the west coast." In the island village of Doeega ("doo-ah"), Moyna took rooms in a local hotel and let the girls "run all over the beaches and across the rocks and the bogs of that wild Atlantic coast of County Mayo."

When they returned to London, Angela was taken in hand by Granny McIldowie, who assumed the task of helping the youngster get over the loss of her beloved daddy. That included taking Angela to "the pictures," as movies were called at the time, and the two of them would march off to the great cinema palaces like the Marble Arch Pavilion and the Odeon Leicester Square. They went wherever they could find the latest from such favorites as Bette Davis, Ginger Rogers and Fred Astaire, or Deanna Durbin.

It was Durbin, the teenage coloratura, who inspired the little girl to sing, and whom she would imitate whenever she was alone. "Just copying," Angela recalls. She liked to mimic and was good at it. "All the young years, I sang everywhere. In the bath, and all over the house, in Deanna Durbin's high voice." Singing was a talent that Moyna wanted to nurture — she had a vast affection for musical theater herself — and so she arranged for a teacher to come to the house and give private singing and dancing lessons to Angela, Isolde, and herself.

Isolde shared a passion for the cinema and, as Angela neared eleven, the sisters were allowed to go by themselves. Their favorite theater was on the Edgeware Road, where the matrons wore uniforms with epaulets and walked up and down the aisles with trays slung from their shoulders on straps, selling ice creams and chocolates. When the feature film finally began, after the short subjects and the Gaumont British News, the matrons turned military, patrolling the aisles and securing the theater, their flashlights at the ready. It was at this cinema that Angela first saw Irene Dunne, in *Roberta,* the movie version of the Jerome Kern–Otto Harbach musical. Her memory of the picture would come back in a surprising way, many years later.

Angela was also discovering books, starting with Nancy Drew, girl detective. "And her dog, Flash," Angela says. "She dashed around in a car, and never for a moment did I imagine that I would be anything like her, a detective." That led to "my first whole novel, Enid Bagnold's *National Velvet.* I was quite young at the time and I remember how exciting it was to read a book that didn't have a picture on the cover and wasn't a children's book but was a real, bona fide book."

More important, it was around this time that Moyna took her to her first play, *Hamlet,* with John Gielgud at the Old Vic Theatre, and once initiated, she was smitten. She promptly returned to the Old Vic, saw *Pygmalion,* was entranced by Shaw's brainy romantic comedy, and pronounced herself a full-fledged "stage freak." After that she went as often as she could, seeing ("the great") Edith Evans and Michael Redgrave in *Cousin Rachel* and all the Noel Coward plays and operettas that were produced "and actresses like Peggy Wood and Yvonne Printemps."

These were surprisingly mature interests for a girl not yet an adolescent, but Angela's childhood was a brief one. She was being rushed into adulthood, having accepted, consciously or not, the fate of being her father's deputy. She was concerned that "Moyna had a terrible time adjusting to our new circumstances. We really had no income to speak of. We were held up by my Grandmother McIldowie. She paid for my music lessons, paid for Isolde's and my tuition at school. We were just managing to hang on."

As for her mother, in those days there seemed only one solution for a woman who had no dependable way of earning an income, and that was a man. Strangely enough, all of Moyna's children, including the twins, who were only six at the time, had a very definite sense of their mother's sexuality. (It was stranger still that, for someone presumably so sexual, she would be without a man for most of her lifetime.) Angela looked on her mother's need for a lover with a certain resentment. "I adored my mother and always wanted to be with her. Her acceptance of a new man in her life took her away from me, and I was desperately unhappy. My sister and I were sort of thrown out a bit on our own, and that was when I discovered for myself the extraordinary mystical qualities of Ireland."

It was a new summer, and Isolde and Angela prepared to return to Achill Island. Moyna arranged for a family friend to come down from Belfast and keep an eye on the girls in Doeega, where she'd rented a cottage for them.

This trip was Angela's first without her mother, and, she later thought, her child self was still grieving without knowing it. The trip seemed to be the only time she simply *played*. It was a pure holiday, strictly for fun, and even the train was part of the adventure. She would remember walking through the coach as they trundled across Ireland. The passengers sat munching on chicken parts that they had brought with them in paper bags. She sat down beside her sister, who was smoking a cigarette and gazing at the passing landscape, sitting on the wood bench of the wood train that was turning north toward the sea. Isolde was very sixteen. She offered Angela a puff, and of course the youngster leaped at the opportunity. They had played at smoking before, but the mischief of life's first serious inhale was a memorable moment in any childhood. She would soon have the smoking habit.

Even in summer, the west coast of Ireland tends to be cool, damp, and sometimes downright frigid, but the day had become unusually warm by the time they reached the bridge across to Achill. The weather was balmy throughout the trip, and the sensuousness of the experience seemed to have its way with Angela. She was thrilled with the physical beauty around her.

With its clear white light and picturesque landscapes, Achill Island had become an art colony and it seemed, Angela says, that "people came from all over the world to paint the sea and the mountains and the sky." She herself had never demonstrated a gift for art, but with so many artists around, painting seemed the thing to do. "It was the only time I ever painted anything," she remembers, "and I did a very simple picture of an Irishwoman wearing a long black skirt and boots and a shawl, pulling a load of turf in a trundle cart . . . but that island was so beautiful and I loved it so that I couldn't wait to paint it. If you really love something, you want to reproduce it so that other people can see where you spent your summer holiday." (In the fall she would win a school prize for "this silly little painting.")

Once again, the girls made do without water or electricity. For swimming, they would hitchhike down the mountainside road to Keem Bay and along the way, Angela was smitten with "a large white house that was tucked into the land below us, with a private lake behind it." That house was called "Corrymore Lodge," and the girls came to spend a fair amount of time in it because there were boys living there.

With those boys came flirting and crushes and local dances. It was a time for growing up, then, and along with the flirting (which was largely Isolde's interest), they spent the four weeks swimming in the sea, sunbathing on the beach, collecting shells, and riding horses bareback across the open fields. They discovered that the roads contained amethyst rocks, and would dig for them for hours. Whether or not they actually found the stones really didn't matter.

Evenings, they would wander through the little village, or stop in at the Amethyst Hotel. Owned and run by a young woman named Thea Boyd, it was a rudimentary sort of place, more like a rooming house than an actual hotel, but it was comfortable and cozy, and Angela would remember it. Everything about this Irish journey would in fact be memorable, for it was not merely a holiday, but a time of spiritual renewal and magic.

That magic would be centered on the house on the mountain, the house that seemed to float in the sky, Corrymore Lodge. Angela "fell in love with that house. In a romantic kind of vision, it symbolized some of the happiest times of my childhood. It was the most halcyon, beautiful time. No wonder I fell in love with the whole memory of that piece of my life. Those trips to Achill Island made an indelible imprint on my psyche! I was so happy there, and Corrymore Lodge was so important a part of that memory of happiness. It was the last of my childhood.

"I wasn't consciously mourning my father," she remembers, "but I think it was this huge adjustment to life without him that I was having to live through. And I know now why this trip was so important.

"It was because he wasn't there."

In London, Moyna was struggling with her finances as well as her solitude. With the twins still so young, she was determined to stay home and not accept any acting roles. She leaned on her mother for help until she found what she had been looking for. By the time Angela got back from Ireland, her mother had begun an affair with a handsome, ruddy-faced Scotsman named Leckie Forbes. ("Leckie" is a fairly common name in some parts of Scotland and not, as might be imagined, a diminutive of "Alexander.") Leckie was a stiff-upper-lip type who had recently separated from his wife. His life-defining career had been with the British army in India — as Bruce put it, "the very British Colonial Service, and he was very *pukkha*."

A former colonel, Leckie Forbes did not seem to have fully accepted the concept of military retirement. He barked orders and kept a sword, as well as a loaded pistol. He was a rigid and conservative fellow who went to work every morning wearing a bowler hat and carrying a walking stick. He was hardly suited to the arty, bohemian, theatrical Moyna Macgill, but she was certainly his type. "He was absolutely smitten with her," Angela says.

She chose not to look upon Leckie as a replacement for her father. Insisting that her mother's "grief over my father was always there," she would point out that Moyna never remarried, and that "Our family was rent in two. My mother's sorrow was very intense." At eleven, she tried to put herself in her mother's place. "It would have been very hard," Angela believed, "for Moyna to live without a man. She needed someone to stand beside her and help her, not only for the companionship. She needed the money. It was for our sake that she entered into that liaison."

Forbes rented a big house in Hampstead for his new, instant family, a three-story brick structure in the Victorian style. It was beautifully set on a quiet, tree-lined street called Kidderpore Gardens, a few blocks uphill from the Finchley Road, Hampstead's main business thoroughfare. The house had plenty of room for all of them, so they all moved in — not only Moyna and the children, but also Leckie Forbes's sons, the twenty-year-old Patrick with a wife and baby, and the teenage Malcolm.

Forbes had a passion for not only small arms but for big dogs. He was still in mourning for Simba, the St. Bernard that he'd lost in the marital separation. After he established the new household for Moyna and the children, he bought her a tiny tan Pekinese called Jalinga and for himself, a bloodhound puppy he named Pluto. That one would develop into a force of nature, requiring a tremendous amount of food and a powerful leash. He even had to be locked in one room so that he wouldn't eat the furniture in the rest of the house. Unfortunately, the room in which he was locked was the library, and Angela remembers, "That enormous bloodhound ate his way through many of my parents' books. He was unbelievable. And he shat all over the floor."

Isolde, who had been off at boarding school, quit at sixteen to study acting with the famous teacher Michael Saint-Denis at the London Theatre Studio in Islington. The twins, now seven years old, were sent to separate day schools because Moyna wanted them to establish individual identities. Angela continued at South Hampstead High School for Girls, which was a day school, only a bicycle ride away through the heavy commercial traffic on the Finchley Road.

South Hampstead High School for Girls was housed in a four-story, redbrick building, known throughout Hampstead as "the school on the hill." It was and still is an elite school in the English educational system. Neither a private nor a public school in the American sense, it is a "direct grant" school, meaning that it is outside the state system. The students attend the lower school from the age of five until eleven years old and then move on to the upper school, where they stay until they are sixteen. In 1938, its headmistress was Muriel Potter, the sister of the Lansbury family friend Stephen Potter.

That year, at thirteen, Angela started in the second form of the upper school, one class behind Glynis Johns, who was already a professional actress and had even appeared in a movie called *South Riding.* After classes, Angela and some of her girlfriends would play tennis at the club behind the house at Kidderpore Gardens. Then she'd go home to practice the piano. The Royal College of Music issued competency certificates, and she was preparing for its examinations in scales, sight reading, and recitation.

But at home, she sometimes felt that she was "my mother's partner in bringing up my brothers. I had become an old lady at ten." Dispiriting, too, was the Leckie Forbes household, which was quite unpleasant, with its "difficult, nitpicking" master, his loaded guns, and his now fully grown, still unhousebroken bloodhound, who seemed unable to grasp the concept of frustration and habitually crashed into any door that stood between him and the edible.

Forbes was also a jealous man, suspicious not only of Moyna's activities while he was at work, but also of her attachment to her children. As Angela puts it on behalf of her sister and brothers, "We couldn't stand Leckie, and he couldn't stand us." They were all unnerved by his tantrums and distrustfulness, and none of them was more disgusted than Isolde. She escaped into her acting, and was already working for her father, Reginald Denham, in his films. The pay was only nominal, one pound a day, but Angela found that "thrilling!"

Isolde finally got out from under the glare and bluster of the oppressive Leckie when she was offered a part in a Christmas pantomime, a children's spectacle that was being produced in Manchester. With that, she quit drama school, telling her excited sister that she was going to be a flying mermaid, suspended by wires. From Manchester she wrote to Moyna, describing how difficult it had been for her to stay in the house and to listen to all the arguments with Leckie. It was time, she felt, for her to move on and move out, and besides, she said, her absence would leave Moyna with one less responsibility.

Typically, their mother shared this letter with Angela.

Isolde, at the time, was "a lovely-looking girl," according to Angela, "not extraordinarily beautiful, but attractive. She had lovely eyes and a nice figure." While studying acting at the London Theatre Studio, she had acquired a boyfriend, whom she had met in a school production of *Wild December,* a play by Clemence Dane. His name was Peter Ustinov, and he was a precocious young man who intended to become not only an actor but a playwright. In fact, when the romance was first blossoming, she joined him in performing one of his own plays at the Studio.

Peter was a few months younger than Isolde and a charming fellow, a youthful version of the celebrated playwright, actor, and wit he would become, and nobody was more charmed by him than Angela. When her sister brought him home to meet the family (including Leckie), she and Peter became fast friends — at least as fast as it was possible for a seventeen-year-old boy to befriend a thirteen-year-old girl. They did, however, share a sense of theatrical fun. Peter had a wonderful sense of humor and was already doing a cabaret turn at the Players Club in London. When visiting at the house in Kidderpore Gardens, he would escape Leckie and the dogs by sitting out back in the garden and entertaining Angela. They would have long, involved conversations in languages that they created as they went along, and he found her "a gawky and very amusing child."

Ustinov could be droll even about Leckie, immortalizing the man in his autobiography, *Dear Me,* as a

> Scottish military gentleman [who] kept his tin hat from the Great War and a loaded revolver from the same conflict suspended from a hook on the bedroom door, threatening to use the gun on himself if ever his mistress should leave him. The expression in his bloodshot eye when aroused tended to confirm his sincerity.

But Leckie's militarism was only decorative. He had little interest in the Second World War, which was now expanding across Europe. Like many in England he insisted that Hitler had no intention of crossing the English Channel. Angela was old enough to be conscious of world events. Her grandfather's influence had made her politically aware, but history was teaching her the flaws in GL's blissfully unqualified pacifism. "The Low Countries were being overrun," Angela says. "Germany just charged through Czechoslovakia and all those countries. And we — the Allies — the French, the Belgians, the Dutch, and the English — were just allowing them to do it."

But when Germany invaded Poland on September 3, 1939, the British government declared itself in the war. Moyna promptly volunteered to drive an ambulance, legitimizing her speeding and freeing her at last from the confinement of traffic regulations. At the same time, the schools began to evacuate children from the city. Bruce and Edgar were sent to stay with a woman in Cornwall, while Angela panicked as her school was being readied for relocation.

"I was a tremendous homebody," she remembers, "and I decided that I wasn't going to leave my mother." She begged Moyna to allow her to remain in London, promising to study history and English at home with a private tutor. ("I was absolutely hopeless at mathematics, so that was out.") She didn't have to plead at length, for Moyna hardly put up a fight, saying simply, "If we do that, then the rest of the time I'll arrange for you to go to the Ritman School of Dancing and learn music and dancing." Angela did not need much time to accept the proposal.

And so her formal education ended before her fourteenth birthday, in the middle of her upper fourth form at South Hampstead High School for Girls. While the student body was scooped off to safety, she rode the bus from the Finchley Road in Hampstead to Baker Street, where she did her musical studies. It was at this moment that she resolved to become an actress. "I didn't have any plans for myself as an actress until I had to make that decision."

In late 1939, Moyna coached her in the nurse scene from *Romeo and Juliet,* and Angela auditioned for a scholarship in the Webber-Douglas School of Singing and Dramatic Art, on Gloucester Road in Kensington. When it was granted, she became the youngest student there, but she would make her stage debut with the more advanced class. "I was thirteen, yes, but I was a very mature thirteen, mature in my attitude — the way I carried myself, studious and very serious about what I was doing."

The part was in a school production of *Mary of Scotland,* a verse play by the American dramatist Maxwell Anderson. The school's Chanticleer Theatre had a stage equipped with lights and wings and curtains. It seated an audience of three hundred. A lifetime later, Angela would still savor her first stage appearance. "That moment. I can feel it, I can smell it, and it all had to do with putting that theatrical makeup on. And whisking my hair up."

She knew why she had been chosen for the play. "I was probably the best in the younger group. That was how I got to play with the big guys. That was an indication to me that I was okay, but boy, I sure had to mind my *ps* and *qs.* I couldn't fool around. From the very, very beginning, when I got that first role, I have worked hard and put energy and attention and focus into what I am doing. Because I'm terrified of being mediocre and not very good; of being accused of not bringing off a part, from the very, very beginning, when I got that first role."

She soon got to play her first Shakespearean character, the rowdy peasant Audrey in *As You Like It.* The young Patrick Macnee, who years later would co-star in the television series *The Avengers,* was Orlando.

The twins came home from Cornwall for Christmas, already quite proper little fellows. Moyna set up a series of holiday parties, many of which, as usual, called for everyone to come in costume and be prepared to entertain. Eddie remembers that his mother had "quite a collection of costumes. She would start out in her Ambulance Corps uniform, but would keep changing. Bruce and I wrote a skit. Moyna and Angela sang 'My Heart Belongs to Daddy' — in harmony and a capella."

Then it was Peter Ustinov's turn in the parlor entertainment. He was already a professional performer, working in cabarets, and so his routine was more polished than the rest. He began by standing behind a curtain, and announcing, "This is Radio Luxembourg," which he followed with a series of "news announcements" in "Luxembourg" dialect.

In Angela's mind, wartime was personified by Malcolm Forbes, who was Leckie's younger son and the object of her first schoolgirl crush. "He kind of took a shine to me," she remembers, "and we had a very sweet, totally asexual relationship." Malcolm enlisted in the military, going off with a Scottish regiment, and so began Angela's serious letter-writing career.

The war left her grandfather an irrelevance. GL's commitment to the belief that decency would prevail among civilized people had led him to pay a "goodwill" call on Hitler, three years earlier. He came home with his faith unshaken, insisting that "pacifism is not on trial," and even resigned from the Labour Party when it endorsed the League of Nations resolution on Ethiopian intervention. He died at eighty-one on May 7, 1940, spared at least the historical ignominy of a Neville Chamberlain reputation. Oswald Garrison Villard wrote in *The Nation,* "A saint on earth died the other day, a man really too good for this kind of world. Of course I refer to George Lansbury, perhaps next to Gandhi the most outstanding pacifist in public life anywhere."

In his request to have his ashes scattered in international waters, GL had written, "I like to feel I'm just a tiny part of universal life which will one day break down all divisions of creed or speech and economic barriers and make mankind one great eternal unit both in life and death."

He would be Angela's lifelong pride and inspiration. In England, he is still the most famous of the Lansburys.

Like most young men, Peter Ustinov expected to be drafted into the military, and like many, he rushed into marriage because of that expectation. He and Isolde were wed in a civil ceremony, which was followed by a small reception at the apartment of his parents, five-foot two-inch Jona ("Klop") Ustinov, and his even smaller wife Nadeszdha ("Nadia"). Both of them were educated, cultured, and aristocratic White Russian émigrés. Their guests at the wedding were also socially well connected, a fact that was going to prove a tremendous and even miraculous stroke of fortune for the Lansbury family. For among the little wedding party that day were Sir Clifford Norton and his wife, who, as Ustinov put it, "was my de facto godmother." Lady Norton was involved in the evacuation of children from London, and her pet project was assembling a group of twelve youngsters to be shipped to safety in America. Prevailing upon her wealthy friends in the United States, she had been arranging for sponsors to pay the cost of passage and then shelter these young evacuees for the war's duration. At the wedding reception, Lady Norton suggested to Moyna that not only would it be possible to include Angela and the twins in the group, but that she might even be able to arrange for Moyna herself to accompany them and then become the group leader after all the children had arrived in America. Even before Moyna could leap at this opportunity, there was a second one. Another of the wedding guests offered to try and find an American sponsor who would provide a home for the four of them.

As excited as they were by these strokes of luck, there arose the question of how to escape from under "the bloodshot eye," as Ustinov put it, of the possessive, paranoid, and, worst of all, armed, Leckie Forbes. Fortune again came to Moyna's rescue, this time in the form of mumps. That highly contagious disease, dreaded by the mightiest of men, chose precisely this moment to infect Moyna, Angela, and the twins.

Leckie's panic was instant. The dread of contracting mumps — and of becoming sterile or impotent as a result — so terrified the Scotsman that he moved out of the house for the duration, leaving Moyna and the children free to prepare for their escape. They were to be the first of Lady

Norton's evacuees to sail, leaving immediately on *The Duchess of Atholl.* The rest of the children would follow on the *Benares.*

The timing of the voyage was perilous, for the German blitzkrieg of London was about to begin. U-boats were already patrolling the North Atlantic, threatening all sea traffic. Moyna sold everything that she owned except for the family antiques, which were loaned out to relatives. Since no money could be taken out of England, they would arrive in America with little more than the clothes on their backs. But ill as they all were with mumps, Moyna, Angela, Bruce, and Eddie were excited as they prepared for their dramatic departure.

The tension was electric. It seemed as if at any moment, an enraged Leckie could come bellowing up the stairs, a saber in one hand, a pistol in the other. Or they might carry their suitcases down to the front door and open it to find the mad Scotsman guarding the gate with Pluto, the bloodhound.

But Leckie's fear of the mumps outweighed all other considerations, and ironically, his fear was for naught. Mumps never causes impotence in men, not even when it spreads to the testes. In only two percent of all cases does it even cause sterility.

Under cover of night, when all was in readiness and the ship set to sail, the little band of adventurers crept stealthily through the front door. Outside of the house, all was quiet on Kidderpore Gardens.

"It was like a midnight flit," Angela remembers. "An escape. You leave in the middle of the night.

"And in the morning you aren't there."

CHAPTER 3

THE BRITISH COLONY

AS SHE hurried along the pier toward the ship, Angela tried to picture how Leckie would react when he discovered their disappearance. She imagined how he would be stunned by the sheer emptiness of his house, and by what Angela describes as "the hugeness of Moyna's gesture." As time went by, she would come to believe that he'd been so shocked, so nonplussed by the Lansbury disappearing act, that he became literally speechless, for he never did try to communicate with Moyna again, nor did he even inquire among friends as to her whereabouts.

An ocean voyage can become unendurable confinement for the average, energetic ten-year-old. One of the officers of *The Duchess of Atholl* endeared himself to Bruce and Eddie by asking confidentially that they act as submarine spotters, looking out for German U-boats. For hours at a stretch, they would scan the ocean expanse, searching for the periscopes, and when that thrill wore thin, there was always the drama of the two ships continuously nearby. One was a freighter and the second, a British destroyer, served as escort for both ships. Were *The Duchess of Atholl* torpedoed, the officer told the wide-eyed boys, the destroyer would rescue the passengers and put them aboard the freighter.

"That was exciting," Eddie remembers, but much to the twins' disappointment, no submarines were spotted throughout the crossing, not even friendly ones.

Below, in their cabin, Moyna opened her valise and took out her husband's crematory urn. She asked Angela to fetch the twins, and when everyone was gathered for the ceremony, she announced that she was going to throw their father's ashes out the porthole and scatter them at sea. She explained that they were now halfway across the Atlantic Ocean, and she could satisfy Edgar's wish to be buried in England while at the same time, "Daddy will be with us in America." The ashes of his father, GL, had also been scattered on the sea.

The children were hushed as their mother unlatched the porthole. She pulled it open, but as she put the mouth of the urn toward the opened window, the powerful ocean wind gusted in. Angela looked on with appalled mirth as "some of the ashes flew away over the water and some flew back in our eyes."

After they docked in Montreal, the four of them continued down to New York by train while the *The Duchess of Atholl* returned to England — or at least set out to do so. Halfway back, as if without the twins to keep the watch, it was torpedoed and sank. That attack marked the end of nonmilitary sea travel for the duration of the war; civilian vessels would no longer be permitted to cross the Atlantic. Moyna and the children had gotten out the door just before it was shut; Lady Norton's other young protégés would never set sail for America.

A welcoming committee awaited the Lansburys at Grand Central Station in the person of Moyna's gentlemanly first husband, Reginald Denham, and his "lady of the moment," as he put it, Mary Orr. (They would later marry, and she would write the famed short story "All About Eve.") Reggie gathered up the weary travelers, shepherded them out of the railroad station, and brought them upstairs to the baking air of mid-August in Manhattan. With everyone jammed into a taxi, the boys on the jump seats, he and Mary took Moyna and the children the few blocks to the Algonquin Hotel on West 44th Street. It was on that ride that they had their first glimpse of New York's soaring skyscrapers, through the sunroof of the Sky-View cab.

They were greeted by Reggie's friend John Martin, who was the manager of the hotel and nearly as legendary as the Algonquin itself. John Martin personified the hotel's reputation as the essence of New York sophistication and wit, which made it a haven for theater people and writers.

And so that was where they spent their first night in America, in August of 1940.

Their luck was holding: Lady Norton had succeeded in finding an American sponsor for them, a rubber millionaire named Charles T. Wilson. He and his family had a country home in Lake Mahopac, a resort area about thirty miles from the city. When Moyna telephoned Mrs. Wilson to report their arrival, she was told that a car would be sent to take them there in the morning.

A "huge" (at least in Eddie's eyes) Packard limousine whisked them off to the Wilson compound, which fronted on the sizable lake. A cottage on the grounds was given over to the Lansbury ensemble, and Mrs. Wilson promised Moyna $150 a month for living expenses for as long as she needed it. She would, as it happened, need it for a while. In order to get work of any kind, a green card — a certificate of legal immigrant status — was required. Applying for it immediately, Moyna was given a quota number, and since Great Britain's allotment was one of the largest, she expected that the wait would be brief. In fact, it would take about a year; until then, they had only visitors' visas.

Although Moyna couldn't work, the children could certainly attend school. Angela was immediately enrolled in the Feagin School for Drama and Radio at Fifth Avenue and 50th Street in Manhattan, with a scholarship from the American Theater Wing. At the same time, Moyna aimed for the best for the boys, and applied to the elite Choate School in Wallingford, Connecticut. (John F. Kennedy was a student at the time.) She paid a personal visit to make her case with the headmaster, Seymour St. John, and came back with both the admissions and scholarships. The boys were promptly shipped off to Wallingford, while Moyna busied herself sending care packages back to her family and doing volunteer work for the Red Cross and "Bundles for Britain."

Life was becoming exciting for Angela, who was just turning fifteen. She made new friends in the country, and every Monday morning she would leave for the city and school. Mr. Wilson provided her with a season train ticket and gave her a weekly allowance of two dollars. More likely than not, he, too, had been instrumental in finding the place where she would live during the week while at drama school. It was nothing less than an elegant townhouse at 6 East 94th Street, the home of George W. Perkins, who was the executive vice-president of the Merck Pharmaceuticals Company and a member of its founding family. (He would later become an undersecretary of state.)

Madison Avenue was then a two-way thoroughfare, and every morning Angela would take the bus downtown to the Feagin School in the International Building of Rockefeller Center. When she got home in the warm dusks of that early autumn in 1940, after dinners with the Perkins family, she would rollerskate the block and a half to Central Park with their eleven-year-old daughter, Ann. When the weather grew cooler, Mrs. Perkins began taking Angela to concerts and plays, a lovely life for this demure and serious-minded English girl who seemed in no way spoiled by her remarkable looks. For as a Mahopac friend, Zella Merritt, vividly remembers, "Bidsie was a stunning girl with a beautiful peaches-and-cream complexion and real golden hair and big blue eyes." During school holidays, the two of them would haunt the Seventh Avenue garment district, looking for modeling work. "She was so striking," Zella remembers, "that when we walked down the street people would turn around and look at her."

If they did stare, Angela was too unaware of her own beauty to know why, or else was simply too distracted, for she was discovering the big, new city. She didn't have enough money for taxis and was not yet bold enough to brave the subway system, so she walked, dazzled and made dizzy as she stared skyward at the buildings.

Mrs. Perkins also gave her the outgrown or outmoded items from the wardrobe of her eldest daughter, Penelope. "I wore only cast-off clothes," Angela remembers, but as a fact rather than a hardship. "I didn't buy one single new thing during those first years. It was such a curious dichotomy, having no money at all and yet living in this incredible and generous Perkins household. I was living in abject luxury."

The drama classes at Feagin were not unlike those at Webber-Douglas in London, but by now, at fifteen, she found their value dubious. Ultimately she would be convinced that "you don't learn how to act. You either got it or you ain't." She knew, though, that her speaking voice was too high and that she needed to work on the placement of it. Feagin also provided acting experience, and that was invaluable. The only way to learn to act, she believed, was by *acting,* and in that respect, the school pushed its students into the deep end of the pool. Her first play was a Restoration comedy, a highly refined and stylized genre requiring not only powdered wigs, hoopskirts, fluttering fans, and beauty marks, but equally extravagant diction, readings, and gestures. The piece was the classic William Congreve seventeenth-century comedy of manners *The Way of the World*.

Its plot revolves around the romance between the beautiful and witty coquette, Millamant, and the dashingly handsome Mirabel. The troublemaker of the piece is Millamant's aunt, the elegantly bitchy Lady Wishfort, whose name reflects her motive — she'd once been seduced by Mirabel and wants more. However, after a considerable flurry of repartee and fluttering of fans, the dashing hero dupes her into approving the marriage.

Angela was cast not as the beautiful heroine, but as the older, nasty Lady Wishfort. It was certainly a sizable part, a major role, and a juicy one at that. Nevertheless, at fifteen, she was having her first experience of playing an older woman. It would not be the last time, nor was it by chance that she was so cast. In real life, she had long been assuming responsibilities beyond her years, and the maturity she had gained from it had already begun to show in her expression and manner.

For another role, she found a Salvation Army bonnet, squashed it, and then slapped it on her head. She was learning the importance of such externals as costumes, props, wigs, and any other kind of physical aid. As for her ability with accents and dialects, it would prove crucial if she were to have any hope for a career in America. There were only so many plays calling for British accents, and she would later acknowledge, "Being able to switch, and being able to pick up and hear accents, has been my single most important ability as an actress."

Meanwhile, at Choate, the twins were a couple of shabby genteels in a crowd of young men with old money. They had to endure a certain amount of taunting about their British accents, but they seem to have been a resilient pair. The only complaint Eddie recalls was "not having the funds to enjoy ourselves in the tuck shop [the school store]."

Bruce's memories are similar. He did get into a fistfight with a boy who razzed him about wearing hand-me-downs, but in the end, he believed that "boys' schools and dormitories are great fun, once you settle in, especially compared to those awful English schools."

Angela knew why her brothers detested them. "The twins had gone to British public schools [in England, of course, private schools are called *public schools*] so they knew about masters putting their hand up their short pants. And being hot for their buns. It had become a joke to them, an absolute joke. Because there were two of them, they were able to reduce its importance and laugh about it."

In the fall of 1941, after a second summer at the Wilsons' Lake Mahopac cottage, the children all went back to school, just as Moyna obtained the green card she'd been so impatiently awaiting. Wasting no time, she found an apartment in the city. The subsidy from the Wilson family continued while she set out to look for stage work.

The apartment was only a studio, one room at 55 Morton Street in Greenwich Village, but the rent was a reasonable $42 a month, and the place was big enough for Angela and Moyna. Once again, John Martin of the Algonquin came to their assistance. "He adored actors," a fact Angela appreciated. "He understood our circumstances and helped us, sending over a couple of beds, some tables, and even a gooseneck lamp."

Even in those busy theater times, acting assignments were hard to come by, and Moyna did not have the reputation on Broadway that she'd enjoyed in the West End in London. In the beginning, she had to invent work. She would give dramatic readings at private schools like Spence or Brearley, and recite speeches from the stage literature, mainly the works of Shakespeare, because that was what was in demand, especially when delivered with a British accent (though Moyna's voice still had a touch of the Irish). Sometimes Angela would tag along, and they would play the Juliet-Nurse scene from *Romeo and Juliet.*

The twenty-five dollars she received for each reading did not go very far, even in 1941, when lamb chops were thirty-three cents a pound in the little butcher shop a block away from Morton Street on Seventh Avenue. One evening, they felt so starved for relief from frugality, so desperate to do anything just to get out of the apartment, that they pawned one of Moyna's coats for the price of two movie tickets. Yet they never felt poor, not even when Bruce and Eddie came home for Christmas and all four of them had to sleep in the one room, with mattresses laid out on the floor for the boys.

Angela says, "We were driven by the need to eat and make some money and get on our feet. We had nothing to go back to in London. We were like everyone else who had made it to the United States. We had nothing going for us except my mother's reputation and our forebears — this tremendously strong family sense of believing in one another and in the desire to accomplish a future for ourselves."

She was also intensely aware that "the desperate background of all this was the war. We felt like we were the luckiest people in the world. Forget self-pity. How could you feel anything but thankfulness at having the opportunity to live in America during those war years?" At ten, Eddie was too young to appreciate his circumstances, but he was aware that they "always had a sense that we were in it together," and Bruce says, "We didn't feel at all put-upon. We had the whole future ahead of us and it was kind of an exciting time. We had nowhere to go but up."

* * *

Feagin was a serious dramatic school, which at the time meant that it did not offer music classes, but Angela was not that kind of theater snob. She loved to sing. "I had a good head voice," she recalls, a reference to the type of singing a soprano does. "But it was small. Not thin, just small. And I didn't know how to project it, strengthen it, use it, or train it. I wasn't very interested in having my voice trained, and nobody at school suggested it."

But Moyna did. She took Angela to see a voice teacher who lived nearby, on West 11th Street, an older woman named Daisy. To Angela, she looked "like someone who had been a Ziegfeld girl, or had been in the musical theater in the World War One years. She was quite elderly and played on a terrible piano in her living room. That was how she made her money, giving lessons to young singers."

Daisy taught the teenager some of the popular songs of the day. She also entranced the girl with stories about her theatrical past and once took her to meet a real star from the old days, an actress named Fritzi Scheff, who had been the toast, as they used to say, of two continents. She'd sung at the Metropolitan Opera, as well as in such operettas as Victor Herbert's *Mademoiselle Modiste.*

A very little lady, Fritzi lived with her little dog in a little Fifth Avenue apartment filled with big, overstuffed furniture. After pouring tea for her guests, she sat down at the piano, and accompanied herself as she sang her signature piece, "Kiss Me Again," which had been her big number in *Mademoiselle Modiste:*

Sweet summer breeze,
Whispering trees

She sang it, Angela remembers "in this high, high, high little voice," the likes of which the girl had never heard. "I was transfixed, and it's the most rangy song. You have to start down in your boots or you'll never hit that high note."

When Fritzi told Angela that it was now her turn to sing, the youngster chose "I'll See You Again," from the Noel Coward operetta *Bitter Sweet.* It was a piece she had been practicing with Daisy, and when she finished, Mme. Scheff was encouraging. "She gave me advice about how to phrase, to breathe, how to bring emotions to the song. So she made a lasting impression on me, even though I wasn't going to become another Fritzi Scheff. But it was all part of my musical education."

A lifetime later, when taking a shower and feeling in good voice, she would sing "Kiss Me Again," just to see whether she could hit that high note. And she would remember Fritzi Scheff.

Moving into her second year at Feagin, Angela showed enough talent to land the title role in a production of *Lady Windemere's Fan*. This time the character was closer to her own age, although Lady Windemere was far more experienced at twenty-one than even the worldly Angela Lansbury was at sixteen. Once again, the play was one that required elegance and extravagant style, this time in the double-edged manner of Oscar Wilde.

In concentrating on the finest of classics, was the Feagin drama school providing useful lessons in craft for its students, or was it ignoring the realities of the working theater? The students were aiming for Broadway, since it was basically the only professional theater in the country, but there, critics were applauding the naturalism of Sidney Kingsley, Lillian Hellman, and Robert Sherwood, or else the witty comedies of S. N. Behrman and Moss Hart. Few classics were produced. With so many new shows available, any classic was called a "revival," and that was a dirty word. This drama school seemed to be preparing its students for a theater that did not exist.

On the other hand, a solid grounding in the fundamentals and a classical training are valuable for playing any style of drama, even if the actor never again has the chance to appear in Wycherley or Wilde. Angela may well be correct in her belief that actors are born, not developed, but she was acquiring an English-style, conservatory training, and with it the solid background that enables an actor fully to exploit any natural gifts.

New York's agents regularly scouted the Feagin productions, and in Angela's audience for *Lady Windemere's Fan* sat the celebrated Audrey Wood, of Leibling and Wood. She immediately recognized the student's talent, and although she did not offer representation, she did start to send Angela out on casting calls with her personal recommendation. Even this early in her career, Angela took her work very seriously and, entering her young womanhood, she was still a girl without frivolity in her life. She hadn't much interest in boys, although she did start going to the Stage Door Canteen on 46th Street, near Times Square. America had been brought into the war, and even though the battle was thousands of miles away, there was no escaping an era's atmosphere. Every aspect of life seemed to relate to the war.

The Stage Door Canteen provided servicemen with a sense of home ties and gave civilians a feeling of patriotic contribution. It offered music, food, and company for soldiers, sailors, and marines, and pretty girls to dance with — stage actresses who volunteered their time. Angela remembers it as "a huge place, and there was a band and a small stage and a big dance floor where you'd dance with the boys. And there was a counter with coffee and doughnuts."

Going there got her a few dates with young servicemen, and gave her a sense of being American. It also provided her with a chance to see some of the stars who entertained at the Canteen, opera singers like Jan Peerce and Robert Merrill, and even Marlene Dietrich. She studied them from the viewpoint of a fellow professional and began to develop a taste for American popular songs.

With her lessons giving her more confidence, she very much wanted to sing as an actress, and a friend she'd made at Feagin encouraged that. He was a slender, good-looking, blond fellow named Arthur Bourbon, an older man (already in his middle thirties). A professional ballroom dancer, he was studying at Feagin because he wanted to learn how to act. Now he offered to help her create a cabaret routine.

His first idea was inspired by Bea Lillie, the eccentric English comedienne who was so popular in the States. His notion was to combine Lillie's dotty humor with Angela's gift for dialect and impersonation, somehow blending them into a musical impressionist act. After Angela would imitate one singer, she would spin around and then do another imitation. The whirls were the first thing to go. "They made me dizzy and sick," Angela admits, and they both soon realized she was not really a vague, Bea Lillie type. Finally, she and Arthur decided that she would start the act with a straightforward rendition of her favorite song, "All the Things You Are," and follow it with the popular "Tangerine." After the two songs, she would introduce her impressions by singing Noel Coward's "I Went to a Marvelous Party."

To Coward's dry catalogue of eccentric and increasingly bizarre guests, she added her own list: opera's Brünnhilde (the Wagnerian soprano, Kirsten Flagstad), a British musical comedy star (the song was "The Biggest Aspidistra in the world"), the British soprano Gracie Fields ("The Lancashire Lass"), and a French chanteuse (Edit Piaf singing "J'Attendais").

Bourbon got in touch with a manager whom he knew from his ballroom dancing days, a man who specialized in replacement acts to play in small nightclubs when the regular entertainers were off, and they came up with the idea of putting several substitute performers together and billing them as "Audition Night."

Angela eventually secured two engagements with this group, a performance at Number One Fifth Avenue and two nights at the smart supper club *The Reuban Bleu*. For these jobs, she borrowed an evening gown from her mother, a navy blue net-and-sequin dress ("It did have a bit of sprinkle") with a sexy halter neck. The dress was too big, but Moyna took it in herself. It succeeded in making Angela look older than her sixteen years.

She found those first audiences "warm and generous," and after several weeks, Bourbon felt that they were ready to audition the act for booking agents. He set up a series of appointments and then steeled his young protégé for the ordeal ahead, the trudging from one office and rejection to another. At the first audition, she opened up her accordion-folded sheet music and spread it out on the piano rack in front of the accompanist. As Arthur looked on with a big, encouraging smile, she launched into the routine.

"I got my first booking after my first audition!" she would always boast with a broad grin of pride.

Moyna was also meeting with success. She got a part in a Broadway play called *Yesterday's Magic,* and while it was not a leading role, she was certainly in good company, appearing alongside Paul Muni and Jessica Tandy. Alas, the play was not as good as the actors and it closed quickly.

She went back to making the rounds and one of the places she looked for work was the 52nd Street office of the Theater Guild. It was there that Moyna met Elaine Anderson, a beautiful young stage manager who was married to the actor Zachary Scott. When Moyna told her about Angela and the twins — who had come home for the 1941 Christmas holidays — and about their flight from England, Elaine invited them all for dinner at her Greenwich Village apartment. "We didn't have much money," she recalls, "but nobody did." And she took her husband's suggestion to offer their guests anything they wanted for dinner.

That called for a family conference. The choice of fruit was unanimous. They hadn't been able to afford any since they'd arrived, and were starved for it. But the most special treat, everyone agreed (having no idea of the cost), would be lobster. The Scotts were pleased to provide the fruit, but they were taken aback by the request for expensive lobster. Nevertheless they decided to indulge the hardy, luxury-starved little family, and Elaine looked on affectionately as they ate "everything except the shell."

Actors are a clubby lot, and Moyna's club included many of her fellow expatriates from the London stage. They had established a British theatrical colony in America, and while some actors were often so vain or insecure that they were uncharitable about helping others get roles, this

English crowd genuinely supported one another. One of them, an actress named "Pixie" Hardwicke — married to the Hollywood actor Cedric Hardwicke — was putting together a bond-selling show to raise money for the Royal Canadian Air Force to train British fighter pilots. The production was Noel Coward's delightful three-parter *Tonight at 8:30*. With the cast — Pixie, Anna Neagle, and Herbert Wilcox — almost fully assembled, Moyna was invited to complete the company.

The rub was that it would be a touring production, opening in Toronto and then traveling westward across Canada to Vancouver. It would keep Moyna away for several months, but of course, she accepted the part. That was an actor's life.

As she left, Angela was preparing for her own three-week booking at a Montreal nightspot called the Club Samovar. It would be her first professional engagement of any kind, and would mark the end of her studies at Feagin. With a paycheck she was a professional, on her way. There was no need for schooling now and, not incidentally, that paycheck was going to be $60 a week, a very respectable salary in 1942.

While both were away, the boys came home from school on summer vacation. Moyna had arranged for them to stay with some friends who had a house at the beach on Long Island, and when Angela returned from her Montreal engagement, she joined them there. At summer's end they all headed back to the Morton Street apartment. Angela was not quite seventeen years old and had to see to their food and laundry and begin the job of getting them back to school. Still, she insists, the responsibility was not a burden. At twelve, she says, "they were almost five years younger than me, but they were very smart kids."

But after Moyna finished her Canadian tour, she did not return to New York. Instead, she wired Angela from Vancouver that she was being considered for a part in a Hollywood movie *(Commandos Strike at Dawn)*, and was going directly to Los Angeles. Her telegram added, very matter-of-factly, "Pack up the flat, send the boys back to school, and come out to Los Angeles. There's more work here than on the New York stage."

It was a daunting undertaking for an adolescent, but Angela says, "I wasn't a little girl; I was an extremely mature sixteen-year-old. I was pretending to be nineteen and was very adult for my age." So she did precisely as instructed, putting the boys on the train to Choate and closing up the apartment. Later on, she would look back on her teenage self and admit, "How I managed to do this, I don't really know."

Bruce and Eddie were now even more isolated, with their mother and sister three thousand miles away in Los Angeles and they by themselves at Choate. They were quite sensitive about having been "parked" in Connecticut. "We were always a family," Bruce says, "which was why Eddie and I were so upset. We wanted to be with Moyna and Bidsie. But my mum had that English thing about *sending the boys away to school* — and it was a way of getting us out from under, so she could go and act."

It had not bothered Bruce before. "We never resented that she was acting, and she didn't do that much of it while we were growing up." But now she was going to California for an indefinite stay, and the boys were certainly not thrilled about that. Even worse, their mother substitute was going as well. Angela was not aware of their resentment, and Moyna certainly wasn't. But duty was the byword in the Lansbury family, and the twins went about their schoolwork, while Angela bought herself a one-way ticket to Los Angeles.

She rode the Challenger which, the lowest-priced westbound train, was definitely not the luxurious Twentieth Century Limited, but "It was cheap," she says, "and it was sit-up until Chicago, but at least, then you got a bunk to Los Angeles."

The train rolled to a halt beside the platform in the Pasadena station on the hottest day Angela could remember, but the weather did not spoil her first impression of California. She had an instinct for gardening and flowers, an instinct that had been stifled by the sidewalks and grayness of London and New York. Her first image now was brilliant sunshine and the "*geraniums* on the platform!"

From her movie magazines she was very aware that "the stars got off in Pasadena, so that they wouldn't be bothered by fans." Fans not being a problem of hers, she continued on to Union Station, where her mother was waiting. Then Moyna took her home to the studio apartment she'd found in a building near downtown Los Angeles, at the corner of Ocean View Avenue and Rampart. Other than having mountains in view, it was a West Coast version of their East Coast apartment, again one room. Angela slept on a pull-down bed in the kitchen.

Warm as it was in the daytime, the apartment became chilly at night. They would heat the room by lighting the oven and then shutting the windows tight. One of Angela's first nights there, she was asleep in the kitchen when she awoke with a frightful start, unable to catch her breath. "I thought I was dying. I almost threw something at the window to open it and get some air."

It was not gas from the oven, as she suspected; rather, a leak had developed in the refrigerator; and the refrigerant was seeping into the apartment. "I almost died from inhaling that," Angela remembers.

Staying alive seemed to be the constant threat, economically at least, as well as professionally. Moyna had arrived in Los Angeles to find that the part for which she was being considered had already been cast. Now Angela watched her mother "trying to get into theater, movies, anything that would put money into our pockets." If she couldn't get work as an actress, she was willing to do whatever was available to pay the rent and put food on the table. She could not keep taking money from the Wilsons indefinitely.

With the onset of the Christmas shopping season, she finally landed a job as a sales clerk in the toy department of Bullocks-Wilshire, the Beverly Hills department store. Angela was hired there, too, as an $18-a-week cashier and gift wrapper. Moyna lasted only a couple of weeks, accused and convicted of spending too much time on her knees playing with the toy trains.

Angela, though, made a great success as a gift wrapper. "There was no trick to it," she shrugs, although she has to admit, "I was a hell of a wrapper. You didn't just put a piece of ribbon around a box. You covered the box with paper, and you had to do special corners, and they all had to be perfect. The bow had to be absolutely precise, because Bullocks-Wilshire was one of the most elegant department stores in the world."

After work she would come home and give everyone in the family lessons in gift wrapping. The twins had come out for the Christmas holiday school break, and Bruce said, "We all learned how to fold the paper and tie the ribbons — even my mother."

In a store like Bullocks-Wilshire, there was always a dress code for employees. "You had to wear a black dress," Angela remembers. "I wore the same black dress all the time I was there." She proved to be so good at wrapping, and so pretty and pleasant that, at the beginning of 1943, with the Christmas season over, she was kept on as a salesgirl in the cosmetics department. With commissions, she was taking home $28 a week.

The boys, meanwhile, reluctantly went back to school in the East. This vacation had been the first time they'd seen their mother in almost ten months "and we weren't so emotionally sturdy," Eddie recalls. "The separation upset us terribly. Even though there were two of us, I was very homesick." In fact, Eddie contracted pneumonia as soon as he got back to Choate. He seems to remember the illness as if it were a way of getting even with Moyna for having sent them away again.

Despite the chronic money shortage, Moyna and Angela were never discouraged. They knew plenty of people who were in the same situation. As usual, Moyna had quickly made her way into the local colony of British actors — at least, those at her level. Perhaps she did not mingle with Hollywood's British elite, the likes of Charles Chaplin, Stan Laurel, Ronald Colman, Ray Milland, Cary Grant, or Charles Laughton, but there were some fine actors in her circle, for instance, the Irish actress Sara Allgood and Moyna's own Othello, Basil Rathbone, who unfortunately was known in the States mainly for his portrayal of Sherlock Holmes. The others in Moyna's crowd were, like herself, second-tier character actors, but Angela would always be proud to be one of their number. She saw them as a "kind of merry band who hung together and saw each other regularly."

One of that merry band, the actress Flora Robson, came up with a better place for Moyna and Angela to live. Robson had just finished filming *Saratoga Trunk* with Gary Cooper and Ingrid Bergman, and was moving out of a house at 8286 Mannix Drive in Laurel Canyon. Blitz or no, she was going home to England. The place she was bequeathing was so small it was almost a toy house, with just a bed-sitting room plus a kitchen and bathroom. Next door, at 8288, was a twin hut, where the British actor John Abbott lived.

These digs might have seemed shabby to some, but to Moyna and Angela their new home was just right. There were many actors living in Laurel Canyon, and the area had an artistic aura. As soon as they moved in Moyna resumed her entertaining, and her life in the expatriate acting community became the life, as well, of her seventeen-year-old daughter. Though she had grown taller, Angela was still shy, and preferred to be with her mother and around adults, rather than with people her own age. As for boys, she insisted that she didn't have time for them. She would sometimes go down to the Hollywood Canteen at Vine Street near Sunset Boulevard. It was similar to the Stage Door Canteen in New York, with a dance floor and a band, and entertainers, but apparently movie actors didn't like to perform in person. "Male stars who weren't in the service would serve at the food table," she remembered, "and some of the starlets would dance with the boys. But they just didn't entertain the way they did in New York."

Angela did date a few of the servicemen she met at the Hollywood Canteen. One night, a sailor from North Carolina asked for her autograph, which made her feel just that much closer to being in the movies. When he heard her British accent he asked, "Are you going to stay in the United States?" She replied, "If I have any success in my career here, I will."

In general, dating itself was either not important to her or else something that she preferred not to do. "I never had any *heavies.* I didn't sleep with anyone. I had a couple of guys I fooled around with — heavy necking — but I also went out with a lot of young men who I discovered were gay. And it was interesting because I was around a lot of gay men. My mother knew a lot of them. It was astonishing how many actors, older actors, were gay."

Although Moyna was having little luck at the studios, she finally began to get stage roles, even if they were nonpaying ones. These theatricals were earnest but frustrating endeavors in a city that had neither a sense of nor an interest in the living theater. Moyna's friends among the Irish acting community had led her to the Gate, a sixty-seat theater named after the famous institution in Dublin and run by the director Peter Godfrey. Angela became involved with the Gate, too, but the closest she came to its stage was working in the box office.

Moyna also did *Horror Tonight,* a Grand Guignol evening of blood and gore at the full-sized Belasco Theatre. She was in good company, working with some friends like George Coulouris, Martin Kosleck, and Sara Allgood. This time, Angela, too, had a role, if not exactly onstage: she played a nurse who walked up and down the aisle, offering smelling salts to the weak-kneed members of the audience.

"Once again," she sighs, "I was on the periphery of acting."

Through it all, like every other would-be movie actor in Los Angeles, she tried to crash the studios, regularly making the rounds of the casting offices and looking for an agent who would do something for her. Only one of them ever accomplished anything, she says, "and that one I didn't trust.

"He was a little man and he was very unattractive. He meant well but he didn't have much class. I wasn't very comfortable. I don't think he understood what I was all about."

He did get her an audition at Paramount Pictures, however, and it actually was an *audition,* not a screen test. The experience was a novel one.

She was excited, of course, as she prepared for the appointment, putting on her best dress and taking an hour to apply her makeup. The agent picked her up in his Cadillac convertible and drove her to the studio. There, her auditors sat in a row of chairs and watched her do a simulated screen test, watching her through a glass window that had the rectangular shape of a movie screen. The idea was to pretend that they were watching a film. On the other side of the window, Angela stood alone in a black room, with spotlights focused on her. "You did your reading. It was like being a bird in a glass enclosure."

For this audition, she performed the cabaret act exactly as she had done it at the Club Samovar in Montreal. "All these crazy voices. Accents. Phoney foreign languages." On the other side of the window, she could make out a row of dumbfounded observers. "They didn't know what to make of it. They really thought I was mad."

Her agent never bothered to tell her what their response had been. It wasn't necessary, but once again, she looked upon adversity as a positive. "Yes, it was daunting, but one was challenged."

Such pluck was partly bravado. She knew that she had the talent, but in the back of her mind was the fear that she simply did not have the looks.

"Remember," she explains, "those were the days of Rita Hayworth."

It was a letdown, that experience at Paramount, "And I had been so hopeful."

Luckily, she was still working in the cosmetics department at Bullocks-Wilshire. With small raises, her salary was not only keeping their little home afloat, but it enabled her and Moyna to "disengage ourselves, finally, from the support we'd enjoyed from the Wilson family. We just managed to keep the pot boiling."

When it began to look as if they were going to stay in California indefinitely, Moyna decided that it was time to bring out the boys, and in the spring of 1943, Bruce and Edgar were thrillingly reunited with their mother and sister. Fortuitously, John Abbott was just then moving out of the other little house on Mannix Drive, and so there was room for everyone. Moyna and Angela lived in one little house, and the twins in the other. They also had a car that Moyna had bought for just slightly more than nothing, an old tan Ford roadster with a rumble seat.

Bruce and Eddie would soon be going off as well. Once more, Moyna managed to get them scholarships to a private school, this time the California Preparatory School for Boys. It was in the Ojai ("Oh-hi") Valley, north of Los Angeles, near Santa Barbara, "and that was great," Bruce says, not only because it was close to home but also because "it introduced us to the out-of-doors and the mountains." In time, Bruce would become the West Coast twin, outdoorsy and jeaned, while Eddie would be the East Coast twin, urbane and tailored. As always, they were mirror reflections of each other, exactly the same only opposite.

Now that she was a Californian, it didn't take long for Moyna to discover what Eddie calls "the pre-New Age religions." Christopher Isherwood, who was part of her British crowd, had introduced her to Krishnamurti, the Indian mystic. Isherwood was only one of many intellectuals in the expatriate crowd. At one of the socials, Angela also met Aldous Huxley, and what was Moyna doing in such company? As Eddie perceives his mother, "She wasn't an intellectual herself, but she wasn't stupid, either. She was a romantic. She admired intellectuals, and they admired her because of her beauty and her personality. She was fey in a glamorous way, like Billie Burke [who played the good witch, Glinda, in *The Wizard of Oz*]. She was always striving to belong among intellectuals, but it was always beyond her grasp."

She also had a special appeal for homosexuals. It seemed to Eddie that "her personality just knocked them out, and in Hollywood they were a lot more open than in New York. Michael Kosleck, for instance, lived with two other German exile homosexuals in the Garden of Allah Hotel. They came to all our parties and were quite open about their situation." Of course Angela noticed that as well. "It only made it delightful that a great many of our interesting friends were gay. They were great company."

The boys fell in step beside Moyna and Angela among the expatriate actors and writers. It was hard not to. The houses were so small, and when there was company there was no place to hide. "Bruce and I would just sit there," Eddie recalls, "while all these wonderful old English actors told off-color stories and anecdotes." Everyone would entertain and Angela had developed a new party routine, a yowling imitation of two cats copulating on a corrugated tin rooftop.

"When she did that," Eddie remembers, "it was the *pièce de résistance.*"

However, Angela was also listening to and learning from her mother's social set. "My real education came out of where I was, what I was doing, who I was around, what I was gleaning. I was an extremely impressionable young person, and I met some extraordinary people during those young years."

But parties like the ones Moyna gave were not just social. They cushioned these out-of-work actors from the frustrations of job hunting by giving them a sense of a supportive show business community, and, more practically, they were also a source of food. One of the most bountiful tables was set by a woman with the remarkable name of Mayflo Roden-Ryan. "She laid out this incredible spread for hungry actors," Angela recalls, and it sometimes seemed as if the entire community of British émigré actors was being sustained at the Roden-Ryan house on Orchid Street in Hollywood on a Sunday afternoon.

Those who were managing to work gossiped about the movies they were making, giving those who were jobless a sense of at least being related to the picture business. They would all hush when Sara ("Sally") Allgood let them in on what was happening on the set of *How Green Was My Valley.*

Then the entertainment would begin, with little Roddy McDowell, for instance, climbing up on a chair to recite "The White Cliffs of Dover," or Moyna Macgill taking a turn at the Kiplingesque poem "Somewhere South of Singapore," and no party was richer in theatrical sensibility.

It was at one of these socials that Angela had a conversation that was to prove a turning point in her life — a demonstration of "networking" before there was such a word. It was at Mrs. Roden-Ryan's house, and the chat was with a slender and delicate-looking young Briton named Michael Dyne.

A would-be movie star with virtually no acting background, Dyne, like many of the people who were drawn to Hollywood, was hoping to get into the pictures purely on the basis of good looks. Sitting beside Angela as they held paper plates full of Mayflo Roden-Ryan's wonderful food, Dyne told Angela that he was being considered for a part in a movie. His screen test was already scheduled.

That was marvelous, she said, what was the movie? Over the buzz around them, and the Hollywood shop talk, the young actor told her that the picture was based on an Oscar Wilde novella called *The Picture of Dorian Gray.*

Then it occurred to him that there might be a role in it for her.

As Angela, by now a chain smoker, lit one cigarette after another, Dyne described the part. An English girl, quite young. Her name was Sybil Vane. She was, he said, "a victimized music hall performer who is smitten with Dorian Gray."

He paused and added, "The part does require that she sing a little."

He swallowed a forkful of food, looked up at her, and asked, "Can you sing?"

CHAPTER 4

HOLLYWOOD SCREEN TEST

MICHAEL DYNE came through on his promise to recommend Angela to Mel Ballerino, who was doing the casting for *The Picture of Dorian Gray,* and afterward, Michael called with his report.

"I made it sound as if you had just arrived in town. I said that I knew this young English girl who was over from London."

"Yes? And?"

"And asked that perhaps they might consider you for the role of Sybil Vane."

"What did Mr. Ballerino say to that, Michael?"

"He said," Dyne answered, "that he would get in touch with you and asked for your telephone number."

Metro-Goldwyn-Mayer was the biggest, the richest, and by far the most prestigious of the Hollywood movie studios. Covering several acres of Culver City land in western Los Angeles, its lot stood at the corner of Washington Avenue and Overland Drive. Through its legendary gates, one *got into the movies.*

Since Angela did not yet have her California driver's license, Moyna drove her to the appointment with Ballerino, and accompanied her on the interview, though not as protection. "Mel Ballerino wasn't the casting-couch type," Angela was relieved to learn. "But he did say something that knocked my socks off. Because he didn't talk about *The Picture of Dorian Gray* at all."

Instead, he announced, "It's amazing that you would be coming in today, because we're looking for a girl to play the maid in *Gaslight.*" That was more than true. The picture had been held up for months because the producer and director could not find an actress young enough and good enough to play this small but juicy part and do it with a convincing Cockney accent.

"We've already cast Charles Boyer and Ingrid Bergman, and the script is finished," Ballerino said. "It's by a Broadway playwright named John Van Druten."

Moyna winked at Angela.

"But they just can't find the girl."

A harrowing pause followed, and then he said, "Why don't we go upstairs? Maybe you can meet the producer, Arthur Hornblow, and the director, George Cukor."

As Ballerino telephoned Arthur Hornblow's office, Moyna nudged Angela and whispered, "I *know* John Van Druten! He's an old pal from London." As the men would not be available until later in the day, they were told to come back after lunch, which they were welcome to have in the studio commissary. Once there, Moyna went directly to a telephone and called Van Druten.

George Cukor was among the most respected of MGM's contract directors. He had a theatrical background, in fact. (Oddly enough, his last work for the theater was a play called *Gypsy,* a title that would figure in Angela's life, although this *Gypsy* had been written by Maxwell Anderson and was a twelve-performance flop.) But it was in Hollywood that Cukor had come into his own. His trademark was stylishness, and he specialized in vehicles for actresses, such as *Camille* for Greta Garbo and *The Philadelphia Story* for Katharine Hepburn. Because of his sympathetic touch, he was known as "the gentleman director."

John Van Druten obligingly called Cukor to put in a word for Angela. "Moyna Macgill is out here," he said. "She's a refugee with three children, and one of them is an actress about fourteen years old." With that mistake, the phone call nearly ended Angela's career before it began. Fortunately, although Cukor was discouraged by what he believed was her age, he was willing to meet the girl. An hour later, she and Moyna were "trooping"

(Angela's word) up to Arthur Hornblow's office, where the director was waiting.

She certainly looked older than fourteen; in fact, she looked older than her real age. Cukor was himself a youthful-appearing man of forty-four, handsome in a dark, slender, and bookish way, and his black-framed eyeglasses contributed to the thoughtful effect. He wore a New York gray suit but lent it a California informality with brown-and-white spectator shoes and an open-collared white shirt. In all, his manner was subdued, but warm and welcoming.

The first thing he learned about Angela was that she was almost eighteen, which was good. The bad news was that she had absolutely no professional acting experience whatsoever, neither in the movies nor on the stage. But surprising even himself, he turned to Ballerino and said, "It certainly is an interesting idea. Let's make a screen test."

"Well, can you imagine?" Angela said afterward. "I hadn't been able to get in the door of the studio. Couldn't break down the barrier. And now?

"What a thrilling moment!"

Cukor asked Angela and Moyna to stay in the office so that he might give them some suggestions about preparing for the test. Picking up a copy of the play, *Angel Street,* rather than the screenplay version, *Gaslight,* he turned to a scene that he was fond of. "We might as well give it a once-over," he said, "since we're already here."

And so with Moyna watching, proud and not yet competitive, the two of them started to read through the scene, an eager beginner (who says that she was calm and confident about her talent) and a famous director (who remembered her being "rather nervous"). From time to time, he stopped to tell Angela exactly how he wanted a line delivered. Then she would read it again, and so they proceeded. She was being coached for her screen test by the very man who would decide whether or not she got the part, and she thought, "It's also going to be great having Moyna's help. She can teach me the words, help me learn the lines, get ready to play the scene." That was exactly what they began to do when they got home.

On the day of the test, Moyna again drove Angela to MGM. After all the frustration of trying to get there, they passed through these legendary portals with a military snap of the guard's hand, and breezed in just like that.

Parking the dusty old family Ford in the studio parking lot, they found the rickety wooden building that housed Character Wardrobe all the way on the left of the studio's main street, which ran down the center of the MGM lot. The famous soundstages were on both sides of that street, first the smaller ones, where sound tests were made, and then the big stages, where all the great movies were filmed. The largest of all was for the swimming star Esther Williams, who needed her own stage with a water tank, which had to be particularly deep because of her high dives. (Actually, a double named Edith Mottridge did most of the diving for Williams, and the more difficult swimming, too.)

Inside Character Wardrobe were glass cases and open racks stuffed with old costumes. The room itself was bare and brightly lit, a barren setting for the glories within. For here was the stuff that America's dreams were made of, and the world's. Even this reserved English girl had been swept away by movie fantasies, and now she marveled at the racks of gaudy riches, costumes from medieval movies and pirate movies, religious movies and circus movies. There were costumes that had been worn by Marion Davies and Greta Garbo. "Fabulous costumes," she thought, "all of this stuff going back to *Ben Hur!* Every costume that had ever been made!" And she shivered at the idea that all the great stars and all the fine actors had come through this door at one time or another.

Alice Whitehouse, who ran Character Wardrobe, approached them, a cigarette dangling from the corner of her mouth. She was a "a gray-haired old bird of a woman," Angela recalls, "with a big fat stomach."

Moyna explained that they needed a costume for Angela's screen test, a Victorian housemaid's black dress with a white apron and a mob cap, as it was called in England. Whitehouse led them to a section that was devoted exclusively to maids' costumes. "There must have been a thousand black dresses there," it seemed to Angela, "and five hundred white aprons, all jammed together."

As she and Moyna poked through the garments, she asked Whitehouse whether the costume would be cleaned before the test. The wardrobe mistress, talking with the cigarette still in her mouth, informed her that the apron was *supposed* to be gray. Angela would soon learn that in a black-and-white movie, pure white was never used because it created too much of a glare. Anything that was white was "teched down," that is, made gray.

The day that she made the screen test, a young actor named Hugh Marlow played Charles Boyer's part with her, and weeks later, she still didn't know whether she had gotten the role. All she did know, and in a way it was worse than being rejected, was that she hadn't been eliminated, and so she was in limbo. "There was a lot of discussion," according to

Cukor, "because the studio didn't think she was sexy enough." He was recommending that they sign her, but even he didn't know exactly what was holding up the approval, which had to come from upstairs. One thing was certain about the casting of this role: the actress who played the housemaid had to be believable as a lure for Boyer, she had to be old enough to pose a threat to Ingrid Bergman, and she had to be sure enough of herself to be intimidating.

In an unusually thoughtful gesture, Cukor, knowing that the young hopeful was sitting by the telephone and waiting for the news, called just to say, "Miss Lansbury, I don't know whether you're going to get the job, but you're a very talented actress."

Angela could only comfort herself with the rationalization that it was not *Gaslight,* but *The Picture of Dorian Gray,* that had gotten her the chance at MGM, and she made that screen test too, playing the scene with the actor who actually was going to be in the movie. And it was not Michael Dyne. Her friend and benefactor had lost out to the incredibly handsome Hurd Hatfield, a classically trained twenty-eight-year-old actor who had made only one movie before, *Dragon Seed,* with Katharine Hepburn.

While they were waiting for Albert Lewin, the producer-director of *The Picture of Dorian Gray,* to arrive for the screen test, Hatfield told Angela not to give up hope on *Gaslight.* After his own screen test, he said, he'd waited three months before getting the part. Even now he was being reviewed. "They want to see how you and I would make out as lovers." That was a tall order because Hatfield was so effeminate that it was hard to imagine him as any woman's lover.

In fact, the real reason for the *Gaslight* delay was that the studio chief, Louis B. Mayer, had been on the East Coast watching his thoroughbred horses race. Mayer insisted on seeing every scrap of film that came out of the studio's cameras. It didn't matter whether it was daily footage from the most expensive of MGM productions or a screen test for a secondary player. Nobody was cast without his approval, and so all decisions were suspended until his return.

When he finally did get back, he sat down in his private screening room to catch up with what he had missed. Later, somebody told Angela that when Mayer saw her screen test for *Gaslight,* he turned to his assistant and said tersely, "Sign that girl."

"I might never even have had a career," Angela muses, "if Mr. Mayer hadn't seen that screen test himself." It was one reason why she came to like this generally reviled man. He made the miracle happen, and she was offered a standard one-year contract, with annual options for another six years. "I was signed out of nowhere!"

Quitting her $28-a-week job selling cosmetics at Bullocks-Wilshire, she moved up to the $500-a-week starting salary that MGM paid young contract players. "So that was a lot of money," she remembers, and not just for herself. This was a family thing, getting the role, getting the contract, and getting the salary. It was as if the miracle had happened to them as a unit. "An amazing event in our lives," is how it seemed to Angela, "to have the financial worries taken off us! After two years of borrowing and depending, at last we had the beginning of a future.

"We were simply over the moon with excitement and joy."

But she did take some personal pleasure in it.

"All right. So I was on my way."

Far from being glamorous, a contract player's first day of work at a movie studio was much the same as the first day at any job, taken up with filling out forms in a personnel office and attending to administrative details. Part of the routine at MGM was an appointment with Billy Grady, the head of casting, one of whose jobs was to prepare a basic fact sheet describing an actor's credits, experience, training, and background. It would be filed along with the fact sheets for all the other players in the studio's giant pool of talent, so that producers could easily find people to fill the slots in their pictures.

The most unexpected question that Grady asked Angela, who at that time was still known as Brigid, was, "What about the name?"

"*My* name?"

"Brigid Lansbury," he said. "You know that won't do."

It had not occurred to her, but she didn't disagree.

Then Grady said, "I see that your first name is really Angela."

She nodded.

"What do you think of Angela Marlow?"

"Pardon me?"

"Your name," he said. "How about making it Angela Marlow?"

"Angela Marlow?"

He might gave gotten the idea from the actor in her screen test, Hugh Marlow. "It sounds good to me," Grady said, "but if you don't like it, I've made a list of some others."

She was not going to let a name change stand in the way of her MGM contract, but as a general rule, a name is considered euphonious if both the first and last names have the same number of syllables. By that measure, "Lansbury" should have sounded better with "Angela," than the two-syllabled "Marlow."

She asked whether she might think about it. She wanted to talk it over with her mother.

There was something else to deal with. According to California law, the state protected young actors from the greed of their parents. Angela herself had heard about "terrible things that had happened with child stars." She was required to make a court appearance, and because she was still a legal minor, the judge declared her a ward of the court. This meant that he would set an allowance for her, to be paid out of her salary. The remainder of her income was to be placed in an escrow bank account and held there until she turned eighteen. Since that was only a few months away, the court protection would be brief.

The restriction on her daughter's income didn't deter Moyna from house hunting, and she promptly found a place on Sierra Alta Way, just off Sunset Boulevard. It was in a part of Beverly Hills that was definitely movie country. Roger Edens, from MGM's glamorous musicals department, lived just down the street and so, coincidentally enough, did George Cukor.

The price was an affordable $18,000, and Moyna charmed a bank officer into extending credit until Angela reached her eighteenth birthday. At that time, she explained to him, several thousands of dollars would already have accumulated in the girl's escrow account. It would be more than enough, she pointed out, for the down payment, and so she got a binder on the house. For the first time since Edgar had died, his family had a home of their own.

Was his daughter resentful about assuming financial responsibility for all the Lansburys? Her brother Edgar thinks she had every right to feel that way, but she insists, "Not for a second. We were a very closely knit little family, and I had no aspirations to leave the nest. We were going to make our way together. I do think, however, that as my father's deputy, it fell to me to create financial stability for the family."

When she wrote to her sister about the movie contract, "Zil" responded with a seriousness that the sisters seemed to share, certainly about acting. In an actress-to-actress letter, written from the house in William Mews where she and Peter Ustinov lived, Zil stressed the importance of retaining one's artistic integrity in Hollywood.

> Garbo and Davis to my mind have mastered it as nearly as anyone. Their performances flow and have depth and line and subtlety. Carole Lombard too. Some of the young ones, Teresa Wright and Durbin in her early films. You've got to be *really good,* not second best. It's the hard way but worth it in the end.

She gave some advice that would prove uncannily relevant to her sister's movie career.

> See that they don't try to alter the shape of your teeth and mouth to impose a synthetic mask on your charming, individual face and personality. You have so much that is good. Retain your guts and strength of character. By tact and grace and diplomacy avoid being made into just another pretty face on yards and yards of celluloid. And be an actress your own way.

She also passed on some practical tips.

> A friend of mine who's working in Larry Olivier's picture says Larry gave him a good piece of advice: "Remember, each department in the studio is only interested in its own job — the make-up man, your face; the hairdresser, your hair; the cameraman, the photography; etc., etc., etc. Concentrating on each one individually, you get the best from each." And all contribute to the complete and finished article!

And she ended on an inspirational note.

> It may sound hard — but acting is a hard life and you've got to work like blazes. Aim for the impossible to achieve the possible. Now go right out and smash 'em between the eyes!
>
> *Zil*

One lucky break, as it happened, led to another: Angela also got the part of Sybil Vane in *The Picture of Dorian Gray,* but *Gaslight* was to be made first.

The source for *Gaslight, Angel Street,* had been a hit play in London as well as New York; in fact, a British film of it starring Diana Wynward and

Anton Walbrook had already been made under the title *The Murder in Thornton Square.* (That movie would not be released in the United States until 1978, the discovery of a print leading to a belated American premiere.) As production began on the American version, Angela was made to appear physically intimidating with body padding as well as very high heels. A tall young woman at five feet eight, she was supposed to look taller than Bergman, who was an inch taller. However, it was not her physical appearance that startled Cukor on the first day of photography. "Suddenly," he said, "I was watching real movie acting. She *became* this rather disagreeable little housemaid — even her face seemed to change, it became somehow lopsided."

During breaks in the shooting, the director lived up to his gentlemanly reputation, treating her with a thoughtfulness that touched on the tender. If the crew was within earshot, he would refer to her as "Miss Lansbury," which made her feel respected. "I think he knew this," she said, "and I loved him for it."

As for her screen name, neither she nor Moyna liked "Angela Marlow," or any of the other names on Billy Grady's list. "We decided we weren't going to change my name. Angela Lansbury was more unique than any of the names they suggested," and Billy Grady did not make a fuss about that.

Because she was still technically a minor, a welfare worker was posted on the set, a woman who would clamp her hands over Angela's ears whenever the gentleman director rattled off a string of curse words. The studio also had to get permission from the Los Angeles Board of Education for a scene in which she smoked a cigarette. Rehearsing it, Angela — already a full-time smoker — pretended that she'd never touched a cigarette before, which Cukor thought was hilarious. He also "laughed uproariously," she remembered, "when I did my Cockney accent. Then he would goad me into being saucy and sexy with Ingrid and Charles."

The picture itself is a thriller about a London townhouse that has lain empty ever since the unsolved murder of its owner. The victim's niece (Ingrid Bergman), still traumatized from witnessing the event, has been persuaded by her new husband (Charles Boyer) that the only way to overcome her anxieties would be by moving into the old place. At first, their marriage is a happy one, but she is soon misplacing small objects, then hearing noises. He insists that she is imagining things, and at first seems concerned for her welfare. Then he turns impatient, and accusatory, and finally contemptuous and even threatening. He begins to suggest that she may be losing her mind, and she starts to believe it.

Angela's character, Nancy, the housemaid, is a dramatic contrivance to provide the first hint that the husband may be untrustworthy. She is flirtatious so that he can be responsive to her; she is disrespectful to his wife so that he can tolerate that. Van Druten's script is skillful in putting flesh on these bare construction bones, and it creates dramatic moments while making these points. For instance, when the husband asks the maid about her evening plans, Nancy replies that she is going to the music hall. She even sings a few measures of a song. Then, with a coquettish toss of her head, she turns away from him.

"You know, don't you," he says, "that gentlemen friends are inclined to take liberties."

"Oh no, sir," she replies saucily, "not with me. I can take care of myself." Here, Angela pauses for several tantalizing beats. Then she adds insinuatingly, "When I want to."

The moment is a memorable one, the pause invented by a born actress, and she gives the picture a sardonic wink that makes the villain himself vulnerable.

As Bergman's character teeters at the brink of emotional collapse, a detective (Joseph Cotton) solves the mystery, revealing the husband as the thief who committed the original murder. It is a stagey ending with the usual explanation before the final curtain, but the picture remains satisfying, and it would make "gaslighting" a euphemism for manipulating a nervous crisis.

Boyer's character is the picture's most weakly drawn, abrupt in his transition from husbandly devotion to melodramatic villainy, but Angela feels that "Charles was a very good actor, far better than he ever got credit for. His 'S.A.' as we used to call it — sex appeal — was so tremendous that women were dazzled by that and they didn't realize that he was acting."

Ingrid Bergman is sympathetic as his bride, by turns loving and fearful. It was important for her to establish that this woman was once confident and strong, and she accomplishes that in clear strokes at the outset. Angela admired her work, disagreeing with Katharine Hepburn's remark that Bergman was "too stupid to be any good." It seemed to Angela that "Ingrid was just stupid where men were concerned. I'm sure that's what Kate meant."

While *Angel Street* was a typical stage thriller, Cukor was justified in his boast that he'd made it into "a movie in the best movie tradition." The settings are elaborate, atmospheric, and convincing as London in the early 1900s. "Those sets," Cukor said, "are an example of the dazzling resources of a big studio." And the drama is cinematic in its flow and use of mood.

The picture was released in June of 1944, and Angela's work drew considerable praise for two reasons: one was simply the strength and definition of her performance. As Cukor said, "Hers is a Cinderella story. Even though it was her first picture, she had the ability to transform herself into the character that she was playing as soon as the camera turned."

The other reason was that she had the advantage of being an unfamiliar face. An unknown actor is often given credit for creating a believable characterization even though he is only playing himself. Subsequent performances are the truer test of a performer's abilities.

Angela reciprocated her director's respect. "Mr. Cukor initiated me into the very best standards of filmmaking. It's true, he was a great woman's director. He knew how to bring out the best in an actress, whether it was Garbo or little Miss Angela Lansbury, who was a nobody. He made me feel that I was an actress and made me feel important enough to be directed."

That credit duly given, she felt free to give a straightforward assessment of her own talent. It was something that she would never vulgarize with pretentions of modesty. She knew how good she was and relied on her gift from the outset. She would never have become an actress if she hadn't the talent, and it was that simple. "I was only eighteen," she says, "but I did know how to prepare. I knew how to play the role and I had a gift, an incredible gift."

Nominated for an Academy Award as Best Supporting Actress *in her movie debut,* she was not disgraced in losing out to the eminent Ethel Barrymore. Moreover, she had accomplished something rarer than winning an Oscar: she had been nominated for one not merely in her movie debut, but *in her first professional appearance as an actress.*

Her abilities, then, were unmistakable. What lay ahead was the time and the experience to broaden, deepen, complicate, and exploit that talent. This was only the beginning.

Because of the painstaking care being taken by the producer-director of *The Picture of Dorian Gray,* the picture was still not ready for production even after *Gaslight* was finished. Studio policy was to keep everyone working continuously and so Angela, who was being pigeonholed as strictly a

British teenager, was cast as another one in *National Velvet,* the movie version of the Enid Bagnold novel that had been her first "real, bona fide *book,*" one that didn't have a picture on the cover. She played the older sister of eleven-year-old Elizabeth Taylor, who was also going to have to get rid of her English accent if she were ever to have a movie future. ("When she grew up," Angela later said, "she lost the accent, but it still comes back if you listen to her. It's never very far away.")

National Velvet was a run-of-the-mill commercial movie that didn't seem to offer Angela any of the acting opportunities that were available in *Gaslight.* While it introduced her to some of her contemporaries at the studio, like Taylor and Mickey Rooney, she didn't feel comfortable with any of the other young actors at MGM. "My situation was different in that I came to work and I went home to my family. I wasn't living in an apartment on Wilshire like some of the girls." She adds, "I simply didn't speak their language, and I don't know what language I *was* speaking. I guess I was really driven — by the need to eat and make some money and get us on our feet. And to try and get somewhere."

Being in the movies was not quite as glamorous as her movie magazines had pictured it. Every morning, Moyna would wake Angela at five o'clock, and prepare a hot breakfast before driving her to the bus stop. Usually the boys came along for the ride, piling into the rumble seat with Fella, the dog. Once aboard the bus, Angela would regularly run into the child actress Margaret O'Brien, going to the studio with her mother.

As soon as she was able to get a California driver's license, Angela bought herself a car, a 1941 DeSoto. (New car production was suspended during the war.) Then, most days, she would pull through the MGM gates at around six, arriving at a studio that was already churning with activity. The lot was virtually a city. There were not only writers and cameramen and scenic designers and directors and actors; MGM built its own scenery and it even had its own foundry, where patterns were made and metal was cast. The studio made its own paint, its own rubber molds. There were automobile shops where "old" cars were assembled. There were electrical shops, glass and plastic shops, so that if a prop could not be found in the studio warehouse, it could be made overnight. That was what made MGM MGM.

The actors, when they arrived, were expected to know their dialogue for each day's shooting and to have allotted enough time for hairstyling, makeup, and costumes, so that by nine o'clock, they would be on the set and ready for the cameras.

Makeup was usually a half-hour job, and many of the players started the day in that department because they could stop in the middle, go off to Hairdressing or Wardrobe, and then come back to be finished. Makeup shared a building with the directors' offices. It had the downstairs level to itself, which was a sensible arrangement given that actors were constantly in and out for touch-ups. The department included a lab and a row of makeup studios, each about eight by ten feet. All of the makeup artists had their own little studios with a dentist's chair that faced a bulb-framed mirror. Beneath it was a counter for the makeup; everyone on the staff wore white smocks.

Actors were not assigned to particular makeup people. At first, Angela went to anyone who was free, whether it was Jack Dawn, who was the head of the department, or his assistant, Billy Tuttle, or one of the staff, like Dot Pondell (whose sister was the actress John Blondell) or Charlie Schramm. Later, when an actor felt comfortable with a particular makeup man or woman, it would become a regular appointment. Schramm became Angela's personal makeup man. "She had wonderful skin, and that youthful, buoyant look," he remembers.

The doors of the makeup rooms were always open, and while the actors were waiting their turns, they would poke their heads inside to chat or stand in the hall and visit with anyone passing by. Some were simply more flamboyant than the rest. It was against Charlie Schramm's doorway that Marlene Dietrich liked to lean and smoke a cigarette, with her robe hanging wide open and nothing on underneath. She would pretend to be unaware of it. "Sometimes she would show off like that," Schramm remembers. "I suppose the habits in Europe were different than ours. For him, "There was nobody like Marlene," but other actors had distinctive characteristics too. "Johnny Garfield had that New York quality about him, and Lucille Ball was flippant." Some of them were difficult. Schramm's biggest nuisance was Bette Davis. "She had an I'm-number-one-in-the-business quality," he remembers. But Angela, "she was never the star; just a nice, well-behaved lady, definitely a little bit apart from the Americans."

The other young British actress at MGM, Elizabeth Taylor, was also an easy subject, and her complexion was so good that she made *National Velvet* without wearing any makeup at all. Then again, young faces were generally untroublesome. "As faces got older," Schramm said, "it required more and more makeup to create the young and handsome look."

There were some skin problems, often relating to the thick "pancake" makeup. It was applied with a wet sponge on a cake of color. "I don't think there's such a thing as 'bad skin,'" Schramm said, "but it just isn't normal to fill up the pores every day with makeup." Actors sometimes broke out just from having heavy makeup put on and taken off.

In other instances, he blamed emotions for the complexion problems. "It was a nervous thing in lots of cases. Insecurities, trouble with the director — all of that can pose skin problems. In one case, I had to make up an actress who had just gotten through the chicken pox. She had picked off all the scabs so that she could get the part. And she did the picture. But I had to fill up all the little holes with wax before I could put the makeup on. It must have left scars, but they were going to replace her, and she was determined to get that part."

There seemed to be more waiting around in makeup than in hairdressing. Some people needed more time than others. It might be a peculiar role that required special face work, like a scar, or an actor might have special, personal problems. A couple of actresses had to get rubber noses, because their real noses had been botched during plastic surgery.

However, the basic, facial makeup was nothing complicated. "In the old days," Schramm said, "everything was in black and white, most people wore bright orange makeup because it gave the best exposure on the film. You could see the actors a block away. When color film came in, we had to go to natural colors. Just some color plus covering up the blemishes and the beards."

Next door to Makeup was Hairdressing, a big, open space with a long row of barber chairs, each facing a mirror. The fluorescent lamps overhead made it a harshly lit place, but lighting was not as critical here. The openness of the room and the proximity of the chairs invited socializing. The atmosphere was chummy, like a beauty parlor, except that the actresses had no say about how their hair was designed. That decision was made by Sydney Guilaroff, MGM's legendary stylist.

The actresses had their hair set every morning, but it was set while dry. The only exception was Rosalind Russell, who insisted on her hair being washed every morning and then set wet. Angela's memory of her was that "she was always under that cotton-picking dryer." Not surprisingly, Esther Williams needed unusual treatment because she was in the water so much of the time. Schramm said that they had to put real lacquer in her hair so that her permanent would hold underwater. Katharine Hepburn generally insisted on having her hair done in private, although sometimes she would join the common folk and let Guilaroff comb her out.

Angela remembers that "Sydney used to roll Kate's hair on huge, round rollers like the cardboard inner roll on toilet paper. She was the first to wear her hair in a big, loose pageboy."

The hairdressing room was a great equalizer. Angela found Lena Horne especially warm, and was charmed by Ava Gardner's earthiness. Some, like the aloof Rosalind Russell, were distinctly unapproachable. "I wouldn't ever have said, 'Good morning, Ros,' to her," Angela remembers, but on the other hand, "Greer Garson and I were fellow countrywomen, so we naturally gravitated toward each other. She was interested and knew about my background and my grandfather, and she was a very intelligent lady."

Somehow, Angela was never awed by the famous names. To her, "the great stars were just human beings. I'd been in the world of grown-ups since the time I was thirteen. I was a very sophisticated kid." However, she certainly didn't socialize with any of the MGM actors after hours, as she had so little in common with them. "There were people from every walk of life," she remembered. "Girls from Louisiana. Waitresses and cheerleaders. Girls who were there because they were the Orange Queen of South Carolina, and Miss Burbanks like the sixteen-year-old Debbie Reynolds." But they, at least, were working. Finally, after going to the studio for weeks and doing nothing, she started production on *The Picture of Dorian Gray.*

This drama, like *Gaslight,* would prove to be one of the last products of the old MGM. It was during the thirties, when Irving Thalberg was the head of production, that the studio had come into its greatness, when it was identified with polish and with such sophisticated movies as *Ninotchka, Goodbye, Mr. Chips,* and *Mutiny on the Bounty.* As the king of studios, it offered serious dramas and smart comedies made by sophisticated directors and played by charming actors. But after Thalberg died in 1936, the artistic tone of the studio was set by Louis B. Mayer, whose background was in finance. During his reign, MGM turned toward pictures with mass appeal, pictures likely to have big box office success, like *The Wizard of Oz, Mrs. Miniver,* and the *Andy Hardy* pictures. The studio of sophistication became a studio of family-oriented entertainments. *National Velvet* had been a typical example of that.

But Albert Lewin, the producer and director of *The Picture of Dorian Gray,* was a leftover from the old days. A man of refinement and intellect, he'd been Thalberg's assistant, and the picture would honor that association.

Like *Gaslight,* it is set in period London, although several decades earlier, in 1886. The source is, of course, Oscar Wilde's novella, a Faustian parable about a handsome and esthetic man of society — a man with a soul as beautiful as his features — who falls in love with a young and innocent actress. But his beauty is the flaw in his spirit. After his mentor and manipulator, Lord Wotton, advises him that "there is only one thing worth having, and that is youth," Dorian wishes for it to be eternal, and the wish is granted at the cost of his soul.

Remaining physically flawless, he descends into a degenerate life, and finally an evil one. Although Dorian does not grow older, his age and decadence are reflected in the portrait of his youthful self that he keeps locked in the attic. At the movie's climax, the horrific painting is flashed on the screen in full color, in what is otherwise a black-and-white movie. It was such a sensational effect that many people remembered the movie for that moment alone.

Although there is no explicit statement of a homosexual theme, it is implicit throughout the story, through oblique Victorian references to "visits to the abyss" and "low dens." A half century later, as mores changed, video stores would be stocking *The Picture of Dorian Gray* in their "Alternative Life Styles" sections.

In the simplest of terms, the character of Dorian Gray is the plaything — the sex object — of the witty but unscrupulous and sadistic Lord Wotton, played by the urbane George Sanders. As Hurd Hatfield said, "Sanders understood the implications of the script, and so did I — the real relationship in the movie was between Lord Wotton and Dorian, but it's just implied. If it had been done in 1997, I would have been seen getting into bed with him, and it would have been a mess. The reason the movie still works is that those things happen offstage."

The manipulative Lord Wotton is the true villain of the piece. He persuades the gullible young esthete to test Sybil's moral backbone by suggesting that she spend the night with him. Wotton knows that the girl's fears of losing Gray will frighten her into agreeing, and that he will consequently turn against her for being immoral. In this, Wotton is more evil than his protégé, for he is ruthlessly contriving the suicide of this innocent girl in order to obtain Dorian for himself, though that is certainly left unstated.

The literary irony of Oscar Wilde's novella is that Lord Wotton, the society hypocrite, survives, while Dorian Gray — an innocent at the outset — becomes a victim. It is because of that irony, and Oscar Wilde's genius, that this movie remains effective. *The Picture of Dorian Gray* is perhaps not as well made as *Gaslight,* but it remains atmospheric and engrossing.

Although Lewin's literary sensibility imbues the film with a certain degree of artistry, his work is in many ways betrayed by inexperience. As an art connoisseur, he had decided to focus the movie on its titular painting. Desiring "before and after" portraits of Dorian Gray, he commissioned two artists who were actually *twins,* Ivan Lorraine Albright (who would go on to achieve considerable reputation) and his brother Marvin (whose painting of the young Dorian was rejected).

The minor roles were weakly cast with contract players such as Peter Lawford and Donna Reed. Moyna had a bit part because L. B. Mayer, for all his tyrannical ways, was oddly family conscious, even giving her a one-year contract. (He also tried to sign the twins, but Angela and Moyna vetoed that idea.)

Some actors look to a director as their guru, others as their protector, some as merely their guide. On the stage, some will even ignore him, but in a movie, they have no choice but to place their trust in his technical expertise. Albert Lewin's greenness rattled Hatfield, and the actor was thrown when the director gave him such baffling instructions as "I won't press the camera button until I see the thought forming in your head." Lewin would also insist on a certain tilt of the head, a lift of the hand, even a curl in the corner of the actor's lip, demands that were exasperating to someone like Hatfield who had been trained in the psychological school of Stanislavsky, as taught by the acting teacher Michael Chekhov.

The highly strung, often petulant actor was also unhappy about the visitors who kept showing up on the set. He could hardly complain when Mr. Mayer came around, but he did object to Katharine Hepburn's showing up "just because she wanted to watch. She just comes onto the set, saying, 'Hello,' to everyone. So they all answer, 'Hi, Kate!' Everything stops. I wasn't used to that. We don't have it in the theater.

"Somebody comes into a theater and stops a rehearsal?"

Lewin finally closed the set to all guests, but tension and petulance weren't what really bothered Hatfield. He had so completely identified with the character of Dorian Gray that he was in full crisis.

Angela was too disciplined as a professional, too reserved as an individual, and just too reasonable to confuse herself with a role. She certainly had no opportunity to do so in this picture, for Sybil Vane is a straightforward part, offering few of the shadings that had been possible with *Gaslight*'s Nancy. Nor was there a mentor like George Cukor behind the camera, encouraging her to dig deeply into the character she was playing. And so she made *The Picture of Dorian Gray* "kind of walking through it in a daze."

Her most creative contribution is in her first scene, when Gray comes to a tavern-theater called the Two Turtles Club and is instantly smitten when he hears Sybil sing a Victorian air, "Goodbye Little Yellow Bird." Angela's voice is light, sweet, and true, and she communicates purity and trustfulness with her song.

Goodbye, little yellow bird
I'd rather brave the cold
On a leafless tree
Then a prisoner be
In a cage of gold

Although *Dorian Gray* was made a year after *Gaslight,* visually, its style is almost that of a routine silent movie. The subject matter, too, seems antiquated, for while *Gaslight* offers psychological drama, *Dorian Gray* is rococo. Finally, its cast seems to work individually, rather than as a coherent ensemble. Yet fifty years after it was made, *The Picture of Dorian Gray* continues to have a unique power, and it remains a mysterious and hypnotic piece. Sanders's cynical manner and personal brand of world-weariness are especially effective, and they were not entirely feigned. While making the picture, he invited Hatfield to dinner at his home. Opening the door, he said, "You should marry a reputable waitress, the way I did. And make her into a lady." Then, Hatfield was led into the living room, where Sanders's wife was playing cards. "This is my wife," he said, and pointing to another woman, added, "and that is my mistress."

The two women glanced up in astonishment. "And this," Sanders said, bowing in Hatfield's direction, "is Dorian Gray."

In a painful way, he was right. Hatfield's performance was so vivid that it came to curse his career. He could not escape being identified with the part, and years later, when he appeared in summer stock, he was still being billed as "The Dorian Gray Man."

As for Angela, *The Picture of Dorian Gray* provided her with a second Academy Award nomination in two years of moviemaking.

CHAPTER 5

SURPRISE!

WHEN Angela began to earn enough money to ensure the security of her little family, it changed not only how they lived but their outlook in general. Her $500-a-week salary "was a fortune, a fortune — when you consider what we'd been living on. Suddenly, we blossomed.

"I mean, my mother and I, we just took it away."

And that salary was only the beginning. Every year that MGM exercised its option, she would be given an increase. Were her contract to run the full seven years, she would be making close to $1,500 a week. Such numbers were stunning after all the years of economizing, and as if a door had finally been opened, whenever she and Moyna simply felt like it, they would go off and buy all the clothes they wanted at Robinson's or even Bullocks-Wilshire.

"Just like girls with some money in their pockets," Angela says.

Being under contract at MGM meant that an actor was on call six days a week for forty weeks of the year. There was a twelve-week layoff period, which was, in effect, a three-month vacation without pay, but the salary was amortized so that there was a paycheck every week for fifty-two weeks.

The assignments were made unilaterally. A producer would ask the actor to read or test for a role, and if he was satisfied, the part would be cast. If an actor was unhappy with a role, a complaint could be registered, but it would seldom have any effect. Interestingly enough, the casting decision that would have the greatest impact on Angela's career, at least according to her, was a minor role in, of all things, a western musical called *The Harvey Girls.*

The role of "Em" is essentially that of a whorehouse madam, although in this family movie, she is portrayed as a saloon dance hall queen in a frontier dime-a-dance, leaving the audience to make of her what they wished. The other actresses who had been considered for the Mae West–like part, Lucille Ball and Ann Sothern, were more obviously the type, both of them older, tougher, big-city, gum-chewing dames. What was Angela Lansbury doing in such company? Why was a twenty-year-old British actress, nominated for the 1944 Academy Award, and still in the running for the 1945 Oscar, playing a thirtyish, dance hall madam in a musical western?

The inappropriateness of the role was exactly what made *The Harvey Girls* so significant to her career. It would not only establish her versatility, but more important, it was a very American role in a very American movie in which she was going to have to speak a very American brand of English ("with a western twang," she said). It would get her out of the British rut.

Unfortunately, the role also settled her classification as a supporting actress. She had to accept the reality that she was not going to be a leading lady, would never be the glamour girl. It confirmed her old insecurities about her looks. The cheekbones were not high enough, the face was too round, the eyelids too heavy. She simply was not beautiful in the manner of the day, which, as she herself acknowledged, was personified by Rita Hayworth. "I got by, for God's sake, but I didn't have whatever it took."

If she was going to have a movie career, then, it would have to be a career as a character actress who could play Americans. To pull that off, she called upon an ability that had nothing to do with training, craftsmanship, or expertise, but rather, her gift for impressions, imitations, and dialect. She knew, above all, that her accent had to be flawless. When an Englishman imitates an American poorly, or even just fairly well, it is not only obvious to local audiences, it is ridiculous. When it is done convincingly, though, the audience doesn't have an inkling that the actor is even doing an impersonation. "Accents," Angela says, "come easy to me. I've got an ear like a parrot. And I don't think it can be taught."

Another reason *The Harvey Girls* was a watershed for her was that it was her first musical, and the musicals being made at MGM were very special indeed. They had a look, a sound, and a spirit that no other studio seemed able to match, a style that was the doing of the famed MGM musical unit, headed by producer Arthur Freed, with the influential assistance of Roger Edens, the musical director, and his assistant, Kay Thompson.

Edens and Thompson worked with anyone who was singing, or even auditioning to sing, in one of the musicals. If a director was looking to cast a singing part, or if the studio was considering signing a singer, Edens and Thompson had responsibility for the final decision. Then, when the film was actually made, Roger would create the arrangement, that is, the rhythm and shape and style of the performance. He also often wrote the orchestrations, specifying which instruments played what sections in which combinations. Sometimes he even wrote the music itself, as for instance "The French Lesson" in *Good News,* or most of the songs for *On the Town.*

Meanwhile, Kay created the vocal arrangements — the way the singer or group of singers would perform a song, choosing the key, tempo, harmonies, shadings, deciding whether or not a verse would be sung, whether anything would be repeated, and so on. A Kay Thompson vocal arrangement was unique, especially when it involved small groups of singers. Syncopated, jazz-influenced, and theatrical, her work could be identified within the first few measures.

While *The Harvey Girls* was not one of the Freed-Edens-Thompson unit's better efforts, it was a major MGM production because it starred Judy Garland, who at the time was one of the studio's biggest and most beloved stars. In its foolish screenplay (five writers are credited), she plays a girl from Ohio who goes to the frontier West as a mail order bride, but on the way changes her mind and joins up with a group of girls who are going off to work in a chain of family restaurants. Trouble starts when the new arrivals are viewed as competition by Angela, the dance hall hostess, her girls, and their tough guy bosses. But the head boss, played by the handsome John Hodiak, has the soul of a poet and rides off into the sunset with Judy Garland.

Handsome men had always had a big attraction for Angela, and she immediately developed "a great crush" on Hodiak. "Crush" is exactly the right expression for it, because she was still utterly inexperienced in romantic matters. She had no friends her own age and spent her evenings with Moyna and the twins. "I really was a homebody," she remembers, "and I was afraid to go out."

But something in her personality seemed to be changing, because *The Harvey Girls* was definitely making her feel romantic and even sexy. She enjoyed the extra attention that Wardrobe and Makeup were paying to her appearance. She liked having her shoulders bared, wearing tights, and being promoted as "Legs Lansbury." She let herself be "pumped up into this voluptuous, sexy woman," and found that it was not only exciting, but that in playing the saloon hostess, "I took on all of those attributes. The picture opened the kind of physical attention to me that I'd never known." All at once, there were young men around the set whistling at her.

"I nearly fell down. How could it be me? I was this naive, overweight English girl."

Although she really wasn't overweight, it remained her self-image, and because she thought of herself as unattractive and unsexy, she had never learned to flirt. When young men approached her, she told herself she couldn't be bothered; that they bored her. When they got close enough to touch her, "Their sexuality didn't interest me, or arouse me in any way. I needed an older man," she said. "A psychologist might have said I was looking for a father figure," so showing off her legs and wearing a brief outfit in *The Harvey Girls* turned out to be of greater satisfaction than the part itself. As she says, "You weren't playing Hedda Gabler here, you were simply playing a type," and the type she was playing did little more than sneer, along with an occasional snarl ("Our profession is entertainment, *see?*"). She was disappointed that she didn't get a chance to sing, but Roger Edens considered her voice so inadequate he had Em's single vocal number dubbed by another singer.

Even so, making the picture proved to be an exhilarating experience. Critics and intellectuals of the period might have considered musicals inferior to dramas, but actors were beyond that. For them, there was something spectacular and elating about singing and dancing in public, and Angela was at least included in the dance numbers. She also felt a sense of *company* making this musical, in contrast to dramatic movies. "Company" is a stage term; a theater cast reads a script together, rehearses it together, and plays it together, making them feel like a family. Movies, however, are made in bits and pieces, and generally, an actor works only with those people who are in his scenes.

In a *musical* movie, though, the big numbers require that everyone be present for group rehearsals, which create a satisfying, company situation. They also generate energy. In working on the big numbers for *The Harvey Girls,* Angela felt the same sense of vigor that she used to enjoy in her London dance classes. "This was very exciting. It was my introduction to Robert Alton, the choreographer, and working with Roger Edens and Kay

Thompson filled me with this tremendous urge to be part of this musical world," a world in which she was still determined to sing.

Because *The Harvey Girls* showed her legs, chest, and bare arms, she had to make a special stop every morning at Body Makeup. This all-female department at MGM was run by a woman known simply as "Fuchsia," and for obvious reasons. Everything she wore was that color, from her nail polish to her blouses. One morning, Angela walked into Fuchsia's place to find Marlene Dietrich having her legs made up. Every day for a week, those famous legs were being given two coats of gold paint for a scene in *Kismet,* a picture Dietrich was making with Ronald Colman. Then, needing to let them dry, the glamorous star untied the silk braid around the waist of her robe, sat down and tilted her chair backward against the wall. Opening the robe completely, she swung one bare, gold leg over one arm of the chair, and the other gold leg over the other arm. The exhibitionist was wearing no underwear. "Nothing on at all," Angela reports cheerfully. "Just airing herself out. That was her style."

Not everything about making *The Harvey Girls* was cheerful. Late starts were a frequent annoyance. The cast would be on the set at nine o'clock, made up, costumed, and ready to work, but forced to wait for Judy Garland to show up. "She wasn't the world's greatest actress," Angela says, "but she certainly was the world's sweetheart, the great personality, and the great problem child at MGM in those days. Everybody adored her, but we all had to take second place to anything that she wanted. She was awfully jolly and a tremendous worker. But it was always on her terms, and when she came to work, everyone had to jump in behind. That is, when she came to work."

Garland usually appeared around eleven o'clock. Apologizing to the cast and crew, and visibly upset, she would blame the delay on problems like alterations for her wedding dress. As everyone knew, she was about to marry the director Vincente Minnelli.

Angela found herself worrying about Judy. "She was such a sensitive little soul with this enormous voice and tremendous success. She was always on edge and up to her neck in pills. I guess she was using drugs to keep herself from eating." One day during production, when the two of them were sharing a limousine, Garland proudly showed Angela her engagement ring. It was an unusual one, with a pink pearl in a black enamel setting. As she held it out for examination, she burst out laughing. It was a frightening laugh, more hysterical than joyous; and it gave Angela the chills.

On the *Harvey Girls* set, the director, George Sidney, kept urging

Angela to work with the studio drama coach. Considering the disparity in abilities at a place like MGM, with actors ranging from Shakespeareans to beauty queens, the notion of a drama coach was somewhat absurd. Nobody could teach across that wide a spectrum. Angela, of course, didn't believe that acting could be taught on any level, but because the MGM drama coach was Mr. Sidney's wife, there was no diplomatic way to escape.

Lillian Sidney's method of drama coaching was to teach an actor every word of every scene he or she appeared in, demonstrating how the lines should be read, and drilling until the duplication was complete. Her great successes, Angela believes, were with the completely incompetent — Lana Turner, for instance. "Lillian tried to do it with me," Angela says, "but I just did not want to be told how to act."

Then again, the production schedule of a movie like *The Harvey Girls* was sometimes a mere four weeks, leaving barely enough time for the actors to learn their lines and speak them for the camera. If the scene was essentially satisfactory, the director would have it printed.

More work was devoted to the musical numbers. Angela rehearsed for three weeks with Garland and Cyd Charisse, learning Robert Alton's choreography, and "that opened all kinds of thoughts in my mind. That was when I decided that I *loved* the musical side of acting. Since I was worried about my ability to become a big star in Hollywood, I decided that I was going to make my name as a musical star on Broadway."

It was certainly a farfetched notion for an actress who had never been on a professional stage in her life — not in a single play, let alone a musical — and who had just been rejected as a singer in a movie. Still she thought, "I know I've got something and one of these days I'm going to show it." And she would nurture this feeling by "imagining," as she put it, or "visualizing" herself getting that opportunity, picturing herself at the center of a big musical, "being able to sing like a bird, dancing like a dream, this is how I envisioned myself."

It was an approach that she had learned at the Church of Science of the Mind, a La Brea Avenue spiritual center that she attended with Moyna. Sometimes, Bruce and Eddie were taken along, too. "It was a free-thought religion," Eddie remembers, "kind of a conglomeration of all religions rolled into one, called *Vedanta*."

Angela had certain reservations about it, but she took it more seriously than her brothers. "My mother was very responsible for starting me on a journey of self-realization. Of course Los Angeles is famous for all kinds of things like that, but they're wonderful for helping people get on the right track."

It was there, too, that she learned to avoid any "negativity" around her. What she got from the Church of Science of the Mind was not a formal philosophy, but a state of mind and a way, she says, "to describe the accepting and searching for the ultimate perfection of life. It certainly helped me. It's basically what I live by. I feel very strongly about the magic of believing."

Perhaps as part of her dream of someday being in a musical comedy, she was more and more drawn to the musical people she was now meeting, particular Roger Edens and Kay Thompson, who seemed to be the MGM musical incarnate. Both were tall and slender and very good-looking. Edens was a Southerner with a fey elegance, and although he'd been married, Angela read him as "gay, obviously." She found Kay Thompson "the most colorful character you could possibly imagine." She was an extravagantly glamorous, brightly bleached blond with a whiskey voice and an easy way with cigarettes. In the MGM commissary, lunch time or no and southern California notwithstanding, Thompson would make her entrance in a long mink coat. Her eyelashes were shamelessly false, but her flamboyance was real and it delighted Angela. Small wonder that to this inhibited twenty-year-old, Roger Edens and Kay Thompson were "terribly sophisticated" and scintillating people. "But," she knew — and this was an important but — "they were also warm and friendly human beings, and they weren't snobs. They were workers, they were musicians, and anyone who really worked at what they were brilliant at, appealed to me."

As far as Angela was concerned, then, Roger Edens and Kay Thompson "were the absolute tops. They were chic and smart and funny but also silly and full of jokes. They were fun to be around.

"They were hot stuff."

Being around such hot stuff made musical performance all the more appealing to the young actress, and apparently Edens and Thompson took to Lansbury as well. Soon she was being invited to the big parties that Edens gave at his home on Schuyler Road, just a few blocks from her own house.

On one occasion, her escort was the composer Hugh Martin ("Have Yourself a Merry Little Christmas," "The Trolley Song"), and by the time they arrived, the party was in full swing, and looking just like a scene in a movie itself. People were singing at the piano, and an electric buzz was in the air. It seemed to Angela that "all the reigning stars of MGM musicals were there, and all the composers, the producers, the directors."

At the center was a concert grand piano and there Edens had a dazzling fluency, but it was not just his musicianship that delighted the young actress. It was "his taste, his style, the way he entertained, and just the way he ran his parties." The glamour quotient at these affairs was always high, and Edens would sit at his beautiful piano and accompany anyone who felt like singing, whether it was Frank Sinatra, Judy Garland, Mickey Rooney, Gene Kelly, Van Johnson, or Lena Horne. As Betty Comden said, "None of us was 'on.' Everyone performed at Roger's because it was like breathing. Anybody who could do anything did it."

Then, if Kay Thompson was in the mood to perform, Edens would slide over and make room for her. "She managed to play," Angela remembers, "with the longest, reddest nails anyone ever saw — on such long, bony fingers. She played and sang with this husky smoker's voice. I always thought she would never make the note with that raspy voice, but she always did. She had the most incredible facility for selling a song," and at those parties, Angela more than enjoyed the glamour. "I certainly listened, and docketed away a tremendous amount of musical education."

Although she had not had a single serious romance in her life, whether for lack of time or inclination, Angela now began seriously dating an actor named Richard Cromwell. He had seen Moyna play a small but juicy part in *The Big Clock,* and was then floored by Angela's performance in *The Picture of Dorian Gray.* He was desperate to meet both mother and daughter, and prevailed upon a mutual friend to get their telephone number.

Hearing from him flashed Angela back to her starstruck childhood, when she collected American movie fan magazines, "bought for thruppence in Woolworth's. I remembered seeing a picture of him and this actress, sitting on a diving board at the Hotel Miramar in Santa Monica." Now life had brought her to the flesh-and-blood Richard Cromwell, in his home on Miller Drive, on a hillside overlooking Sunset Boulevard.

The house was small but exquisite, and with Angela seated beside him at dinner, he told her all about its history. To her mind, "it was a rarefied and marvelous little house," and Cromwell was pleased that it was stylish enough for Cole Porter to borrow whenever he came to California. Richard also talked a great deal about art and architecture and antiques. Although

Angela had always been taken with knowledgeable older men, Cromwell had something else to offer: he was gorgeous, blond and suntanned, with a beautiful and resonant voice. He was funny, too, and better still, the admiration went both ways. "He thought I was the prettiest thing on two feet."

As a contract player at Columbia Pictures, Richard Cromwell had played featured parts in a half dozen films. His biggest role was in *Lives of a Bengal Lancer,* which starred Gary Cooper, but he'd never been more than a second-string actor, and now he was not even that. His movie career was all but over, which left him, in the cruel clarity of a Hollywood cliché, somewhere between a has-been and a never-was. To make matters worse, he was aging. He didn't look it, but he was sixteen years older than Angela.

He told her that although he still looked for parts, he spent most of his time making this beautiful house even more beautiful. He maintained a lovely flower garden. He had a kiln and made ceramics and life masks, which, he said, frightened people because the process required that the subject breathe through nostril straws while the clay was setting. When he was preparing a life mask of Bea Lillie, as he related to Angela with a chuckle, "I told her, 'It'll be hard in a minute.' "

The comedienne mumbled, "Isn't that what the sailor said?"

It was Hollywood dinner table talk, and there were movie stars at elbow distance and the names of others being dropped and trashed all over the place; the party atmosphere was brightened by dirty jokes and wine, both of them good. For the young actress, this made for a heady mix, and as Cromwell focused his attentions on her, he raved about how he'd been "absolutely dazzled" by her performance as Sybil Vane in *The Picture of Dorian Gray* — just floored by the "apparition" he'd seen on the screen.

He insisted that she call him "Roy," as all his friends did, his real name being Roy Radabaugh. He seemed to know everyone, and Angela found him a "wonderful and dear man." They began to see each other frequently, and after several weeks, he became the twenty-year-old virgin's first lover. To the sexual neophyte, their physical life was "not great but all right" — all right enough for her to fall "madly in love with him."

Now a couple, they would drive off to Palm Springs for weekends. She had plenty of free time, since it was the layoff period at the studio. He introduced her to some of the most famous stars in Hollywood — Cary Grant, Joan Crawford, Gary Cooper, and William Holden — and their various wives, husbands, and lovers. There were a lot of gay men in his circle, too. Cromwell's next-door neighbor was Jerry Asher, the head of publicity at Warner Brothers and he made no secret of being homosexual. Hollywood's double standard meant that being gay was acceptable as long as it was kept within the movie community. It could not be revealed in public, where everything had to be played straight. The hypocrisy made for a nasty bargain.

Roy's crowd, then, was a crowd of movieland insiders. He even knew Angela's old friends, Zachary and Elaine Scott, who had given the Lansburys their first American lobster, and he introduced her to the actor Scott McKay and his wife, the writer Maggie Williams, who became her new friends.

But Angela and Roy's life was not all social. When they were alone, he would share with this very unworldly and inexperienced young woman all his interests, and he was interested in many things — most excitingly, for Angela, music. His taste ranged from popular music to jazz, and he would play records of pop singers like Russ Columbo, Jo Stafford, and Peggy Lee, jazz singers like Billie Holiday, Ella Fitzgerald, Sarah Vaughan, and Lee Wiley, and Broadway original-cast albums, too, which she had never heard before. Listening to his recording of *Annie Get Your Gun* she heard Ethel Merman for the first time. "That," she remembers, "was one of the most exciting voices I had ever heard in my life."

Angela gives Roy credit for introducing her to "the singers and the voices that really gave me the backbone of my musical training; people who sang and knew how to phrase and were totally individual in the way they performed and sang songs."

Roy was a native Californian, and his mother, Fay Radabaugh, lived in Long Beach, just outside of Los Angeles. On first meeting she seemed to Angela "a little drink of water of a woman, tiny like a feather." Meeting Mrs. Radabaugh was, of course, the first step to getting married, which the couple did on September 27, 1945, before a justice of the peace in Independence, California. From there, they drove to Lake Tahoe, Nevada, where Roy had arranged a honeymoon hotel. It was all like a dream to Angela. "I never really thought through what I was doing, getting married. I was just carried away with the idea."

For a wedding present, Roy gave her a Steinway grand piano, and they embarked on a marriage of entertaining. There was always somebody for lunch, often Maggie and Scott McKay. "We would do silly things," Maggie remembered, such as dancing around the pool with high kicks, imitating a Broadway show. "We gossiped about the studios. Nobody talked about the war's ending. We were so removed from the real world."

When the summer hiatus was over, Angela returned to work, starting with a cameo appearance in *Till the Clouds Roll By,* an all-star musical biography of Jerome Kern. It reunited her with Roger Edens and Kay Thompson, and in this film Roger gave her the chance to sing a song in her own voice. ("I knew that with a little coaching, I could do it.") The song was a Cockney turn called "How'd You Like to Spoon with Me?," and Angela looks positively tickled performing it. When she watched herself in the movie, she wondered, "Who is that girl? How did I ever get it together to do all that?"

The studio loaned her out to United Artists for *The Private Affairs of Bel Ami,* which reunited her with George Sanders and the director Albert Lewin, both friends from *The Picture of Dorian Gray.* Lewin used Moyna in this movie, as well, but no loan-out was necessary in her case, because MGM had not renewed her option.

Angela knew that she need have no such worries about her own option, but even with that confidence she was not thrilled with the direction her career was taking. After starting out with two wonderful roles in *Gaslight* and *The Picture of Dorian Gray,* she had made no progress toward bigger parts, and those she was cast in were for mundane projects. It was of little consolation that she was being noticed and written about in fan magazines, the ones she used to dream over as a London teenager.

One of the articles mentioned Roy, as well, describing Angela as being married to "former actor Richard Cromwell." He was complaining of increasingly painful migraine headaches and was suffering asthmatic attacks. He was already an alcoholic.

His frequent dinner parties had now become their frequent dinner parties, which were no great burden on Angela, since she had a housekeeper to do the cooking as well as the cleaning, and Roy liked to do a lot of the menu planning and the flower buying himself. Since he usually invited her mother, her life was not really so different from the way it had been. In fact, Moyna was at Angela and Roy's so often that it seemed to her son Bruce, "as if she wanted to be a third party to that marriage." She even went with them to the Academy Awards dinner in March of 1946, and it turned out to be a good thing she did. A year earlier, simply being nominated might have been recognition enough for Angela, since *Gaslight* had been her first movie. In that case, she could hardly have been insulted, being beaten out by the likes of Ethel Barrymore (for *None But the Lonely Heart*). When she lost again, this time to Anne Revere — in a movie that, ironically, she'd been in herself, the lightweight *National Velvet* — it was a real letdown, and she sounded as if she was delivering a frustrated acceptance speech when complimented, during the evening, for her work in *The Picture of Dorian Gray.* "I really can't take credit for that performance," she remarked. "I have to credit Albert Lewin, and the cinematographer, the music, the role, and the art direction. I was framed in the most perfect way and I would like to be remembered for that part."

On that night she lost, Roy wasn't even at her side to console her, but was deeply engaged in conversation with Bette Davis. Angela had only Moyna to give her a hug and tell her to put on a brave face.

A few months later, she came home to find his car gone and his closets and drawers emptied. The note was left on the piano.

I'm sorry, darling. I just can't go on.

He didn't say why he couldn't go on or what had prompted his departure. He simply disappeared.

She was staggered, and reeled next door to Jerry Asher's house, as if he would somehow be wise enough to figure everything out and explain it to her.

"What was wrong?" she pleaded. "Where did Roy go? *Why* did he go?"

Asher had no answers, nor did anyone else. She assumed it was her fault, that she had failed him as a wife. She floundered beneath waves of rejection. A sense of inadequacy became self-criticism. She had been spending too much time at the studio; her success had hurt his pride. She was to blame.

In the agonizing months that followed, the young bride rocked with pain. Finally, desperate for an explanation, she contacted Roy's psychiatrist, Dr. Bertram Frohman. "I just wanted him to explain what it was that had gone wrong. What it was I didn't understand."

At a meeting with Dr. Frohman, she brought up Roy's sinus attacks, his headaches, his drinking. The psychiatrist listened but said little. Professional ethics, he explained, forbade him from violating his patient's confidence. Although his evasions annoyed her, Frohman reassured her that Roy did not leave because of anything she had done wrong. "Dr. Frohman told me," she remembers, " 'You are the most balanced person. You have no problems. You see things in a sane, adult way. You are not in any way an emotionally disturbed person.' "

It was of little consolation, for she had never doubted her own sanity. When she continued to press him, insisting that she needed some rationale to get a grip on her situation, he ventured a "guess" as to why the marriage had not worked — could not work — but it was frustratingly vague. She "had been badly let down," she pleaded, but despite the urgency of her need, it seemed to her that the psychiatrist was being "very careful and tender" when she needed specifics.

Gradually, she sensed that there was something peculiar about the entire situation. It was as if everyone knew something that they did not want to tell her. She hadn't asked Moyna's opinion about why Roy had left her, which in itself was strange. Perhaps (she would later speculate) she was afraid that her mother had information that she did not care to hear.

And then the truth dawned on her, and she thought back in a rage about her meeting with Roy's psychiatrist, for she realized that his tiptoeing around the subject was not tender, but cowardly. "He just didn't have the courage to tell me that my husband was a homosexual. He never said, 'Your husband is a homosexual and therefore he is incapable of having a relationship with a woman, sexual or otherwise.' He implied that Roy wanted to have that relationship with me, and just couldn't, but Dr. Frohman never really said anything to me that helped, and there I was, absolutely shattered."

Having finally recognized Roy's homosexuality, she realized that not only "everyone knew it except me," but "Moyna *had* to have known." Her brother Bruce thinks so, too. "Why not? Eddie and I both knew. She might have gone along with it because she wanted to keep her relationship with Angie intact."

Finally Angela realized what a child she still was, and how immature her approach to marriage had been. "I must have been going through life with blinkers on. I'd been leading a totally unreal existence. I had never thought about where this marriage would lead or whether I wanted a family. I never thought about anything beyond the current five minutes."

Her growing self-realization, and the cycle of psychological reactions served to ease, but not overcome "the biggest emotional punch that I ever experienced." And what seemed to hurt her most was not the revelation of his being homosexual, "but his leaving like that."

In August of 1946, after eleven months of marriage, she obtained a Los Angeles divorce from Roy on the grounds of incompatibility. The legal action didn't stop the gossip, however, and there were whispers that Angela had stumbled onto a bedroom scene. Even some of her friends insisted on that scenario. "That was absolutely made up," she says. "Homosexuals like that cliché, but it only happens that way in the movies."

As the shock subsided, and as she collected her emotions, she finally concluded that Roy had married her in the hope of changing his sexuality. Perhaps he'd identified with Dorian Gray. "I know," she says, "that he himself was carried away with this glorious idea that he was marrying Sybil Vane; that I would straighten him out. It made him ill," she says. "He couldn't do it."

She never resented him for it, and they would even remain friends, but it was now evident that beneath her mature facade and her ability to convincingly play an adult in a movie, she was a very young and hurt twenty-one-year-old. She resolved that she was going to take charge of her life and that nobody was ever going to hurt her like this again.

CHAPTER 6

UPLIFTERS

ANGELA plunged into her work as if driven to it, and MGM provided enough to distract her from all of her pain and confusion. In the year and a half following the divorce, she made four movies, ranging from the absurd *The Hoodlum Saint* to the smart *State of the Union.*

The lead players in *The Hoodlum Saint* were a novel combination, a sure William Powell and an unsteady Esther Williams, playing her rare role above sea level. "She was out of her depth," Lansbury jokes, and as for herself, she played a sexy nightclub singer who had a half dozen numbers, all of them sung by another actress.

Nearly as strange as the pairing of Powell and Williams was the combination of child actress Margaret O'Brien, tap-dancer George Murphy, and stage comedian Barry Nelson for *Tenth Avenue Angel,* which was Angela's next picture. Despite her opinion of this script, which was low, she looked down on neither her fellow players nor her assignment. "I was acting in the movies, and it required a different set of tools. These roles were not demanding but they did require the ability to turn on a character and be believable." She prepared for them with as much diligence as if the characters were challenging. She studied her lines, learned and practiced them, and made sure that she got plenty of sleep. "When I was working, I would never go out. I wouldn't take the chance of being exhausted the next day. I had a tremendously unhealthy feeling of responsibility about what I was doing. I would take it to a point that didn't make sense."

Despite her commitment, her work was beginning to seem more like a job than an actor's life, and she was increasingly frustrated by her inability to be cast in a leading role. No matter how serious her approach, there was a part of her that bought the Hollywood fantasy — that movies were about being a star. She started to dwell on her doubts about having any ability to become one. "I don't conform to any of the accepted types," she thought. "I'm not the girl next door. I'm not like the girls under contract. If only I were a bit more glamorous, or a bit more sexy, or a bit more intelligent, or a bit more funny, or smart . . ."

Evenings, she stayed at home. She never had gone out when she was working, and didn't feel like it when she wasn't. She was too distracted by the healing process of her emotional life.

Concentrating on the good things that Roy had given her, like the pleasure of creating a beautiful home, she pulled herself together. "I said, all right, I'm going to make an incredible life and home for us." So she bought a spectacular place in Rustic Canyon, just inland from Santa Monica and the Pacific Ocean. It was in an enclave known as "The Uplifters' Ranch," a name that had originated with a drinking club Will Rogers and some of his businessman cronies had formed in the 1930s.

Rustic Canyon had a special appeal for Angela and Moyna. It was in a pocket of climate that was unusually moist for southern California, nurturing deciduous trees and dark greenery that was reminiscent of the damp and verdant English countryside. The house had been built by Richard Neutra, a member of the Frank Lloyd Wright school, and some considered it an architectural landmark. It was expensive but, Angela thought, worth the money.

Neutra designed his houses to conform to their surrounding landscapes. This one jutted out from a mountainside, with trees around, above, and below it. The rooms were unusually big, and a spectacular sliding wall, which had been installed during Prohibition, dropped from the living room clear down to the basement, revealing a full-sized bar.

As breathtaking as the outside of the place was, Angela and her mother made its interior into a showplace. She found making this house, and creating the home within it, to be rewarding and even therapeutic work, and she realized she was starting to become a *house person.* She was also responding to Moyna's need to share in her life. It was either that or be competitive, "because she was an actress, too. We were vying with each other, and what happened? I was shooting ahead, and in some ways my success was very difficult for her.

"Nobody has any idea of what lies behind people's lives."

In England, Isolde's marriage was disintegrating. The sisters hadn't seen each other in six years and communicated only by mail, but Isolde was just as private as Angela, and she had never even mentioned marital trouble. There was no reason to suspect any. She had become pregnant when Ustinov came home after the war, and in July of 1945 they had a daughter they named Tamara. But soon afterward, Isolde fell in love with a writer named Derek Dempster.

Dempster was an aviation journalist, and one who seemed to cover a lot of aerial territory in his work, including flying saucers. That and assorted otherworldly interests of his appealed to Isolde's mystical side, a side that had never exactly impressed Ustinov. Nor did he appreciate (when he learned about it later) that his wife was "audacious enough" to bring Dempster around for an introduction while they were still married and living together. Only a month later, Isolde announced that she wanted a divorce so that she could marry the man. The procedure, Ustinov recalls, was "very English and very reasonable," although "we did have to go through that ludicrous charade of sending a detective to a prescribed room in a transient hotel, where Isolde would be discovered playing cards with a hired adulterer — a rented gentleman in underwear."

Isolde finally came over to visit and to introduce Moyna to the first grandchild, and also, not incidentally, to find some relief from the rigors and shortages of postwar London. By then, the house in Rustic Canyon was finished enough for entertaining, and Moyna was inviting all of their pals.

Hurd Hatfield was one of the regulars, having remained friendly with both Moyna and Angela after *The Picture of Dorian Gray.* He was still very good-looking, but with no movie roles to follow up on that showcase, he had a melancholy air. The gloom seemed to weigh him down even when he was having fun, although he almost overdid his good time at one of Moyna's socials. He'd run into the great English actor Michael Redgrave, who was in Hollywood filming *Mourning Becomes Electra.*

Redgrave was also a homosexual and, Hatfield remembers, "We chased Eddie and Bruce all over the living room. We had them jumping over the sofa."

The twins both insisted that they were not confused by such antics. There had always been gay men around Moyna "because she was attracted to them," Bruce said. "Eddie and I had to sort of fight them off. They absolutely did come on to us. It was no big deal. When you're fifteen years old you laugh in their face. It's no problem if you have a sense of humor about it and you grew up with those guys around. We were thoroughgoing heteros so it didn't matter."

Isolde's visit gave Angela a chance to talk out her situation at MGM. With nine pictures under her belt, she was wondering where her career was going and what, if any, intentions the studio had for her. She did not want to believe she was doomed to play drabs forever. Experience was giving her more poise and confidence, and her opinions of scripts were becoming outspoken. For all of these reasons, when she made *If Winter Comes* she was "very, very upset" about it — more upset than by any picture she had yet done. A big reason seems to have been the way MGM was treating Deborah Kerr. She was the leading lady, she was also English, and she was six years older. Yet Angela, at twenty-one, was cast as the thirty-five-year-old mean-spirited wife of Walter Pidgeon.

Frankly, she didn't want to accept the role. "She is dowdy, and such a bitch," she thought, and even complained about it to Benny Thau, who was second in command to Louis B. Mayer at the studio. Confronting authority was not her favorite pastime, and so this protest was really out of character, not that it did any good. "There wasn't much chance of convincing Thau," she says, "because you couldn't call your soul your own, as far as what you were going to play. They owned you, lock, stock, and barrel."

There was, however, something very pleasant emerging over her horizon. Hatfield had invited her to a weekend party at a friend's house in the Ojai Valley, but she was not enthusiastic. It was only five months after her divorce, and she was barely over the shock of it. Hurd insisted. It was his birthday, he argued, and she knew most of the people who were coming, including his mother and Maggie Williams and Scott McKay. The house was wonderful, too, he said, set in the middle of a big orange ranch that stretched all the way to the Pacific.

"Even if I wanted to go," she asked, "how would I get there?" Moyna didn't want to drive that distance (eighty miles), and Angela couldn't leave her without a car.

"I'll get you a ride," Hatfield said. "I know this English guy who's under contract at Metro. He's just out of the British army and he's been going out with Joan Crawford, so you know he's good-looking. He's coming, too, and I'll have him pick you up. So he'll drive you there and back."

"I don't know," Angela said, "he sounds like an awful wolf, bragging about going out with Joan Crawford."

"Wouldn't you?" Hatfield asked.

"No, I wouldn't," she replied.

The next morning, Hurd found Peter Shaw on the MGM lot, and asked whether he knew Angela. The Englishman replied that he'd seen her around the commissary, and that it would be no trouble to give her a lift. On the morning of the trip, however, she was still vacillating, and even telephoned Hurd to cancel the plan.

"You've got to come with him," Hurd said. "He's really a very nice man," and by then it was too late anyway, and she knew it.

When Peter Shaw showed up in his checkered shirt, gray trousers, and rented car, Angela looked out the window and saw "just the most gorgeous thing ever seen on two feet."

Shaw was his stage name. His real name was Peter Pullen, he was six feet three inches tall, his hair was thick and dark, his shoulders were broad, his hips were narrow, and he looked like Errol Flynn. Otherwise, he was all right.

They talked all eighty miles to the Ojai Valley, and by the time they got there, they were both feeling pretty rosy about life in general.

Peter Pullen was born on June 24, 1918, in London, where he grew up and went to school. In fact, he'd been a classmate of Peter Ustinov's at Westminister School. As a boy, he would visit the Ustinov house, and the two of them would play with toy railroad trains in the basement. Ustinov called him "Pulley," not that they were great pals, for they were quite different. Ustinov was already a linguist and a brilliant student, and would grow up to be a man of the mind, while Peter, although bright enough, was no intellectual. He was a superb athlete, though, especially at cricket and tennis.

At twenty-nine, he was seven years older than Angela and also an actor. But he did not have the theater in his blood or even his heart. (The closest his middle-class family came to show business was through an uncle's wife, a musical comedy actress.) Leaving school at sixteen, he'd joined his father's business, which was making concrete blocks. Then, London's Central School of Dramatic Arts offered him a scholarship. ("The students were all wealthy girls," he remembers. "They were desperate for boy actors.") Mild as Peter's calling was, he did get a part in a movie called *Sons of the Sea,* and it was then that he took the name of Shaw. Wherever his career was leading, though, it was interrupted by England's entry into the war. While Angela, Moyna, and the twins were sailing for America, he was enlisting in the army.

Upon graduation from officers training, he returned to his original unit in London. There he met and married a model named Mercia Squires, and she soon became pregnant. He was shipped to Europe and while he was stationed in Brussels, Mercia gave birth to their son, David, in 1944.

Never firing a shot, Peter spent the war as a staff officer, moving on to Hamburg, where he became an aide to Field Marshal Bernard Montgomery. He was with the British army when it triumphantly entered Berlin, and it was there that he started planning for his postwar life. He traded a carton of English cigarettes to have a set of professional photographs made and on his return to London, he brought them to his agent, who forwarded them to contacts in Hollywood. A response with an offer followed almost immediately.

At the time, Peter found himself in an emotional state common to many returning servicemen, for he discovered that his wife had fallen in love while he was away. Glum being the situation, Peter accepted the offer to go to America, even though it meant that he had to leave his son, and there was no way to explain such things to a two-year-old.

By the time he arrived in Los Angeles, he had a contract at MGM worth $350 a week, without ever having taken a screen test. That's how handsome Peter Shaw was, and because he was so good-looking, he soon was going out not only with Joan Crawford, but with Lana Turner and Rita Hayworth. He took them to the Mocambo, Ciro's, the standard Hollywood itinerary. The studios hired the limousines and sometimes paid for the dinners, but Peter says the dates weren't just studio-arranged. These were "sort of" romances, he remembers.

"Fun? It was okay."

He was, in his way, as reserved as Angela, but that by no means ruled out passion. At the party in Ojai, he remembers, "we got along like a house on fire."

Hatfield had been decorous in arranging the accommodations. The men were placed together in the two back bedrooms and the women in front. Even so, "It was a madhouse," he remembers. "I put the mistress of one of the men in the same room with his wife. Oh, I was full of fun!"

In the morning Peter was so eager to be with Angela that he brought her breakfast in bed. He took a seat at the foot of it, there in what Hatfield liked to call "the pink room." She had the pillows propped up behind her, with the tray balanced on her raised knees, when a tap was heard at the door. As it opened, they saw Hurd standing there, dressed as a maid. "I put my hair up," he remembers, "tied it, and got a feather duster. I was clowning. I wasn't serious the way I was in *Dorian Gray.* I don't know what kind of maid I was supposed to be, but I started dusting Angela's face."

Putting her tray aside, she drew the blanket up under her chin, and whispered in Hatfield's ear, "He's wonderful!" And so she and Peter started dating three times a week, "doing," she says, "the whole nightclub thing." They were expensive places, but "We were both under contract, and we were both earning money. We'd get all dressed up to the nines," she says, "and off we'd go."

It was at Ciro's that they saw Kay Thompson turn professional with the act she'd first performed at one of Roger Edens's parties. It was a fast, sophisticated, and slickly arranged singing act, performed with four backups called The Williams Brothers. (Andy Williams was one of them.) Angela was certain that "nobody had ever seen anything like it," and afterward, she went backstage to tell that to Kay. While she was at it, she whispered a small request.

"Where do you get your clothes?"

While Thompson was a flamboyant dresser, Angela was beginning to worry that she looked as dowdy as the roles she was playing. Not only did she consider herself less than a beauty, she seemed skeptical about any possibility of making herself into one. Certainly, she distrusted her own taste in clothes, but if she was going to hold onto this man who had courted some of Hollywood's biggest stars, she was going to have to look better than she did. "I'd always been a girl who wore a dress bought 'off the peg,' or a pair of slacks. Or suits. But I was seeing now that when people went out to these places, everybody *dressed.*"

Kay Thompson told her that her costumes for the show, and many of her own dresses, were made by a woman named Zorin, who had a little shop on Sunset Boulevard (which, to a 1940s Hollywood insider, was known strictly as "Sunset Strip," or, to definite insiders, simply as "the Strip"). Angela paid a call on Zorin and had a complete wardrobe made up. "That," she says, "was the first time that I started to think of myself as a fashionable-looking young woman. Kay helped me so much to become aware of what I was really putting on my back."

It wasn't merely the thrill of Peter's courtship that was catching Angela's breath. "The thing that we share," she believes, "is our *Britishness.* That is the most comfortable, comfort*ing* part of our relationship." As she put it, "We're not hysterics, but we do have our different emotional climates. I won't stand there and be rolled over, but I'm not temperamental.

"Peter blows up faster than I do, and I think that's very good."

She was accurate in that assessment. If Peter was angry about something, he would turn aggressive, focusing an almost fierce nastiness against the object of his anger. Then the rage would emerge, tough and mean, but once expressed would then pass, and he would forget about it.

He still hadn't been given any movie assignments, but a screen test was finally scheduled, and Angie (as he called her — she called him Pete) offered to coach him. She suggested that, instead of using a script, they write the test themselves. They adapted a scene from her last picture, *If Winter Comes,* giving its soap opera plot a detective twist. Peter wore a dark blue suit to the studio and wore it beautifully. "I was sort of Robert Taylor with a gun," he remembers. "Angie was Barbara Stanwyck."

However, after the test was made, she didn't even wait for the official verdict, whispering to her British gumshoe as they left the little studio, "Darling, I love you very much, but an actor you aren't."

Yet something good did come of the experience. The celebrated director Frank Capra had been watching as the test was filmed. He was looking to cast a major character in a movie version of the Broadway hit *State of the Union,* and Katharine Hepburn, who was to be one of its stars, had been urging him to consider Angela. ("Kate related to me," Angela says. "I think she recognized her kind of 'iron willed' thing in me.") Capra had replied that Lansbury was too young to play anyone's mistress, let alone Spencer Tracy's, but Hepburn was persistent. Since Lansbury happened to be making a screen test with Peter Shaw, Capra decided to go downstairs to the testing studio and watch for himself.

His reaction was, "The English guy is really awful, but I'm going to use her," and so he did, casting Angela as Kay Thorndyke, an assignment that made her "very, very proud. This," she points out, "was a Frank Capra movie, with Spencer Tracy and Katharine Hepburn. This was top-drawer, real class" and, she rather proudly thought, "I was moving into *such company.*"

Even so, she had mixed feelings about the assignment. She assumed that the script by Anthony Veiller and Myles Connolly would be "pretty good," based as it was on the Pulitzer Prize–winning play by the reputable Howard Lindsay and Russel Crouse. (In fact, most of the script *was* the play.) She believed that *State of the Union* would make a "hard-hitting, fascinating film," but she definitely did not appreciate being cast, yet again, as a bitchy woman "out of my age frame and the very antithesis of me."

The role of Kay Thorndyke is a tough, Katharine Graham–like publisher of a newspaper chain that is headquartered in Washington, D.C. Seeing herself as a kingmaker, Thorndyke contrives with a power broker — played by Adolphe Menjou — to parlay a Mr. Average Guy into a viable Republican candidate who can defeat Harry Truman in the 1948 election. The candidate she has in mind is her married-but-separated lover, played by Tracy, who is not only a smart and successful middle-American businessman, but positively glows with decency.

He is so decent that he has no patience for compromised principles, and is sympathetic to everyone except politicians. The newspaper publisher and the power broker love that quality, utter cynics that they are. To them, his homespun idealism only makes him seem an even more viable candidate. The trouble begins when it turns out that he actually means what he says. That antipathy to both Big Business and Big Labor is downright unacceptable to Kay Thorndyke and her political partner. The weakest link in the screenplay — and the play — is her managing to convert the Tracy character — temporarily, of course — into just another double-talking politician.

In the meantime, his estranged but still loving wife — the Katharine Hepburn role — has been persuaded to keep up appearances by accompanying him on a speaking tour. The twenty-two-year-old Angela — besides playing a domineering, homewrecking bitch — was supposed to look and act at least as old as the thirty-eight-year-old Hepburn. She was also supposed to be credible competition for the attentions of Spencer Tracy, who at forty-seven was more than twice her age. Naturally, she loses the competition against Hepburn, and is left to gnash her teeth as the credits roll.

Lansbury accomplishes all of this believably and with energy, seeming to join with relish the interplay with Tracy and Hepburn. Those two play with such relaxed discipline, are so at ease with their performances and are so masterful at them, that their dialogue seems spontaneous. They act as if they are unaware that they are being photographed and yet they never lose a sense of where the camera is. In short, they are very professional movie actors, as well as true Hollywood stars. Hepburn, looking beautiful enough to just drink in for two hours, can break the heart with a sideways glance and a momentary closing of her eyes. She seems to have invented her own appeal, in lines like, "Mister, you are looking at a mighty dry waffle." She brings her unique combination of wit, radiance, and warmth to this crisp movie, and there is a touching reminder of her long romance with Tracy when, in character, she asks him, "Do you want a divorce?"

As for him, he is so comfortable in his role, and his screen persona seems so natural, that it makes one wonder why, if it's that easy, nobody else can do it. As a duet, their timing is flawless, and their presence palpable. Their energies make this picture entertaining a half century later, and Angela keeps step with their heady pace, looking the complete veteran. The truth is, she was never intimidated by them.

"The only confidence I *ever* had," she says, "was in my ability as an actress."

She felt a special kinship with Hepburn. "Kate knew I was a worker, and that's what she was. Coming to work prepared and being ready was terribly important to her." Angela found Tracy "the most snuggly, attractive man you would ever hope to work with, and he really helped me. I mean, here I was, a kid, having to play almost a love scene with him. Can you *imagine?*"

She vacillated between enjoying his warmth and being bowled over by his presence. "He was such an icon. When you were working with Tracy or Gable — any one of those *great guys* — those behemoths at MGM, you were so awed by them when they just opened their mouths. What was I doing there with those people? Even Adolphe Menjou, for God's sake."

Her adulation of those "behemoths" was not the same as her respect for classical stage actors, but it was another kind of honor. To her, these great Hollywood movie stars were performers who had created vivid personalities that they would bring to every role. "They play that personality," she says. "They learn how to use it effectively, attractively. Cary Grant, Gary Cooper — they presented themselves in a way that is disarming, attractive, wonderful to listen to and watch. And that can be enormously affecting, particularly in their kinds of movies."

Certain directors were particularly adept at bringing out the essence of such stars, and Frank Capra was one of them. He was Angela's first director from the top rank since George Cukor, and there was no mistaking why these two were in the top rank. Still, she finds the comparison between them an interesting one. In her view, Cukor felt responsible for every moment, "every breath that the actor takes on the screen. He wants control. He would push until he got it."

Capra, in contrast, "went more for the scene as a whole. He played the situation in the scene, and if the situation worked — if the fireworks in the back-and-forth dialogue were landing where he wanted them to — well, then he was happy."

She does consider Cukor to have been the more versatile of the two.

Capra's movies, she feels, tended to deal more narrowly with social and political subjects. "He was fascinated by the political framework in our country," she says, "but although he has a reputation for being a conservative, he wasn't a rabid Republican." It would be a mistake, she believes, to narrowly characterize him as a reactionary.

Although *State of the Union* plays at a brisk tempo, the making of it was as tedious as that of any other movie. While sitting around waiting for the sets to be dressed, the lights set up and the camera positioned, she was taught how to play gin rummy by Menjou ("the old Nazi"), and by the time *State of the Union* was finished, she considered herself a master of the game. Louis B. Mayer thought so, too. When he invited her to a dinner party at his home on Benedict Canyon Road, he asked if she might come an hour earlier, just so they could play a few hands.

Mayer was "practically paternal" with Angela. "Maybe," she thinks, "it was because I was an English girl." It was certainly because she was English that he'd invited her to this particular dinner party. The guest of honor was the Earl of Harewood, who was a cousin to the Queen. She had also been instructed to come alone. "Being a Brit, I was seated next to the earl."

She started drinking gin and tonic as soon as she arrived. As dinner was served, a different wine was poured with every course. She drank every drop of that, too. "By the time dessert arrived, I was looped."

The thirty-mile drive back to Rustic Canyon was a harrowing one. As she "sailed along" on fast, curving Sunset Boulevard, she gripped the steering wheel with all her strength and tried to will herself sober. "In those days, Sunset wasn't graded on the curves. It was *scary.* I was taking my life in my hands. I knew it.

"When I think about it, it seems to me, goodness gracious, Mr. Mayer should have sent for a car to take me home. He should never have let me go home by myself."

Peter, it seemed clear, had no future as an MGM actor. If he hadn't realized that after he finished his screen test, he knew it for certain when the studio canceled his contract. While trying to figure out exactly what to do next, he painted houses. In a way, the work was not so different from his father's business of making concrete blocks. That was all part of the physicality of Peter Shaw, the undiluted masculinity that Angela had noticed from the outset.

Finally, he landed a job with the Paul Small Agency, a "boutique" personal management agency, and he began to learn the business of agenting. "It was like boot camp," Angela said. "Paul really made an agent out of him."

It was only an entry-level position, negotiating "smaller things," but it was a valuable apprenticeship, and early in 1949 Peter Shaw negotiated his first important deal. It was made with Angela. One day he suggested that it seemed a bit crowded, the two of them in his cramped studio apartment. It would be more intelligent, he suggested, if they got married and found a house.

Angela replied that she thought it was a good proposition and made the deal.

CHAPTER 7

CHILDREN

ANGELA wanted to be married just outside central London in Bow, the place where her grandfather had lived, where her father had grown up, and in the church where her family had worshipped. Peter was enthusiastic about that plan, too, because his family could come to the wedding, and so Angela had Zorin design and make a wedding dress, and she booked sea passage for Moyna, Bruce, and Eddie. At nineteen, they were now both sophomores at UCLA and too big to be called "the boys," too individual to still be "the twins." Eddie was going to give her away because he was the older of the pair by twenty minutes.

But just when everyone's bags were packed and Angela's dress was finished and Peter had arranged time off from the office, they ran into two snags. The first was that although Mr. Capra had told her, for God's sake go off and get married, MGM kept delaying Angela's release from *State of the Union*. Every time she asked whether she could leave, she was told that she was needed for one more week's work.

The other problem was that the Church of England would not sanction the wedding because both Peter and Angela had been previously married. They were still trying, and failing, to convince the church that they deserved its blessings. Even after MGM finally released Angela, early in August of 1949, the wedding couple did not know where or when the wedding ceremony would take place. Still, they flew to England, Angela's first trip back since leaving in 1940.

By then, she and Peter had accepted the finality of the Church of England's refusal, and were considering other alternatives. She wouldn't have minded being married in a Catholic church, for when she was a child, Moyna's Irish maids had taken her to early morning Mass. "I loved all the incense and the chanting," she remembers, but aside from the fact that neither she nor Peter was baptized a Roman Catholic, as divorced people, they could not be married in a Catholic church, either.

They scrambled from one denomination to another, in a hectic and embarrassing search for acceptance. One newspaper even printed an editorial about their plight, complaining about the narrow-mindedness of the Church of England, as well as its hypocrisy, considering the exceptions that had been made for royalty. This attention was less a reflection of Angela's celebrity than of her grandfather's: it was, after all, George Lansbury's granddaughter who was being rejected.

Finally, Angela and Peter won approval from the Church of Scotland and were married on August 12, 1949, in St. Columba's Church in London. Both immediate families were present — Moyna and the twins and Isolde, and Peter's younger brother, Patrick Pullen, his sister Clover, and their father Walter Pullen.

After the ceremony the newlyweds flew to Paris and honeymooned in Les Roches Fleuries, in the south of France. Then it was back to a rather different, Hollywood version of France as Angela returned to MGM to make *The Three Musketeers.* The picture provided her with yet another role that she didn't like, and she spoke up about it. Whether emboldened by her marital status or having Peter behind her or her gin rummy partnership with Mr. Mayer, she felt confident enough to go straight to him — "Louis B," as everyone called him (never "L.B.").

It wasn't the movie that she found objectionable. *The Three Musketeers* was hardly Shakespeare, it wasn't even Dumas, but it sounded amusing enough, like a musical without music, a splashy Technicolor production with a leaping, dueling Gene Kelly. Angela was looking forward to working with him, and with the others in the cast as well — Frank Morgan, June Allyson, Van Heflin, and Vincent Price. What she did not like was her role, the villainous *and older* Queen Anne. "I'm just too young," she groaned, wanting to be cast, instead, as the glamorous Lady deWinter, a part she'd heard was going to be assigned to Lana Turner.

She paid a call on Ida Koverman, who was Louis B. Mayer's executive secretary and the guard at his palace gate, because "First, you had to convince her that you'd a good reason to speak with Mr. Mayer." Only with that task accomplished could the supplicant then proceed to the next plateau, entering the throne room itself.

Angela swears that she was not even momentarily intimidated by "the long walk down to the big round white desk" where the little man would be waiting, at the far end of his huge office. As Mayer surely knew, the expanse of carpet terrified many an actor. She had heard all the stories about others who had dared to question the studio chief, but she remained unfazed. "I just sort of sat down and talked acting to him. I wasn't afraid to state my case and tell him what I wanted to do and what part I wanted to play."

As she spoke Mayer watched her through his wire-rimmed glasses, with hands clasped in front of him. He heard her out, and when she finished her speech, he said he had complete confidence in her, and that he was positive she would be wonderful as always — playing Queen Anne.

It was then she knew for certain, "I would not go to the top of the class at MGM." What she did not realize was that her life at the most regal of studios was now all but at an end. MGM itself was changing, and the executive vice-president, Dore Schary, who operated out of the New York office, was already preparing to challenge Mayer's artistic administration. Schary was viewed as an East Coast alien, yet Mayer, who had always seemed unassailable — even his name was given to the studio — lost out when the board chairman, Nicholas Schenck, sided with Schary.

Whether it was the new administration or a more fundamental shift in American taste, MGM would never again have quite the same luster. Schary soon dismissed the famous actors in its fabulous roster, and "the whole climate changed" in front of Angela's eyes. Gone were the star-filled entertainments, and in their place were tough, realistic movies like *Battleground.* "It was Eastern air that had blown in," and she accepts that. "Maybe it was fresh air, but it didn't make for blockbuster movies."

Stars who had been contract players and those who had worked elsewhere were now hired on a freelance basis. Suddenly, it seemed as if the studio had forgotten exactly what their appeal had been. Glittering personalities who had histories of popularity and success were finding themselves cast in unlikely roles, and because of that, their public turned away from the pictures — Elizabeth Taylor in *The Big Hangover,* Cary Grant in *Crisis,* Burt Lancaster in *Vengeance Valley.* Even the combined charms of Spencer Tracy and James Stewart could not transcend their peculiar presence in *Malaya.*

Angela's own contract was one of the few renewed, perhaps because Peter was still working for Paul Small, who was Dore Schary's brother-in-law. But her assignments were worse than ever, from the Communist-baiting *The Red Danube* to the ridiculous *Remains to Be Seen,* which was "the bottom of the barrel," as far as she was concerned. When even MGM had no roles for her, she was loaned out to other studios. Yet still she was not soured on Hollywood. While at Paramount Pictures, making *Samson and Delilah* with Victor Mature and Hedy Lamarr, she was excited about the chance to work with Cecil B. De Mille, even if his primary concern was her feet, and how they looked in sandals, and even if his final inspiration was for her character to be actually speared to the wall. She chose to regard working with this legendary director as "a challenge. I was still trying to make it on the Hollywood scene." And, she sighs, "still trying to be a movie star . . . working and working and not being a star.

"But if I wasn't, I had the billing. As long as I had the billing, I maintained my position."

Billing. The size and location of the name in the credits, or on the poster, or on the marquee, or in the advertisements and the program. Billing represented both ego and job security to an actor, in a show business that was treacherous in both of those crucial emotional areas. Billing was the traditional measure of position. If it was a painfully public measure, was that not appropriate to work in the public arena?

By now she had faced up to the fact that her earliest roles, as Nancy in *Gaslight* and as Sybil Vane in *The Picture of Dorian Gray,* were "the best ones I ever did at MGM, and the only ones that made any sense in terms of acting." But she didn't yet seem to grasp that they made perfect Hollywood star sense, in that they were the only parts for which she had been typecast. Everything else she'd done was character work, whether the film was good, mediocre, or trashy. Movie stardom in Hollywood, however, was in fact the last word in type casting, rather than character acting. It was those actors who played themselves — who had unique, extroverted personalities that they exploited — who became the stars.

"What I did in the movies," Angela says, "is what a lot of actresses did in the theater." Of that type of acting, she says, "The only other movie actress who did it — and she did it to a fare-thee-well — was Bette Davis. She wasn't afraid to put white flour on her face and come out as Mrs. Skeffington. She altered herself constantly, with wigs and makeup and costuming.

"That is why the audience adored her."

The respect is deserved, the conclusion debatable. Bette Davis's stardom was likelier based on the personality she projected. She was so easily and frequently imitated and caricatured not because of disguises like Mrs. Skeffington, but because she was so extravagantly and uniquely herself in her most popular pictures.

In short, a star is a personality the mass audience pays to enjoy again and again. It was Angela's reluctance to reveal her personality at all, let alone extravagantly, that was holding her back. Character acting was an admirable calling to be sure, but not a gloried one, and while it served as a respectably unthreatening niche for the introverted, it would always be a second-best alternative if the goal was stardom.

Sensing that her assignments could only get worse at an MGM in decline, she told her agent that she wanted out. It seemed to her that "all of us who had come up through the ranks with Mr. Mayer, we really didn't fit into the new scheme of things with Schary." She could also see that with television's growing popularity, the studio was cutting back on feature film production. Her agent, Harry Friedman of MCA, negotiated her departure.

That left her with more free time than she'd had in many years, and since it seemed that "I couldn't get arrested in Hollywood," she and Peter decided to spend an open-ended stretch of time in England. "We thought of it as a second honeymoon," she remembers, "and we even thought we might conceivably stay there and make our lives in England."

They sailed on the *Queen Elizabeth* and it was a festive crossing, with lots of Hollywood people aboard. Angela happily ran into "Gertie Lawrence and Ty Power and a whole bunch of friends that we knew." They would all go to the ship's famous Veranda Grill, where they "dressed every night in gorgeous clothes and danced and had a marvelous time."

One of those nights, Gertrude Lawrence took Angela aside and whispered, "You know, you have the most beautiful hair." That was a welcome remark, for she had gotten a new cut, close to the head. An "Eton crop," it was called in England, because it was so prep school boyish. "And it's very flattering," the celebrated Ms. Lawrence added, "because your head is beautifully shaped."

Angela tucked the praise away for saving, "because from one woman to another, that was a very nice thing to say."

After three months in England, she faced up to the fact that she wasn't getting much work there, either. At least "I was known in America, but in London they just weren't interested in me." She was also pregnant, and along with the excitement of that came a sense of the need to settle in one place. And so she and Peter decided to return to California "and make America our home." She promptly became a citizen and a year later, so did he (although they would always maintain dual citizenships).

With the change in their circumstances, the cancellation of the MGM contract took on a slightly different tone. It might have made her feel better but, financially speaking, her timing had been terrible. Their plan to begin a family was proceeding exactly as they had wished, but they did not seem to have planned the money situation nearly as well.

As long as her condition permitted, she flew East for television assignments. They weren't lucrative, and she certainly would have preferred movie work, but as usual, she looked to the positive side. "I rocked to my feet with good television," she says, and appeared on such dramatic shows as the *Lux Video Theatre, Playhouse of Stars,* and *Four Star Playhouse.* In such works as Somerset Maugham's "Cakes and Ale," with Robert Montgomery, and "The Pearl," with Ronald Colman, she felt, "I was starting to really act again."

All of that came to an end with the final term of her pregnancy.

Rather than go to a hospital, she decided to give birth at home, which was a house they'd bought on Balboa Avenue in Encino, in the San Fernando Valley. It was a small but beautiful place perched on a three-acre plot of hilltop land, and there, in the tiny, sun-streamed guest room on the brilliant morning of January 7, 1952, Angela gave birth to a boy they named Anthony Peter Shaw.

Natural childbirth was not common in 1952, but she was glad she did it. "Pregnancy was easy for me," she says. It proved to be easier than delivery, for in the middle of her labor, Angela cried out to her husband, "For God's sake, forget the washing up!" It wasn't Peter who was running the water in the kitchen, however, but the nurse, who was sterilizing the obstetrician's instruments. But finally it was done, and Angela was resting in the little bed in that sunny room as the nurse came in, cradling the infant boy in her arms.

Three months after giving birth to Anthony, Angela agreed to go East and act in summer stock, bringing the baby with her. She would be doing two plays, *The Gramercy Ghost* and *Affairs of State,* touring a circuit of East Coast summer theaters in smart resort communities like Westport, Connecticut, and Bucks County, Pennsylvania. She bought a second Cadillac, a used convertible, to transport herself, the baby, and a nursemaid named

Mildred Burgess from one booking to the next, and she started out by driving them across the country. Like her mother, she loved to be behind the wheel of a car.

Moyna was back on the stage in summer stock, too, spending that season at the Windham Theatre in New Hampshire. And as Angela had brought her own little family along, so, too, did Moyna, wangling apprenticeships at the theater for both Bruce and Eddie. Bruce had just finished his army stint. As a British national, he could have avoided it, but only at the price of never becoming an American citizen (which he did two years later).

He was not smitten with the stage, however, and come fall he would take a job as a junior executive for a shoe company. Eddie, who had completed his military service after dropping out of college, was more susceptible to the theater's charms. He started the summer painting scenery, and was finishing it designing sets. Since Moyna felt inspired and ready to try the New York stage again, Eddie decided to go with her, and perhaps make a career of stage design.

Angela's theatrical summer was also one of discovery. Many movie actors find the stage intimidating. They aren't accustomed to memorizing an entire role, and are used to close-ups that show their every blink. The camera focuses the audience's attention for them. But theater audiences are further away than the lens of a movie camera and the actor must seize attention by projecting not only his voice but his energies.

Angela had no problem with that. Confidence as an actor was set in her bones. She found projection easy in summer stock theaters, which were "small houses with small audiences," and believed she had a head start with the audiences because "I had a little bit of a reputation from the movies." She loved that summer, and even enjoyed the traveling, playing each theater for a week before driving on to the next. She and Anthony (she would always pronounce it "Antony") and Mildred stayed in rooming houses and rustic hotels, and more than once, the baby was bedded down in a bureau drawer, just as in stage lore. At the end of the tour, exactly as she and Peter had planned, she was pregnant again. She worked as long as she could, but was forced to stop abruptly when she went into labor three weeks prematurely. Instead of another natural childbirth, her obstetrician had her go straight to Hollywood Presbyterian Hospital, where he delivered a daughter on April 26, 1953. They named her Deirdre Angela.

When Angela was ready to go to work again — and now they needed the money badly — there was no work to go to. She had no studio contract, no assignments, and no regular paycheck. She was grateful to get a summer stint as a panelist on a television game show called *Pantomime Quiz.* It was not acting, it was not dignified, and it involved charades, which she hated, "but $300 a week paid the grocery bill. Peter wasn't getting a huge salary at the agency, and we had two children. It was a rocky time."

As she had never had to before, she was now taking roles in B pictures like *Mutiny* and *A Life at Stake,* and westerns (*A Lawless Street*), and even a Tony Curtis swashbuckler called *The Purple Mask.* That last she considered even worse than *Remains to Be Seen,* "a new all-time low point," but the Skid Row of her film career was yet to come with *Please Murder Me,* which was actually filmed in a supermarket. Produced by a fly-by-night company called Distributors Corporation of America, its sets were dragged into an empty store at the corner of Yucca and Franklin. To make matters worse, she wasn't even the star — that was Raymond Burr. After the epic was finished, Angela went straight to the California State Welfare Department and signed up for unemployment insurance.

"We were just patching it together, and we just plain needed the money. I was socialistic enough to think, 'Well I've been paying into this and since I need it, I'm going to go and get it.'

"So I lined up with everyone else."

It certainly was not the best of times, but better ones were about to start for Peter. He was finally finding himself in his work as an agent. As Angela saw her husband, "He is an English gentleman, a man of lovely manners, which is something sadly missing in our world. His life work as an agent was the perfect vocation for him, because he is so expert at taking care of others. He doesn't want to talk about himself, *ever;* in fact, he is incapable of having such a conversation. He wants everyone else to have the limelight. And he is a master strategist, with more charm than most of the actors he represented!

"This is who Peter really is."

His progress began with an offer from the William Morris Agency to be an assistant actors' agent. It was a step into the big leagues, and the family could well use the $200 a week that came with the job.

Business entertaining also came with the job, and for the first time Angela found herself being a company wife. That was a novelty, to be better known as Mrs. Peter Shaw than as Angela Lansbury, and she liked it. They did a lot of socializing, seeing to William Morris clients and mixing with people in the business. "We were typical young marrieds," she remembers, "real thirtysomethings, with children growing up. We were friends with other movie stars and writers and producers."

A few years earlier, Peter had won custody of his son, David, and now he and Angela agreed that the time had come to bring over the ten-year-old. Within a week the boy left England on a DC-3 "airsick," he would remember, "from the moment I took off." He retreated to his sleeping berth, and the stewardesses looked after him for the twenty-four-hour-plus duration of the flight.

Peter met him at the airport and drove the boy straight to a toy store, where he was properly equipped with a set of silver cap pistols. David would always remember, "We didn't have that kind of thing in England," and then they went home to Encino, although it would not be home for much longer. With the addition of a second son, a bigger house was needed, and Angela found one quickly, a three-bedroom home north of San Vicente Boulevard, at 116 Twenty-sixth Street, which was just on the Santa Monica side of the Brentwood borderline. She thought the house was not only beautiful, but perfect for two growing boys who — she could already picture it — would be able to ride their bicycles right out in front, for Twenty-sixth Street was a quiet, dead-end street, ending in a polo field.

It was more than wonderful to David. After growing up in belt-tightened, bombed-out, fog-drenched London, "life in California," he says, "was breathtaking. All these lights, this vast land, the clearness and the warmth. It was amazing."

Meanwhile, Moyna was back East and far from the Hollywood take on domestic life. Having married off one of her sons (Edgar — to Rose Kean, whose brother would become governor of New Jersey), she returned to the world of theater and, living out one of her great ambitions, was appearing in a musical comedy. She was playing a society dowager in *The Boy Friend,* a British spoof of 1920s American musicals. She hadn't much of a singing voice, but then her part didn't call for any singing ("and," Edgar says, "a good thing, too"). The show had become the surprise hit of Broadway's 1955 season, in the process making an overnight star of nineteen-year-old Julie Andrews.

Angela was going British, too, in a wonderful Danny Kaye film called *The Court Jester.* Nobody had ever thought of casting her in a comedy, and she discovered the pleasure it is "to be in something hilarious. To really enjoy yourself. That," she says, "is the absolute best." Although the movie had originated as a vehicle for Kaye, this unique and witty spoof of Robin Hood adventures turned out to be the best picture of his career, and one of the best in Angela's, as well. It allowed her to play not only a princess, but a princess her own age. She was made up to look young and lovely. She got to wear beautiful clothes that showed off her fine, slender figure. She got to read droll dialogue, and while she did not end up with the hero (her former schoolmate Glynis Johns did), Danny Kaye never really came across as the sort of romantic male figure with whom a heroine would likely end up. Off-camera, too, Angela found him mysterious and remote.

The movie, directed with comic grace and balletic precision by Melvin Frank, from Norman Panama's literate script, gave Angela the chance to work with a company of "ace farceurs," and although she hadn't any experience with the genre, by the end of filming, she was proud to consider herself one of their number. As she defined it, "a farceur is somebody who can seem to be playing straight when he is, in fact, playing high comedy. Danny Kaye [although she admired him] was a comedian, never a farceur. But Basil Rathbone, Cecil Parker, Mildred Natwick, Glynis Johns — my fellow players — certainly were.

"And I learned how to be a fairly good farceur in that picture."

That education was about to come in handy, for soon after *The Court Jester* was released, and possibly because of it, she received a telephone call from the British stage director Peter Glenville. "Vividly" remembering her work in *Gaslight* and *The Picture of Dorian Gray,* he wondered whether she might consider doing a French farce on Broadway. He hastened to add that good movie acting did not necessarily translate into good stage acting. He wasn't even sure whether Angela could be heard on stage.

If she was interested, he advised, she would have to fly to New York and audition for him, which she was more than willing to do. It was an important moment in her career, she realized. "This was what I wanted to do; go to Broadway and prove myself as an actress."

She found a new nanny to take care of Anthony and Deirdre ("because Mildred wanted to go look after more babies"), and went to New York to appear in a *Playhouse 90* television drama and, not incidentally, to meet with Glenville. He told her that nobody else was being considered for the role; she simply had to convince him that she was capable of it. He even rented a rehearsal room so that they might work together — on what, she did not know, but she'd already proved that she could project in a theater. As for her diction, it was a fundamental skill she had already mastered.

"If you're going to be in the theater," she says, "you learn how to enunciate." But she also knew that Glenville would demand work on lowering her British-style stage voice, because it was too high for American audiences. She considered technical things like that tools of her trade, and if improvement was required, she would make all the necessary adjustments. But as for the basic, unlearnable gift of acting, "I knew I had the essence, the ability to characterize," and Glenville agreed. Within a month, he gave her the part and rehearsals began.

The play was *Hotel Paradiso,* written by France's master of farce Georges Feydeau. It was typical of the genre, its characters' sexy hopes frantically illicit, fundamentally ingenuous, and finally unfulfilled. In this plot, a henpecked bourgeois is desperate to have an assignation with a married woman (Angela's part) who is as frustrated as he is. Once they arrive at the titular would-be love nest, so do their wives, husbands, children, and, finally, the gendarmes. As Angela's fellow cast member Sondra Lee said, "Everybody talks about going to bed but nobody ever gets to do it. They are too exhausted from talking about it."

Hotel Paradiso had first been produced in Paris as *L'hotel du Libre Exchange,* in 1894, when Feydeau was at the peak of his success, with four new plays in that year alone. Glenville's production was based on the version that had just been presented in London with Alec Guinness and Irene Worth. The same beautiful belle époque look was being used, with lots of palm trees for the hotel lobby. Guinness and Worth's satin costumes were being altered to fit Bert Lahr and Angela.

Casting Lahr was a calculated gamble. He was an inspired buffoon and had starred in several Broadway musical comedies, but he had neither dramatic training nor classical experience. Both were critical to the success of this type of ballet-theater, as was a respect for discipline and ensemble performance. Lahr's forte was as a solo turn, even in a company; he was a self-centered clown. That made Angela even more of a risky choice, for how could this young, inexperienced British actress hold the stage with a wily old master of low comedy?

She roomed with her mother until she was certain the part was hers and then moved into the Algonquin Hotel for the run of the play. When Moyna had begun *The Boy Friend,* she'd found a tiny apartment over the only drugstore on upper Park Avenue and she stayed there after the musical finally closed. Angela was starting to sense a hint that "suddenly my success was difficult for her to take," but Moyna transcended that to come through with maternal warmth and fellow professional advice.

As the premiere approached, Angela was "nervous but excited about opening in my first Broadway show — and hopeful." She had acted on the stage before, of course, "but Henry Miller's Theatre and *Hotel Paradiso* were quite a step from summer stock or the Chanticleer Theatre at the Webber-Douglas School of Singing and Dramatic Art, on Gloucester Road in Kensington." While it was true that she was still being cast in parts older than her years — at thirty-two she was playing the love object of the fifty-eight-year-old Lahr — playing older in the theater did not seem to bother her as it did in the movies. As she saw it, "I was really playing a lovely, flighty woman of no determinate age."

She rehearsed by day and when she got home, Moyna ran lines with her, reading all the other dialogue. Moyna also helped to design her makeup. With footlights, Angela points out, "You have to wear a lot of makeup for your face to emerge, for your eyes to emerge. Otherwise, you blank out." The show's overall lighting scheme was white, "with just a couple of pink gels." She learned from her mother "how to bring out the eyes and give the whole look. She showed me how to use good old Leichner 'Five and Nine,' two sticks of greasepaint wrapped in gold foil. Number Five was the lighter shade, the base, and Number Nine was used for shadow, to contour the face. As for eye shadow, we used only blue."

Rehearsals were stressful for Lahr, and Angela watched him "sweating his way through the role, always questioning our director. 'If I do this, then what? Would it be better if I did that?' 'What's he doing if I say that?'" A year earlier, he had made a powerful impression in Samuel Beckett's *Waiting for Godot.* However, his role in it was Chaplinesque, which was less of a stretch for him than French farce. Feydeau might have been less esoteric than Beckett, but it was arguably harder to do.

During the Washington, D.C., tryout, Lahr's approach was often maddeningly old-fashioned. "When Bert was going to deliver a punch line," Angela was beginning to learn, "everyone had to stand stock still. He absolutely demanded that, and when he wasn't the center of the action, he was not willing to support anyone else. Also, he was quite dizzied by the number of people whirling around him." But by the time the show came to New York, he was achingly funny, and she considered working with him an education. "He could give a college course in playing comedy," she said. It was from him that she learned comic timing, and how to milk a laugh. He was perhaps a different kind of professional than she'd ever known, but he was a professional nevertheless.

On opening night, April 12, 1957, Moyna kissed her daughter, whispering, "Be smashing, my angel," and then took her seat in the front row. Backstage, Angela was suffering her first attack of stage nerves, and to make matters worse, her feet were killing her in a pair of "little satin shoes, tiny and tight. Leather gives with your foot. It stretches. Satin is a whole different thing, and it's impossible."

As she waited for the curtain to rise, her mouth turned dry as salt, her sweat made the silk blouse sticky, and her stomach hollowed out, but she wasn't the only one nervously awaiting the audience confrontation. A young actor named Carleton Carpenter was hunched over in the wings, throwing up into the fire bucket. But once the house lights dimmed and the show began, Angela felt at home, and the next morning, the play was a hit. There were "endless belly laughs," drama critic Brooks Atkinson wrote in the *New York Times,* and "As Madame Cot, Angela Lansbury gives a wonderfully whirling, high-paced, bridling and billowy performance."

She wasn't surprised and she wasn't humble. "It was all gift and hard work. One has got to recognize that you have it in the first place and you don't mess around with it. You don't waste it, you don't put it to the wrong tests. Once you know it's there, you build on it, add to it, embellish it, learn how to use it."

Ultimately, her nerves disappeared, but not Carleton Carpenter's. The young actor would throw up every night of the run.

With the show up and running, Angela sent for five-year-old Anthony and four-year-old Deirdre so that they might be with her for the run. An avowed homebody, she hated to leave her house and found it "an awful wrench to be away from Peter." But she talked to him on the telephone every day, and she was determined to have the children with her.

The new nanny, Jane Fyfe, could have stepped off the pages of a book of Nannies. Hired on the recommendation of Greer Garson, she was a fortyish Scotswoman, a disciplinarian who ruled her employers with a code of responsibility and moral propriety. The Shaw household quickly became Jane Fyfe's domain, and it had to be run her way, just as the children had to behave the Fyfe way. "She put the fear of God in all of us," Angela admits, and as for the tough agent, Peter Shaw, "those two," she says, "had an armed truce."

But Jane Fyfe also excelled at her job, and at more than one job, in fact. She took on the duties of secretary to Angela and tutor to the children, and she was an excellent driver, too. "She was a totally responsible woman," Angela had to admit.

When Fyfe and the children arrived in New York, they all moved directly into a wonderful old, Early American house rented in Westport, Connecticut. Angela had wanted Anthony and Deirdre to be in the country. Always the car lover, she'd brought her Jaguar convertible from Los Angeles for the daily round trip to and from the city. Every afternoon, she would brew herself a strong cup of tea and then drive off to New York, and she would return home after every evening performance, six nights a week. "That drive up and down the Taconic Parkway was a schlepp," she said, "but it was worth it."

She would sometimes have company on the road, bringing a house guest, such as Sondra Lee, from the cast of *Hotel Paradiso.* Sondra was young and bright, and she was already a feisty Broadway professional. If they drove to Westport after the Saturday night show, they wouldn't have to go back until Monday, giving them two days for cooking, gardening, and wearing sloppy clothes. Angela wore jeans by day, caftans in the evening, and pajamas to bed. To Sondra, a tiny thing, "Angie" seemed "a big and big-boned woman. She has big hands, big fingers, and her nails have never been girly."

Eight performances a week in the Feydeau play was a schedule to be treated with the usual Lansbury respect. "The only problem with the play," she remembers, "is that it's like a terribly funny joke that somebody tells you and you fall on the floor. Two hours later, you've forgotten it. That's boulevard theater."

But it was never tedious. Some people suspect that actors grow bored when they are in a success, performing the same part for six evenings a week, and twice on the matinee days. But while the same words must be spoken in the same story at every performance, there is always room for exploration, and there is even time for pranks. Bert Lahr, cast as he was from so different a mold than the others, all but begged for horseplay. At one performance, Sondra Lee threw him a line that was not from *Hotel Paradiso* at all, but was, instead, from Lahr's previous play, *Waiting for Godot.* He absentmindedly responded to her cue with his dialogue from the Beckett piece.

Another prankster was the actor John Emery, who would try to break the others' concentration by playing tricks with one of his eyeballs. He had the dubious talent of being able to stand sidewise to the audience and — while not moving his downstage eye (nearest the audience), move the upstage one. Nobody but the actor to whom he was talking could see this rather strange demonstration. Since Emery was playing Angela's husband, she bore the brunt of the trick, which never did break her up, but it was sometimes a struggle, and she was not always amused.

When the play closed after a disappointing run of only fifteen weeks, Angela and Fyfe shared the driving all the way back to California. The children sat in the backseat playing cards while the two women smoked cigarettes and chatted.

Arriving home, Angela was faced with a situation that required attention immediately. For several months Peter had been watching with dread as 26th Street was extended all the way to Sunset Boulevard. A land developer had bought the big polo field at the end of their street, and within a year, a development would be built on their doorstep. There already were many cars driving through. One of them struck and killed their sheepdog, Angela. Peter and Angela knew that they had to move yet again. Her whole life, it seemed, had been transient, with many houses but no home.

CHAPTER 8

AWAY FROM HOME

THE concept of home became almost theoretical when a string of location assignments fell into place. First, she would make *The Long Hot Summer* in Baton Rouge, Louisiana. Then, much of *The Reluctant Debutante* was to be filmed in Paris. These roles would keep her working steadily and would also revive her Hollywood career after the two-year absence that followed her dismaying movie-in-a-supermarket. Finally, and by no means least, they would restore her status as an A-picture actress. Perhaps some of this renewed demand was due to her success on Broadway, but even that achievement did nothing to raise her to stardom. Her recent roles were not big parts, nor did they reflect any change in Hollywood's perception of her as an older woman. Lansbury continued to experience history's longest and earliest middle age.

In *The Long Hot Summer*, even though she was only thirty-one, she was cast as the mistress of a 61-year-old tyrant played by Orson Welles, who was only forty-one himself, but so fat that his age was indeterminate. The picture was typical of Twentieth Century–Fox, a studio that seemed cursed to forever play runner-up to MGM, unable to discover the secret of class. As a glossy exercise in ersatz Tennessee Williams, everything about *The Long Hot Summer* is imitative. The screenplay draws on two William Faulkner stories as source material, but the obvious inspiration is Williams's 1955 hit play *Cat on a Hot Tin Roof.* The idea seems to have been to glue and staple together a facsimile of the play and to get it out before MGM could film the real thing.

In *The Long Hot Summer,* Welles plays a copy of Tennessee Williams's "Big Daddy," the fabulously original character at the center of *Cat on a Hot Tin Roof.* More precisely, Welles plays Big Daddy in the celebrated way that Burl Ives created the part on Broadway. Likewise imitative is Paul Newman, the picture's leading man, who at the time was in his Marlon Brando phase. In this picture, Newman presents a scrubbed version of Brando's legendary Stanley Kowalski (from *A Streetcar Named Desire*), even wearing a neat new undershirt in place of Brando's famously filthy and shredded T-shirt. (The unthreatening Newman approach to a Williams stud was so successful in *The Long Hot Summer* that MGM hired him to star in the real *Cat on a Hot Tin Roof* a couple of years later.) Such sanitizing efforts seemed to have been a Twentieth Century–Fox specialty, for the studio likewise came up with the scrubbed Pat Boone as a safe version of Elvis Presley.

As for Lansbury's performance, it is brief, and notable only as a demonstration of her southern accent. For her, the most memorable part of the experience was making two new friends. One was the young (twenty-three) actress Lee Remick, who was appearing in her first movie since making a startling debut in *A Face in the Crowd.* The other was the even younger reporter Rex Reed, who was then a student at Louisiana State University, interviewing the visitors from planet Hollywood for *The Daily Reveille*, the local college newspaper.

Immediately after finishing *The Reluctant Debutante*, she joined the cast of *The Dark at the Top of the Stairs*, which was based on a Pulitzer Prize–winning drama by William Inge. Although he was a highly respected playwright, Inge did not write the script himself and was displeased with the changes made by those who did, Harriet Frank, Jr. and Irving Ravetch.

The director was Delbert Mann, a specialist in soft-edged and pensive, commercially Chekhovian drama. "My pictures have no villains," he says, "and nobody is mean-spirited. My attitude is that everybody deserves compassion." It was an attitude that made Angela wonder, "How did a man as mild and sweet-tempered as Del Mann ever make it in this business?"

The revisions to her character in the picture were among the changes that bothered Inge. Mavis Pruitt is a decent, warmhearted, lonely beautician who seems to be having an adulterous affair with the central figure in the story, Rubin Flood, played by Robert Preston. Flood is in male ego crisis, out of a job and — as in so many of Inge's plays — sexually frustrated.

Old-fashioned masculinity, it seems, has become as obsolete as the horse-and-buggy equipment that Rubin used to sell.

In the play, only passing reference is made to his friendship with Mavis Pruitt, but the screenwriters chose to expand that relationship into a scene in which Rubin and Mavis play out a close call with marital infidelity. (The revision also adds another location, serving to, as they said in Hollywood, "open up" a stage-bound story.) The new material begins with Rubin losing his job, getting drunk, picking a fight with his wife, and then driving over to Mavis's beauty salon. When she agrees to go to dinner with him, he can't start the car. He gets out and turns the crank while she pulls the spark down, trying to help him. It was supposed to be happening on a hot midsummer night in Oklahoma, but as director Mann remembers, "It was one of the coldest nights on the back lot of Warner Brothers that I have ever seen. Just freezing, damp and awful, and we tried to keep both actors huddled in coats and around fires.

"Luckily, no breath was showing."

The abortive Mavis-Rubin love scene that follows is but ten minutes long, and is peripheral to the main action, but it provides rich acting material. As Del Mann reconstructs it, the setting is the foyer of Mavis's home.

> They come in the door, with the lights off in the room; the lighting comes from a street lamp outside, through the glass pane in the front door. They close the door behind them, and the two stand facing each other, almost in complete silhouette. Very slowly, they move toward each other and kiss as the camera moves in, also slowly, to a very tight two shot. And then they separate just enough to play some lines of dialogue in which she tells him of her life — that, yes, she is still in love with him but that she understands why he cannot begin an adulterous affair — she knows he's going to get back to his marriage. It's a very sweet, very tender, very true love scene — it's just one of the nicest, if not the nicest that I've ever had played.

It had taken ten years in Hollywood, and twenty-five movies, for Angela to have her first screen kiss, and it was with a married character who was going to do nothing about it except go back to his wife.

She and Preston act their way through the scene with beauty and controlled energies, like a duo piano team, harmonizing and counterplaying, anticipating and supporting each other. She has only one other scene in the picture, when Rubin's wife (Dorothy McGuire), having heard the gossip about her husband and Mavis, comes to the beauty parlor for a manicure and a confrontation. After reading this scene, Angela told the producer, "You've got to be kidding. It's too much for a woman to behave like this. These words — I don't think I can get my mouth around some of what I'm saying here. It's too *purple.* Listen to this, 'Every time a woman turns her face away because she's tired — or unwilling — there's someone waiting.'

"I mean, *really.*"

An actor must read whatever lines are written, but a creative actor can sometimes spin gold from dross. As Lansbury ultimately delivers this dialogue, she takes care to savor the sentiments, while timing her phrases to minimize the clichés. She alternately focuses on Rubin's jealous wife or gazes into the distance in self-contemplation, creating for her character a quiet strength, a will for survival, finally a suggestion of the depth of her personal wounds. Only after several beats, at the end of that small "purple" speech, does she conclude, "There's someone waiting," with the final, and lonely, "Someone like me."

Mavis Pruitt comes to life through this fine work, and as interplayed with Dorothy McGuire, the scene could serve classes in acting, even though Angela brushes it off.

"We did it," she says. "It was okay."

Upon completion of *The Dark at the Top of the Stairs*, she wrote to Moyna in New York,

> Sweetheart, I've got me still another picture. It's going to be made in Australia, so I've made a deal that they pay Jane [Fyfe] and A and D's [Anthony and Dierdre's] airfares. They will come too — as it is a ten- or twelve-week shooting schedule!! Pete will take his vacation and come over with David during the Christmas holidays. I think it is a most interesting play. Anne Baxter, John Mills and Ernest Borgnine are the three stars and I'm the fourth! So it should be a good follow up to "LHS" [The Long Hot Summer] and "Debutante."

As it would turn out, Peter couldn't be away from the office long enough to justify making the long trip to Australia. He stayed home, taking advantage of the rare chance to spend time alone with his son David. Their relationship had developed into a curious combination of closeness and

Angela's paternal grandfather, the statesman George Lansbury, and his wife, Elizabeth, his beloved "Bessie." They were married for fifty-three years.

Angela's Irish maternal grandmother, Elizabeth ("Cissy") Magean. "When we were on our uppers, she paid for my music lessons, paid for my tuition at school."

Angela's Irish grandfather, William ("Willie") McIldowie.

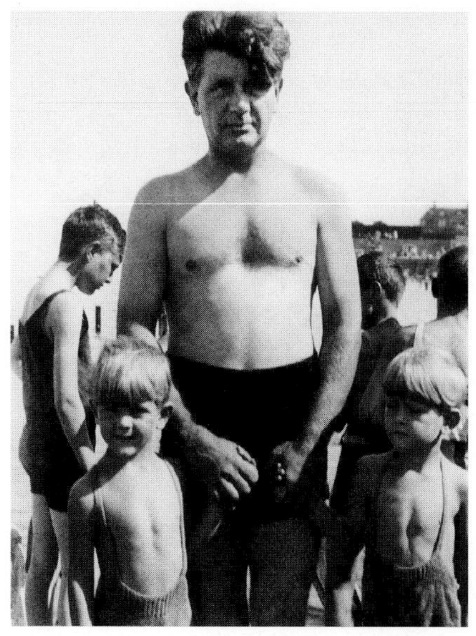

Angela's father, Edgar, with her twin brothers at three, a year before his death.

Angela's mother, Moyna, on the London stage in Jean Cocteau's *Orphée.*

Angela (then called Brigid) at three, with her eight-year-old "complete" half sister, Isolde, and Moyna, 1928.

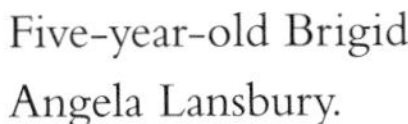

Five-year-old Brigid Angela Lansbury.

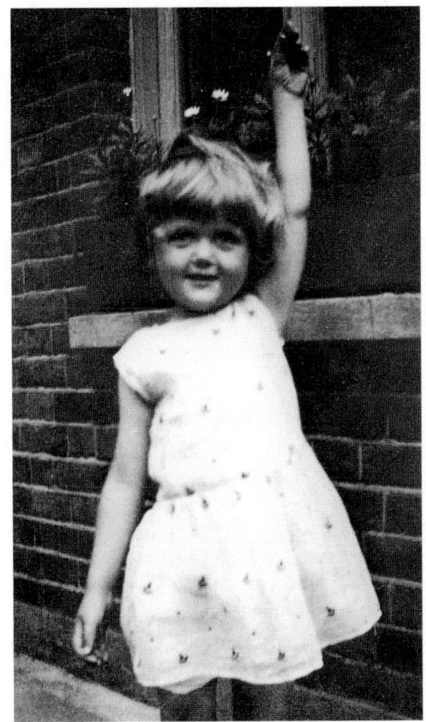

Isolde was an actress who was not competitive with Angela. "She absolutely got behind me, and encouraged me, and pushed me. She really was my best pal."

Eight-year-old Angela at the Lord Mayor of London's fancy dress ball. "Isolde went as an eighteenth-century shepherdess. I was Madame Pompadour."

The young acting student at New York's Feagin School for Drama and Radio.

With Canadian airmen and dressed to look older than sixteen at her first professional job, as a singing impressionist at the Club Samovar in Montreal, 1942.

Isolde and Peter Ustinov at their London wedding in 1939.

The powerful gossip columnist Louella Parsons wrote that in *Gaslight,* Angela "gave a performance worthy of a trouper twice her age."

With George Cukor on the set of *Gaslight,* her first movie. "Even though she was only seventeen," the celebrated director said, "and had no experience, she was immediately professional."

Singing "Good-bye Little Yellow Bird" in *The Picture of Dorian Gray,* a movie of which she is "very, very fond." Hurd Hatfield is at right.

On the set of *The Harvey Girls* with Moyna. "To wear all those clothes and have a great deal of money lavished on one was pretty exciting, [but] once I took all those clothes off, I was back to being Angie again."

With Frank Capra, director of *State of the Union,* 1948. "Everything made him laugh. And he was smart."

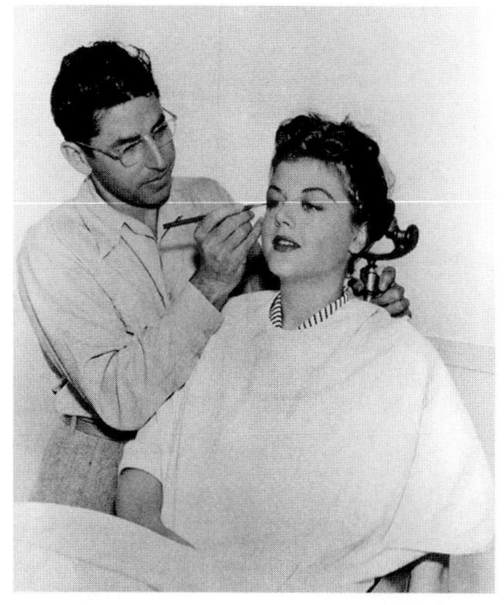

Being made up for *State of the Union* by MGM's Charles Schramm: "We didn't try to make Angela look older for older parts. She had that mature look and just acted older."

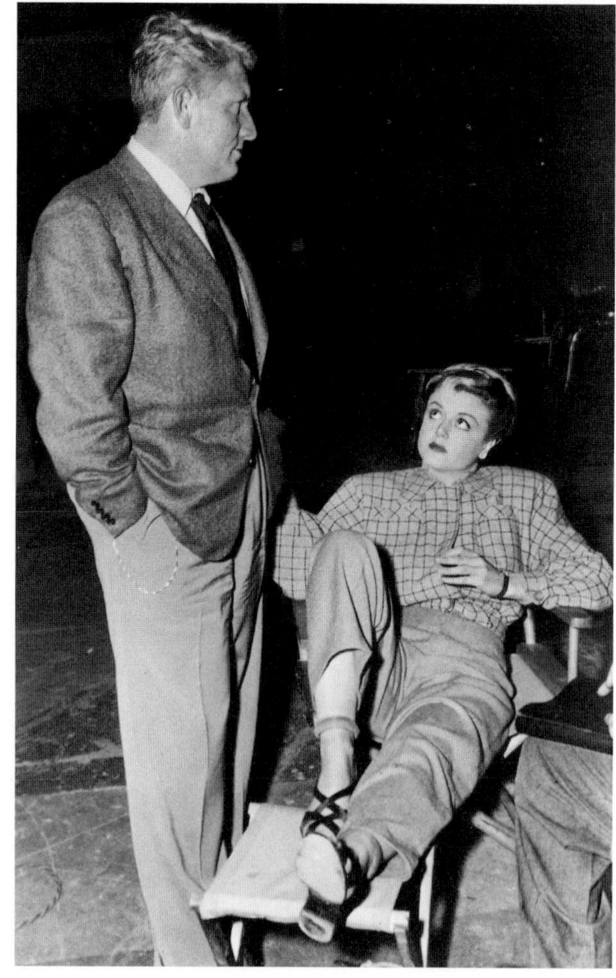

The twenty-three-year-old Lansbury with Spencer Tracy, forty-seven, on the set of *State of the Union*. "His greatness was his absolute, no-nonsense, no-temperament devotion to what he was doing."

Angela with *State of the Union* co-stars Katharine Hepburn, Spencer Tracy, and Van Johnson. "I was so impressed by Kate, and we just understood each other. Tracy was the only one who treated her like a woman."

Angela and Peter Shaw at their wedding, August 12, 1949. Moyna is grasping Tamara (daughter of Isolde and Peter Ustinov). Isolde is at Angela's left, next to Peter's stepmother. The twins are in the back row, Bruce on the left, between Peter's brother Patrick and sister Clover, and Edgar on the right, standing beside Peter's father, Walter Pullen.

Angela and Peter at a screening with John Agar and his wife, Shirley Temple, and Judy Garland with her husband, director Vincente Minnelli.

With three-year-old Anthony on the set of *The Court Jester.*

With Peter's son David, shortly after his arrival in America.

In the 1956 Danny Kaye vehicle *The Court Jester,* Angela was given a rare chance to play movie comedy. The picture reunited her with British schoolmate Glynis Johns.

With Raymond Burr at a low point for both, *Please Murder Me* (1956), the movie that was made in a supermarket.

With Deirdre at the Malibu house, 1961. (*Stephen Paley*)

With Deirdre, eight, and Anthony, nine. (*Stephen Paley*)

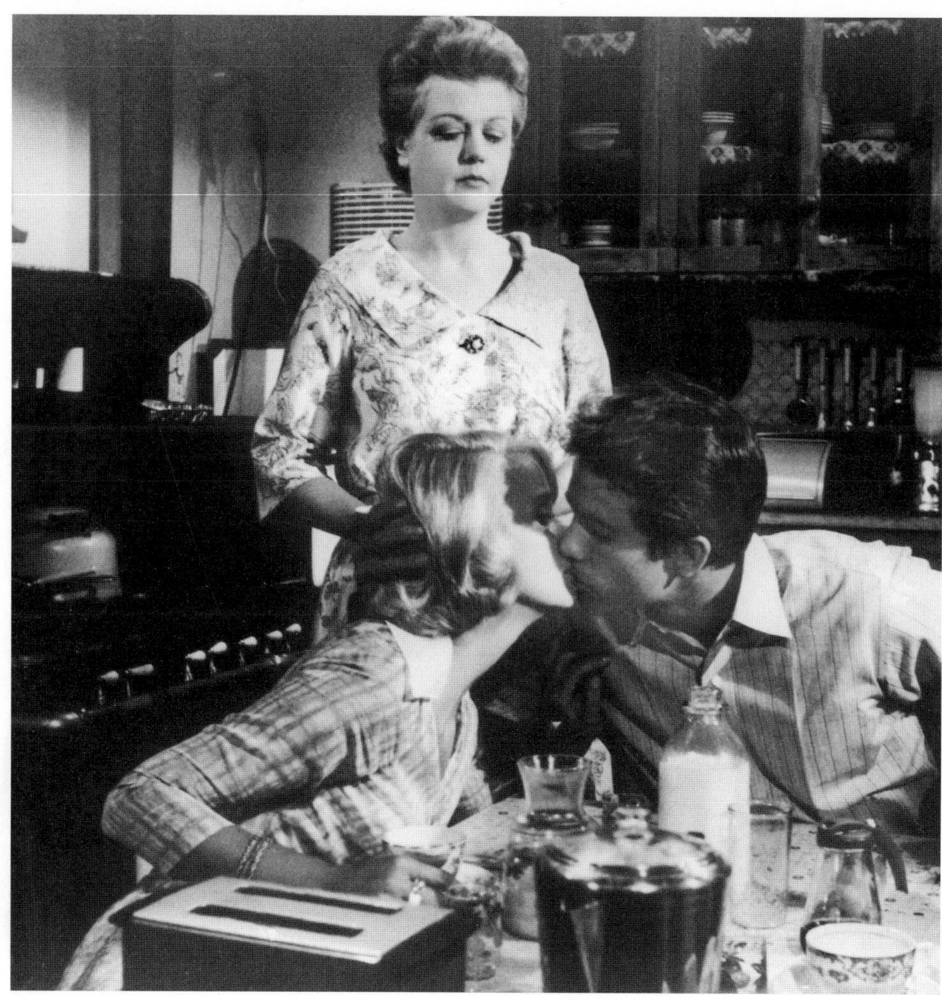

Watching Eva Marie Saint and Warren Beatty as his all-but-incestuous movie mother in the 1962 *All Fall Down*. Most of the cast were Method actors. Lansbury "was hardly one of them. I learn my lines and play the scene. I discover, myself, who my character is and run with it."

distance. Peter's reserve was in the marrow, and in that respect David emulated his father. He would come to feel that "the feelings we have for each other are greater than anything we could ever say."

Halfway across the ocean, Angela was having a "wonderful, wonderful time" making *Season of Passion* in the Australian outback, and while she worked on the movie, the children were in the sure hands of the redoubtable Jane Fyfe. With Anthony six years old, and Deirdre — called Dede ("Dee-dee") from the beginning — only five, the children had only just started school. Still, Angela did not want her work to be an excuse for their play. Besides, Jane Fyfe wouldn't have allowed it, so the children did their lessons every morning, based on the curriculum that had been provided by their Los Angeles schools. "They didn't suffer from that at all," Angela insists. "Jane brought all those school papers along, and they were given credit for their work with her. They never fell behind, like some other children in the movie community who sometimes weren't even promoted at the end of a term."

Season of Passion was an oddity in Angela's career. It was based on the play *The Summer of the 17th Doll*, which had enjoyed a moderate success in New York. It was written by an Australian (Ray Lawlor), and proud Australian money was now financing its movie version. The picture would be sparingly distributed in America and go all but unnoticed.

She came home to join Peter in the search for their ultimate house, for they agreed that after so much moving, the time had come to buy the permanent home. To Angela, that meant the perfect one, and she found it in Malibu, perched on a spectacular, two-acre site high on a bluff, with a panoramic view of the Pacific Ocean. Her profound interest in houses, her longing for them, her clinging to them, had led to an absorption with residential architecture. At first sight, the Malibu home was as magic to her, and she knew why. It reminded her of childhood and Corrymore (in her mind misspelled as "Corymore"), the magical place on the hill in Ireland. Yet it was its own self, "the most ingenious and wonderful house, with a lot of light, all timber and glass."

An illusion of floating was its essential quality. "You had the most marvelous sense of hanging in space over the sea. It was kind of an island in the sky," and this, she vowed, would become her own personal Corymore. Ever since those holidays so long ago, she had carried with her the memory of that house, and those summers on Achill Island, "that halcyon, beautiful time." She identified the magical site in Ireland with coming to terms with her father's death. It symbolized, for her, "the extraordinary mystical qualities of Ireland." It had become "a kind of talisman for everything that I dreamed of."

The new address was 24818 Pacific Coast Highway and the house was both Japanese and American in spirit. On the one hand it was spare and light and airy, yet it was close to the soil in its integration with the surrounding topography. Like Richard Neutra, who'd designed the house that they were leaving, the architect of this house, Aaron Green, was a Frank Lloyd Wright disciple. He had built the place with redwood walls and stretches of floor-to-ceiling glass, and had landscaped the grounds in the manner of a Japanese garden. Angela knew she would keep that Eastern feeling and that her floors would be kept bare. There were no rugs in the big living areas, only tatami mats. Still, there had to be practical concessions. She agreed with Peter that they needed at least two additional bedrooms.

She was never happier than when she was creating and shaping a home, but even so, she decided to call in a decorator. "It was one time," she admits, "that I put on the dog, as they say. It was what everybody was about at the time, 'Keeping up with the Joneses.' And I enjoyed doing that too. "It was the same with cars. Just like the rest of our friends. Cars were important. I loved them and I always had the best. I had a Mark VII Jaguar."

With all of this to keep her emotionally plump, she responded with predictable uninterest to an inquiry about doing another play in New York. The last thing she wanted was to leave her husband, her children, and this wonderful new home, for they were all just getting accustomed to it. "Malibu," Anthony remembers, "was pretty much cut off, and out in the middle of nowhere, just a stretch of dirt roads and ocean. Later on it would become fashionable, but then, it was just beautiful. Sun and sea and cowboy boots. We were very much *not* Hollywood kids." Instead of their old Beverly Hills life of children-of-celebrities parties and a protected education at the private John Thomas Dye School, he and Dede were now enrolled in a public school. They liked that, and so did Angela, and she wanted to get more used to this new way of life. Peter, however, thought otherwise. He encouraged her to do the play, and then, she remembered, "he began to cajole me." He told her, "This is a marvelous role. You're perfect for it. You *must* play it, and why not? Jane is here to take care of the children." He said that it was a great professional opportunity, especially as the offer was coming from the most famous theatrical producer in New York, the already legendary David Merrick.

The play was called *A Taste of Honey*, and it was the debut work of a nineteen-year-old English playwright named Shelagh Delaney. It had achieved a great success in 1958 at London's prestigious Royal Court Theatre before moving on to a successful run on the West End. The critic Kenneth Tynan could have been speaking directly to the actor in Angela when he reviewed it as bringing "real people onto the stage, joking and flaring and scuffling and eventually surviving." The opportunity to act in a play by a female writer had added appeal for Angela, as there were virtually none in America or England.

The role she would play was appealing too, being truly female, and that was a rare thing in the theater. Male playwrights, she felt, seldom wrote dialogue the way women actually talk, or had female characters think the way women do. She had a strong sense of the womanly, which was what her involvement with and her passion for homes was all about. It was why this new home was so heavenly to her. "We were living out in Malibu," she remembers, "in the most idyllic circumstances." She did not care how interesting a play *A Taste of Honey* was. She did not even want to discuss leaving her husband, her children, or this new home. But the agent in Peter could also turn the screws when it came to work opportunities, and he persisted. Still she demurred, even as David Merrick, George Devine ("De-veen"), and Tony Richardson pulled into their driveway one day in a powder blue Cadillac convertible, on a mission to apply group pressure. Richardson was the famous director who would be staging *A Taste of Honey.* He had been in demand ever since directing *Look Back in Anger,* the first of the "kitchen sink" plays (of which Delaney's was another) that were revolutionizing the London stage. He was in California making the movie of William Faulkner's *Sanctuary,* which explained the presence of George Devine, who was also a director. The idea was for Devine to begin work on *A Taste of Honey* until Richardson could take over. Because of that, as the three men took turns in explaining to Angela, rehearsals would be held in Los Angeles. She would not even have to leave home. Yet.

Siding with their visitors, Peter continued to pour on the enthusiasm. It was obvious to her that "he was conspiring to get me to do it." One of his selling points was that she would be working with the splendid actress Joan Plowright, which, he suggested, would make for a stimulating stage experience. Moreover, Plowright was romantically involved with Laurence Olivier, who was already on Broadway, costarring with Anthony Quinn in *Becket*. Wouldn't Plowright, Olivier, and Angela make for a good British theatrical family?

Once again, she insisted that she wanted to stay at home. She intended to work on the house. "The children," she said, "are just getting to an age when they are fascinating. Anthony is coming up to third grade."

The men ganged up on her, again urging her to consider the importance of the project. Peter became still more adamant. Angela felt, "I was faced with this terrible pull. Should I leave the children?" But finally worn down, she sighed, "Well, all right, but I'll only do it for six months."

This was an unprecedented stipulation, one that would have been querulously met even had it come from a major star. All eyes turned to Merrick, the terrifying producer who was known as "the Abominable Showman." To everyone's amazement — most of all Angela's — he agreed, and afterward, she said, "I think it was the only time David Merrick ever made a deal with an actress to play for six months."

It wasn't her only condition. Turning to Peter she said, "Once the show opens in New York — if it's a hit — I want the children to join me."

She admits that at that time, she was focusing more attention on them than on Peter. "They came first, as far as I was concerned. Their comfort, their education, nothing could interfere with that. I felt that my presence in their life was most important. The fact that they missed their father on those occasions — well, at least one of us was there."

That attitude had never bothered Peter, and he certainly had no quarrel with Anthony and Deirdre's going to New York while Angela was in the play; they'd done so for *Hotel Paradiso*. But even with these concessions, there was still conflict in her heart. "I was dragged kicking and screaming into that. I just didn't want to go and do it.

"It was Peter."

Rehearsals for *A Taste of Honey* began at Royce Hall on the UCLA campus, a half-hour drive from Malibu. Inside the rehearsal space, the play's milieu — a tenement apartment in the drab industrial city of Lancashire — could not have been more incongruous with the reality outside, the sunny skies and palm trees of southern California.

A Taste of Honey is about a seventeen-year-old girl (Plowright), who has been made pregnant by a black sailor (Billy Dee Williams). After he abandons her, she pluckily survives, cheered up by her homosexual roommate. Her mother (Angela) arrives with a very young lover (wearing an eyepatch and muttering that "it brings me halfway to Oedipus"), and somehow, this shabby but brave little band muddles through.

Angela's role was a rich one, a sexually indiscriminate slob who, for once, might have been the actress's own age, for a thirty-four-year-old woman could well be the parent of a seventeen-year-old. That was of little consolation, however, considering that Joan Plowright, at thirty, was playing the daughter.

Rehearsals with Devine would begin every day at noon and run through the afternoon. After a dinner break, Richardson would take over and continue through the evening. "It was kind of frustrating," Angela felt, because "George Devine was a great director, a collaborator in the building of a character, the creating of a role. He was really responsible for most of my performance in that play."

Despite the distraction of alternating directors, the *Taste of Honey* rehearsals went smoothly, as did the Los Angeles opening at the Biltmore Theater. The bump came when the company was preparing to leave for the Cincinnati tryout engagement. With bags packed and a car waiting to drive her to the airport, Angela leaned down to pick Deirdre up for a goodbye kiss and then she lifted Anthony for his big hug.

Once out the door and inside the car, she fell apart, and wept to her depths. "It was terrible, terrible," she says, and for the first time in their marriage, she was resentful of Peter. "We were so happy during that time. It was a wonderfully level period. He was doing well, his career was zooming. He was a young man on his way, and that was terribly exciting for me. I was just as interested in his career, and helping him to get there, as I was in my own.

"At that point I probably could have stopped and quit and been a wife and mother."

She ponders that idea. "At that point," she said, "to be truthful, I probably could have."

She considers it again.

"Yes. For sure, I could have.

"And I probably would have missed it, too."

A Taste of Honey opened on Broadway at the Lyceum Theatre on October 4, 1960. Moyna sent a note backstage that night: "The very, very best of luck, my Angel. You'll be marvelous!!" Pinned to it was a bit of blue fabric, which Angela recognized at once as snipped from a dress that Moyna had herself worn in the movie *Interference.* The blue cloth had become a good-luck token for the whole family. Everyone had a piece of it somewhere with them, and Angela slipped it into her neckline, stood up at her dressing table, tucked in a stray wisp of hair, took a deep breath, and was on her way.

The reviews were excellent, and the play settled in for a healthy run. Angela found an apartment on East 97th Street at Fifth Avenue, and sent for the children. She was also able to spend time with her mother, who as she aged had found a new source of charm as a doyenne of the theater. If Moyna could not be on stage, she could at least entrance at a cocktail party. It was a characteristic that Angela did not share and she certainly could not play *the actress.* "When I'm doing it, I love the work, but when I'm not in the immediate experience, I cut off. I don't want to be in that place and I don't allow for it. I can't allow for it."

She was always able to turn off the actress and become the person, something that Moyna seemed increasingly less inclined to do as she faced the end of her acting career.

With *A Taste of Honey* off and running, Angela had two new chums, "Joanie" Plowright and her boyfriend, "Larry" Olivier. Angela was beginning to appreciate that one of the most compelling arguments made by that sales team back in California had been the prospect of getting to know this man who was probably the finest living actor on the English-speaking stage. "His kind of British actor," she felt, "*that* is greatness. Olivier, Sybil Thorndike, Ralph Richardson, Peggy Ashcroft, John Gielgud, Michael Redgrave, Edith Evans." She aspired to their level, and the budding friendship with Olivier and Plowright made such acting seem within reach.

After the show, she would regularly go to their Sutton Place apartment for midnight supper. "They'd rented this small, elegant flat and had a wonderful cook. We would have incredible meals." But she had her own cook, too, and reciprocated. The occasion that seemed warmest among those, she felt, was a real Thanksgiving Day dinner. "That," she knew, "is always a special treat for Brits," because the holiday is strictly American. Olivier and Plowright sat down to a traditional turkey dinner with all the fixings — along with Jane Fyfe, Dede, and Anthony (who thought the handsome visitor was a basketball star named Larry Oliver).

On the street below, a crowd of reporters and photographers loitered around the entrance to the building. There was a rumor that Joan Plowright and Lawrence Oliver were about to elope. At the two theaters where Olivier and Plowright were playing, the press, desperate for gossip, would hound the casts for any crumbs of information. They waited at the stage door after performances, and followed Olivier and Plowright wherever they went. Making the situation all the more dramatic, Olivier's famous ex-wife, Vivien Leigh, was also in town.

Her proximity didn't bother him. Before every evening performance of *Becket,* he would pick up the telephone in his dressing room and call Joan in hers. When her dresser, Dolores Childers, answered, Olivier would always say the same thing: "Be sure and take care of my baby." Dolores certainly would — in part because that was a dresser's job, but primarily because she would do anything for Mr. Olivier. ("When he came to the dressing room and greeted me like a long-lost friend, I nearly fainted, he was so wonderful.")

Dolores was a pretty young woman, small and blond, a former dancer herself. As she explained her duties, "a dresser not only takes care of the costumes but also makes sure the actor gets into them so that they're on right and look okay. And then you have to handle the clothes afterwards as far as cleaning, pressing, and taking care of them as far as mending and sewing."

A dresser could do more than that. A dresser could be secretary, confidante, even friend, as long as the friendship was understood to be between unequals.

Although Angela had her own dresser, a woman named Billie White, Joan Plowright's dresser, Dolores, was becoming a regular visitor, stopping in to chat and gossip, especially between performances on matinee days. Most of her conversation was about the newlywed Oliviers, for Joan and Larry had finally eloped. They'd done it from Angela's apartment, leaving by the kitchen door, going down the back stairs and slipping out through the building's service entrance. A car had been waiting to whisk them to a justice of the peace in Connecticut.

Olivier and Plowright seemed to be reminding Lansbury of her essential Britishness. "American actors," she says, "are a little more social. We British are more reserved. In England, acting is a job. Everybody comes to the theater, does their job, and leaves." Of course the greater part of the Anglicizing was done by *A Taste of Honey* itself, in which she had to speak in a Cockney accent for eight performances a week. A serious actor frequently takes a role home after the curtain comes down, and while she wasn't going home a floozy, she was certainly walking out the stage door still a rather British person. She discerned another difference between British and American actors. "British actors," she says, "are much more a breed apart from ordinary citizens than American actors, and I am part of that breed; that was how I'd been brought up.

"That may be why in Hollywood, I always felt like a stranger in a strange land."

It was to that strange land that she returned, as guaranteed, at the end of her six-month excursion to Broadway. Hermione Baddeley succeeded her in the play, and Shelagh Delaney never wrote another one of consequence. Ultimately, the only thing remembered from *A Taste of Honey* would be its title song.

If Peter's career had been taking off before Angela left California, the momentum was still strong when she got back. He was representing some of the William Morris Agency's most important talent (as they called the artists) and was negotiating major deals for them. Among his clients was Carol Reed, then directing one of the most expensive movies MGM had ever produced, a remake of *Mutiny on the Bounty*.

One night, Shaw remembers, Marlon Brando — who was starring in the film — got into "such a terrible row" with Reed that the agent thought they were going to come to blows. To make matters worse, it was all happening in front of Sol Siegel, the head of MGM. He looked on with no little concern as the studio's gigantic investment threatened to go up in ego.

"I managed to calm things down," Peter remembers, and after the smoke had cleared, Siegel invited him out for a Scotch and a proposition. "I would like you to come with me at MGM. I'd like you to be my executive assistant."

It was an extraordinary opportunity, a wonderful job with a handsome salary. In six months it would get even better, for when Siegel resigned so did Benny Thau. Thau had been second in command, responsible for all the talent. Thus, Peter was sprung into the right place at the right time. He took over Benny Thau's job as the second man at the studio. It was a major position, of course, and he was represented in that contract negotiation by no less than his former boss, Abe Lastfogel, the president of the William Morris Agency. The glittering contract that Lastfogel brokered for him was a matter of friendship, at least as far as an agent could be friendly in business dealings.

Certainly, there was another motive. In Peter, the William Morris Agency would have a friend indeed at MGM. Ironically, Angela would not. "I never did hire Angie," Peter says, because he would not risk the appearance of nepotism. She did do her old studio a favor that was kept secret for a while, dubbing the entire part played by the Swedish actress Ingrid Thulin in *The Four Horsemen of the Apocalypse.* That item of trivia aside, although she made no films at MGM in 1961, the year was, in fact, going to be her best in the movies.

It was also going to be her oddest one, and her last as a full-time Hollywood movie actress.

CHAPTER 9

THE MAGIC OF BELIEVING

BLUE HAWAII was Elvis Presley's first movie after being discharged from the army in 1960, and although Angela had experienced her share of the cinematically ridiculous, from *Samson and Delilah* to *The Purple Mask,* not to mention the movie filmed in the supermarket, it seemed particularly embarrassing to be involved with an Elvis Presley opus.

To be sure, she'd hesitated before agreeing to do it. The family finances were no longer desperate. While she was accustomed to playing older characters, she was for the first time being asked to actually play a mother, and that dashed any remaining hopes for Hollywood stardom. Moreover, just as in *A Taste of Honey,* she was to play the mother of an actor who was too old to be her child — in this instance, she was thirty-six and Presley was twenty-nine.

"So I was sort of insulted to be asked in the first place."

But, she rationalized, she would be playing a Southerner, and she felt strongly about "the importance of dialects. And also, I recognized that she was a kind of funny character." "It is ridiculous," she says finally about *Blue Hawaii,* "but quite charming." Perhaps some of her conflict about the assignment was related to her husband's Presley connection. When Peter had negotiated the singer's movie *Kissing Cousins,* he had gotten to know Elvis's manager, Colonel Tom Parker. In fact, Angela says, "Peter had a real feeling for Elvis and the colonel." The Shaws spent several social evenings with Parker and his wife, "so," she explains, "I was kind of in the loop as far as Elvis was concerned, even though he was never there on those occasions."

She did learn, from Parker, that "Elvis never read a script. The colonel read the scripts and said, 'We're gonna do this, ma boy,' and that was it."

Perhaps inevitably, then, she agreed to *Blue Hawaii,* insisting that, in the end, it was her own choice, not Peter's. "I was a freelance. It was a professional job. I was well paid. It was a lovely location. There were good costumes and attention to detail. It was a good cast — and Elvis was a very nice young man in those days. And so I did it. I'm not apologizing for it. I was a journeyman actor. I did what was proffered. If it was applicable to my talents and I could bring it off, I would do it. As long as I got the billing and the money. That was the important thing — and that I didn't disgrace myself."

Blue Hawaii was the first of her assertive mother roles. The next one was even more dominating, Warren Beatty's mother in *All Fall Down.* The movie's director was John Frankenheimer, a tall and rangy thirty-two-year-old who had grown up in the New York area, prepped in a Catholic military academy, and graduated from Williams College in the class of 1951, a year ahead of George Steinbrenner, Dominick Dunne, and Stephen Sondheim (in whose school musicals he performed).

Frankenheimer was a child of television's "Golden Age," having directed the first and last dramas on *Playhouse 90* and scores of its programs in between. He says that he had Elia Kazan's advice in mind when he hired Angela to do *All Fall Down.* The great director had advised him, while they were at the Actors Studio, "You want to work with them on their way up or their way down." Frankenheimer admits he saw Lansbury as being on her way down. "She had never really made it as a young leading lady and was already in her middle thirties, an age when it's difficult for actresses."

The script for *All Fall Down* was adapted by William Inge from a James Leo Herlihy novel. The playwright had recently fled Broadway in despair, having been hit with a series of flops. He was now on the brink of alcoholism, but Frankenheimer offered him a protected environment, populated with Actors Studio people, just as Inge's plays had been. Not only was the director himself a Studio man, but with only Angela excepted, so was the entire cast — Karl Malden, Eva Marie Saint, and Warren Beatty (who had even been in one of Inge's failed plays, *A Loss of Roses*).

In *All Fall Down* Frankenheimer reaches for a hothouse atmosphere and achieves it. He also creates striking imagery. Much of the picture is shot from oblique angles, focusing on stark and deserted, surreal, de Chirico-like streets with very high-contrast black-and-white photography. This styling seems to be in frank homage to Orson Welles and *Citizen Kane,* and overall the movie appears determined to be artistic. But while Frankenheimer is particularly proud of *All Fall Down,* it can seem a shapeless and even incoherent film.

As for the performances, Angela did not care what anyone's acting approach or process was — so long as it was professional and responsible. Actors Studio or no, she very much admired both Malden and Saint as actors and Frankenheimer as a director.

Beatty, however, was driving her quite mad. His character in the picture is a young man with the peculiar name of "Berry-Berry." He is a sulking, James Dean–like youth, who never explains exactly what is bothering him. In his inarticulate gloom, he knows only that he has to get away from his family, particularly his strong mother, with whom there is an unmistakable sexual attraction.

What bothered Angela most about Beatty was the disparity between his shallow acting abilities and his deep devotion to the Actors Studio system. To her, "He was visibly putting The Method into practice." The way Frankenheimer saw it, "We were all Actors Studio people, but the others didn't practice it the way he did. Angela was a team player. She thought Warren was egotistical, self-centered, and looking out for himself."

That was not her notion of professionalism. She could not accept Beatty's apparent disregard for the rest of the cast while he ran three or four laps around the set so that he could arrive for a scene and appear to be out of breath. ("We all stood around and waited," she remembers, "and tried not to look embarrassed for him.") But despite all of his elaborate meditations and rituals, the thinking and preparing before he pronounced himself ready for the camera, Lansbury was "appalled at how there was nothing in his face. It was completely empty."

At one point during the filming, Frankenheimer says, "Angela was supposed to berate Berry-Berry, and he was supposed to look awful. I put the camera on Warren and got *nothing.* It is very tough to get reactions out of him." The director took Angela aside and whispered, "When you berate him, tell him what you really think of him." She strolled onto the set, assumed a dark expression, and turned on the young actor, suddenly crying, "You conceited asshole! You are a horrible brat!"

Beatty showed no reaction, and there never would be any change of expression on his face throughout this movie. Angela's final word on The

Method, and its psychological approach, was that no matter what the actor is thinking, no matter what the actor is feeling, no matter what technique the actor is using, if it doesn't show up on the face, the camera can't see it, and if the camera can't see it, then it isn't going to appear in the movie.

As for Beatty's legendary sex appeal, "Warren certainly is beautiful looking," she says. "I'll give him that and I certainly realize and appreciate an attractive man. But I was married to the most attractive man in town.

"Warren's intelligence has seen him through. It has allowed him to have an incredible career."

During a break at a looping session, rerecording dialogue for *All Fall Down,* John Frankenheimer walked up to Angela and slapped a book down on the table in front of her.

"That," he said, "is your next movie. Read it."

The book was Richard Condon's novel *The Manchurian Candidate,* and she found it "one of the most exciting political books I ever read." More important, she could see that her part was "one of those great roles that an actress dreams about."

Ever since Frankenheimer had read this McCarthy-bashing political thriller, he'd wanted to make a movie of it. He felt that the book had important things to say and said them in an entertaining and highly dramatic way — a way that was readily adaptable to cinematic language. But even seven years after the downfall of Senator Joseph P. McCarthy, the project was being turned down by every major studio, and Frankenheimer suspected they were still intimidated by the political right wing.

The director knew that a major star's commitment could turn a cowardly movie studio into a courageous champion of righteousness. Frank Sinatra was such a star and he was interested in making the picture, but he told Frankenheimer that because of the anti-McCarthy theme, he was going to have to consult with his great and good friend President Kennedy.

As Sinatra relayed it to Frankenheimer, the White House was enthusiastic. "Jack told me he loved the book. He said it's going to make a great movie." There was but one presidential question: "Who's going to play the mother?"

That was the paradox about both the book and the eventual movie. The central figure in the story is an army intelligence officer (Sinatra's part) who senses something peculiar about a Medal of Honor winner (Laurence Harvey), who is the second most important figure, and who turns out to be a brainwashed assassin. Yet it is his mother who dominates the story, much as she dominates her husband and son. Even when she isn't in a scene, she is an unseen presence. Her intensity, her viciousness, her extravagant malevolence bestride the story, and because of her, *The Manchurian Candidate* rises to a level beyond that of a mere political thriller.

In response to the Oval Office's concern with movie casting, Sinatra told President Kennedy that he wanted Lucille Ball for Raymond's mother. He thought she would be marvelous in the role, and since his contract would assure him of casting approval, he pointed out that she would indeed get the part. More important to Frankenheimer, "Once the United Artists people heard that the President wanted the picture made, there was no resistance," and they agreed to finance it.

But the director did not want the mother to be played by Ball, and after finishing *All Fall Down,* he knew exactly whom he did want. Finally, he telephoned Sinatra and said, "Look, I don't want to go to the mat with you on this one, because I don't think there's any point in it. But I believe very strongly in Angela Lansbury for this part. I'd like you to come over and see a rough cut of my movie *All Fall Down.*

"If you don't feel the same way as I do after seeing that rough cut, then we have something to talk about."

He arranged a screening of the unpolished (no credits, no music) movie for just the two of them. When the lights went up at the end of the picture, he rose and turned to Sinatra, who looked up from his seat.

"Enough said," he smiled. "You wanted Angela Lansbury, we'll have Angela Lansbury."

The political thesis of *The Manchurian Candidate* is that at the height of the red witch-hunt, the anti-Communists were, ironically, the greatest help the Communists could have wanted. The point is not subtly made. The gruff and ranting Senator Johnny Iselin is the scourge of traitors, a list-waving, "point of order" shouting, barely disguised Joe McCarthy. He is targeted by Soviet and Chinese Communists as a weakling through whom they can seize control of the American presidency. Iselin's own wife is their chief American operative, and her son, from a previous marriage, is the Medal of Honor winner who has been brainwashed by the Chinese Communists into becoming the assassin who will implement the plot.

But an intelligence officer who was in the son's unit begins to dredge up memories of the brainwashing sessions, to which he, too, was subjected.

He nearly has a nervous breakdown before he realizes that the war hero has been conditioned to murder a presidential candidate, which would lead to the nomination of the vice-presidential nominee — Senator Iselin.

Were that plot the center of the movie's dramatic gravity, *The Manchurian Candidate* would be a good political thriller but merely that, linked to its era and perhaps already forgotten. But an artistic energy is provided by the depiction of the bizarre mother and her intense relationship with the "two little boys" she emasculates — her husband ("I keep telling you not to think") and her son, who is not even allowed a girlfriend ("My mother always wins — I can never beat her").

It was the "Oedipal thing" between Berry-Berry and his mother in *All Fall Down* that prompted Frankenheimer to cast Angela in *The Manchurian Candidate,* but in the latter case the Oedipal thing is so vivid that it displaces the center of the movie away from its political themes. Indeed, the politics of *The Manchurian Candidate* seem its clumsiest and most dated aspect, while the mother-son relationship provides an enduring electricity. In the novel, Condon attempts to make psychological sense of Raymond's mother by describing an incestuous adolescent relationship with her father, a plot element that was probably too controversial for any studio to handle. It was daring enough for the movie to show this mother planting a full kiss on her son's mouth — while ordering him to murder a presidential nominee. That certainly was more daring than denouncing McCarthyism in 1961, seven years after Edward R. Murrow had already skewered the senator on television.

Moreover, in dealing with a son who is enticed by his mother, and murders his father (a stepfather — one goes only so far), *The Manchurian Candidate* is not only the *Hamlet* story in essence; it presents a stereotype homosexual, mother-father-son relationship, one drawn in such extravagant — even absurdist — terms as to resemble a play by Tennessee Williams or Edward Albee. These qualities do not dilute the story, but add to its fascination.

From the outset, Angela "recognized what an incredible challenge this was — a role above and beyond anything that had ever happened to me." It was not only a great part; in terms of its dramatic impact, it is the leading role, even though, oddly enough, her character has no name. In the picture, she is known only as "Raymond's mother."

To be sure, her fellow players also give good performances. Frank Sinatra, in particular, makes the intelligence officer convincingly exhausted, emotionally as well as physically, and then energized by the hunt. Sinatra is, of course, a very different sort of actor than Angela Lansbury, but she gives him his due, considering him "an extremely effective performer who has played the character that he has devised for himself. That works wonderfully well for him, and sometimes he takes a good step beyond that. He did in *The Manchurian Candidate.* He's very good in it. I think it was one of the best performances I ever saw him give."

Laurence Harvey is effective, too, although he is no Lansbury when it comes to defeating a British accent. He was playing her son even though, at thirty-two, he was only three years younger than she. Yet, without looking old or dowdy — in fact, looking dangerously sexy and quite beautiful — Angela makes the mother utterly and dreadfully believable, and Frankenheimer considers hers "one of the finest screen performances I've ever been associated with."

Its brilliance is the result not only of artistic but of cinematic professionalism. It is a combination of dramatic technique and a knowledge of the particular requirements of movie acting. As Angela describes it, "I am always aware of the camera, and where it is. I don't *play* to the camera," she says, "but I think of what the camera needs to tell that moment." Frankenheimer, coming as he did from the theater, ran more noncamera rehearsals than most movie directors. "But," Lansbury points out, "when we do start rehearsing with the camera, it's terribly important to know just where it's going to be. Then, you show the director what you think you should be doing in this scene. Finally, the cinematographer and the director decide where the camera should be put to most effectively get that moment."

To her, such technical knowledge was simply a requirement of the professional movie actor — part of the arsenal supporting and supplementing one's natural talent. In the case of *The Manchurian Candidate,* the role, the technique, the talent, and the actress come together under ideal circumstances. It is not surprising that the performance won her a Best Supporting Actress nomination for the 1962 Academy Award.

"Everyone kept telling me, 'You're a shoo-in,' and I sat there with my speech prepared." When the envelope was opened, the twelve-year-old Patty Duke was declared that year's winner for *The Miracle Worker,* leaving Angela in a state of shock. "It was like your stomach has fallen out of your body.

"It bothered me desperately," she admits about this third fruitless nomination.

Although *The Manchurian Candidate* is the strongest, the most memorable, and the best picture she ever made, and while she gives her finest film performance in it, she was left with one negative and by now all too familiar afterthought. More than ever before, she was weary of playing older women, bitchy women, and most of all, malicious mothers. Raymond's was the final straw. "I'd played a number of women of that ilk, but none with such vitriol. She was the most evil woman I could possibly imagine.

"That was kind of the zenith of those roles and I didn't want to do any more after it."

Frankenheimer thought she was wrong. "It's typically the actor who's good at something who says, 'I don't want to do this anymore.' But basically, Angie is very good at playing very strong, powerful characters who have a lot of dimension to them."

She had her limits and he might have understood limits. His own intense liberalism was not going to last beyond the assassination of Robert F. Kennedy. That took all the hope out of him. "Ever since then," Frankenheimer says, "I don't have strong political convictions anymore."

Despite Lansbury's "huge" reviews, as Frankenheimer describes them, for *The Manchurian Candidate*, there was no rush of directors following up on them to wave great parts in her face. She accepted that, for she knew her Hollywood. "Parts like Raymond's mother don't happen every five minutes and besides, that role was still a one-up [featured part]. It wasn't going to guarantee a tremendous movie career, and I didn't get a lot of offers because of it."

Her next assignments were no better or worse than before, "good small parts, but always small. I was still never the romantic lead or the heroine." So she continued doing standard Hollywood fare, working with Jane Fonda and Peter Finch in *In the Cool of the Day* (memorable only as a title to prompt the later *In the Heat of the Night*) and with Peter Sellers in *The World of Henry Orient*.

A camping trip was the Shaws' idea of the perfect vacation. Angela had bought a big station wagon ("a Chrysler New Yorker," she enthused, "a great car"). With five in the family, they needed something roomy.

Even so, it always seemed as if there was never enough room for all there was to pack. Everyone would help carry the tents and sleeping bags and provisions out of the house, and start loading up, but invariably, halfway through the job, the children would get to giggling. "The amount of stuff

Mom brought along," Dede thought, "was incredible," and even Angela had to laugh at the comprehensiveness of her preparations, admitting, "They thought I was crazy." Besides obvious things like the poles and the pegs for the tents, there were necessary blankets and pillows, and a kerosene stove. Perhaps the sewing kit wasn't essential, but a button *could* come off. "She was like something out of a movie," Anthony remembers.

There were the usual coolers and cooking utensils, dishes and silverware, battery lamps, candles and waterproof matches and flashlights. There were water skis and fishing rods and reels. There was food, naturally, two weeks' worth of canned goods and canned drinks, can openers and bottle openers. And cigarettes and charcoal. There were also extra sweaters and slickers and first aid kits and endless tools; an axe and a screwdriver; a sledgehammer for the tent pegs. Eventually, there was so much stuff piled up in the driveway that sixteen-year-old David, eight-year-old Anthony, and seven-year-old Dede were all but rolling around on the ground, hysterical with laughter.

Angela just took it smiling, standing there in her jeans and sneakers and zipper jacket, holding an armful of bathrobes. "Laugh all you want," she said, "but you've got to be prepared." And she added, "Sure, we could camp with much less but you wouldn't like it very much, and God help me if you ask for something I forgot to bring."

When the wagon was crammed so full that its sides seemed to be bulging, the back door was slammed shut. Then, after Angela backed it up, Peter and David hooked the car up to the sixteen-foot launch that they used for water skiing, and the camping expedition was ready to roll.

Peter waved goodbye (he would join them later) as Angela eased down the driveway with the boat in tow and headed south on the Pacific Coast Highway. She veered eastward onto the Santa Monica Freeway, continuing in that direction for seven long hours of driving until she approached the Nevada state line. Just before reaching it, she left the Interstate highway and a short distance later was rolling into the marina at Meeks Bay, at the edge of Lake Tahoe. Then the laughter started all over again as everyone helped unload all of the stuff from the car so that they could lug it onto the already crammed boat. Finally, they launched it into the water and Angela steered over to Emerald Bay, another inlet off the immense body of water that is Lake Tahoe.

Angela always called ahead to the park rangers, reserving a tent space providing their own private little clearing with its picnic table, fieldstone grill, and fire grate. Once they had the tents up, Anthony and Dede broke out the charcoal and lit it. Soon a campfire was glowing behind them in the dark, and they all sat down to dinner at the candlelit picnic table that Angela had set with the tablecloth she'd brought along, and paper napkins, and the special camping dishes and glasses and eating utensils, and of course salt and pepper and ketchup and mustard.

She set the alarm for five o'clock, and when it went off, each new morning seemed to be dependably sharp and clear and chilly. The water of the bay was always sleek, "and terribly cold," Angela remembers. "Icy." They warmed up with hot cereal, tea, and cocoa, and as the sun rose higher in the morning sky, the kids jumped into their bathing suits and grabbed the water skis. Clambering aboard, David and Anthony and Dede arranged their rotation while Angela manned the wheel. "All you would hear was the motor starting up," she remembers, and then someone would yell, "Hit it!" That was the signal to zoom out across the bay, and, she says, "The kids would just take off like flashes across the water."

A week later, Peter would arrive, sometimes with his brother Patrick. Then, Angela would be relieved at the helm of the boat and she, too, would take a turn zooming around on the water skis.

One spring day in 1963, Angela received a small blue air mail letter. When she saw who had sent it, a tingle of excitement ran through her. She tore open the envelope and read the message that she had long hoped would arrive through "the magic of believing."

The note read "Would you be interested in a musical on Broadway? Stephen Sondheim is writing the music and lyrics. I am writing the book."

It was signed by Arthur Laurents, the author of *West Side Story* and *Gypsy.*

CHAPTER 10

I JUST WANT TO BE LOVED

WOULD *she be interested in a Broadway musical?* The words all but jumped off the stationery, and she thought, "This is it! The most exciting letter I have received in years!" She hurried through the house, clutching it in her hand and calling out, "Pete! Pete!" while under her breath, she whispered, "God, this is exciting!"

Not content to let him read it, she insisted on reciting it aloud. "We are coming out to California and would like very much to hear you sing. Would you consider auditioning for us?"

"Consider it?"

She stared at her husband.

"A musical on Broadway! It's the most exciting thing I can possibly imagine."

It was ten years since she had tried to will herself into a musical comedy future by the process of "visualization" — picturing herself glamorous and sensational, "singing like a bird and dancing like a dream." Now those hopes seemed on the verge of materializing, and she would save the letter for years, "with its blue lightweight air mail envelope and the name of Arthur Laurents looming on the back flap."

When she calmed down, she realized that she was only vaguely aware of who Stephen Sondheim was — a lyricist, she believed (he was — of

West Side Story and *Gypsy*). Like most people, she didn't know that he had also written the music as well as the lyrics for the current hit *A Funny Thing Happened on the Way to the Forum*. But she had certainly heard of Arthur Laurents, as a playwright (*Home of the Brave*) as well as a librettist. In her mind, "he was a member of the Broadway elite," and she promptly responded to the letter, indicating that she was flattered to be asked, and would be delighted to audition for them.

Then, since "there weren't any movie offers hanging there anyway," she began to prepare for this heady occasion — daydreaming, too, about the musicals she'd seen while doing *Hotel Paradiso* and *A Taste of Honey*. Such shows as *My Fair Lady* and *Bells Are Ringing, Candide* and *Damn Yankees, Fiorello* and *The Sound of Music*, and most of exciting of all, Ethel Merman in *Gypsy*. Such musicals, she found, were "like alcohol, they go to your head, and you think, 'That's what I want to do — get out there and perform!'"

As Angela explains it, "There's much more of the entertainer in the musical theater performer than there is in the actor, and I love music so much." She went to work on her singing with a songwriter friend who had a songwriter name — Buddy Pepper. He wrote commercial jingles and even the occasional hit ("Vaya con Dios"). Since Pepper was not familiar with Stephen Sondheim's music and had no idea what kind of songs would be in the show, he suggested that Angela prepare one with a medium tempo that had been written for a Broadway show, and that included low and high notes. It would demonstrate that her voice was flexible, and with that in mind, he suggested Gershwin's "A Foggy Day" because it is "a very rangy song."

It was that piece she sang when she finally met with the small and wiry Laurents, forty-six years old and debonair, and the thirty-four-year-old Sondheim, who was the very picture of eccentric genius — shy, squinting, a generally twitchy collection of tics, so badly dressed that if he weren't brilliant, he might have been taken for an ordinary slob. Angela could hardly have realized that the moment was as thrilling for him as it was for her. For on that same afternoon, Sondheim and Laurents were also auditioning Lee Remick to play their romantic lead (as usual, not that part for Angela). To the starstruck Sondheim, this one-day trip to Los Angeles was "a very glamorous moment in my life, hearing both Angie and Lee sing on the same day."

A few days later, both women had their parts; the decision was that simple because Laurents was also going to direct the show. He informed them that rehearsals would begin in New York that winter of 1963, and Sondheim suggested that, in the meantime, Angela contact Herbert Greene, who was working in Los Angeles and was going to be their musical director, and who might work with her on strengthening and projecting her voice.

The title on the black vinyl cover of her script was *Anyone Can Whistle.* The play is set in an imaginary town that has recently gone bankrupt. To rescue its finances, the tough, bossy, and unpopular mayoress, Cora Hoover Hoople (Angela's role), and her political cronies decide to create a tourist attraction by faking a miracle — curative waters spouting from a rock in the town square. Soon the lame, the halt, and the just plain nosey begin to arrive, and so does a group of mental patients led by the skeptical Nurse Fay Apple (Remick's role), who intends to use her charges to discredit this "miracle." When the snarling mayoress orders the patients arrested, Nurse Apple sets them loose, at which point Hapgood arrives.

He is simply a new patient, but he is mistaken for a psychiatrist, and the mayoress prevails upon him to separate the sane from the insane. Instead, he declares everyone mad. The play's ultimate point is that "normal" is a euphemism for self-control, orderliness, and conformity — as well as for sexual repression (such as that of Nurse Apple). This was an attitude popularized at the time by the Scottish psychiatrist R. D. Laing, who argued that mental illness was really just unconventionality; that society rejected its individualists (those enumerated in the show ran from Sigmund Freud to John Dillinger and Christine Jorgensen) until they conformed. And so at the end of *Anyone Can Whistle,* Hapgood voices a moral, to wit, that the true miracle is "being alive. Either you die slowly or you have the strength to go crazy." With those words of wisdom, Nurse Apple falls into his arms.

Angela was certain that Arthur Laurents got the inspiration for casting her as Cora Hoover Hoople "from watching me playing tough, domineering women." She also noticed that in *Whistle,* he had his own idiosyncratic take on that type of woman. "It was a very campy part," she explains. She also believed that Laurents and Sondheim were expecting too much musical talent of her. "Arthur knew I could carry a tune but that's all he knew, and it's all Steve knew. They didn't know whether I could sing the songs that Steve had up his sleeve," and the score did indeed include some tough music.

She finished reading the script, "unable to make head or tail of it," but liked its spirit, and thought, "It must be good, because these guys wrote it. I was dazzled by Arthur Laurents and, after hearing his music, this young genius Sondheim." Heading east, she checked into the Dorset Hotel on West 54th Street, and within a few days, found an apartment — Gore Vidal's place on 50th Street and First Avenue. From there it was just a walk to Sondheim's townhouse on 49th Street, where she heard him run through the songs that she would sing, while Laurents explained what would be happening onstage.

Her first number was the opening of the show, a crucial moment, and it was a long, vocally involved piece that would be staged with a great deal of dancing. It was called "Me and My Town," and was performed like a nightclub act, with Angela escorted by four male dancers. It starts out sung as mock-blues.

Everyone hates me — yes, yes
Being the mayor — ess, yes

The number turns intricate, mixing jagged melody with intricate lyrics and interpolated patter.

And I'm so depressed
I can hardly talk on the phone

The vocal arrangement becomes syncopated, with rhythmic hand-clapping. There is even scat singing, and then rhythmic chanting.

But a lady has responsibilities —
To try to be
Unpopular with the populace

The number culminates with South American rhythms. Nobody had to tell Angela that all of it was modeled on the performing style of the flamboyant Kay Thompson, the MGM musical specialist who had become the quintessentially smart nightclub act.

Nobody did tell her, either, but it wasn't out of any ill will. Sondheim, a congenital worrier, simply feared, "She can't possibly know what I'm writing about. This is all high camp. Big gestures, a big presentation. How could Angela know that nightclub style? Why would she be familiar with Kay Thompson?" And Laurents agreed. "The whole thing that Kay did in a nightclub with the Williams Brothers — I wouldn't think that Angie knew that."

For once, the Broadway sophisticates were the naïfs, while the Hollywood person was the insider. "The dream is happening," she thought. "I'm Kay Thompson!"

Then, one week before rehearsals were to begin, she announced to Sondheim and Laurents, "I can't play this part."

"Why can't you play her?" the director asked.

"Cora's a cartoon," she protested. "There's no substance to play."

Laurents replied, "That's true, Angela, but the *show's* a cartoon."

"Yes," she answered, "but of the three main characters, she's the most cartoonish." She paused. "And besides, Lee Remick has five numbers, and I only have four."

Both of the collaborators grinned. "All right, Angela," Steve said. "That I can handle. I'll write you another one."

The song he wrote for her was called, "Is a Parade in Town?" By letting Cora express the feeling of being left out, it gave Angela an emotional dimension to play. Sondheim felt that in it he had written a good song, but one that was wrong for the musical as a whole because, he said, "The idea of the show is to see what happens when you put two real people — Fay Apple and Hapgood — into a world of cartoon people who are either venal or saintly."

When it came to musicals, there was nobody smarter than Sondheim.

Work began, the rehearsal pianist pounding away at the scarred upright in the tradition-soaked Variety Arts rehearsal studio on West 46th Street. The place was a rickety walk-up that was so steeped in Broadway lore, its walls were all but caked with greasepaint. "Is There a Parade in Town?" proved to be an especially difficult song for Angela to sing. Sondheim considered her voice strong, but within a limited range. He could hear her straining whenever she tried to hit higher notes with her chest voice, and she certainly was aware of that problem herself. "That song," she sighed, "nearly ruined my voice."

Dance rehearsal was tougher, but less painful because it was new to her, and was the kind of work that made her muscles feel good. Mornings, she would show up in gypsy mufti (Broadway singers and dancers call themselves "gypsies" because they go from show to show) — leotards, leg warmers, dance shoes, a sweater, and a leather dance bag. At night, she would leave Variety Arts sopping wet, too sparked by excitement to even shower. The musical rhythms still rippling through her body, she would "practically dance across town."

As before, Deirdre and Anthony were to come East once the tryouts began. For the time being, Angela was "on my own, completely and totally happy — so energized, so filled with the excitement and the prospect of this show that we're doing — difficult as it all is."

Rehearsals alternated between book, songs, and dancing, and Herbert Ross's choreography was difficult indeed. But it was also funny in the same spirit as the music. Angela was involved with the show's big number, "The Cookie Chase," a classical ballet pastiche that took off from the search for the mental patients. Between that and her opening number, which had her dressed in a flashy nightclub costume and being carried aloft by her chorus boys, Ross made it appear that she was actually dancing as much as everyone around her. Although at thirty-eight, she was practically elderly for a dancer ("the show's den mother," Laurents said), she took all the classes with the dance chorus and did all the exercises and danced enough to become lean and hard. She walked like a Broadway dancer, too, and looked like one, and she was swept away by "the whole sense of being part of the musical theater. It was heady stuff, absolutely marvelous. A wonderful, wonderful time."

After rehearsals she would stride across Times Square and head back to the East Side and the apartment. She'd stop to buy hamburger or lamb chops and a vegetable, and while she cooked and ate, she studied her lines, but the dramatic part of the show was not as satisfying as the music rehearsals. For one thing, a musical's script is too short to be a complete play. But there was another problem: although Angela and Lee had known each other since *The Long Hot Summer,* Remick had become something of a name after being nominated for an Academy Award for *Days of Wine and Roses.* Now, Angela says, "Lee had the star dressing room, and I was the second person; she had billing over me, and one felt that she carried around her reputation as a movie star. I think Bill, her husband, encouraged her to take that position, and it was unfortunate."

Angela also knew that Remick was nervous. "The score was horribly difficult for her, and although she was the romantic lead, I was playing a far more showy part. Everything that I was doing was paying off, because that's the way the part was designed."

One of the biggest payoffs was in her second-act dance number, "I've Got You to Lean On," in which she had to sing Sondheim's complex lyrics quickly and clearly while his music ranged up and down the scale, changing keys with daunting frequency. It was her second Kay Thompson kind of song, and its staging required her to deal with a gay taste that was particularly Broadway.

"I camped around in that song," Angela admits. "I was led down that road by Arthur and Herb [Ross]. It seemed to lighten things up." She does realize that "Cora could have been a drag queen, but I certainly didn't play her that way. Yes, it's a very campy part. Arthur had written it that way and he loved it.

"He would roar with laughter in the middle of rehearsal."

Remick was not getting that kind of feedback from the director, and she wasn't having Angela's kind of fun with her difficult songs. Then again, neither was her leading man, Harry Guardino. He had started out with what Sondheim calls "a natural, big, terrific Italian voice," the best singing voice in the cast. But, as Angela noticed, "he drank and smoked cigarettes, and was trying to sing, all at the same time." She could hear his voice deteriorating, but as she had to admit, she also noticed that he was "a very charming, attractive fellow and a real ladies' man." As Peter would notice, too, she had a bit of a crush on him, the way Sondheim was smitten with Lee Remick. While Lee was singing, the composer would nudge Angela and whisper, "When she crosses her legs, her knees have faces in them."

Remick never had a strong singing voice to begin with, but what really ruined Guardino's voice, and, according to Sondheim, nearly destroyed Lansbury's, was the strange vocal technique practiced by the show's musical director, Herbert Greene. He would press two of his fingers against a singer's larynx in order, he said, to relieve throat tension. "Trying to sing while he had his fingers on your throat," Angela thought, "was like being strangled."

Still, with Remick on one side and Guardino on the other, neither in great voice, she felt as if "I'm the Tebaldi in the group." She worked on it too, trying to broaden her range and develop a smooth flow from low notes sung in a chest voice to high ones in a head voice. "One smooth range," she says, "is very hard to do. Somebody who can do that is Barbra Streisand [whose musical, *Funny Girl,* was already in Philadelphia and in classic road trouble] — she can sing from the bottom of her boots right to the top. That's a marvel, a true gift." But Greene would grab Angela by the throat and demand of her, "sing high, high, high" all from the chest, with no head in it. She hadn't the musical confidence to refuse, although she could feel her throat hurting when she did that. Lee Remick had already developed a bad respiratory ailment.

A few days before the company was to leave for the ten-day tryout, Laurents assembled everyone in the rehearsal room to hear the music played by the full orchestra. After rehearsing for four weeks with just a piano, they were used to the sound of their voices overwhelming that bare, banging accompaniment. As the big company crowded into the room, Greene stood on a chair in front of the musicians. In the back were Sondheim and Laurents, the orchestrator, Don Walker, and the producers, Kermit Bloomgarden and Diana Krasny. There was a collective intake of breath as Greene raised his baton before the twenty-six assembled musicians. Then the trumpets blared, as trumpets invariably did at the start of traditional Broadway overtures. At first, this one sounded traditional, too, but it paused for a drum roll and a long hiss of the cymbals, and then the entire orchestra broke into a cacophonous version of circus music, filling the small room with the rich, crashing energy of young Sondheim's modern approach to the Broadway idiom.

Suddenly, the work, the repetition, the aching muscles, and the repeated criticisms all blossomed from an abstraction into something recognizably a *show. Anyone Can Whistle* was a reality at last — it was going to happen — and all the work was rewarded. Tears welled up all over the room, from the stars to the standbys. The next day they played their "gypsy run-through" — a full-dress rehearsal for an invited audience of fellow actors and dancers — and then they were off to the Wilbur Theater in Philadelphia.

With the first few previews, it was apparent that the show was not exactly winning its audience's love. Even eleven-year-old Deirdre and twelve-year-old Anthony could see that. They had just arrived from California with Jane Fyfe, and were in the front row for every performance. Both of the youngsters were dismayed by the crowd's reaction to the first-act finale, when the actors would suddenly appear in two rows of theater seats — facing front, holding programs, and applauding, mocking the real audience. Guardino looks out into the house and says, "You are all mad."

The audience was mad, all right. They booed as the curtain dropped, and as previews continued, they started to actually talk back. The actors behind the curtain could hear cries of, "This is disgraceful!" and the concise "Bullshit!"

After the official opening, the Philadelphia critics spelled out the problem — the show's message was sophomoric and trite, and its absurdist style was not clear — but Laurents worked on only the music and the dancing, insisting that his libretto was fine. That is often the problem when the writer is also the director. "I knew that something was wrong with the show," he remembers, "but I didn't know what." What he did know — and if Arthur Laurents was not always a nice man, he was certainly a smart one — was that "Lee Remick, who was darling, couldn't sing. Harry Guardino couldn't sing. And it was a musical. Not only does that hurt the score, but they know it, and it makes them shaky, and the whole show suffers."

Yet, although he thought Angela was doing "just fine" with her singing, a rumor arose that she was about to be let go. Part of an actor's tryout ritual is the fear, real or imagined, of being replaced. Although Laurents would deny it, both Sondheim and Lansbury knew that in this case, the possibility was real when the actress Nancy Walker arrived in Philadelphia to see the show. Sondheim also knew how unhappy Angela really was, for he'd found her in tears when he went backstage after the reviews had come out. She didn't know that critics tend to blame a show's inadequacy on everyone in sight, including the actors. Sondheim thought he knew exactly what was lacking in her performance: "An old pro in the show, Henry Lascoe, was wiping her out in every scene, taking the stage away from her because she had no confidence."

Laurents, too, was frustrated by her holding back on stage. He believed, "She had to take control of her scenes. That was necessary to play the role. She wasn't good at that point and she knew it." He was also urging her to play Cora bitchier, "but she was laying off."

Why, she complained, did they "want her to be this monster?" She knew that her character was both Sondheim's and Laurents's favorite in the show, but she did not yet understand *why* they adored the tough, bitchy lady.

Laurents would try his best to explain, telling her, "Cora is a ruthless woman, but she's demented, so it makes her enjoyable." At the same time, Henry Lascoe, the very actor who was taking the stage away from her, was also warning her that she was coming across as too tough and mean, something she did not want ever to be again as an actress.

As her own song put it:

Me and my town,
We just wanna be loved

It was a number she sang directly to the audience, not only the first song in the show but the first time she ever performed that way in a theater. The technique is called "playing in one," because the actor stands where the front, or number-one curtain would drop, and goes head to head with the audience. Sondheim could see its appeal for dramatic actors. "There's something," he says, "about standing there with an orchestra and directly addressing the audience. During a play, the actors have to talk to each other, or least pretend to. But in a musical, they can go out there and face front. They may pretend they're talking to another actor, but they know they are delivering their number, and that gives every actor a huge kick." Angela felt that, playing directly to the audience.

> It wasn't frightening. It's a technique you learn. You're singing to an imaginary focal point — a person, a group, and everyone in the audience thinks you're talking to them. I can't see anybody out there. I'm looking at nothing. Some actors might say they're playing to that exit sign in the back of the house. I always try to include the whole house, including the people who are down below because the tendency in the musical theater is always to play higher, to play up, up, to the first balcony and the mezzanine.

To make this delivery effective, the performer has to step out and grab the audience, and she wasn't doing that. She was not selling — either her songs or herself. She was caught between wanting to come through with what Laurents wanted, and not wanting to come through as nasty, a dilemma that rattled her. After a week of revisions followed by performances followed by notes to the cast, followed by more revisions, her nerves simply started to unravel. Before each performance, she would be collected and eager, warming up her voice in the dressing room by singing "Skylark," the Hoagy Carmichael-Johnny Mercer classic. "If I could get through that," she would say, "I was okay." Then, after each performance, she would remain on stage with the rest of the cast, while Laurents and Sondheim made their comments.

Back in her dressing room following yet another of those sessions, dabbing at her makeup with a sponge and cold cream, she suddenly broke. "I don't know what to do," she realized. "I don't know how to give them what they want." And she jumped up from her chair, opened the door, and, in a burst of rage, shrieked down the backstage stairwell at the men she referred to as "The Group" — Laurents, Sondheim, and Ross — *"What do you want? What do you want me to do?"*

But of course, she knew what Laurents wanted her to do. He wanted Cora Hoover Hoople to be a monster. "Play her," he urged, "as if she were Ilse Koch," referring to the Nazi who ran the Buchenwald concentration camp. Then he burst out laughing while Angela thought, "What an image!"

So it continued until the dispute came down to a couple of lines spoken between Cora and a henchman, who tells her, "They say they need police dogs. We don't have any." Her response is the snarl, "You can borrow mine."

Angela hated the line so much she would mumble it. "That was pretty stupid of me," she admits, "but as a human being I couldn't make myself say it." In her mind, the exchange meant, "Set the dogs on them!"

Laurents finally agreed to cut it, Angela calmed down, and in a bizarre stroke of misfortune, Henry Lascoe, the actor who had been taking attention away from her, had a heart attack on stage and died. It wasn't the only tragedy. One of the dancers overran the stage, fell into the orchestra pit, and landed on top of the saxophonist, who also had a heart attack. "I mean," Laurents laughs, "we were killing them off."

Henry Lascoe's replacement was not nearly so assertive a performer and "From that moment on," Sondheim says, "Angela's performance clicked in. She became wonderful, completely confident."

Anyone Can Whistle, subtitled "A Wild New Musical," opened in New York on April 4, 1964, at the Majestic Theater. The reviews were generally negative, and Laurents defended himself with the rationalization that Walter Kerr of the *Herald Tribune* "didn't like the show because he was a Catholic. The idea that there's no miracles drove him up the wall." Such a self-protective imagination made Laurents more resilient than Sondheim, who was so discouraged that he talked about quitting the theater entirely. The show closed after nine performances, ultimately becoming a cult musical — meaning that if everyone who says they saw it, actually saw it, it would have run for years.

On closing night Sondheim stood backstage, watching the show from the wings. Nearby, Angela waited to go on, huddled with the four dancers who were about to carry her aloft for the last time.

"All right," she said to the guys. "Let's give 'em hell."

And, it seemed to Sondheim, who had never felt that she enjoyed doing the show, "She was saying, 'fuck the audience and fuck those critics, let's just go out and have a good time!' "

The closing night of a show is as emotional as its opening. The theater is filled with friends and fans. The cast is preparing to disband and break up the intimate family they have become. When Angela ran out for her curtain call, she stood at center stage and curtseyed. Looking out into the house, she burst into tears and, as Laurents, who was also in the wings, observed, "Then everyone went. You could have floated the stage away."

Anyone Can Whistle was her first project whose failure genuinely hurt. She had been involved with letdowns as well as successes, but because of the way movies are made, the actors and writers and directors do not develop the theater's sense of personal involvement, common enterprise, and company. Few of a movie's creators are present throughout the entire process, and if a picture fails at the box office, it happens long after the work has been completed and its makers have disbanded. Many are already involved in new projects. And if the failure was not merited, if the picture was simply ahead of its time, for example, it still exists, to be seen exactly as originally made.

A play, however, is a living thing, and all of its life ends with a closing, even after a long run. Of course a sudden death is especially shocking, but any closing is premature. The show could have gone on.

Angela took the loss not personally — the failure, she knew, wasn't her fault — but to heart. The show had given her something she'd not had before. She had sung, danced, and glittered on the musical stage. As for *Anyone Can Whistle,* it was a flop, to be sure, and the jolt was painful to everyone involved, but it was a show that would be remembered long after most of the 1964 hits had run their unadventurous courses.

Angela did have Anthony and Deirdre along to comfort her. It was uncommon for a sister and brother to be such close friends at eleven and twelve years old, but these two were practically inseparable. They were sweet and bright children, and both of them were breathtakingly good-looking. Each had Angela's thick, light brown hair, and her blue eyes, and Peter's dazzling white teeth and smile.

For the children, the failure of *Anyone Can Whistle* meant that they would be free to go home to Malibu. The traveling back and forth was easier for their mother, who had mastered the technique of living two lives.

Her life as an actress was as far away from her life as a mother as the East Coast was from the West, but for her, both lives were rich and rewarding. Now she would shut down her actress world and be thrilled just to be home. It was a quality that made her unique among actors, and it wasn't only for love of hearth. She believed, "If you want to keep the marriage going, if you want to have a great family life, you've got to pay attention to the domestic side of your marriage."

She refused to hire a secretary or a staff. "If you have somebody to do those things for you, it's not the same. If you delegate all of that to minions who are paid to do it, that's not having the whole marriage. And I like to do it. I love having a home and family; having a house, buying my husband clothes, all of those things. It isn't a conscious decision, it's just the way I am.

> Looking after *stuff.* Domestic things. That is a very big part of my life. And that's the hardest part of the balancing act — to keep one's hand on that part of your existence. Women do — they have to think about — fifty thousand more things in the home than men do. And half the time, because of the difference between men and women, men don't realize how much has to be constantly thought through by women — to do with the domestic side of the marriage. And the domestic side of the marriage is terribly important.

Moyna came back to California with them for a long visit. She enjoyed playing grandmother, and the kids loved her being there. She even cut their hair, and she certainly had a special charm for them. As her son Edgar said, "Moyna had this strange *power* about her — for good and bad. She liked to do a lot of touchy-feely closeness, and mystical stuff."

An example of the mystical stuff that awed everyone in the family was the time that Deirdre's arm was covered with dozens of tiny warts, so ugly they made her cry. As Angela looked on, Moyna calmed the child down and sat beside her, instructing the youngster to close her eyes and feel restful. Then, running a hand along Deirdre's arm, she began "smoothing over" the warts. She closed her own eyes, and as long moments passed, she passed her hand up and down the little arm, from elbow to wrist. Then she paused and said, "You are now going to leave Deirdre's arm. And be gone. Go away!"

Then she whispered, "Soon they will be gone, my little angel," and, indeed, after several days, the warts receded and disappeared.

Perhaps they would have disappeared anyway, but her cure certainly made Deirdre a believer. As for the more traditional spiritual avenues, the children were being given no formal religious education beyond being taught to recite the Lord's Prayer before going to bed. Anthony and Dede were aware that the official Shaw denomination was Episcopalian. "That's what we were told we were, technically," Deirdre explains. Angela and Peter belonged to no congregation, but Angela would teach the children to "believe in themselves and believe in the power of God — God being energy and light." She would not instruct them what to believe, only share what she herself felt, and it was not a religion so much as a religious philosophy. "I try to eradicate negation in my life. To think affirmatively. I believe that we have the power within ourselves to bring about the circumstances that become our lives.

"I believe that God is within all of us; that we are perfect, precious beings, and have to put our faith and trust in that. About the hereafter, I really don't know. I tend to think that we all become part of the greater consciousness. And that light and energy are the forces that propel us through our lives; that keep our bodies ticking over.

"And that's about it."

CHAPTER 11

THE AUDITIONS

AS A NANNY, Jane Fyfe may have treated the entire family with classic sternness, but beneath it all, she was a comforting presence around the house. She and Angela, being habitual smokers, would frequently share a chat and a cigarette in the kitchen, but the little tradition was under siege of late. Peter had been conducting an anti-smoking campaign. It was the usual, "What are you going to tell our children if you are going to die of cancer of the lungs?" and "How can you excuse yourself for not stopping smoking?" He himself was a pipe smoker, and considered himself exempt from such accusations.

She could hardly disagree, for she believed that anyone could stop smoking. "I don't think anybody is so weak that they really can't give up smoking if they want to. They just don't want to." But just the same, she turned to Jane Fyfe for quitting support, "and we both decided to quit cold turkey."

Angela went through her break of habit in the classic style, suffering every withdrawal symptom from cold sweats to a lump-in-the-throat desperation. For three months, she says, "it was absolute hell," and even then it wasn't over. Just as she thought she might break under the strain, she got into her car "with a whole bunch of candy bars on the seat beside me," and drove north. When she got as far as Fillmore, she turned around and drove home, eating candy bars all the way. By the time she pulled into the driveway, she was so disgusted with herself that she backed out again, drove down the Pacific Coast Highway to the Mayfair Market — a place that seemed to be the hub of Malibu — and bought a pack of cigarettes. She didn't light up until she was home again, sneaking into the garden and kneeling down in the grass like a guilty child, so that nobody would witness her capitulation, craven and undisciplined.

"I lit one and took a huge drag on it. I didn't let anyone see me. And I threw up. And I was so sick with that cigarette, after not smoking for three months, that I never smoked again.

"But I sort of relish the idea of smoking a cheroot when I'm about eighty. Because I know by then, it'll be too late to kill me."

The children were becoming ever more involved with the Malibu way of life. As Anthony describes that world, "It was so cut off from the rest of Los Angeles that it was sort of a strange reality. Dede and I had grown up with a certain amount of culture in our lives. Out there, if you weren't completely enamored of the surf, there wasn't a lot to do, but for a kid growing up, it was pretty terrific."

David had quit high school, and Peter helped him get a starter job at CBS. From there the young man followed his father's path, becoming a junior agent at Creative Management Associates. Then he landed a job at Peter's old office, the William Morris Agency. It certainly helped to have a father in the business.

Angela had movie assignments to keep her busy, but after the intensity and excitement of a Broadway musical, they were dispiriting experiences, minor parts in minor pictures like *Dear Heart* and *Harlow.* Then she went from the insignificant to the absurd with the Biblical epic *The Greatest Story Ever Told,* for which she joined a novel cast that included Max Von Sydow, Charlton Heston, John Wayne, Sidney Poitier, and Sal Mineo, "with Pat Boone as the Angel at the Tomb."

In New York, a team of Broadway producers, Robert Fryer and Lawrence — always called "Jimmy" — Carr had, for a year, been trying to put together a musical version of *Auntie Mame,* which they had produced as a play some seven years earlier, in 1957. That dramatization, written by Jerome Lawrence and Robert E. Lee, was based on Patrick Dennis's bestselling mock memoir about his fictitious aunt.

Like the book, the play is set in the Manhattan of 1928. Mame Dennis is an archetype of the smart East Side sophisticate, rich, sharp-tongued, and fabulously clothed. She is also a madcap, with a flair for the outrageous and a Ph.D. in ephemera. She parties as a way of life, inspired by the motto that "Life is a banquet — and most sons of bitches are starving to death."

When her brother dies unexpectedly, she finds that her nephew, the elevenish Patrick Dennis, has been appointed her ward. Although seemingly the unlikeliest of guardians, the unconventional Mame develops into an endearing, if eccentric, mother figure.

In a series of short scenes constructed in much the same manner as a libretto for a musical, Patrick goes off to prep school and Mame loses her fortune in the 1929 stock market crash. Forced to work, she fails at various jobs from sales clerk to stage extra, always because of her exuberant antics. When a rich Southern plantation owner named Beauregard Jackson Pickett Burnside is smitten with her, she marries and becomes wealthy again. But while Beauregard is taking her traveling around the world, he dies in a mountain-climbing accident, which saddens Mame, but not unduly or for very long.

Patrick, meantime, has grown up to be a pompous Ivy Leaguer, engaged to the lockjaw daughter — "a girl," as Mame puts it, "with braces on her brains" — of a couple of bigoted arrivistes. When Mame calls Patrick "one of the most beastly, Babbitty little snobs on the Eastern seaboard," their relationship is almost destroyed, but of course all ends happily.

This play had been a fabulous vehicle for Rosalind Russell, who played the ultrachic hoyden to great success on stage and still greater success in the movie version. That very success was proving detrimental to bringing the prospective musical to the stage. For one thing, the play was still fresh in everyone's mind, and the movie still fresher. Secondly, both had been so lavishly produced, with so many costumes and changes of locale — and Rosalind Russell's interpretation of Mame had been so extravagant — that there were people who would swear *Auntie Mame* had itself been a musical. Finally, the producers believed that a star was necessary to safeguard their anticipated half-million-dollar investment, and Broadway's leading ladies (Ethel Merman and Gwen Verdon, for instance) were not interested in playing a role that was so closely identified with Russell.

The obvious solution was for Russell herself to play the musical

Mame, and the producers visited her in Connecticut to offer the part. She not only turned them down, saying, "I don't like to eat last week's stew," but she and Patrick Dennis tried to stop the show from being done altogether, hoping to turn *Auntie Mame* into a television series. That, presumably, would be a stew of another, bankable kind.

Despite these obstacles, Fryer and Carr persisted because they owned the dramatic rights and because they loved *Auntie Mame*, as so many did, particularly homosexuals. One gay Broadway producer said, "The movie of *Auntie Mame* is an absolute staple of the gay community. If you stopped 90 percent of the gay men on the street and quoted some lines from it, they could give you the next line."

Like *The Manchurian Candidate,* the story plays to a stereotypical homosexual family pattern — a possessive mother, a dominated and adoring son — a sex-tinged relationship between them — and an absentee father. What gave this example of the species a mass appeal was its celebratory quality. Mame is not malicious but marvelous, not the villainess of the piece but its heroine. The play is a love letter to an Auntie Mame who might be bitchy but certainly is no bitch. The risk in playing the character as a Tallulah Bankhead sort of female caricature would be that Auntie Mame could be mistaken for a drag queen. Rosalind Russell, attired in countless flashy dresses and brandishing a signature cigarette holder, had taken it close to that limit.

The musical *Auntie Mame,* now called *My Best Girl,* was to be written and directed by the once celebrated but recently erratic Joshua Logan. Its music and lyrics were to be provided by Jerry Herman, the hottest songwriter on Broadway, currently with a hit of hits in *Hello, Dolly!* As that show was demonstrating with Carol Channing, he was masterful at showcasing a musical diva.

The diva Joshua Logan anointed for *My Best Girl* was Mary Martin, who was so enthusiastic about doing the show that scripts were already printed with her name on the cover. His libretto marked a considerable departure from the original play. Among other changes, Logan had moved Mame's marriage from the Deep South to England, not to mention opening the show with Patrick's father dropping dead on stage.

Such wrenches did not seem to throw Mary Martin, who had been pals with Logan since their fabulous success with *South Pacific.* She was positive about *My Best Girl* in every way, except when it came to signing a contract. It was only after the producers and Jerry Herman embarked on, as the composer described it, "a rather monumental journey into the Brazilian jungle" (where Mary Martin actually lived), that she definitely decided against doing the show.

As soon as word of Martin's withdrawal became public, the producers' telephones started to ring. The name of almost every musical comedy actress seemed to be suggested. Lauren Bacall was interested, but her singing voice was considered weak, and she had not yet established herself as a box office attraction. The producers added her to their list, but only as a possibility for Mame's "cobra-tongued" friend, Vera Charles. The great dramatic actress Geraldine Page auditioned for the title role in the producers' office. Standing at the grand piano and singing, she was so off-key, which she obviously knew, that even before she could finish, she burst into tears and fled.

News of the search reached Los Angeles quickly enough. Angela was, of course, very familiar with *Auntie Mame* as both a movie and a play. The similarities between Mame, Cora Hoover Hoople of *Anyone Can Whistle,* and Kay Thompson did not escape her. This was a role she already knew how to play.

She told her agent that she would pay her own airfare to New York to audition for the part. Her brother Edgar encouraged the approach, and he knew his show business. He had made wonderful progress in the theater, from designing plays to producing them. That very season, he and a partner named Joseph Beruh were having a resounding success with the Frank Gilroy play *The Subject Was Roses.*

To one of the *My Best Girl* producers, Robert Fryer, "Angela Lansbury was not a name that would immediately come to mind as Mame." He didn't think that she could be "as acerbic" as Russell, and he was afraid that she was too old for the part, "because she was always playing mothers in the movies." Fryer, however, was concentrating on *Sweet Charity,* which the team was also planning for the 1965–66 Broadway season, while *My Best Girl* was his partner's baby, and Jimmy Carr was much more positive about Angela. He still remembered the closing performance of *Anyone Can Whistle,* when he'd marveled at Lansbury's "ability to keep you interested in a very unsavory character." Even then, he had mused, "She'd make a wonderful Mame," and so he invited her to audition, even though he found that whenever her name was mentioned to potential investors, they all but hung up on him.

"Angela Lansbury?" one of them said, "Who's going to see her?"

* * *

She checked into the Dorset, her usual hotel, and had the valet press her pink linen suit. Then she headed straight for the Fryer and Carr offices at 445 Park Avenue, where she found a tall, slender, good-looking young man sitting on the floor, refinishing a wood chest. An associate producer of the show, his name was John Bowab, and he was Jimmy Carr's companion. He ushered her into Carr's office, where everyone was waiting, and introduced her to Josh Logan, Jerry Herman, the choreographer Onna White, and the team of producers — red-haired, freckle-faced Bobby Fryer and the tall, heavy-set, white-haired Carr, who, in Bowab's description, was "aristocratic — he looked like English royalty." Then they all went crosstown to the Lunt-Fontanne Theatre for the audition.

When they arrived, the auditorium was dark, as somebody in the office had forgotten to arrange for a grip to turn on the stage lights. Since union regulations forbade anyone else from even touching a switch backstage, all the doors were opened to let in whatever sunshine could make it through the theater's entrance. Then, as everyone sat down a few rows back in the orchestra, Angela groped her way onto the stage and started to sing.

Halfway through, she heard a voice call out, which was terrifying to any actor in the midst of auditioning. It was Logan, a big man with a big voice, and she stood at center stage, confused and upset. "It's too dark up there!" the director cried. A young stage manager named Bob Linden offered to shine a small work light (a bulb in a reflector) toward her. As he came and crouched at her feet, aiming the lamp at her face, she thought, "It's a damn good thing I'm used to making movies with all those lights in my face."

She started once more, and again Logan interrupted her, crying out, "Why don't you take a script and tape it on top of the light, so it doesn't glare in her eyes?" By then, "the whole gang" was marching down the aisle and up onstage, which was supposed to be actors' territory. "They were right up here with me, getting a close look, for God's sake, in all these raincoats and dark glasses."

When she was finally left alone to finish her song, nobody was overwhelmed. Speaking for the group, Carr thanked her very much and said they were still undecided. She would hear from them, he promised, adding that perhaps her singing was "not as strong, vocally, as we wanted."

She returned to California and made a couple of movies but through it all, she refused to accept defeat. She found a vocal coach to help strengthen her voice and filmed an episode of *The Man from U.N.C.L.E.*

that had her playing an Auntie Mame type of character. That appearance was not just a stroke of luck; her brother Bruce had long since left the world of shoe manufacturing to become a television producer, and *U.N.C.L.E.* was his show. She notified Carr and Fryer when it was going to be aired (November 12, 1965).

As the new year rolled in, preparations for the show inched along. The producers had gone to Boston, where Logan was trying out another musical, *Hot September,* based on William Inge's drama *Picnic,* which had been a celebrated success in the 1950s, when Inge and Logan were in their primes. Now, alas, both men were in serious emotional distress. Inge was destined for suicide, while Logan had lost control of his talents. *Hot September* was a mess, sending Fryer and Carr back to New York convinced that they had to replace their director. Theater people can sometimes be pretty tough. Since Logan's career was in disarray, his mental state precarious, and his relationship with Mary Martin no longer relevant, they dismissed him. While looking for a new director, they continued the auditions.

The *Man from U.N.C.L.E.* television episode and the failure of a Mame to emerge from the crowd of applicants earned Angela a second hearing a full year after the first one. Whatever it was about this part, in this show, that meant so much to her, she was going after it with fierce determination. If, as she privately admitted, she was "dispirited by the rejection," she did not show it. If she was "exhausted" from working on the audition, she would make sure to appear energized, and she refused to be embarrassed. She even called Jerry Herman from California, asking to meet with him the day before her second audition. They set the appointment for noon at his home.

The handsome composer, who appeared even younger than his thirty-three years, lived in a stunning Greenwich Village townhouse that he himself had restored and redecorated. (He would make a second career of buying, renovating, and selling houses, making even more money at that, he would insist, than writing shows like *Hello, Dolly!*) When he greeted her, she was standing in his doorway with, he thought, "that combination of cool elegance and warmth." At that moment, Herman says, he knew that he had his Mame. Ushering her into the living room, he sat down at the baby grand piano and played some of the show's songs for her.

This was the first time that she heard any of the actual material, and it was plain to Angela that Jerry Herman was no Stephen Sondheim. His music was not brilliantly complex, and the lyrics were not sophisticated, but she was caught up in songs that were catchy and even thrilling. The openness of Jerry Herman's style — the unpretentiousness of his lyrics and his endearing melodies — were lending a new and softened focus to the sharp-edged *Auntie Mame.* He might have intended to capture the archness and sophistication that were associated with this character, but except for a duet between Mame and Vera called "Bosom Buddies," those qualities just were not in him. Instead, he added benevolence to the piece. He was a heartfelt man and it showed in his songs. "He brought a warmth to the character," the associate producer, Bowab, says. "It was a warmth that might not have been there had the composer been — I hate to say *more sophisticated* — maybe a *more jaded* writer. If Cole Porter had done it, who would have been the choice a generation before, you would have had another kind of show. But Jerry, in songs like 'It's Today,' 'Open a New Window,' and 'We Need a Little Christmas,' well, he brought his mother's philosophy and his own humanity to the character.

"It was a major contribution, maybe *the* major contribution."

Indeed, Herman's songs were going to make this flamboyant character into something paradoxical, a glamorous earth mother: It was a strange combination, but one to which Angela Lansbury was singularly suited.

Jerry Herman's reaction to her singing was that "she was very raw," but instinct told him that "she had a real instrument." Her efforts with the California vocal coach had not been in vain. She'd added two or three notes to the top and bottom of her range. "With some work," Herman thought, "she'll be able to sing everything I've written for the character."

The "some work" began right there in his home, as he changed keys to fit more comfortably into her range and eliminated one very low note in "It's Today!" Then they broke for lunch, walking around the corner to Longchamps restaurant with Herman's secretary, Sheila Mack.

There the mood turned curiously awkward. The occasion had turned from professional to social, and they were, after all, strangers. But when Angela looked up from her food, glanced over at the others' plates, and cried, "I've got to taste that!" as Sheila Mack remembers, "That started it. Everybody ate off everybody else's plates, and it broke the ice. We became fast friends."

With coffee, Herman suggested they return to the house. "Let me teach you two songs that no lady who has auditioned for this part has had the privilege of knowing."

Some composers talked that way.

"These producers," he said, "have only heard me singing the songs, which is not very exciting. But if *you* step out on the stage and sing these two songs, they won't know what to do with themselves." Hyperbole notwithstanding, he was giving her an extraordinary gift, the opportunity to audition for a new musical singing actual songs from the show.

The songs he played were "If He Walked into My Life," which was a beautiful ballad by almost any measure, and "It's Today," a vibrant show tune. (In fact, it was called "Show Tune in 2/4" when Herman first wrote it, for a 1958 revue called *Nightcap.*) They worked through the afternoon, adjusting keys and tempi until Angela felt comfortable. Then, to Herman's delight, "She started to sound terrific," and he asked her to come back early the next morning for a brush-up. "Tomorrow," he promised, "somehow, I'll get myself into the orchestra pit. I'll be your rehearsal pianist."

Angela's second audition for *Mame* — as the show was now called — was in the Palace Theater, and this time the stagehands had been alerted. No new director had been named yet, but the producers, the choreographer, and the composer were all present. As the house lights dimmed, Jerry Herman whispered that he had to go to the men's room, and, he remembers, "went down to the bowels of the theater and got myself into the orchestra pit." As planned, Angela stepped out from the wings, dropped her mink coat to the floor, and strode to center stage. At the piano in the orchestra pit, Herman began to set up the song with a flourish. Then Angela sang out:

Light the candles,
Get the ice out,
Roll the rug up, It's today!

"End of story," Jerry says. "It was just maybe the greatest experience I ever had."

But not quite for the others. They looked at each other uncertainly while Angela picked up her mink coat, put it on, and came down the stairs from the stage. They were starting to talk among themselves about having to make a decision immediately. There was the old concern about whether she could play the archness and sophistication that Rosalind Russell had brought to the part.

The demure choreographer, Onna White, wondered, "She can sing well enough, but can she dance?" One of the producers asked the bottom-line question, "Would she sell tickets?"

As she came up the aisle, they stopped talking. Carr thanked her a second time. To an actor, that added up to, *Forget about it.*

Angela again returned to California and told Peter and the kids that it looked like another wasted trip. But in fact, it wasn't *forget about it* yet.

On Onna White's recommendation, Gene Saks — with whom she had just done the hit musical *Half a Sixpence* — was engaged as the new director. After reading Josh Logan's script, he strode into the producers' office, tossed it on the coffee table, and said it stunk, beginning with the very first scene, where Patrick's father not only dies, but cues the opening number by having a heart attack on an exercycle in a fancy athletic club. (John Bowab would say, "When people tell me this show could never have missed, I think, 'I'll show you how it could have missed.'")

Then Saks picked up the script of *Auntie Mame* — the play — and said, "You've got this, so why do we need that ridiculous thing?" (It wasn't all that ridiculous; in the end, Logan would wind up with a one and a half percent royalty of the show's gross receipts.) And so a new libretto was written by the play's authors, Lawrence and Lee, or rather, it was extracted. Essentially, they edited out all the dramatic scenes that Herman had now musicalized, leaving a lean *Auntie Mame* neatly fitted with song cues. With that accomplished, the producers told Saks that although Jerry Herman had his heart set on Angela Lansbury, as far as they were concerned, the title role was still open. Every one of them had a favorite, Carr said, but so far she was the only one they could all agree on. It wasn't an enthusiastic endorsement, but it was a consensus. He then threw the decision in Saks's lap.

"If you're going to be the director," Jimmy Carr said to him, "you're going to have to be the one who chooses the star."

Saks understood. "They wanted me to take the responsibility for that decision."

When he got home, he talked through the situation with his wife, the actress Bea Arthur. She was herself a proven musical actress; at the time she was playing Yenta the matchmaker in *Fiddler on the Roof.* It was not the leading role, but it was a juicy one with lots of funny dialogue, and she was getting a great deal of attention in it. She'd been getting even more attention when *Fiddler* was trying out in Detroit. Bea Arthur was an assertive performer who could easily take the stage away from anyone who wasn't looking. It was for that reason that the director, Jerome Robbins, cut back Yenta's part. "Look," he said to her, "it's not a play about this matchmaker."

And so when her husband pondered the decision that he had to make about *Mame*, naturally she asked, "Why can't *I* do it?"

Why not? he thought. She did have a marvelously dry, comic style and a Rosalind Russell–like baritone, perfect for zinging off barbed remarks. When he suggested her to Carr, it was accepted as a possibility. As the associate producer, John Bowab, said, "If you were re-creating the acerbic image of Rosalind Russell, wouldn't Bea be a likely choice?"

But Saks still had not seen what Angela could do, and so he asked for another audition — her third. She had no choice but to come in yet one more time, and this time Saks wanted line readings as well as songs. When she was finished, Jerry Herman caught her eye and pleaded and begged for patience. She flashed Carr, Fryer, Bowab, and Saks her best bullshit smile. She was furious.

The next morning, she telephoned Carr from her room at the Plaza Hotel.

"Look," she said, "this has been going on for a long time. Right. But this is it. I am going back to California and unless you tell me" — she paused, struggling to contain herself — "I mean, let's face it, I have" — her voice nearly broke — "*prostrated* myself. Now — *yes or no* — that's the end of it. I want an answer. I must know before I leave New York because *I'm not coming back again!*"

There was silence at the other end. Carr asked her to give him just a little time — a half hour. He called Saks and said it seemed to him that while nobody was all out for Angela "with banners flying," she came closer to general approval than anyone else. Gene gave his best pitch for Bea, pointing out that she was "a wonderful actress, a terrific comedienne, and a good singer."

It did seem that, if they were interested in re-creating the Auntie Mame of Rosalind Russell, Bea Arthur would be the likelier choice, but as John Bowab said, "Who wants to re-create the Rosalind Russell performance?" Saks agreed with that, too, and so when he hung up the telephone he turned to his wife and said, "You have got to play Vera."

There was a pause. Like Angela, Bea Arthur was frustrated by a career spent playing secondary roles. As she put it, "What can I say? I wanted to play Mame. And I was married to the director." She considered the part of Vera, and thought, "We're not worried about money. Why the hell should

I play Vera? Why go into something if I'm not going to come out for the star's curtain call?"

Watching her go through all this, Gene repeated, "You've just *got* to, honey," and she shot him her best glare. While she mulled it over, he pointed out that *Half a Sixpence* was only his first musical. Were this show to prove a second hit for him, he would be established as a director of musicals. Rather than Bea fighting for the lead, if she took the featured role there would be two good actresses in the show, and that would be in their family interest — if more in his interest than hers. It was not easy for Bea, but she finally agreed.

Soon after her casting was announced, she started telling people, "You know, the real name of this show is *Vera*. The only reason they changed the name was because Jerry couldn't think of a rhyme for it." After a pause she would add, "Steve Sondheim could have."

She was perfect for Vera.

Saks called Carr with the decision and then the producer walked out of the office and over to the Plaza, where he went up to Angela's room and told her, "We are offering you *Mame*." And so, after twenty-three years as a professional actress, having performed in thirty-six movies, twenty-six television plays, and three Broadway productions, at the age of forty-one Angela Lansbury finally had a leading role.

She felt an eerie lull in Malibu while she was waiting for rehearsals to begin in New York. Time had no purpose, and although she was physically in California, her mind was already on Broadway. The difference between movies and theater, between California and New York, between drama and musicals, never seemed so vast.

Nevertheless, Angela picked up the homemaking routine. She started Deirdre off on piano lessons, a pursuit that would prove a lifelong satisfaction for the girl, and which was typical of so many middle-class homes in America. But then, "It was a regular home," Deirdre says, "with regular rules. We weren't allowed out at night during school. We had our Sunday dinner, always together, always around the round table. Mom would cook it. Our Nanny, Jane, was always around."

Of course, it wasn't an average home, in the sense that their mother was a well-known actress. Anthony saw this as a mixed blessing. "There were advantages to having a famous mother," he admitted. "Other kids were always intrigued with her, so they were intrigued with me." But there were also disadvantages. "I had problems wondering if people really liked me, or if they just liked my mother, because my friends' parents would always bring her up."

Deirdre didn't have that problem. "Mom always thought it bothered us, the autographs and all that. But it doesn't bother me," she says. "I'm proud of her."

As for Peter, he had none of the married-to-a-star problems that bother some actresses' husbands. He was now a powerful and busy executive at MGM.

With the new musical looming in the near future, Angela went on a diet, signed up for dance classes, and began to work herself into shape for the arduous rehearsals ahead. She also hired a vocal coach, and could have had coaching from one of the best of all singers. At a big party given by Merle Oberon, she sat down in a corner with Frank Sinatra. She hadn't seen him since the end of production on *The Manchurian Candidate.*

She was bubbling over with excitement about *Mame.* "Frank was very familiar with *Auntie Mame,*" she says, and he was "enormously enthusiastic" about her doing the show. Better than that, he said, "Listen, Angie. I can help you with this. I will teach you how to phrase every line of every song that you have to sing in the show."

She was deeply touched by the offer and thought, "What a perfectly terrific chance." And even though she knew that his reputation for meanness and violence "was not undeserved," she felt that "he was a man of many facets. His offer to me was the most extraordinary, open, warmhearted gesture."

She only regretted that she hadn't the time to take advantage of it, for she was about to leave for New York and rehearsals and her chance for Broadway stardom.

CHAPTER 12

TAKING STAGE

WHILE still in California, Angela had spoken to Dolores Childers about becoming her dresser for *Mame.* She already knew that a dependable dresser is a stage essential, but she'd never had a role with so many costume changes. *Mame* would require two dressers, and Dolores was the first person she contacted after checking into her regular hotel, the Dorset. She planned to stay only until she could find an apartment, but her real home, in any case, would be Variety Arts on 46th Street, where she would be rehearsing for most of the time. The old place would be the focus of her energies and her life for the next five weeks, that spring of 1966.

Dance rehearsal always had a one-week head start on script rehearsal. The principals did not have to attend. Their songs would eventually be staged by the choreographer, but that would be done later and individually. Angela, however, was slated to be in all of the dance numbers. She was not only in them; she was going to be *the focus* of every one of them, so she had to show up at dance rehearsal from the outset.

She came to the show as someone who may not have been a trained dancer, but who certainly could tap-dance and high-kick. "Those kicks were way up, over her head," the dance captain, Diana Baffa-Brill, remembers. "She always looked good doing them, too. She had great style and was very limber."

By this time also, Lansbury knew from her *Anyone Can Whistle* days just how a dancer was supposed to look, and she came to rehearsal like one of the girls, carrying a leather dance bag and wearing black tights and long, loose, billowy work shirts. Later on, she would also put on the standard dancer's low-heeled shoes with T-straps, but the first thing each morning, she warmed up with the others. "I got down on the floor and did pushups, leg stretches, everything to get myself in absolute top physical condition." The only difference was that she was forty-one, and they were in their early twenties.

Then she joined the ballet-trained dancers at the barre. "She couldn't do triple pirouettes and she didn't dance *en pointe,*" Baffa-Brill says, "but she could do a little bit of everything."

Lansbury learned right away that "a little bit of everything" was going to include sliding down a banister into the arms of two dancers. Besides putting a little heat on her rear end, that slide put understandable fear in her heart, because she was going to have to trust those guys every night as she swooshed down toward them. Part of her professional code was that a frightened actor is a bad actor, so she asked Onna White that the chorus boys who were chosen be big and dependable. Since the same two fellows would also be doing "star over your head" lifts, carrying her all over the stage, it was even more important that they be strong and steady. The two who were eventually selected, Ron Young and Gene Kelton, would become her pals — her "bookends," she'd call them — because they would always dance on either side of her, and they were indeed strong. They were also tall, which helped lessen the effect of her own height — and besides, she liked her men tall.

As dance rehearsals continued, Gene Saks started coming in to watch and make suggestions. In the theater, with egos so exposed and vulnerable, a strict code applies about who can criticize whom, but every part of a show is the director's business. Saks, having worked with Onna White before, was confident enough to give his opinion and smart enough to express it humbly. He would begin by saying, "You know how dumb I am about choreography." Then he would practically stammer, "I don't know why, but watching that number I was kind of losing interest. Maybe you could throw those two parts together, and get to the other part a little faster?" Constructive criticism could be accepted, so long as it was humble.

Angela was not always inclined to observe such niceties when her own work was involved. She didn't like her choreography for "We Need a Little Christmas," and said so. "Look, Onna," she said sternly, "this number shouldn't be about dance steps. We've got a story about a family, a maid, a housekeeper, and this little boy, Patrick. They're trying to make Christmas when they haven't got two cents to rub together.

"They haven't got money for the decorations. So this song is about that, and the Christmas they are inventing for themselves. When they dance, it has to look as if they're making it up as they go along. Not *steps*, for God's sake."

Onna White reworked it.

Then the rush was on. A show has only four weeks to rehearse, and a musical is not just rehearsed — it is created in rehearsal. Before Onna White was able to finish her choreography, the jump start on dance rehearsal was over, and Angela had to use mornings for learning her songs. Of the show's twelve musical numbers, she was involved in ten, and four were solos. In addition to "It's Today!" and "If He Walked into My Life," she was to sing "Open a New Window" and "Love Is Only Love." She also had three major duets, two with Bea Arthur, "The Man in the Moon" and "Bosom Buddies," and the original title song, "My Best Girl," with young Frankie Michaels, who was playing Mame's ward, Patrick Dennis, as a child.

Angela was taught these songs by Don Pippin, the show's musical director, and she practiced them with the rehearsal pianist, Dorothea Freitag. She had already warned both Pippin and Jerry Herman that, for this show, she was not going to strain her voice the way she had during *Anyone Can Whistle.* "I know I can sing this score," she insisted. "I can make it work, but I will not go through those vocal gymnastics again. That was strip-your-voice-to-pieces time."

Pippin not only promised that he worked differently; he agreed with her judgment, for he believed, "If *Whistle* had run, she would have risked real vocal cord injury." Instead of demanding that she sing high from the chest, he showed her how to blend her head voice into her chest voice. "We got a nice mix," he says, "and she had control of it, so that she could go for a real chest belt if she wanted, but she could also go into the upper voice and have very good control." Toward that end, they went through a series of exercises each morning, starting with the breath, then working the lower register, finally moving into the upper range.

Pippin found it easy to teach Angela the songs "because she has this infallible ability to remember everything you tell her. So you'd better remember what you're asking her to do." And as far as pitch and rhythm were concerned, "You don't even have to discuss it with her. She's a natural singer." As a result, the show's orchestrator (Philip J. Lang) did not have to back up her voice by doubling her melodies with instruments. He could concentrate his orchestrations on the harmonies.

After the songs were learned, they were staged. Such work is normally the responsibility of the choreographer, but it was director Gene Saks who staged the way Angela sang her big ballad, "If He Walked into My Life." He took that responsibility because "It was like a scene, it was an acting number, a monologue of inner thoughts." It was also a crucial moment in the show, the "eleven o'clock number," which is supposed to be a guaranteed showstopper.

Saks kept it simple. "She was all alone on stage with just a garden chair and a table. She did it absolutely stunningly. That was one of my happiest moments, working one on one with Angela."

By the time he brought in the whole company to begin book rehearsals, most of the cast already knew each other. The principal players, besides Angela, Bea, and Frankie Michaels, included little Jane Connell as the comedic Agnes Gooch (Mame's secretary-maid), Jerry Lanning (the grown Patrick Dennis), Charles Braswell (Beauregard Burnside), and Willard Waterman (Dwight Babcock, the executor of the Dennis estate). They knit quickly; the risky nature of a Broadway show, the prospect of printed criticism, and the nightly quest for applause invite huddling, if only for self-defense.

From the outset, Bea Arthur was class clown, because that was her style. Funny people often have a compulsion to reveal their feelings, and Bea lost no time cracking wise about having wanted to play Mame and blaming her husband, the director, for her not getting the part. The laugh was truthful and pained, but it was on her, which made it all right.

While the atmosphere around *Mame* rehearsals was chummy, it was subject to the inevitable backstage caste system, which was especially true of musicals. The chorus people eat with the chorus people, the leading players lunch with each other, the creative team (authors, choreographer, director) sticks together, as do the lighting and costume designers, and nobody eats with the "suits" — the producers and general manager. Above it all, Angela assumed the role of mother hen to the entire company. She inquired about their families, she wrote notes, she sent little gifts. In her mind, she was responsible for every one of them, offstage and certainly on. It was she who would have to set the professional tone, she who would have to capture and hold the audience, and she who would have to become the box-office attraction to keep the show running and everyone employed.

The last number that Jerry Herman wrote, just weeks before rehearsal, was the show's title song and centerpiece, "Mame," which was to end the first act with, he hoped, a high. It was one number Angela would not sing, but as the subject of this paean, she would be at center stage while it was performed by the twelve singers in the chorus. Inspired by a banjo strumming "Way Down Upon the Swanee River" on the *Auntie Mame* movie soundtrack, the song was Jerry Herman at his most Broadway. It was an irresistibly catchy tune, and as Dorothea Freitag, the rehearsal pianist, kept playing it for the singers, Pippin expanded his arrangement so that the number built to enveloping size. Yet even so, something about it remained unresolved when the group concluded with

Your special fascination'll
Prove to be inspirational,
We think you're just sensational,
Mame.

As Pippin realized, "it seemed to just lie there, totally unsatisfying," and the worst thing about it was that it was his own arrangement.

He mentioned the problem when Jerry Herman came in to hear it, and suddenly had an idea. Asking Dorothea to slide over and make room for him on the piano bench, Pippin played a variation on the song's ending, repeating "Mame" five times, each repetition coming on another chord progression. The composer's grin was all the approval Pippin needed, and he spent the rest of the morning rehearsing the piece.

As the cast was concluding its run-through of the number, the studio door opened, and Bea Arthur was seen walking by on a rehearsal break. Somebody shouted, "Bring her in so she can hear it," and then the ensemble began to sing from the beginning, starting out in a whisper,

You coax the blues right out of the horn, Mame,
You charm the husk right off of the corn, Mame,
You've got the banjoes strummin'
And plunkin' out a tune to beat the band

As they sang, Bea took a seat. She was their first audience, and the first to hear this number in full arrangement, even though it was accompanied only by Freitag's piano. But when they got to the end of it, with the repeated, cascading chords of "Mame," the tough and glib Bea Arthur burst into tears.

When Onna White stuck her head in to ask whether the number was finished, they sang it again, but unlike Bea, the choreographer was not carried away. "I suppose it's great," she said to Pippin, "but they're all going to be kneeling at the end. Now what the hell am I going to do for choreography with all those goddamned 'Mames'? How many times do you need to have them sing them?"

The conductor's heart sank at the thought of losing his brainchild, until Bea Arthur piped up. "When they sing it," she said to Onna, "why do they all have to kneel at the same time? Why can't they kneel in little groups — with each 'Mame'?" Pippin immediately knew that it was a wonderful idea, and of course it was the solution. It exemplified the collaborative aspect of show-making. "Here was a musical thing that was exciting," he said, "but it wasn't exciting to the choreographer. Teamwork, the group thing. That was what came up with the answer."

It inspired another idea in Angela, and she told Saks, "You may think I'm crazy, but with the 'Mame' number, I would like to have my back to the audience."

The director was incredulous. The suggestion, he said, was "plain nuts. You don't turn the star's back to the house."

"I can act that way," she insisted, and turning to Onna, she said, "I know I can." She had a very particular effect in mind.

The choreographer simply thought, "She's smart, that lady."

While rehearsals were running, the design team was rushing sketches of sets and costumes toward completion. As a play and a movie, *Auntie Mame* had been a glamorous thing. The musical *Mame* aspired to be even more than that. The set designers, William and Jean Eckart, were known for their sleek elegance, and as for the costumes, Jimmy Carr told the designer, Robert Mackintosh, that he was determined to make the show "a super-stylish, leading-lady musical."

The first costume meeting involved Saks, Onna White, Carr, and Angela. First, they decided what they did *not* want, which, as Mackintosh put it, was "anything that was like what Rosalind Russell had done." In the original play and also in its movie version, Russell played Auntie Mame as a fashion overdose who changed her hair color every twenty minutes. As Bob Mackintosh saw it,

> Instead of being true to what high fashion in *Vogue* and *Harper's Bazaar* had been, we wanted — and this came from Jimmy Carr — to do the Hollywood version of fashion, so that it was like the clothes that women wore in the movies. Those clothes really didn't have anything to do with what anyone else in the world wore. Not even Paris couture. They were the world of Adrian of Hollywood.

Mackintosh began sketching his dresses, and as he turned in the designs, he and Carr would play which-designer-does-this-resemble? And what-movie-is-that-from? One dress might be "so Joan Crawford," another "a perfect Kay Francis." Sometimes, Mackintosh says, "Jimmy Carr would show Angela how to wear the clothes. He understood clothes. He knew, without being a drag queen, how to flip the fur over the shoulder."

Angela thought the show was "their chance to go wild. For a heterosexual man, that would be hard to understand, but oh gosh, it was a show about costumes! Absolutely. Every time I came into a scene I had a different outfit."

Mackintosh decided that she would wear a body stocking throughout the show. Such an undergarment was necessary if she were going to make it through twenty-seven costume changes. "The dresses could just go on and off it," the designer says, adding, "She's not known as chic, and she's long-waisted, but that isn't a problem because she was slimming down. She had the figure to wear clothes and she was tall enough." And she had few complaints about his designs, except that she was touchy about necklines ("I have a short neck") and about baring her arms, for she feared they'd gone flabby after she lost weight. Because of that, he added sleeves to the splashy gold pajamas she was to wear at the start of the show. She also suggested that when she wore hats, they be turbans, "and she was right about that," Mackintosh says. "Turbans are easier to get on and off, because you don't have to worry about the hair."

Her fittings were done at Variety Arts, because she couldn't spare the time to leave, and because the producers, Carr and Fryer, wanted to watch. Barbara Matera, who was executing the costumes (and would become one of Angela's closest friends), was responsible for making them not just beautiful but stageworthy. "The quick changes were the problem," she says. "All the closures had to be made simply. On couture gowns, it's very hard to use Velcro or things like that because everything has to be invisible — and still, easy to put on."

A special rehearsal was set up just to work out the costume changes. Because some of them had to be done in as little time as forty seconds, Dolores Childers actually had to plot carefully these changes for herself and the second dresser, Corinne Bishop.

> One of the big costumes, for instance, was a bouffant skirt. I'd lay it down and fix it so Angie could step into it — and then someone would stand with a stop watch while one of the dancers would get into it and we would have to put it on her and hook her up and get the jewelry on and everything and see how long it took us. If we didn't make it in the right time, we would have to keep practicing until we did. We had to know exactly how much time we had because every change meant a change of shoes, change of costume, earrings, and then the hairdresser had to do her hair. Each one's got their place and what they have to do.

Only then did they call Angela in, to show her how all the changes would work. As they began, she started to unzip her dress. Dolores pulled back, put her hands on her hips, and said, "Look, Angie. It's natural to try and help, but if you're going to put your hands in my way, I can't make these changes. We've got all this choreographed, so just stand still!" And then Corinne grabbed the dress and yanked it off while Dolores was snatching at the star's turban. Almost before letting go of one dress, they would be slipping on the next one. When Angela finally learned to stand still and let them do it, they got the whole procedure right.

During one rehearsal break, she was sitting on a leatherette hallway couch, next to Jane Connell, adrift in thought. With her voice at a distance, Angela softly said, "I really shouldn't be here. I should be home taking care of my roses."

It wasn't the roses she was thinking of. She was thinking that perhaps she should be back in Malibu with the children. Jane Connell was an unusually smart and sensitive young woman, but Angela was not about to share her personal concerns with even so sympathetic an outsider. She shook herself out of the daze, got up, and hurried back to work. "The theater," she was perfectly aware, "is an extraordinary escape because, if you're the star of the show, it demands your whole concentration, presence, and involvement. It enables you to get through some pretty tricky periods. Through the worst times of family troubles."

On the day the theatrical trailer truck backed up to the loading dock of the Shubert Theater in Philadelphia to "load in" the *Mame* lighting equipment and scenery, a line of 150 people had formed around the corner at the box office, waiting to buy tickets. The only explanation Saks could think of was the hit recording that Eydie Gormé had made of the show's big ballad, "If He Walked into My Life." All those people certainly weren't on line to see Angela Lansbury. "She wasn't a big attraction at the time," Saks says.

"You think you know the business," he shrugged. "It must have been the character of Mame. She had become like a folk heroine."

It was on the late evening Jack Paar show that Saks and the rest of the cast were able to see Eydie Gormé sing their song. The bunch of them crowded into the director's hotel room to watch it together, but the one who should have been most interested — the composer, Jerry Herman — was looking, instead, at Jane Connell, who was playing Agnes Gooch.

When the song was over, he said to her, "You know, Jane? I think you should wear your own hair instead of the wig." Any criticism was enough to worry an actor, but the mention of a woman's hair put her especially on the alert. Connell's poor heart began to thump. She knew that her real hair was at best "wispy and babyish" and was sure she was about to be replaced, until Herman added, "I noticed in rehearsal that your own hair kind of 'floats.' I like that look." She sighed with relief. Such were the anxieties besetting an actor in a Broadway tryout.

There was work yet to be done. The technical rehearsal was for the stage crew's benefit — to allow them to set their scenery changes and lighting setups. The production stage manager, Terry Little, checked out all the final choices and then marked the technical cues in his master script. The show would be run from that script at every performance. What was becoming worrisome to everyone was not some unmanageable problem but rather, the unbelievably smooth sailing they were experiencing. It was enough to petrify the superstitious, and just before the curtain went up for the first preview, Saks facetiously said to the the show's general manager, Joe Harris, "Well, Joey, we just blew another five hundred thousand dollars."

He gave Angela one last note as they got ready for that first public performance. "Everything you're doing is terrific," he assured her, "but you don't yet own the stage. Technically, everything you're doing is great, but *you've* got to take the stage. This is your show, this is your part. You are the pivotal point of this thing. *You must not be afraid to own the stage.*"

It was a pep talk, yes, but it reflected his continuing and genuine concern about her assertiveness. Angela responded well, considering it "a wonderful, wonderful note, because I think from that moment I knew that I could take it and make it my own. Certainly that was the beginning for me as a Broadway star."

Of course, that would ultimately be up to the audience.

As the song "Mame" got under way, its first theater audience started to cheer *in the middle of the number.* At the end of it, after the five cascading repeats of "Mame," there was a dramatic coda while Mame — on a stage filled with singers and dancers in riding habits and plantation finery — notices young Patrick, standing alone at the side. She hurries to embrace him, but her dialogue could not be heard. The ovation would not hush. "It was so strong as the song ended," Saks saw, "that she couldn't play that little tag to the scene."

When the curtain then swept downward, ending the first act, the theater roared with the approval that show people usually just dream about. The applause and cheers and whistles continued even after the house lights went up. As the audience started from their seats, to surge up the aisle for the break, Saks, standing at the rear of the auditorium, knew that there was still work to be done and he knew that Angela was still not at the level he was seeking. But he also recognized that this show was already a hit and he relished the audience's love for it.

Walking up the aisle toward him was Arthur Laurents, who had directed *Anyone Can Whistle.* Like many theater people, he often went out of town to see the tryouts of new musicals. He took Saks's arm and offered no congratulations. Instead, he said, "The show's problem is that the music is at war with the book." He meant the contrast between Jerry Herman's warm music and the bitchy style of the original *Auntie Mame*, and he was right as usual, but the show was working, and that was the main concern.

Saks was incredulous and simply gaped at Laurents, shocked by the insensitivity of the remark, and its impropriety, coming from one director to another at such a moment. Then he laughed at the absurdity of it in the face of this ecstatic audience, and wondered, "What world are you living in?" Without replying, he turned and walked away, thinking "You never heard an ovation like that for *Anyone Can Whistle.*"

Philadelphia's Main Line audiences, which monopolized the seats on the official opening nights, were infamous for leaving early because of their long rides home. As the stage manager, Terry Little, could see, checking his watch, *Mame* needed some twenty minutes of cuts, but he also noticed that "not one person walked out. We knew it was a hit from that night in Philly."

Little skipped the opening night party because he had been trapped in the theater since they'd arrived. The show was so technically complicated, with choreographed scenic changes in full audience view, and fast lighting changes, that he and Jim Brennan, who was his head technician, and the whole crew, had to work not only during all the rehearsals but before and after them as well. Dinner breaks were all take-outs, and so on opening night, Terry and Jim took themselves to celebrate in the African Bar, on Broad Street, "where everything was black and there were phosphorescent lights so that if you smiled your teeth glowed."

They sat down at a table and were sipping martinis when the ladies came through the door, Bea first, saying, "So you're too good for the party?" Angela was right behind her. "Well," she said, "we don't want to see the rest of the company, either." They sat themselves down and the four of them stayed long past midnight, in the little joint with the black light, drinking, putting quarters in the jukebox, and dancing.

"In the theater," Angela says, "there are times when you are really thrown to people by the proximity of your work, by the camaraderie and the feeling of family. So backstage romances are the most natural thing in the world. I really don't know anybody it didn't happen to.

"It isn't just theater people who are sexy. It has to do with men and women. Most people would be amazed at the amount of sexual promiscuity that goes on *outside* the theater, I mean in everyday life. But I suppose there's something sort of different about backstage affairs. People don't seem so emotionally involved.

"And it certainly gives a lift to the proceedings."

Angela and Peter's marriage could not have been as good as it was if they weren't so emotionally and temperamentally similar, and of comparable sensibilities. It also wouldn't have worked so well had they not both been in show business. Angela was more possessive than Peter, who was not by nature a jealous or suspicious person. She knew him to be "a very sophisticated man, now that I think about it. *Was.* In his years as an agent, and at MGM, well, I know who was available to him."

Even as Saks was certain that *Mame* was going to be a hit, he knew there was work to be done. Those twenty minutes had to be cut, and there was still the problem of Angela's performance. He was more certain than ever that at the root, she was suffering "from a lack of real confidence." As a result, Bea was stepping into the vacuum and taking the stage. Although she was playing a supporting role, she was the dominant personality in the show. He was hoping that Angela could "grow into" playing Mame with flamboyance and verve, but was it possible to grow into charisma? Could an introvert become an extrovert? Could a character player ever become a star?

As the company moved on to the Colonial Theatre in Boston, the next stop on the tryout tour, Saks went to work. One of his changes was dropping the ballad "Love Is Only Love." In musicals, the only ones who like the slow songs are the composers and singers. For everyone else, they are stage waits, and for directors and choreographers, they are stage deaths. Jerry Herman was a good soldier and replaced "Love Is Only Love" with the sprightlier "That's How Young I Feel." Set to a Charleston rhythm, it was expanded into a dance number, exploiting Angela's mastery of not only the Charleston but the tango and the lindy hop. An inorganic number, making no contribution to plot or character, but simply a diversion for the sake of a diversion, it was everyone's least favorite number in the show.

The tougher problem remained Angela's assertiveness, which had to be established as she came down a flight of stairs for her first entrance. "We talked to her about playing bigger," Saks remembers. "Onna and I tried to make her confident enough to come down the stairs like Tallulah Bankhead or Ethel Merman." Both of them were campy performers, outsize personalities, and even self-caricatures. Saks says, "I think Angie recognized what we meant, but you can't do much about it unless you have that feeling of confidence.

"Some people can't learn that."

In her dressing room, she was sitting and pondering this problem and had come up with the idea of a special dress to wear just for the curtain call. It was as if the star's dress might make the star, and suddenly, the show's costume designer, Bob Mackintosh, was tapping at her door. "Funny," she said, "that you should come in right now. Because I was just thinking about a dress for the curtain calls — like the one that Irene Dunne wore in the movie *Roberta* when she sang 'Smoke Gets in Your Eyes.'"

Mackintosh stared at her. "That is so bizarre," he said, "because it is exactly what I came in to suggest."

CHAPTER 13

THE WHITE DRESS

Then she goes to Broadway and gets the makeover of all time, a new body, a wardrobe to choke a horse, and she opens in a show called "Mame" and gets worldwide acclaim as a glamorous leading lady for the first time in her career and becomes the kind of shining star that she had dreamed about. So let's examine that.

GENE SAKS

FOR MANY WOMEN, hairstyle is not just a matter of appearance. It is often an expression of the self; a mood changer and a mood setter. It announces image and self-image, even a new image.

Angela was still striving to beat back her reserve and take stage, but the suggestions by her director and the producers did not seem to be helping. She began telling herself, "I will no longer do what I'm told, or advised. I will simply take this role and make it my own." Alas, this was only intellectualizing. She was still dealing with performance as if it were an acting assignment. If Mame Dennis was supposed to be flamboyant, then Angela Lansbury would act flamboyant, but that seemed to be the problem. She was only acting.

She decided to chop off all her hair. She had the celebrated hairdresser Kenneth come up to Boston from New York. What she had in mind, she told him, was a boyishly short cut. It was the Eton crop that she'd worn on the Queen Elizabeth when she sailed on that second honeymoon with Peter.

The hairstylist went to work, and when most of the Lansbury mane lay shorn on the floor, what remained was dyed a honey blond. Then it was restyled into a breezy, boyishly female cut, flat on top and parted to one side. Finally, it was swept back along the sides.

When she looked at herself in the mirror, she saw a brand-new face to go with her brand-new body, and smart as she is, she knew exactly what she'd been after. "Cutting my hair enabled me to reinvent myself. It took away every vestige of the Angela Lansbury who had played this, this, this, and this. It allowed me to emerge as Mame."

At least she hoped so. Her body had certainly been renewed. The weeks of tough rehearsal had left it lithe, sinewy, and long-muscled. She'd been dancing fearlessly, unconcerned about the flying skirts that exposed her thighs. When she appeared backstage with the haircut for the first time, just before the first Boston preview, Gene Saks gazed upon her with delight. So did "the boys," as she referred to Carr, Fryer, Mackintosh, and Jerry Herman. "They were mad about it. No question, it worked."

At the premiere, a few nights later, the Colonial Theatre's house lights dimmed. In the orchestra pit, Don Pippin raised his baton in the glow of his music stand's lamp. Angela waited behind the door at the top of the staircase for her first entrance. The overture ended with a cascade of trumpets and rolling kettle drums, firing the audience with electric anticipation. The curtain whooshed up on little orphan Patrick and his nanny, Agnes Gooch, as she was escorting him to the Beekman Place home of his new guardian, who they assumed was the proper and responsible maiden aunt Mame Dennis. The stage lights rose on the set of Mame's penthouse apartment.

A wild and glamorous party is in progress. As Patrick innocently looks on, his not-so-maiden-aunt Mame makes her entrance at the top of the stairs. She is the wildest and most glamorous thing at the party, fabulous in gold pajamas, a trumpet in hand and bursting with song.

Tune the grand up.
Dance your shoes off,
Strike the band up,
It's today!

She slides down the banister into the arms of her chorus boy bookends, spinning, prancing, and high-kicking her way across the stage. The audience erupted, and the next morning, Boston's critics were as enthusiastic as Philadelphia's. Everybody seemed to love this show, and best of all (rarest, too), it continued to enjoy a trouble-free out-of-town tryout. It was the perfect hit — and yet Saks was still dissatisfied with Angela's energy output. He thought that she remained reluctant to "come down the stairs," which to him meant not merely igniting the show with a spectacular entrance at the start, but going through its two acts with the same powerhouse energy. Certainly, the show was going well; but just how well and how far it would finally go depended on Angela. For *Mame* was an unabashed star vehicle and there had to be a star to drive it.

The star herself was confident enough about the show's prospects to take a one-year lease on a handsome town house on East 64th Street near Lexington Avenue. She needed all of that room for the kids, who were coming to stay in New York and go to school there. Because they would be arriving at the end of May, she was already arranging for them to escape the miserable heat of a New York summer by swapping places with Patrice Munsel, the opera singer, who lived near the shore, in Oyster Bay, Long Island. Angela hoped that the beach would remind Anthony and Deirdre of California.

Since *Mame* was set to open on May 24th, 1966, when Anthony and Deirdre were finished with school, they were going to be able to attend the big event. Deirdre had a special opening-night dress that her mother had bought even before leaving for New York and rehearsals. Anthony, too, was given his first blue suit, but they really weren't suit-and-dress youngsters. They wore their hair long, their jackets fringed, and their pants bell-bottomed. As Angela put it, "They were 'California Dreamin' kids," and neither of them wanted to leave Malibu. Their friends were there, and their lives were linked to their friends, the beach, and that way of life. It was exactly what Angela wanted to get them away from.

It was at the Winter Garden Theatre, where *Mame* was playing previews, that Angela finally got to have a star dressing room on Broadway. Every Broadway theater had a dressing room that was considered its most prestigious, usually closest to the stage. The one at the Winter Garden was a two-room suite, up the spiral metal backstage stairs; it was the only dressing room with a private bathroom, as required for the star by contract. It was big enough for a sofa and an armchair in one room and the makeup table in the other. If *Mame* was successful, the suite was supposed to be redecorated, and the producers were already arranging that.

They were also ecstatic about Bob Mackintosh's final design, the white "bow" dress. It was finished at last, and even the designer had to admit that his Irene Dunne–inspired creation was "gorgeous, gorgeous." The dress thrilled even the costumier, Barbara Matera, as she was fitting it on Angela. It was of white chiffon, with a wide, billowing skirt and a big raised collar and it had luxurious white fox fur trim along the neckline, around the upturned collar, and encircling the generous hem. Every actress in the show seemed to be awed by it, from the understudies to Bea Arthur. Besides being breathtakingly beautiful, it seemed to symbolize a distinctly female ideal of stardom that had inspired them to become actresses. Soon, a murmuring began among the women in *Mame.* As Bea put it, "Whether it's Molière or Edward Albee, I want to be wearing the white dress."

Dolores and Corinne approached this "bow gown" from a more pragmatic point of view. They would have no more than forty-five seconds to get Angela out of the black velvet coat with the red fox collar that she wore in the closing scene and into that white dress — her twenty-eighth costume — in time to reappear for her curtain call. That meant they would have to be ready with it as she started up the stairs with the nephew. They would be poised as the final curtain fell, waiting as she clambered down toward them in the wings while the rest of the cast was taking curtain calls.

Onna White restaged the curtain calls. She lined up the whole cast diagonally. When their bows were done, they would all turn toward the stairs in unison and gaze upward. Angela would then appear at the top of the staircase in her spectacular white dress. After descending, she would move down the line, past the company, and toward her audience.

Would all of this attention and support, all the theatrical resources of staging and music, all the manipulation of audience emotions, capped by the fabulous white dress — would all of that set the stage for Angela Lansbury to come down the stairs in the greater sense? Would she dominate entirely and then detonate, setting off the explosive reaction that means *smash hit?* Could she do it from the outset? Could she muster up the flair, the power, and the pizazz for that?

It wasn't only Peter and the children who were coming to New York for the opening night of *Mame.* Bruce flew in with them, Edgar was going to be there too, and of course, so was Moyna. She was escorted by Hurd Hatfield, who hired a limousine for the occasion.

A New York opening night is like no other, but Angela was prepared for it. As she waited in the wings, Dolores hugged her for good luck and gave a strong yank at the back of the splashy yellow pajamas. Then Angela climbed the flight of stairs for her entrance in the opening party scene. She took a deep breath and was ready to go.

The show began and suddenly she was out in the open, blowing the first notes of "It's Today!" on her bugle and then singing the song with full-throated joy. Her golden hair sparkled in the bright pink-and-blue spotlights. Below was the company of actors. No longer Angela's beloved stage family, they were now Mame's party guests. She spread her arms wide and came storming down the stairs. Then onto the banister, sliding down, kicking her legs, up in the air, carried aloft on the strong arms of her bookends, and singing all the while.

Bruce Lansbury, watching from close up and dead center, could see that it wasn't his sister, but his sister-as-Mame who was becoming a star before his eyes. "It's the actress in her, creating a character that the public believes. When she came down that staircase, she projected that character to such an extent that she made herself a star. She couldn't will herself to *become* one, but in that role, as an actress, she found the character that the audience loved so much. *They* made her a star."

This was the ultimate projection. Inhabiting the part, she was letting Mame's flamboyance work for her. The reserved Angela became the exhibitionist Mame Dennis so believably that the audience saw one as the other, and so she was welcomed into the engulfing arms of that awesome creature, the audience, and things stayed that way all through the first act, until the big "Mame" number began.

Angela took her place at center stage, her back to the audience as the ensemble serenaded her. All of those dancers and singers were dressed in wonderfully nonsensical plantation finery and hunting clothes, which provided a bright spray of color to frame her riding outfit, which was black from silk topper to boots. There was no missing her against that brilliant background of red-and-white riding habits and pastel-colored dresses.

They swung their elbows with swaggered ease.

You've brought the cakewalk back into style, Mame

As the number swelled, something began to happen that had not happened during previews. Even with her back to the audience, Angela was communicating with the audience. Her movements were contained—mere hand gestures, really—yet, as Jane Connell observed from the midst of the ensemble, "you could see that just from the way she moved her back, the audience was getting the whole impact of this number." Jerry Herman had the same impression, standing at the rear of the theater. "You could see her almost start to quiver with emotion. You could tell from Mame's back that a tear was coming down her cheek."

In the wings, the associate producer, John Bowab, could watch what Angela was doing from the actors' point of view. "She operated during that number. The chorus would be singing and she would be looking at one of them, then at the next and the next, and then back to the first one. Her eyes would linger [with an extra twinkle sometimes, one of the chorus boys swore]. It was as if she fell in love with one chorus member, then another, and it was all accomplished with her back to the audience. Nor was she doing it for herself. She was doing it because she knew that for the chorus member to do the job, she had to.

"Angela's internal acting — in a song that she did not sing one note of — turned that production number," Bowab says, "into a fantastic emotional experience."

The first act ended with rousing hosannahs from the audience, and the excited buzz that is money to a producer's ear, and after intermission, things continued to go swimmingly as the evening arrived at the biggest of her songs. She had been singing with strength, clarity, and a great warmth. Her intonation was pure, and she was always precisely on key, yet it wasn't just "singing" because she also acted as she sang.

Now, alone on stage, she began quietly with the verse that, in a musical, is the link between the dialogue and the lyrics, between a character's speaking and singing. Mame is forlorn that the little boy she'd loved so much has grown up to be the rather obnoxious young man she has just told off.

Where's that boy with the bugle?
My little love who was always my big romance;
Where's that boy with the bugle?
And why did I ever buy him those damn long pants!

Gene Saks's simple staging put full focus on the song's ravishing melody, its rueful lyrics, and Angela's overwhelming blend of musicianship, acting intelligence, and radiance. As she sang, her voice soared across the audience, engulfing it, and elevating it.

Did he need a stronger hand?
Did he need a lighter touch?

Was I soft or was I tough?
Did I give enough?
Did I give too much?

This was not a Broadway belter, nor an opera singer. The chest voice/head voice issue seemed resolved. It was simply a natural voice with character across its entire range.

Though I'll ask myself my whole life long,
What went wrong along the way;
Would I make the same mistakes,
If he walked into my life today?

That was a high-ish note, yet she was not singing in a head — or falsetto — voice, but in the flowing range of a singing voice that was musical and still seemed like the character's speaking voice. Then she started upward toward the song's big finish. The arrangement was shamelessly melodramatic. She did not flinch from the high note that brings the song to a finale, and now she belted it out:

If that boy with the bugle
Walked into my life — today!

It brought the house down. They were simply roaring, and it was all Angela could do to keep herself from reacting, but she held character, and if there was a moistening in her eyes, or a lump in her throat, who was the wiser?

The show headed down the home stretch, and it was breezing to the finish now. The evening had begun with a head start, for every opening night audience arrives ready to cheer. There are always friends at a premiere, and investors in the house, and an eagerness to be the first to see the latest smash hit. But the first night *Mame* audience seemed honestly overcome, and when the final curtain plummeted down, they were ready to explode. Jerry Herman looked on from the back of the house as the applause rang out from the balcony and washed down across the orchestra floor in waves of approval and reward and everything that being a Broadway smash means — love in massive and repeated doses, and a lot of money, too. The applause grew as the leading players took their curtain calls, running out to bow and grin and thrill for themselves, taking their places along the dramatic diagonal that Onna White had devised for the ritual.

The cheering rose another level as Bea Arthur came out in her black dress, and there was an accolade for her, and then the noise grew thunderous, an expanding rumble as Angela's appearance was anticipated. She stepped out from the wings at the top of the stairs, a glorious vision in the ravishing white bow gown, and at the first sight of it, there was an audible gasp from the oceanic audience. In that pregnant moment of love and magic, time seemed suspended, and then Angela felt "a roar that hit me" — and the cheers came crashing down upon her golden shoulders.

Jerry Herman wept for her, and felt, "When she came out in that angelic, glamorous gown, and when the audience realized that they had just seen one of the great performances of all time and had discovered a new star who was the image of goodness and decency and fairness — well, after the Hollywood years and the character actor stuff, she suddenly became the lady in the white dress.

"She was it, the one in the spotlight."

At a theater in California, a New York director named Billy Barnes was invited to a glamorous benefit party. He was seated beside Rosalind Russell. A few minutes later, Dinah Shore came into the row and took the seat on his other side. The two stars then began to talk, paying no attention to Barnes in the middle. Dinah Shore said, "Isn't it just wonderful about Angela?"

Russell replied dryly, "Isn't *what* wonderful about Angela?"

The beautiful and bright singer said, "Why, her great success in *Mame,* honey."

Russell responded, "Oh, that. After I did it, anybody could do it."

Shore smiled sweetly and said, "Well, *I* couldn't."

Rex Reed, the young Louisiana college student whom Angela had met while making *The Long Hot Summer* in 1957, had nurtured that meeting into a friendship. They'd since exchanged letters, or he would telephone, or — when she was in a show — he would come north to see her. He'd hoped to be a movie actor, but college experience had led him into celebrity journalism. By 1966, he established himself by writing a Barbra Streisand article that was sharper and less sycophantic than the usual star profile. Now, he was thrilled to have a Sunday *New York Times* assignment to write a piece about Angela, coinciding with her *Mame* opening.

However, when his mother slipped into a leukemic coma, he was unable to deliver it on schedule. Angela came to his rescue. "She wouldn't let anyone else do it," he remembers. "It was the test of a friendship. She put everyone off while she waited for me to come back."

He wrote that she was

> something to scream about. Angela Lansbury blowing a trumpet in backless canary yellow spangles on top of a grand piano. Angela Lansbury doing a slow Theda Bara burn across a speakeasy floor in silk lame and monkey fur. Angela Lansbury leading an imaginary parade into theatrical history with a peppermint stick. A happy caterpillar turning, after years of being nose-thumbed by Hollywood in endless roles as baggy-faced frumps, into a gilt-edged butterfly.

Offstage she was also transformed, and playing out a dream. "I was living the life of a star, you bet — a glamorous, *Broadway star* life. It fed my need to act my age" — and by "act my age" she meant the opposite of the usual. For a change she was acting as *young* as she was.

> To some extent I took the part offstage. I felt attractive. I'd never believed it before. And that's really the crux of the whole thing. I never thought of myself as an attractive woman.

She already had the fancy town house, and next came a full-time limousine — and a chauffeur to go with it — in exchange for appearing in a series of liquor advertisements. Then the producers assumed that expense, and they redecorated her dressing room, too ("on the cheap," she dryly noted). They also gave her a raise, but at $1,750 a week, she was not breaking any Broadway salary records, despite having been acclaimed a star, and having become a major box office attraction. She was, however, "going and doing," as she put it — all over town. She had an offstage wardrobe that was almost as sensational as the twenty-eight costumes she wore in *Mame*, with lots of flimsy little dance dresses. One night Ron Young, who was one of her "bookends" in the show, was startled to see her in "a mini beaded dress clear up to her hips. She posed for pictures in it. She was just thrilled to be that sexy. Great legs."

She topped it off with a flamboyant white mink coat when she went out in those chilly autumn evenings in New York, and she went out most every night after performances; for dinner, or to parties, and — when *Mame* was dark — to Broadway opening nights. The novelist James Leo Herlihy told her, "You are the golden girl of New York."

She thought, "I guess I am, except I'm no girl, I'm forty-one years old."

Midnights, she went to the new hot disco, Arthur, "and danced the night away." And when Peter came into town, both of them would "do this very glamorous life. It was a chapter of our lives that was filled with glamour." Her private life not only fed off the stage role but seemed to improve it. Every night at eight o'clock, she was growing more assertive as Mame. Yet, ironically, she was still not really more sure of herself. There was a difference between acting confident and being confident. She knew that the audiences "loved the show, and they loved me playing Mame," but tellingly, she would add, "They were so pleased for me. That I had pulled it off."

Not every director keeps tabs on a production after it opens, which is why some shows grow stale or sloppy. Gene Saks checked in regularly. Among other things, he did not want Angela to go too far with her newfound flamboyance, taking Mame toward caricature and beyond, into the realm of the bizarre and even the grotesque. She never would. "I would not let myself fall into the campy pitfalls," she says with mixed pride and relief. "I mean, a musical version of the great *Auntie Mame.* The possibilities are pretty frightening. But I kept the kernel of truth and played Mame as Madcap Polly — absolutely straight."

This required a fair amount of ego control, because performers bask in approval and audiences like their stars to play pet roles repeatedly, in an ever more exaggerated style, no matter what show they are in. Carol Channing tried to resist that audience pressure, but as the director Harold Prince put it, "There are certain artists that people want a certain way, and Carol is one of them. When she replaced Roz Russell in *Wonderful Town,* George Abbott asked me to direct it. Carol Channing is a wonderful woman and so smart, and is another person, not just that kewpie doll in a blond wig. And she is a wonderful actress, so she decided to play not 'Carol Channing,' but Ruth Sherwood.

"She was just grand, but the audience didn't want that. They wanted this oversized, quirky blond that Carol Channing meant to them and they wanted her whenever they came into a theater, so what is she doing there in *Wonderful Town,* with red hair and another voice, looking totally different?"

Angela didn't fall into the trap.

As *Mame* moved into its second year, Angela enjoyed the novel experience of a long-running show. One of the most common questions asked of actors is how they keep fresh, performing the same part hundreds of times. The theater, by its very nature of being live, with a diverse group of individuals on stage and a different audience at every performance, is inherently volatile and unpredictable. Yet, some actors will still walk through — *phone in,* as it's said — their performances.

As this show passed its five hundredth performance, Lansbury grew relaxed enough to sip tea in her dressing room between acts and even see visitors. On stage, however, she kept herself stimulated by the challenge of making every performance seem fresh, treating Mame Dennis as a dramatic character who could be constantly explored and reevaluated. Meanwhile, Anthony and Deirdre finally persuaded their mother to let them go home to Malibu and their friends, leaving her with feelings of guilt and too big a place for just herself. She moved out of the town house and into an apartment in the handsome UN Plaza condominiums, on First Avenue at 44th Street, facing the East River and across the street from the United Nations headquarters.

David was also moving eastward from California to New York, courtesy of the Selective Service System. His father was still upset about the young man's electing to enter the army when he might have evaded it by exercising his British citizenship and going back to England. In this time of war in Vietnam, Peter would even have had his son flee to Canada, but David — like his Uncle Edgar before him — did not want to sacrifice his chances for American citizenship, which that would have entailed.

In her dressing room, Angela could hear the angry anti-war demonstrators marching along Broadway past the Winter Garden Theatre. Before David had made his decision, she'd weighed in with the argument that the Vietnam conflict was pointless, futile, and probably unjust. There had been no "probable" in Deirdre's mind. She was "very sore at David" about his being in the military at this time, and possibly going to Vietnam, but then she was angry about a lot of things. The way Anthony describes it, "at the time there was a certain hostility toward the status quo. She was very concerned with social inequities and political principles." Mixed with her anger about Vietnam was concern for her father. "I was worried about how upset Dad was," she remembers, "saying good-bye to David."

The young man went through basic training at Fort Ord in California, and was assigned to an Army movie unit in New York City, because he had a film industry background. The unit was based in Astoria, Queens, and with his remarkably good looks, David was often asked to play scenes in military training films. But Peter had apparently passed along his acting genes, for even in these pictures, the young man was no better an actor than his father had been.

He spent his weekend passes in Manhattan, staying with Angela, until the dreaded orders did indeed come his way, and he was sent to Vietnam as a combat photographer.

Angela was preparing to leave the New York company of *Mame*, and although she had always meant to come home after two years it was not easy for her to leave. This had been an extraordinary time. She'd finally gotten the starring role that had eluded her all of her professional life. Now the producers were searching for a replacement, and many middle-aged movie actresses were applying for the part, hoping to follow Angela's example and also start second careers as musical comedy stars. In Hollywood, an actress in her forties was considered over the hill; on Broadway, the age factor was not only overlooked, but older women were glorified. The greatest leading ladies in musical comedy, Ethel Merman and Mary Martin, were both sixtyish.

Jane Wyman inquired about playing Mame, and so did Jean Arthur, on whom Angela had modeled her own performance. Judy Garland asked for an audition, and of course, one was granted. Her career was in decline, but the Garland legend endured. She had long since left Hollywood, establishing herself as an extraordinary concert performer, but in recent years she had suffered a series of psychological setbacks that resulted in humiliating onstage lapses, even momentary breakdowns, and terrible audience assaults that left her in flight from boos and catcalls — and that was when she managed to show up for a performance.

Now she came to the Winter Garden, to see *Mame* and plead her case with Angela, who swallowed hard as she greeted the tiny and frightfully frail Garland. The once glowing, hugely gifted performer was pathetically hollow-cheeked, dark-eyed, and desperate. She was wearing "this rather tawdry little evening gown," Lansbury sadly observed. "It was the sort of thing you would wear if you were doing a club act, only she came to the theater in it." Both of them were roughly the same age — Garland was only forty-four, but she looked ancient as she reminisced about the old days at MGM, when they did *The Harvey Girls* together, and Angela grieved for her. "It was so sad, it really upset and blew me away."

At the first warning buzzer for the performers, she arranged for a folding chair to be set out so that Garland might watch the show from the wings. The audition was scheduled for the following day. For weeks, Garland had been calling the producer, Jimmy Carr, telling him how badly she wanted the part, and how urgently she needed it. She was, she said, in the most terrible of financial straits. Just talking about bounced checks was reducing her to tears. Then, with a sort of mad childishness, she started to mewl and pout about punctuality and discipline. "Don't believe anyone who tells you I'm a bad girl, I'm not a bad girl," she pleaded. "I promise I'll be a good girl.

"Mr. Carr, I need this job."

Jerry Herman offered to accompany her at the audition, just as he had for Angela, and he met Carr and Bowab at Garland's town house. "That first meeting," Bowab remembers, "she was two hours late. *At her own home she was two hours late.*"

That didn't matter to the composer. He was yearning for her to get the part, but her state of mind was heartbreaking. She hadn't even been able to learn the songs. They finally hired Janice Paige, and Judy Garland was dead only a few years later, at forty-seven.

Meanwhile, Bea Arthur had finally gotten to wear a white dress, only it wasn't in *Mame.* She had left the show a year into the run when, at long last, she was offered the leading role in a new musical. It was based on the Bruce J. Friedman novel *A Mother's Kisses*, and when rehearsals were finished, the show shipped out to New Haven for a tryout engagement. It was there that Jack Hutto saw it.

Hutto had formerly been Bea's agent (and would later be Angela's), and they'd remained friends, so when he went backstage after the performance, it was on a strictly personal basis. Naturally, the first thing she asked was what he thought of it.

Many theater people devise devious responses to such questions, for they are so virtuous and have lived such saintly lives that they simply cannot bring themselves to lie, even when an artist is still emotionally vulnerable following a performance. Elaborate evasions are conceived to safeguard such honesty — for instance, "I never saw anything like it," or "You were simply unbelievable." Everyone knows what such remarks really mean, and perhaps that is the subversive point.

Jack Hutto was too smart and too old a friend for such nonsense and so when Bea asked what he thought of *A Mother's Kisses*, he told her exactly what he thought of it.

"They hated it," he said, "and they hated you. They wanted to throw shoes at you."

In her wonderful basso profundo, Bea said, "I don't believe you. I felt waves of love coming from the footlights the entire night."

Hutto burst into gales of laughter. "Then you were drunk," he roared, "absolutely drunk."

At that moment, another visitor tapped at the dressing room door, and when she came in, Bea nodded in Hutto's direction and said, "He came backstage and then he tells me they hated me."

"And," Hutto said to the visitor, "that's why we're still friends."

Photographs taken of Angela at the curtain calls for her final performance of *Mame* are heart-wrenching. Her cheeks are wet with tears but her eyes betray her mixed emotions as she raises her arms to hush the audience. She told them that "Performing *Mame* has been the longest running love-in in Broadway history," but as she loved her stage family, so she feared for her children. And warmed as she'd been by her life doing the show in New York, so she was chilled by the possibility of what was awaiting her in California. She was torn by the inability to be in two places — not just geographically but also mentally — at the same time, and she was profoundly troubled by the thought that her two years as Mame might have been enjoyed at the expense of her children's welfare.

From Los Angeles, she wrote a letter to Terry Little, the production stage manager at the Winter Garden Theatre. It was dated April 3, 1968.

> *Dearest Terry,*
> I am addressing this letter to you, but I would be grateful if you would sort of pass it around to everyone. I don't want it to go

up on the board because it's really very private and so much from my heart to *all of you.* If time permitted, I would want to tell personally each individual who was in the Winter Garden on Saturday night March 31st the following —

I wonder if you realized that it was impossible for me to look any single one of you in the eye? If I had I would have broken completely before the curtain ever went up! I tried to fill my head with myriad thoughts — anything, to avoid facing the reality that it was my last time to bat with you all as "Mame" at the Winter Garden. Two marvelous years suddenly at a total end. But you pulled me through it, buoying me up and jollying me along until that final curtain.

All the days of my life I will remember the moment when I came on to take my bow — suddenly the air was filled with flowers and all of you were there — every dear face etched in my memory, the cast, the crew, the orchestra with Don reaching up with the bouquet of red roses and then my old battered bugle. All this sounds very sentimental — *well it was,* probably, one of the most warm, loving, sentimental evenings ever on Broadway. Every person from the front of the house to the back of the house including the audience was caught up in the emotion of the moment and it was BEAUTIFUL.

My little speech did not make much sense because in fact I would have liked to have sat down and given the audience a good half-hour on the subject of all of you! What you mean to me now and always. But I think they understood.

I'll never forget what we shared together for two years — I look forward to seeing you again more than I can tell you.

HAPPINESS IS BEING "YOUR MAME."
BLESSINGS AND LOVE TO EVERY ONE OF YOU.

Angie

CHAPTER 14

FIRESTORM

MAME went on to run another year without her. Jane Morgan succeeded Janice Paige, and the final stretch was played by the movie dancer Ann Miller. She would go offstage in the midst of the Charleston number "That's How Young I Feel," strap on her tap shoes, and then come out for a tap specialty. While she was perhaps the most ridiculous of the Mames, none of them was truly satisfactory, simply because Angela Lansbury couldn't be replaced. It wasn't just a matter of talent. There were other actresses who could sing and dance and be funny, and some of them were, in fact, among the various Mames — Susan Hayward, Celeste Holm, Ginger Rogers, and Juliet Prowse — who took the role in the touring companies.

But they could only play the part as it was written in the script — read those lines, sing those songs, and follow those stage directions. The actress in Angela Lansbury added a warmth and softness that made for a uniquely lovable chemistry of a role, an actor, and the audience. Certainly, *Mame* was a hit by any standard, but its final figure of 1,508 performances would come to seem disappointing, especially since many felt that it was a better show than Jerry Herman's previous musical, *Hello Dolly!,* which ran a thousand performances longer. The likely reason for the shorter run is that the *Dolly!* audiences were satisfied with Carol Channing's replacements, but *Mame* just was not *Mame* without Angela Lansbury.

Angela herself was far from finished with the show. According to the producers, she was "desperate" to play it for the ten-week California tour, perhaps hoping to show Hollywood exactly how wrong they had been about her. After that, she was going to take the musical to London, for a spectacular homecoming and stage debut.

It was quite an exhilarating plan, but it got off on the wrong foot when the sponsor of the West Coast production, the Los Angeles Civic Light Opera, suggested that the actress Nanette Fabray might be preferable to Angela. According to John Bowab, "They didn't think the West Coast audiences would find Angie a big enough star. It was a tough sell, but they were finally convinced to go along with her." Luckily, she was spared that information, but Hollywood was certainly resolute in its pigeonholing. It seemed as if no matter what she did, however high she scaled, as far as Los Angeles was concerned, she would always be (in her phrase) a *one-up* — a supporting actor.

At the same time, Peter was changing jobs. He respected the advice of Abe Lastfogel, his former boss at William Morris. Lastfogel had made the MGM deal for him, and now his advice was "Metro is going to be changing. This guy [James T.] Aubrey is coming in. It's time to get the hell out of there.

"Come on back to William Morris."

Peter took his counsel, and also the opportunity to get his son David a position at the agency. Safely home from Vietnam, the young man went to work in the management department, assisting with such clients as the actress Sarah Miles and the singer Cat Stevens. It meant that for the first time in a while, all the Shaws were in California, and Angela looked forward to enjoying the best of both her worlds — private life and public, home and the stage.

Mame was not going to be the first opportunity for Los Angeles to see the glamorous, singing and dancing, theatrically triumphant, new Angela. A year earlier, she had electrified the Academy Award audience with a dazzling Broadway-style musical number nominating the song *Thoroughly Modern Millie.* She was given a spontaneous, standing ovation for her performance ("It was a very exciting moment for me"), but *Mame* was her own personal star vehicle, and she harbored hopes that such a showcase might yet lead to her still unfulfilled dream of a leading role in a movie.

The show was a hit, and so was she. The California producer who had been reluctant to hire her was pleased enough to present her with a hundred red roses on opening night, but alas, stage success meant little to Hollywood. This was a movie town, and if it had once been impressed with Broadway success, that was no longer the case. Angela herself noticed that "Bob Preston wasn't a star before *The Music Man,* and he wasn't a star after it." Nor did *Mame* do it for her.

Perhaps she'd had enough of *Mame* for a while, because she decided that, instead of playing the show in London, she would do a new Jerry Herman musical on Broadway. She was no longer thinking about movies, nor even plays, only musicals. "I was in love with the life and the work. It can be a drug, absolutely."

Nevertheless, the new musical was one about which she'd already expressed doubts. It was based on a 1945 play, *The Madwoman of Chaillot,* by Jean Giradoux. The show had been written for Katharine Hepburn, but she changed her mind about doing it (ultimately making a movie version of the play instead). Now, Gene Saks, who'd been asked to direct it, had his doubts as well. "The script really wasn't very good," he says frankly, "and the score wasn't very good," a combination that, one might say, did not make for an auspicious beginning. Even so, he'd still been the director of record when Angela initially turned it down. Then, when he changed his mind about doing it, she said she would reconsider. "Maybe," he muses, "she just didn't want me."

That certainly was possible, because Saks was directing the movie version of *Mame* for which, incredibly enough, Angela had been passed over in favor of Lucille Ball. That rejection stunned her, and she still had not recovered from it. Even Saks could understand her sense of betrayal, although he insists that by the time he was asked to direct the movie, "Lucy was the centerpiece. Warner Brothers never considered Angela." Their reasoning, according to Robert Fryer (who was producing the movie, as he had the show), was that "Ball was an internationally syndicated television star, which meant that abroad, at least, Warner would get their money back." There was also the incidental matter of Ball's being an investor in the picture — she had made a fortune producing the various *Lucy* television shows.

The *Mame* movie lumbered into production with the star's seeming to carp about everything from Bea Arthur's clear nail polish to the care of the props, which she felt she was paying for, to the casting, when it did not duplicate that of the Broadway company. It was for that reason that she had

Madeline Kahn replaced as Agnes Gooch, demanding, "I want the New York show," which meant the Broadway cast except for, of course, Angela Lansbury.

Saks — Ball wanted him fired, too — insists that he went to Frank Wells, the second in command at Warner Brothers, and begged for a different leading lady. As the director describes it, "Wells asked me, 'Would you take Angela?' and I said, 'In a minute.' So he said, 'Wait a second. Stay here.' "

Wells then went off to see Ted Ashley, the studio's board chairman. When he returned he told Saks, "If we don't do it with Ball, we don't do it. She's the whole reason for the picture."

In fact they would have been better off not doing it at all. "Making it was just a nightmare," Jerry Herman says, and the finished product fits that description. The movie of *Mame* is a professional embarrassment, and it is difficult to imagine an actress's looking more inappropriate or more uncomfortable in a role than Lucille Ball does in this one. As Bea Arthur's agent, Jack Hutto, put it, "The movie was dreadful and Lucy was dreadful. Just awful. Angie thought it would have been a different movie had she been in it, but I'm not so sure." What he meant was that by that point, all Broadway musicals were beginning to look clumsy on film.

Far from blaming Jerry Herman for the disappointment, though, Angela now went ahead with his *Dear World,* which was what the musical version of *The Madwoman of Chaillot* was finally called. She would forever regret canceling the London *Mame,* even though it would also have meant working with Gene Saks, which, as with *Dear World,* may have influenced her decision. She was quite capable of holding a grudge ("If somebody does me wrong, I don't forget it"), and never would overcome her disappointment about the *Mame* movie — or even see it. As for the London *Mame,* Ginger Rogers would ultimately play the role, "which was not a happy experience," associate producer John Bowab remembers. As a sign of Angela's intense identification with *Mame,* she uncharacteristically criticized the Rogers performance, telling a British interviewer, "The New York production was more intimate. I didn't take any theatrical license. I didn't play to the audience. I didn't do any of the things one associates with musical comedy actresses."

Before the start of rehearsals for *Dear World,* Peter and Angela approached its producer, Alexander H. Cohen, with a personal request. They wanted a $50,000 advance against her salary, which was to be $5,000 a week, and a percentage of the weekly gross receipts. It was a considerable jump from the $1,750 a week she'd been paid for *Mame,* but then it was the first time Peter was involved with Angela's management and, Cohen felt, "He negotiated a tough but fair deal." The producer readily conceded, "Peter Shaw is one of the great agents of all time. Sophisticated beyond belief."

Just as the producer was wondering why the Shaws would even have a money shortage, Peter said, "You know Alex, when we got finished with *Mame* we didn't have any real money."

He let Angela explain that the loan was for an investment opportunity. She said that, like many people in show business, they were not financially prudent. "We've always lived kind of hand-to-mouth, although we are certainly very comfortable. Peter has his job and there's no problem, but this is an opportunity we have through Lefkowitz and Company to get into a kind of annuity."

Team that they were, Peter then covered the financial details. That, after all, was his business. All she knew was that "It was mutual funds or something."

Under ordinary circumstances, such a request and the giving of an explanation would have meant unthinkable self-exposure for the intensely private Shaws, but, Angela admits, "Peter and I felt that the family was so important it was worth approaching Alex about it. And it was indeed worth it. That was the beginning of us being able to solidify our financial arrangements."

The Madwoman of Chaillot was certainly an odd choice for a Broadway musical. The Giradoux play is an unsubtle anti-capitalist satire whose title character is the elderly eccentric "Countess Aurelie." The title derives from the bizarre way in which she lives in poverty in the Chaillot district of Paris. Her grotesque appearance certainly makes her look mad, and her cronies are likewise unconventional — a group of relentlessly quaint proletarians who go by such names as The Dishwasher, The Rag Picker, and so on.

The villains of the story are the money folk, likewise labeled as The President, The Broker, The Baron, and, most villainous of all, The Prospector, who is willing to destroy all of Paris in his greedy drilling for oil. These people congregate at the Café Francis near the Place de l'Alma, where the Countess crusades against such avarice. From there, she lures the capitalists to her cellar on the pretext that she has an oil well. Instead, they meet their doom.

This exercise in leftist whimsy was pared down to libretto size by Lawrence and Lee, who had done the job for *Mame,* and Herman provided a musical score that was restrained by Broadway standards. The costumes and settings were exquisitely designed, and Angela was put into appropriately stylized, even grotesque makeup that included wild wigs, huge darkened eyes, and a big crooked nose, all of which rendered her unrecognizable. That was not exactly what her *Mame* fans wanted and the audience let her know its feelings.

> On opening night in Boston, they were furious and practically booed. They were furious with me — *they'd come to see Mame.* They thought I was going to throw my legs around and be that golden girl out there again. And for me to come out looking like this crone was too much. I wasn't afraid of looking like that in the first place, but I sure was convinced that I had to modify my look to bleed some of myself into this character. Otherwise, we weren't going to last for five minutes.

That opening night left her in tears in her dressing room, and the changes came swiftly. Her false nose was modified, and her "Mame" picture was put in the show's advertisements. The director, caught in the crunch, tried a quick fix by converting the chamber-sized piece into a traditional, flashy musical. With that, the show's fate was sealed. Life as the cast knew it was racing toward disaster. The way Jane Connell (again playing alongside Lansbury) put it, "It was around the time that Jackie Kennedy married Aristotle Onassis, and we thought, 'Oh God, the world's going to pieces. Our show's falling apart — and now John Kennedy's wife is marrying *Aristotle Onassis*?' "

Dear World opened on Broadway on February 6, 1969, and while most of the critics disapproved, Rex Reed gave its star the praise he felt was her due. A few days alter, she sent him a note.

> Darling, I've just been read your excruciatingly lovely review. You are a true and wondrous friend, my angel. You inspire me to work harder every moment I am on that stage just to approach the performance you gave me credit for. My love and thanks to you.

In the first few weeks of the Broadway run, there was still hope of making the show a hit simply on the basis of Angela's box office power.

"Wrong as it was," conductor Don Pippin recalls, "Angela worked and worked. Even so, I don't think she ever enjoyed any part of it, to be this wonderful star performing this show, which wasn't easy and wasn't her favorite show by any means."

Dear World closed after only 132 performances, a run of about four months. Angela won the Tony Award as the season's best actress in a musical, as she had for *Mame,* but on Broadway, the play is the thing and this one certainly was not.

Just as Anthony had got his first car, an MG roadster, the previous year, now Deirdre was given a Volkswagen minivan, which was a vehicle of choice among California's youth. That would have been unexceptional in a well-to-do community, but Peter and Angela were increasingly concerned about their particular community. Malibu was becoming a dangerous place for young people. The drug activity that had been growing insidiously in recent years, and had been kept secret by the guilty, the confused, the self-deceptive, or the simply frightened, was now surfacing. More and more youngsters were in trouble, and their parents were confounded by this unprecedented plague. Angela, hoping that Germany would put real distance between this threat and her children, took both Deirdre and Anthony along with her when she left to spend three months in Fussen, making the movie *Something for Everyone.* The conditions could not have been more desirable, for the film was shooting in a stunning summertime location in the midst of a couple of glorious castles looking down the Bavarian mountainside to a sparkling lake.

Here was a starring movie role at last, although the movie would finally have more of a Broadway feel than a cinematic one. *Something for Everyone* was being made by Harold S. Prince, an acclaimed stage director who had never before made a film. The forty-year-old Prince was a man of essential New York sophistication, stylishly informal in his blazer and pressed jeans. Yet for all his urbanity and success, he was a straightforward individual who would frankly admit, "I'm a theater man. I'm learning about movies on the spot. I never had the desire or the time to learn the craft."

Prince armed himself with a first-class cinematographer and editor, but his script was written by a Broadway playwright (Hugh Wheeler) who was equally inexperienced. The source was a novel called *The Cook,* written by Harry Kressing; the story is set in postwar Germany, where the beautiful and arch Countess von Ornstein lives in opulent poverty. Her home is merely the fairy-tale Neuchwanstein castle, the original cost of which — in real life — nearly broke the royal bank of Bavaria (although the place ultimately returned a handsome profit in tourist revenues). The countess's negligees are exquisite, she has strawberries for breakfast, and the castle is falling apart. Symbols of postwar emptiness and cultural decadence are everywhere. The character herself is yet another bitchy and venal mother with no husband and a gay son.

A penniless but wily and sexy stranger (Michael York) insinuates himself into the household and embarks upon a campaign of seduction, violence, and, finally, murder in order to take power over its members. Bisexual and thoroughly amoral, he gets as far as an engagement with the countess, but her mousy daughter ultimately blackmails him into marrying her instead. The story's mordant irony is typical of postwar German literature.

Lansbury is excellent as the countess and looks beautiful, yet, for all its attention to scenery and costumes, the picture is more verbal than visual, and develops holding power only late in the game. *Something for Everyone* also ends up focusing, probably mistakenly, more on the Michael York character than on Angela's. As her friend Rex Reed correctly points out, "It may be about York, but she still dominates every scene she's in." She succeeds in doing so with dialogue that is at times self-conscious ("When your world has gone, you're your own ghost") or strained ("These are the bad news days"). Other speeches are simply difficult to read ("Common and caution are two words which have never been and I hope never will be applied to me"). It is a curious picture, then, as its British title — *Black Flowers for the Bride* — suggests, but it remains one of Lansbury's own favorites.

In the filming of it, she sometimes grew impatient with Prince's inexperience as a director. If there is ever any area in which she can be short-tempered, it is in regard to professional expertise. When, for instance, she forgot her lines during a scene, Prince shouted, "Cut!" She glared at him as he stood beside the camera. In the chiding tone of a schoolmarm, she said, "Why are you cutting? I'm fine. Just keep going and I'll find it again."

That was the way it was done in the movies but not in the theater. There, Prince points out, "If you don't get the dialogue right, you start again from the beginning." But in filmmaking, he soon realized, "all these professionals, they even talk to the camera while it's rolling. They don't worry about their voices being recorded, or the film being wasted." Brilliant onstage, he would never seem comfortable behind a camera.

The situation was exactly the reverse — much professionalism but little artistic sensibility — in the next Lansbury picture, in which she was also featured in a starring role, this time for Walt Disney's Buena Vista company. This studio produced technically flawless, G-rated pictures that supported whatever was meant by "family values." Impersonal in their sheen, vulgar in their sentimentality, they seemed to be dependably profitable.

Bedknobs and Broomsticks was palpably a Disney attempt to clone *Mary Poppins,* which had been a great success for the studio and its star, Julie Andrews. *Bedknobs and Broomsticks* is likewise British in setting and tone and involves children with a quirky nanny figure; it also has a score by the *Mary Poppins* team of songwriters. As a singing and dancing apprentice witch, Angela is game at best, but uncharacteristically detached from the material at hand. At times she seems downright bored with the picture, and is virtually blank-faced during a long stretch of stupid animated action late in the proceedings. But the picture was a great commercial hit and Angela is partial to it, saying, "it secured an enormous audience for me."

The spiffy yellow Mercedes-Benz convertible was one of a pair of identical models that she and Harold Prince had bought while making *Something for Everyone.* She carefully backed it out of the Malibu driveway and set out with Moyna for the Paramount Pictures lot. It was a bright but unusually windy afternoon in September of 1970, and they had a lunch date with Angela's brother Bruce. Afterward, driving home on the Pacific Coast Highway with the top down, she noticed an acrid smell in the air. As she approached the traffic lights at the Malibu intersection, she could see the flashing beacons of police cruisers. Slowing to a stop, she got out of the car and asked a state trooper what the problem was. He told her that there were brush fires ahead, a not uncommon occurrence after southern California's dry summers. She could feel the warm wind in her face and knew, "When we get the Santa Ana winds in the fall, *watch out!*"

Now the highway was closed to all traffic except fire engines.

"Our house is up there," she pleaded with the trooper, pointing toward the bluffs along the ocean side of the highway. "I've got to get my animals out. That smoke could hurt them."

She could see a "huge ball of smoke" in the distance.

That would be impossible, he said. Although the Pacific Coast Highway was closed to northbound traffic, she talked him into letting her turn west, toward the Pacific. From there she was able to drive north along the old Malibu Road. She parked below the house and told Moyna to wait. Then, using trees and brush as handholds, she scrambled her way up the steep incline, which was "not an easy task, let me tell you," she recalls. "I had to claw my way up, but it's extraordinary what we can do under the stress of a situation, and I had to get to the house."

Her home was deserted and still. She figured that Anthony was surfing, but in fact he was up by Mulholland Drive, overlooking Los Angeles, stretched out on the mountainside, he remembers, "with three sports cars and twelve guys." Deirdre, she remembered, was "up north with her friends and her minivan and her dog, George." Angela knew, then, that the only animal in need of rescue was Nosey, the cat, and as she walked through the house in search of it, everything was so serene that she thought, "Well, the fire's not going to happen." To be on the safe side, though, she packed all of Moyna's clothes into a suitcase ("because I thought she didn't have a lot of money to replace her clothes — isn't that strange?"). It was so quiet that she could even hear the dryer "spinning and clicking" in the kitchen, "and it was all kind of still and perfect and lovely."

She found a note from the cleaning lady. "I'm leaving early today. See you tomorrow," and was calmed by the normalcy of the message. "The house is going to be all right," she thought with relief. "The wind is going to change, and the firefighters will stop the flames before they hop the highway." She knew that the Pacific Coast Highway was her ribbon of protection from autumn brush fires, for the flames would have to jump all four lanes of that highway to ignite her side of it. Even so, she telephoned Peter at the office to alert him, "You've got to come out. There is a bad fire, and it's coming this way. The chances are it won't hop the highway and get us, but I think you should be around."

Peter said that he would leave right away, and they agreed to meet at the Malibu traffic lights on the Pacific Coast Highway, where the Mayfair Market was. He ran down to his car, and "shot back."

Still on Mulholland, Anthony was suddenly aware that he was looking at "this wall — we're on the top, looking at the valley — this wall of fire coming towards us. It's forty or fifty miles away, but the winds are *howling*." With that, the boys' mountainside reverie was abruptly shaken, and they roused themselves and hurried to their cars. "Everyone took off," Anthony says. "It was plain fear. Everybody went to their homes. We all lived around Malibu. I drove off with a friend, and took the back roads to my house because the Pacific Coast Highway was closed off."

He arrived home to find only his mother there, and she told him and his friend that Moyna was sitting in the car, down at the bottom of the hill, and that they had to drive her there to get her car so that she could get to the Malibu lights to meet Peter. She grabbed Nosey the cat and they fled.

Up north, Deirdre heard the news about the fires and immediately headed home in her minivan. Meanwhile, her father managed to get permission to drive back up the highway to the house, and by then, the fire had indeed begun to jump the highway. Pulling the car over, he and Angela could see that the flames were rolling inexorably toward their house, the blaze whipped along by the raging wind. Fire engines were racing up the highway. "We weren't able to get any of them to stop," Angela says. "We felt literally like lying down in the roadway and saying, 'Please stop. Please come wet down the house.'" When one of the engines did stop, a fireman told her that they couldn't do that. "If we stop and wet down one house, six other houses would go in that time."

Getting back into the car, Angela and Peter sped up the access road to Corymore, which, Peter could see, "was already beginning to smolder. There was no danger yet," he says, "but the winds were amazing."

The two of them dragged what they could from the house, throwing it all into the swimming pool. Southern Californians learn such things, accustomed as they are to nature's critical rhythms, like autumn brushfires and periodic earthquakes. Peter grabbed a small picture of Angela, painted by an artist friend, Paul Clemens, and threw it, too, into the pool. Then they fled to the adjacent lot.

There they watched as Corymore, their island in the sky, burned to the ground.

"We just stood and stared," she says. "The heat was unbelievable. The bricks of the chimney and a couple of brick walls just melted. Even all the metal melted from the heat, until there was nothing left."

Only moments after they had departed, Anthony and his friend returned to the house. "The fire was coming fast," he could see. "It was still about five miles away, but you could hardly see anything else because the wind was so powerful. It was coming in from the ocean and blowing everything toward us." The brush was already catching fire. "There was a lot of brittle eucalyptus," he says, "and there was all this dry tumbleweed, thick with fire, floating through the air, blowing up toward the house. It would light a tree just by the gust of the wind."

The two of them got it into their heads that "we're going to save the house. We'll get some blankets and wet them down in the swimming pool." After that, they figured, they would "walk up the driveway with them."

They proceeded to do just that, holding the blankets out in front of them. "We were thinking that we were going to literally *stop the fire*."

Before they could even see the fire at the edge of their property, though, "the blankets disintegrated from the heat. The wind was blowing a hundred miles an hour," Anthony was certain. "We stood there, and then our shirts went on fire. And we turned up there at the top of the driveway — we turned and ran for the ocean."

As they hurtled down the side of the cliff toward the highway, the trees on all sides of them were engulfed in flames. "The actual fire hadn't got there yet," he says, "but the trees caught fire from the heat and the flying embers."

Still they kept running, "running down from the house, and then everything was on fire, everywhere we ran. It must be what napalm fires are like. And we kept running, down, down the hill, with the fire all around us."

When they got to the Old Malibu Road, they fled across it, and still the fire followed, jumping the road after them. They pulled up short at the barbed wire that fenced off the beach. There was no choice but to climb over it, for they both knew that the only safe place now was the ocean, for even the beach houses along the old Malibu Road were aflame. Scaling the fence, they dropped down on the other side and fled down the beach, into the water. "The smell of smoke was so thick," Anthony says, "that you could only breathe about an inch and a half over the water, where there was oxygen. So we literally had to go parallel to the shore for about a mile in the water. Down to where — at the Malibu colony where the Mayfair Market was — you could finally come back to shore."

"It was," Angela would later say, "what they call a firestorm."

CHAPTER 15

IRELAND

BY THE TIME Deirdre got home, she found only smoldering remains. "All that was left," she says, "were ashes and two Harley Davidsons."

Emerging from the ocean, Anthony walked toward the Mayfair Market. With all the soot-blackened, woebegone, formerly poised souls milling about in front of the store, it seemed to him that "the place looked like the Red Cross in a war movie." In the parking lot, the animal lovers huddled around their fire-frightened horses and dogs, those they'd been able to rescue from the tidal wave of flames. An eerie silence lay over the scene, but with no trees around the lot, it was at least a safe place, one of the few that the blaze could not reach.

Inside the haven, from the checkout area through the aisles and in every food section, the market was crowded with well-to-do refugees. It looked to Anthony as if "everybody from Malibu was gathered there," and he peeled off what shreds of wet clothing remained. "Everything had been burnt off anyway" but nobody seemed to care, or even notice as he walked through the store, looking for friends or family.

* * *

After the fires were quelled, the entire family — Peter, Angela, David, Anthony, Deirdre, and Moyna — moved in with Bruce and his wife, until John Bryson, a *Life* magazine photographer, let the Shaws use his place while he was away on assignment. Eventually they rented a house from Bob Hope's son, Tony. Their nomadic existence seemed to suit the hellish atmosphere.

Firestorm has a biblical resonance, as if this had been a storm to ravage a decadent landscape and force a clean start. If so, then it was a mundane Gomorrah that had been razed, merely Malibu and the mindless hedonism it symbolized. Danger, however, is not always exotic and Angela understood exactly how menacing the place was, and how confused were its people, flailing as they vainly sought to help their drug-plagued children. "We could see," she said, "that no matter what the approach, these young people, including many of Anthony's friends, were dying of overdoses. Some of them had parents who were churchgoing people. Some of those children were in 4-H clubs. It did not alter their inability to resist this enormous temptation.

"Even the son of our next-door-neighbors — and those people were rough, tough parents. They literally abused their children to stop them from doing drugs. It didn't stop them. And they died. So many died.

"Even the son of the principal of the school."

As for the loss of her "island in the sky," Angela would never recover from that. "It was a huge family tragedy," she says. "It rocked all of us." Such was this moment in time for Angela Lansbury, star of stage and screen.

Grim, then, was her mood, and grim her homeless state, when she left California to, of all things, start work on another Broadway musical. Given the weird contrast between the harrowing reality of their loss and the song and dance of her work, the new show was appropriately bizarre. In the words of the librettist, Bob Merrill, it was "the story of a Southern woman who becomes alcoholic and schizophrenic, desperately blocking out the sins of a brutal husband/law officer, suddenly deceased."

Adapted from *Prettybelle,* by the gifted novelist Jean Martin, it was a story to make *Anyone Can Whistle* seem like *The Sound of Music.* Angela's role was that of the title character who, aside from being a psychotic drinker is, in the bargain, also a nymphomaniac and a prostitute.

Like *Whistle,* the new show had ambitious and unconventional intentions, as well as a creative team of established Broadway figures — in this case, the composer Jule Styne, the lyricist/librettist Merrill, and the director/choreographer Gower Champion. However, as the courtly producer, Alexander H. Cohen, readily conceded, "Let's face it, the three of them weren't intellectual heavyweights." They certainly were not in the brainy category of *Whistle's* Sondheim, Laurents, and Ross.

Nevertheless, the start of a new show is always a time of hope, and rehearsals of *Prettybelle* began, like those of any production, with the feeling that another *My Fair Lady* was in the making. It also, like any Angela Lansbury show, began with a diet. "I was never a big eater," she says, "but I can sit down and eat cheese and French bread and butter and consume vast amounts of calories. Or ice cream! And big quantities of meat. A ten-ounce steak. When somebody weighs a hundred and thirty pounds, they shouldn't eat a ten-ounce steak. You need a four-ounce steak."

Yet, she found losing weight to be as easy as gaining it.

> I have a very strong will but I cheat. I do all the things that dieters do. But finally, I do do it and I get a great kick out of it. For *Prettybelle,* I knew that I had to dance for Gower Champion, and I had to dance in a slip, with my legs exposed and everything. I really had to be in very beautiful shape from the neck down. And I devised a way of getting it off. I made up this concoction of egg, protein powder, orange juice, and a banana. That was my breakfast. For lunch I'd make a sandwich and have a good dinner. I wasn't concerned about fat, so much as about starch. It was the whole grains and all that. But I couldn't stay on a diet longer than three weeks, so finally I devised a style of eating over the long run. You don't eat anything but fruit until noon, and then you have a lunch of vegetable and whole grain. Then have a small amount of meat for protein. That's basically what it is. And that works very very well.

Prettybelle was not esoteric, just disastrous — notwithstanding Merrill's lofty intention of transferring to a stage the "techniques and abstractions in avant-garde films." The show's director, Gower Champion, was famously gifted, but he was also a famous eccentric whose eccentricity now outdid itself. Cohen, the producer, puts it bluntly: "He was a dictator and a fascist, and he had strange sexual alliances. First [his wife] Marge, then a girl in the show, then a guy in the show. And he wouldn't let anyone into rehearsal, wouldn't even speak to anyone about it."

Of course, all of this would be considered simply colorful if the show were a hit. However, as *Prettybelle* started previews in its Boston tryout, late in January 1971, the audiences at the Shubert Theater derided and hissed it. They began with the cheerful opening number ("Manic Depressives"), and by the final curtain, it seemed to producer Cohen that they "loathed every minute of Angie and the show." She told Dolores Childers, her dresser, "I'm not going to let them bring it into New York unless it's fixed."

The opportunity to fix them is precisely why musicals have out-of-town engagements, but when even the producer cringes every time the curtain rises, little can be done. The Boston critics were almost as abusive as the audiences, and when Cohen went backstage to tell Angela of his decision to close the show at the end of the week, she threw her arms around his neck in gratitude.

After the final performance and into the dawn, Rex Reed drove Angela back to New York. They stopped only for gas and to eat fried clams at a Howard Johnson's restaurant at three o'clock in the morning. She was plainly depressed. As her brother Edgar said, "It was a tough stretch for her, first *Dear World* and then *Prettybelle*." He was himself sitting on top of a huge hit as co-producer of the musical *Godspell,* but he had compassion for his sister, and admiration for her ability to maintain performing standards even with failing shows. "It's difficult to give everything you've got, every night, and still know that the production isn't working."

The two flops notwithstanding, she herself had "no sense" of being in a jinx zone. "I always figure that it was the material's failure, not mine. I know that Hal [Prince] thought *Prettybelle* was some of the best work I had ever done in the theater, and it probably was, but it was just an unfortunate root idea for a musical."

There were more important matters on her mind, however. Home and family were, as always, at the center of her consciousness, and she felt driven to make a new home, one removed from southern California and its threat to her children. "I've got to snatch them away from this," she thought. "Nothing else matters. We've got to get out, and it has to be as far from Malibu as we can get." As she remembers, "After the burning of our house, the house that was Corymore, I got on an airplane and flew to the place where I as a child had flown to get away from the unhappiness and loss of my father.

"Flown to innocence."

That was the meaning of Ireland for her.

Anthony asked her to take him along, but she was being deliberate about this trip, and cautiously told him, "Let me go ahead and pave the way." As if operating on blind maternal instinct, she seemed impelled to "find that earth base which I had suddenly lost in the fire. "It meant a brief abandonment of her family and an indefinite sabbatical from her career, but she accepted these conditions. She was even prepared to give up her career entirely, if need be. ("I was quite prepared to stop.") For she knew she had to give weight to the family side of the balance board. To do that, she first had to be secure within herself, and she believed, perhaps even mystically, that she would find that security in Ireland.

> I wanted to get away to one last piece of peaceful green earth again after living in cities and chaos so many years. I wanted to see the bogs and the hills again, and after the fire wiped us out I wanted to start life over again in an uncluttered way and live a simple life.

Peter did not join her immediately. He had a job, and besides, whether or not the idea was fashionable, she considered homemaking to be woman's work. It was her specialty, and so this, she says, was the "one great area where he allowed me to have my head. He gave me the permission to go to Ireland and find a house, any house, because like me, he was so concerned about the children. So he gave me leave, and I did it."

She did not know what kind of house she was looking for, only "to create a place of safety and warmth for my family." It had to be a place where she could garden. "It had to do with my desire to be part of the earth." And a big kitchen was a necessity. "Food and making food for people is so pleasureful. It gives people who come a good sense of coziness and home to sit down to a terrific meal of just wonderful food. Chicken, meat loaf, lamb chops, stews. Good fresh mushroom soup, vegetable soups."

Once in Ireland, she rented a Morris Mini-Minor and set out for Achill Island, her childhood Eden. The winter was barely over, the landscape barren, "and the winds of March were howling" as she headed directly for the village of Keel, where she had gone as a child with her sister, Isolde.

The place had not changed in any significant way. Except for being a little smaller and somewhat seedier, the Amethyst Hotel was much as she remembered, "sort of wind-washed, artistic and charming," with Thea Boyd, "a bit older but the same," still running the place. Thea rustled up a hot meal and then showed the weary traveler to a long, narrow room. Saying good night, she provided a hot water bottle, "which," Angela remembers, "burst in the bed, making it wet and cold."

That first night, she slept in her clothes while the gale outside came off the sea to batter the shutters of the little room. By the light of day, there was an even greater contrast between the simple Amethyst Hotel and the lush southern California she had left. "There was this filthy old kitchen downstairs," Angela says, "where Thea kept these great pots of stuff on the back of the stove — all the time — to reheat them and make gravy and stews." Filthy or not, she felt it could not have been more perfect.

It was time to start the house hunt, and to suit the task, she bought a Renault Four "for practically nothing." After a week at the Amethyst, she moved to a considerably more luxurious country inn, Ballymaloe ("ballymaloo") House, in the village of Shanagarry in southeast Cork. Then she began criss-crossing the countryside.

The search would end near Cork, that much she had already decided. Cork is a medium-sized port city on the River Lee, by her description a "grimy and industrial" city. "On first sight," she admits, "you think it's a 'redbrick city,' but it has a kind of wonderful charm and it grows on you." It would take three months, this search for a new home, but fifteen miles north of Shanagarry, near the village of Conna, she found what she was looking for, a property called Knockmourne Glebe (*knockmourne* means "high place" in Gaelic). It was, she says, "in the most extraordinarily beautiful part of County Cork."

The site was a full twenty acres, with a five-acre field in front and the fifteen remaining acres facing on the River Bride, and it came with two barns. The house itself was an old stone Gregorian rectory that had been built in 1825 for a minister of the Church of Ireland. It was a house, Angela says, "like the ones you draw when you are a child, with two rooms upstairs and two downstairs and a door in the center. You even had to crank the telephone to get the lady who was the telephone operator in the post office."

It was important and good to her that these basic stone walls were smooth and clean enough to be left bare with the plaster removed, and that these rooms were "all the same size." She was also ravished by the property.

"The most beautiful trees, elm trees, oak trees, enormous trees three hundred years old, and a marvelous old-fashioned Victorian garden."

> I am what they call "an earth person." I'm very rooted to the ground as far as my physical being is concerned. My mental being can soar and fly and imagine and I use that, but to enable me to do that, I've found that I need to be very much in touch with the soil, the ground, with growing things, with very basic, rather boring creature comforts: a home, an environment that is warm and encompassing — not just for myself but for all those that I love; my family around me.

So she telephoned Peter and said, "I've found the house I think we should buy. I'm going to put a down payment on it and send you a photograph." She told him that it was going to cost $50,000.

Money is a difficult subject with almost any couple in almost any circumstances, but Angela felt that she and Peter handled it well. In this case, he simply said, "It's your money," but it would not be quite so simple. Once the house was purchased, her husband grew very interested in how much the remodeling was going to cost, and between such tasks as rebuilding the cellar and creating what Angela considered "a dream kitchen," it was going to cost a great deal.

His interest was not just economic. Peter's was a double-edged sensibility, a macho man's and an agent's, which added up to a double dose of domination. It had been different earlier, when the children were growing up, but he had since turned assertive, and his current springboard was the spending on this house. Angela says, "He felt that I trusted people too much, that I was too openhanded. He wanted to be sure I wasn't 'done in.'"

But it was hard to control the situation from eight thousand miles away, and she knew her independence wasn't easy for him. "When I went there," she says, "I literally decided that I was going to start a new life for us, and I did it without Peter. That was rather difficult for him to go along with. He went along, but he made a few waves along the way."

The extensive renovations finally got under way, an anticipated three months' worth. In the meanwhile, Angela lived in a prefabricated cottage on the edge of the property, facing the road. It had two bedrooms, a living room, and a kitchen, and she bought a few pieces of furniture "to make it cozy." By the time Peter came over, the work on the house was well underway. He had only seen the house in photographs, and he certainly did not know how much or even precisely what it meant to her; just that it meant a lot. Her pleasure in it was apparently enough for him.

Then, the whole family moved in. Angela found Deirdre a job as a waitress at Ballymaloe House, which had an acclaimed restaurant with its own cooking school, and Anthony would also be working there as a bar assistant. She herself plunged happily into "the adventure of creating this home." In its walled garden, she discovered that just about anything could thrive. "We planted every kind of vegetable, and every kind of fruit. Loganberries on the wall, black currants, gooseberries, raspberries. It was an absolute dream world, and everyone was going to learn how to cook properly."

Peter, meantime, "wanted to put in his twopennyworth and be part of the redesigning," which created a conflict, because she felt very territorial about her homes.

> He made some waves about my going ahead with certain people to do the work on the house. I'd had to entrust certain things to new friends that he didn't know. It was a little tricky. He would get annoyed and uptight. Peter can get very, very angry. His sense of ownership is tremendous. He has a very strong sense of ownership and responsibility. And he doesn't want anyone else usurping or taking his position in any decisions that I make.

"Once we got over that hump," she says, "he threw himself into the house, got into the garden and landscaping and rock hauling and making rose gardens for me. He was doing everything possible to make the children happy.

"That was our quest."

He was also adapting to a new life of his own, becoming, as Angela puts it, "a country gentleman. It was an adjustment but, God bless him, he did it," and she slipped comfortably into the role of country wife.

Anthony was expressing interest in becoming an actor, and his mother suggested that he apply to Webber-Douglas, where she'd studied as a girl. When she had to go to London to promote the English release of *Bedknobs and Broomsticks,* she suggested that he follow her over, and they would visit the drama school together.

It was now some ten months since she had come to Ireland. For the first time in her adult life, she had not been working steadily; in fact, she had not worked for more than a year when Peter Hall, the eminent director of England's Royal Shakespeare Company, offered her a lead role in Edward Albee's play *All Over.* In addition to its summer Shakespeare productions at Stratford-Upon-Avon, Hall's company presented a winter season for contemporary plays at the Aldwych Theatre in London's West End. These were performed in "rotating repertory," that is to say, alternately. It meant that Angela would only have to play three performances a week.

She mulled it over. Anthony had been accepted at Webber-Douglas and was living in London. "He had this real desire to become an actor, and I was delighted. I knew it was a hard row to hoe, but he already had the basics — he was an enormously attractive young guy, and he had a very good speaking voice."

Isolde, too, was in London. If Angela accepted the offer and agreed to do the Albee play, the sisters could begin to make up for all the years apart. Back in Ireland, Deirdre was settled in, waiting on tables at Ballymaloe House, and Peter was there to keep her company. It seemed to be the ideal opportunity to make a British stage debut, and "in an auspicious way," she thought. "Besides," she rationalized, "it'll cost me only twenty-five quid to fly from Cork." She had never outgrown the thrift learned in childhood.

All Over had been a failure on Broadway, but Angela regarded Edward Albee as a prestigious playwright, and in any case, most actors tend to separate the role from the play. They see the whole as the director's concern, and of less interest to them than the individual parts. Angela, being in so many ways the archetypal actor, shared more of this attitude than she cared to admit, although she did concede that "the big lure was the opportunity to work with the great Peggy Ashcroft," and so she began her return to acting. "I didn't go there as an American movie actress, or a star of Broadway musicals. I went there," she says, "to prove my mettle as an English stage actress. This was terribly important to me, my first play in England, first play on the West End, first outing with the English critics. It was vitally important for me to make it; to be accepted by them as a bona fide stage actress."

She found a flat in Pont Street, in London's fashionable Belgravia section, and with Isolde's assistance, began work on the script. "She helped me immeasurably, just learning this difficult text."

"Difficult" was perhaps an understatement. As succinctly described by the British critic John Barber, *All Over* was set "in the master bedroom of an ornate home. In a four-poster bed lies the dying master, a man of wealth, success, and power. Seated around, in deathbed watch, are his wife, his mistress, his best friend, his son and daughter. They talk about themselves, they barb each other. Most malicious is the deserted wife, faithful after fifty years. . . . She vents her bitterness on her son, a confessed failure, and her wretched daughter. Her venom drives both from the room more than once."

At rehearsal's start, none of the cast had a clue as to what the point of the drama was, or even what the characters were talking about. "With Albee," Angela says, "half the time, you don't know what the words mean." The playwright was present at rehearsals, but when queried, would only answer that there was no "ulterior" meaning to the play. When asked directly what it meant, he said, "Well, I don't know. What do *you* think it means?"

Angela was "rather frightened by somebody like Edward Albee — I'm not smart enough for him." She soon realized, in any case, that "Edward didn't really want to carry on that kind of conversation with me. He preferred to gossip."

That *All Over* was supposed to be *meaningful* was obvious enough, since the characters had descriptions for names. Angela was playing The Mistress, Dame Peggy Ashcroft The Wife, and so on. But when rehearsals were finished, on the eve of the premiere, Angela stepped out from the ranks of actors who, in intellectual insecurity and emotional need, bow in trust to the presumably superior intelligence of playwrights and directors. Fully confident, she asked Peter Hall directly, "Where the hell are we with this play?" The only thing he could say was, "Just play it for all you're worth. Just give it everything you've got. That's all I can tell you. Make of it what you feel."

Such paternalism no longer carried any weight with her, and she knew, then, that "Peter was just as flummoxed as all of us players were."

A play's incomprehensibility is not necessarily a shortcoming. Ambiguity is a perfectly respectable literary device and can be very effective when cleverly used, as it is by such playwrights as Harold Pinter and David Mamet. Were such ambiguity Albee's conscious intention, he ought to have communicated that fact to his actors, so that they might play his lines accordingly. Lansbury and her fellow players, deprived of such guidance, were sent out before an audience to play characters whose dialogue simply made no sense.

How is that done? Brave as the bravest of actors, Angela considers it "surprisingly possible to make something seem interesting even when you don't understand it. You *sing* the words. That's what happens. You make the words sing and keep the audience's attention."

This is the sort of courage that gives actors such charm, and makes them so admirable and beloved.

Acting in *All Over* with Dame Peggy appealed directly to Angela's theatrical upbringing. Having been away from the serious stage for ten years while she played the musical comedy star, she was returning not merely to her British roots but to her dramatic ones as well. As she focused her energies upon the work, she soon felt as if she'd never been away. It seems to her that "in other professions, people do so many other things at the same time as their specific job. But most ladies of the theater who have big roles to play actually spend most of the day getting ready. I've known people to stay in bed all day. And sometimes I'm inclined to want to do just that, and not open my mouth. Certain jobs require this kind of dedication."

Acting took concentration, but sometimes even she felt she overdid it. "I have perhaps an oversense of responsibility about what I'm doing," she acknowledges. "And not to fail. Not to be less than my best. I'm driven by the desire to do it right. I don't think of it as professionalism. It's an absolute requirement for me, personally. I'm taken aback when actors put their personal lives first. This is a tricky thing for me to say. I might be accused of not paying attention to my family because I was so busy being professional. But I don't believe I could be found guilty of that. I always made provisions that everything was taken care of, and I was always on the end of the phone — in my dressing room — available to the kids.

"But when it comes to the actual acting work, I guess I'm a bit of a bore. No, not boring. I guess I set a very high example, so people are very intimidated by the fact that here's this woman who's prepared to work her butt off to get something right. And they're expected to do the same, and sometimes they don't have the same vested interest as I do. When one's the star of the show, one does take that responsibility as the star. When you get ten percent of the gross, you take on a lot of responsibility, and you feel it very strongly. The responsibility is to the producers, the audience, and to my fellow players. That's part of the deal. And it includes getting to bed early and eating the proper food. And not drinking. And when you're a singer, all you worry about is your voice. Ask Julie Andrews, or Liza. That's all we talk about. In the morning, you sing a high note good and loud, just to see if your voice is still there. And sometimes you wonder, because you really killed yourself onstage the night before, and you think, 'Oh God, I blew it. I won't have a voice tomorrow.'

"I probably take my professional responsibility many, many steps too far. If I'm asked, 'How can you hang on these many, many years? How can you produce what's needed at any given time,' I answer, only by concentrating on that one thing: To do it well."

All Over opened on January 31, 1972, and while the play itself was all but physically assaulted, her own reviews were excellent. Irving Wardle of the *London Times,* for instance, dismissed the piece as "ponderous" and "banal," but gave Lansbury credit for "expressive variety" and "tactical brilliance." Whatever that meant, the main point was that Lansbury had made good in her hometown, and that achievement meant a lot to her. Moreover, working in a classical British company with the likes of Dame Peggy, and being directed by Peter Hall, restored to her the classical acting tradition for which she'd been trained.

> The British actor takes risks, does things on stage that I've never seen an American actor do. Except a few. There are a handful — John Malkovich, John Lithgow, Frank Langella — they are the exceptions, and only a few more. Meryl Streep is an extraordinary actress, a British type of actress and I love it that she's got a huge family. She spends time with them. She's had a marriage and children, a whole life. . . . But these are the only ones in the American group who take the kind of chances and perform in a style that I consider parallel to the British theater. But for instance, Woody Allen, he has his own persona. He's quite short and because of that he has to take roles which play into that, so he's going to be attracted to all those kind of strange out-of-the-ordinary characters. He has evolved totally his own style and he brings that to everything he does. Mind you, I do admire him. He's created a person that he plays and does it in a fascinating way. Just like Michael Gambon in England. He's always himself, too, but he's very good at being *successfully theatrical.* And in the same way, so is Pacino. He's an original actor. He's a good example of an American actor.

Once she gets started on American movie actors, she is not afraid to express her opinion. "Take Kevin Costner," she says.

> Now I think Kevin is a very good actor, but I think because he's a man — well, it's very difficult for male performers not to

allow their own personas to leap very largely into everything they do, finally. Because they become so *aware* of their personal magnetism with an audience and the fans and the crowds and the women, it is quite difficult for them to not fall into the trap of suddenly playing that person rather than playing a character.

I think of seeing Kevin in *The Untouchables.* I went to the first performance in New York. He and Sean Connery were in the lobby, kind of greeting people, and I remember walking up to him and saying, "You know, you have an enormous future. You are stunning in this picture." Because I knew that he did have that future. I think he's wobbled because his own ego got in the way of him. But he does some very good work, and some not-so-good work, which we all do.

Also, there are choices of material. That is very, very difficult for actors and actresses. And the bigger you get, the more difficult it is. I think Tom Cruise has been extraordinary in his ability to find material. He's got a hell of a good crowd around him who are bringing him terrifically interesting scripts. And he's trying to grow. I was terribly worried about some of these young actors. Because I felt that they were going to run out of steam and there wouldn't be anything to replace those initial great roles. Tom Cruise, I think, is the golden boy — in my estimation.

When the engagement of the Albee play was completed and the commuting between Cork and London came to an end, Angela resumed her Irish earth-mothering, tending to the garden and keeping house. That life was keyed to the fundamentals. Whether she was dealing with linens, flowers, or cream, she dug into the details with relish, and with a commitment equal to that of her actress self.

The cream in Europe is so different from in America. Because they don't whip everything. They have what they call "pouring cream," which is thick cream that comes out of a bottle. Very, very high butterfat content, but it's the real thing. If you're serving a summer pudding — late summer fruits done with bread in a bowl and then turned out served with that kind of cream — I mean there is nothing on this earth that is more delicious. Gen-

> erally berries. And some apple for filler. If you use too much it counts against you. That kind of cooking is a combination of the best English, the best French, but it's all provincial cooking. It's not what you would call gourmet cooking, but it *is* gourmet cooking, of course, because it's sort of *high provincial.*

She even doted on her cooking equipment, hopping over to London for "the great kitchen shops" in Sloane Square. She threw out all of her aluminum pots and pans and replaced them with stainless steel. She decided that good cooking started with good ingredients, and made everything "from scratch. I wouldn't use anything that came out of a can. It was sort of ridiculous in a way, except it wasn't. I learned to make bread. I learned to make mousses. I would only use fresh eggs. I got cream at the creamery."

Deirdre was inspired by her mother's industry. Angela had already taught her to cook, but now the twenty-year-old was learning what Angela describes as "seriously high provincial" cuisine where she worked. Ballymaloe House was owned by the Allen family, and according to Angela, "Myrtle Allen was really the premier cook in Ireland. She was single-handedly responsible for raising the standard of Irish cooking." Myrtle was not only letting Deirdre watch her work; she was letting the young woman attend classes at the Ballymaloe Cookery School.

But just as everything seemed to be humming happily along, the contentment of the Shaws was suddenly threatened when an offer arrived from America.

CHAPTER 16

SCREAMING AND YELLING

THE OFFER was one that Peter considered irresistible, a three-month, summertime tour of *Mame* through an East Coast circuit of music tents. Angela, however, could hardly have been less interested. She was leading an idyllic family existence, singing "That's Amore" while making beds and scrubbing floors, cooking and mending and fussing and digging shoulder to shoulder with "the most wonderful gardener."

> He was an old man called Paddy O'Brien who had worked on this garden from the time he was a lad. He was rather particular about where he worked and who he worked for, and he wasn't about to come just because I offered to pay him. I wooed him over by asking him to trim the apple trees, there were a lot of apple trees, so he did. And I think he sort of liked the idea of this madwoman who'd moved into this house which he liked, and this garden that he'd known all his life, so he came to work for me. He had no idea who I was. Nobody there did. I was just Mrs. Shaw, which suited me down to the ground. I had absolute anonymity in those days, which was wonderful.

She found it perfectly satisfying, the ordinariness of this life and the regularity of it. That was much more gratifying to her, and it was certainly more important than a *Mame* tour, but Peter disagreed, and he was now in charge of her management. She had convinced him, after long stretches of separation and constant commuting that, for the sake of the marriage, it would make sense for him to quit the agency business. "We would be centered in Ireland," was her idea. "Pete would remain with me and be my business manager, because it had been a bad situation. I'd been in Ireland for months, and he'd been in Los Angeles. So we put our eggs in one basket."

Now he was being insistent about the *Mame* tour, telling her, "You're crazy if you don't do it. This is your great role. This is a chance to make a lot of money."

She knew that assuming financial responsibility was *his* great role, but she also felt he was pushing the tour merely because of the money. "Peter wants to keep the numbers going. I couldn't care less. Well, I do care — I can be a pretty good businesswoman, too — but I know that enough is enough, sometimes."

She did give him credit for having a motivation beyond mere profit. He was concerned about the considerable amounts of money that had been spent buying and remodeling the house. She was certainly aware of the costs, but she was also sure that there was no crisis. "We weren't wildly well fixed but we were okay. We didn't need to do the tour, I didn't think."

So now there was a conflict in Paradise, and it was over the same issue that had caused trouble in Malibu, when *A Taste of Honey* came up: Angela's leaving the homestead and going back to work. This time, however, the friction between these two extremely civilized people was about as hot as it could get. It was exacerbated by Peter's irritability over his hip, which was bothering him so badly that he was wincing while walking, and he moved around with a pronounced limp. A hip replacement operation seemed inevitable.

They actually "screamed and yelled" whenever the subject of *Mame* arose, and that kind of behavior, Angela says, was positively unheard of in their temperate climate. Neither one said anything so awful, though, that it couldn't be taken back. As she puts it, "We're not the kind of people who say things. Screaming and yelling, that happened maybe once in ten years."

But it did happen, and that year was one time when she felt "the marriage was almost in a little bit of danger. I think it was because we were on different wavelengths," but she was willing to share the responsibility for that. "We're no angels and we're no saints," she says. "I've got my problems and I know that I'm not the easiest person to live with. There are just times when frustration moves in." She was certainly frustrated then, because she absolutely did not want to leave when she was "so entrenched in the Ireland life, and in our home and in the family — the feeling of being very comfortable."

But Peter continued to press her about the tour. "He said he could hold the fort, stay in Ireland with the children," and added, "You're either in the business or you're not. You must keep doing something." She found that when he got this adamant and she was cornered in a disagreement with no escape, her husband could reduce her to tears.

"Finally," she admits, "I was just worn down. I know that's easy to say. I could have said no. That's why I feel guilty. Because I know damned well I could have *not* done it.

"If I hadn't, it wouldn't have been the end of the world."

And so it was with some resentment that she left Cork in the spring of 1972 to tour *Mame* through musical tent theaters in the American northeast, from Valley Forge, Pennsylvania, to Cherry Hill, New Jersey, and Westbury, Long Island.

The show had to be restaged for the theater-in-the-round style of the music tents, and with all the costume changes, she had to make her exits on the run, dashing down a ramp to get out of one dress and into another in time to run up a different ramp and make a new entrance. There were also performance problems unique to working on an arena stage. For instance, in order to make everyone in the audience feel as if they're being played to, the cast has to keep turning around. "It's distracting to the actor," she says. "It becomes mechanical. I got used to it and went through the motions, but it was difficult."

As she was leaving the theater after one of these performances, she noticed a teenage girl whom she had seen repeatedly among the autograph seekers. The fan phenomenon was hardly new to her. When she'd made *The World of Henry Orient,* a young man began "hanging around, watching the shooting . . . always lurking, always around a corner, just fascinated and dazzled by me," but the adulation began in earnest when she was doing *Mame* on Broadway. "I receive some of the most wonderful letters from people," she says, "and I respond to them — insightful, thoughtful letters. Not fan letters. Letters from people who thoroughly enjoyed my work.

"But there are all kinds of people who get hooked on stars," she says, "and lots of adolescents, fourteen-year-old girls who become absolutely transfixed."

> They usually start by writing and sometimes they inadvertently hit a chord in you and you write back. And that's a big mistake. Unfortunately, it never pays to start a correspondence with a fan. There have been very few exceptions in my experience. The trouble starts when they are becoming too familiar and are looking for too much feedback from me. Looking for attention for themselves, trying to bring some drama into their own lives. Some managed to maintain their place in their lives and maybe write once or twice a year, simply keeping up. But there's the other kind of fan, who really wants more and more and more and more, as if they don't have a life of their own. They suddenly think they've taken on an importance because you have paid attention to them, and they become almost selfish and self-important about it. They take on an attitude that "I'm going to tell you about myself, and you must now pay attention to me."

It was just such mail that Angela began receiving from the teenage girl who regularly waited for her outside the music tent. There was an unmistakable similarity between this girl's attitude and Eve Harrington's in *All About Eve* ("that script really hit on something"). Angela became concerned when the letters began to take on a tinge of competitiveness, "As if she was ready for stardom because she'd done the high school play." Soon, Angela had chills when she felt as if the girl was "lurching up against me, and referring to 'we.'" Even when she tried to write brief and discouraging replies, the letters continued, but by now, she had other things to concern her.

Specifically, her mother had developed throat cancer, and as a result, her larynx had to be removed. A terrible turn of events for anyone, it was a devastating loss for an actress. Now Moyna was voiceless, and trying to be brave about it. She had already begun learning to speak with blurted bursts of air. A great deal of effort and patience was required to produce this strange-sounding, difficult-to-understand, and guttural speech, but she worked at it. She found it extremely frustrating when most people could not comprehend what she was trying to say — she, who'd always been such a loquacious and funny lady.

One day, her telephone rang, and she answered it the only way she could, exploding a "Hello?" with one of her bursts of air.

As she told Angela, "There was this silence at the other end of the telephone, and then I could hear a woman saying something to somebody, 'They've trained a dog to answer the phone. What do I do now?' "

Angela laughed out loud, and grieved for the wonder of Moyna managing to hold on to her sense of humor in the face of such a tragedy.

There just seemed to be so much that was wrong at the moment. Was the tour worth it? In retrospect, Angela says, "It was enormously successful. I made a lot of money."

Rex Reed came over to spend the 1972 Thanksgiving in Ireland with the Shaws and promptly saw an item in the *International Herald-Tribune* about a planned production of *Gypsy* in London. Reading it to Angela, he pronounced it perfect for her, a great role in a great show, and it would not take her far from Ireland.

She knew all about it, she told him. "They asked me to do it. I turned it down."

"What? Are you nuts?" he cried, adding with a certain amount of hyperbole, "This is the greatest part ever written for a woman." He sat her down for a long talk about the fabulous songs written by Jule Styne and Stephen Sondheim — "Everything's Coming Up Roses," "Together," "Small World," "Some People," "You'll Never Get Away from Me," and the marvelous eleven o'clock number, "Rose's Turn" — and with exaggerated patience, Angela replied, "I know all about those songs, Rex. The cast album was a treasure in my house, but I can't sing that role. *I can't sing like Ethel Merman.*"

The legendary Merman had originated her role in *Gypsy* in 1959. It was the singular triumph of her career, Reed acknowledged, but argued, "The British don't even know who Ethel Merman is. *Gypsy* has never been done in London." That much was true. Merman had declined to perform it there in 1961 (because her leading man, Jack Klugman, with whom she was smitten, wouldn't go), and had declined again when asked to star in this revival.

Reed also pointed out that Arthur Laurents and Stephen Sondheim were Angela's old *Anyone Can Whistle* writing and directing team. She wasn't thrilled about Laurents and hadn't forgotten that they'd not had the best of times on that show. Even so, Reed made so strong an argument, with Peter concurring, that she promised to reconsider. She was even "willing to give Arthur a shot."

Peter promptly telephoned Fritz Holt and Barry Brown, the Americans who were planning the London production, and told them that he and Angela were coming to America for Christmas and still might be interested in their show. She eventually committed to the part, and when Brown and Holt found themselves $90,000 shy of their budget, she even suggested they try Edgar. "My brother is a producer," she said. "Why don't I talk to him, and see if he wants to come in on it?"

Edgar certainly had the funds, as productions of *Godspell* were then playing all over the world. "Edgar and Joe [Beruh, his partner] each wrote out checks for forty-five thousand dollars," said an awestruck Barry Brown. "Right in front of us! I don't think I'll ever be rich enough to take out a checkbook and write out a check for forty-five thousand dollars. That's good. That's not so bad."

Not long afterward, when her casting as Rose had already been announced, Angela ran into Ethel Merman at a party. "I hear you're going to do *Gypsy,*" Merman said. The moment might have turned awkward but Angela replied, "Nobody but you can do *Gypsy,* but I'm going to have a go at it." Four months later, in April of 1973, she was rehearsing in an old military training hall for a May opening at London's Piccadilly Theatre.

Gypsy, of course, is the story of Mama Rose, a frustrated performer and the overbearing, ambitious, and finally horrific stage mother of the striptease dancer Gypsy Rose Lee. As Merman played her, she was a one-dimensional monster, abrasive, frenetic, ruthless, and, were it not for the emotion expressed in her songs, totally unsympathetic. Rather than venturing into dangerous Merman territory as a singer, Angela took the serious approach of an actor, seeing the character as a woman of many contradictions, fearful but childish, insensitive and yet vulnerable and guileless. "She has so many sides," Angela says, "that in the end you feel vitally sorry for her. She's a tragic figure."

Ethel Merman had not been an actor capable of such complexities, but she was so much like this woman in terms of loudness and crudity that, to be convincing enough for the demands of this script, all she had to do was be herself. The songs were another matter, and nobody could sing like Merman. Her voice was a trumpet, her vocal presence inescapable, and it was to that instrument of hers that this musical score was dedicated. These are songs of such theatricality and propulsion, set with such brilliant lyrics, that the songwriters in ASCAP voted the score the best ever written for a Broadway show.

Arthur Laurents knew that Angela was loath to compete with so historic a performance. Merman owned *Gypsy* the way Marlon Brando owned *A Streetcar Named Desire* or, for that matter, the way Angela herself owned *Mame.* It would take more than these fourteen years for Merman's fearsome shadow to fade from the role. Then again, had not Rosalind Russell owned *Auntie Mame* a mere six years before Angela wrested the character from her?

Laurents's approach, in directing Angela, was to make the part seem fresh by emphasizing its dramatic nuances rather than the songs. Rarely modest, he believed that "A lot of my dialogue is elliptical — it has enormous subtext." He was able to point out the levels that Merman had never explored. "Angie was challenged," Laurents says, "by the stupidity and vulgarity of Rose. She could play stupid," he says, but the vulgar aspect was not as accessible to her. "It's very hard to find any vulgarity in Angie."

Merman had had no such problem; as Sondheim put it, she was "innately vulgar." The lyricist also understood how Merman's practically mythic performance might intimidate Angela, even if the London audiences had never heard that unique voice. At the same time, he appreciated the difference between Lansbury and Merman as "the difference between an actress and a comic. What people don't remember about Ethel is that she was a comic — a comic with a big, brassy voice."

As an actress, though, he called her "the talking dog."

Laurents draws his own distinctions between the two with his usual shark-toothed brilliance. "Ethel," he says, "was basically the same in every scene. She came on, she screamed and yelled, and she went off. And Merman had a habit of tapping her foot when she was singing. When you're supposed to be begging your father, and your foot is tapping away, it isn't exactly right. But Angie had all kinds of subtleties."

As the London opening night approached, Angela, rather than growing anxious, was relaxed and confident. At the final preview, she was not even fazed when a fifteen-foot pipe, fitted with heavy spotlights, came crashing down just yards from her, in the midst of a scene. Her concentration was so focused that she continued without interruption. But things were different on May 29, 1973, the actual night of the premiere.

> That first night was an excruciatingly nervous event for me. Here I was, coming into London playing the great Merman role in a

> *Gypsy* they had never seen. It was a dynamite situation in every respect, because I had to sell myself to those critics.

Her son Anthony, who was working with the company as a dialogue coach, was allowed to man the ropes and yank at the pulley to raise the curtain on this very special evening for his mother. With that, she sailed on stage, and when the show was over,

> the night was a tremendous success, made so especially by a group of people called "The First Nighters." This is a famous group of theatergoers who attend every London opening. They sit up "in the gods" [the top balcony] and they just took to the show, screaming and yelling and stamping and carrying on. It was unbelievable, and the reviews were terrific. London took me to its heart, but not the way it happens in New York. You're not the celebrity, you're the actress, and I was given the critical greeting that I had hoped for. And also they gave me the Plays and Players Award.

That award was for the season's Best Actress. It was the first time this prize had ever been given to a performer in a musical.

Katharine Hepburn was in the audience that opening night, and after the cheers finally subsided, she sought Angela out. Unwilling to do anything the usual way, and not likely to wait in a crowd outside a star's dressing room, Hepburn clambered into the orchestra pit and ducked under the stage. "She was Hepburn," Barry Brown says, "and nobody dared stop her."

After starring in *Gypsy* for seven months, Angela went on tour once again, and this time she could not put up a struggle, because Edgar was involved in the production, and the tour had been part of the original agreement, assuring a payback. She left the London company to take a second *Gypsy* from Toronto to California, and ultimately to New York.

As Broadway loomed in the near distance, Laurents knew for sure that "she was scared because of the Merman thing. My only concern was that she be recognized by the critics. At the opening night party, [co-producer] Fritz Holt stood on a chair and read the *New York Times* review. It was a rave and it was a rave for her."

But the excellence of her work was essentially in the acting. It's true that Mama Rose had never been played with such depth of characterization, but while Arthur Laurents convinced Angela that his script was "incredible," *Gypsy* simply is not a brilliant drama. The libretto is essentially traditional in its short scenes, quick strokes of character, and song cues. The most colorful and characteristic dialogue is in Sondheim's lyrics. The show is certainly a great one, but its greatness lies in the magnetic music, the marvelous lyrics, and the songs' connection to the powerful central character. As Sondheim concedes, "Those songs were written with Merman's attack in mind, her personality; the presence, the color." Those songs and that singer, as if a single entity, had grabbed the original audience and all but shook it to attention. Angela was valiant in putting an actor's artistic energies into the role, but *Gypsy* was geared to a different kind of dynamism than *Mame,* and the Lansbury humanity finally had no relevance for this character. Among her star turns in Broadway musicals, this was certainly admirable but not the most exciting.

She won her third Tony Award for *Gypsy,* but it ran only 120 performances. Evidently her initial instinct had been correct. "I can't sing like Merman." Nobody knew the actress Angela Lansbury better than Angela Lansbury did, and what roles she should and should not accept had become a recurring subject. It arose again when the movie director Milos Forman offered her the part of Nurse Ratched in *One Flew Over the Cuckoo's Nest.*

Five years had passed since she'd made *Bedknobs and Broomsticks,* and she was eager to make another movie, but not this one. After reading the Lawrence Hauben and Bo Goldman screenplay, she said to herself, "This is a wonderful role, but I simply cannot play it. She is so awful. So evil." She was determined to never again play a malicious woman or, for that matter, a merely unlikable one. Her decision led to another disagreement with Peter. "I thought she should have done that," he says, and once again he tried convincing her to reconsider, now using an argument that he knew appealed to her: the longed-for Academy Award. He was certain she would win it for *Cuckoo's Nest;* he thought, in fact, that "whoever played that part would win it." Nor was Peter the only one making a sales effort. Milos Forman took her to lunch and, she says, "did a number on me. He really wanted me to play the part, but Nurse Ratched was a horrific woman — and another thing, I didn't want to work inside an insane asylum. I knew I would be there for five or six weeks and I just couldn't face being in an actual hospital with actual inmates. I chickened out totally. There were real inmates in the film. They were used as extras."

This time, she would not be persuaded. She acknowledges that, in

America, "They tend to gauge how successful you are by how much money you make," but something more important than money was at stake here. It went to the heart of her professional experience, for she was not only disgusted with all the years of playing bitches; she was convinced that the reason she'd finally gotten to be a leading lady was that Mame Dennis, besides being a great role, was a lovable woman. That had made Lansbury lovable, and she concluded that audiences make stars of actors they like, and like to see — again and again and again.

She also enjoyed an audience's embrace. As Rex Reed put it, "She's in love with being loved," which she did not deny. "I'm buoyed up and supported by that wonderful acclamation that I feel. It's so huge, so tremendous. Do you have any idea?" Can you imagine?" And so, as Peter continued to press the case for *One Flew Over the Cuckoo's Nest,* she felt, "It's very hard to decide to do something that you know is going to turn eighty percent of your audience off you."

It didn't bother her when Louise Fletcher won the Academy Award for playing Nurse Ratched, and she admired Jack Nicholson's work in the picture as well.

> He's so attractive, and so original and so fabulous. He's a great movie actor but he couldn't do it on the stage. He has to move and walk around the way he moves and walks and raises the eyebrows and flashes that smile. Although I must admit that in *Chinatown* he didn't use any of those tricks. But since then, his public persona has bled into his work to a great extent. And vice versa. Anyhow, he probably doesn't even want to act on the stage and, who knows, if he did, he might fool you. . . . And I could have played the pants off Nurse Ratched.

It was a quite a jump from *Gypsy* on Broadway to *Hamlet* in England, and quite a moment when the National Theatre of Great Britain invited her to play Queen Gertrude to Albert Finney's melancholy Dane in the inaugural production at its new home. There was hardly another actor alive who could have demonstrated such astonishing versatility. Yet, although she had been "brought up with Shakespeare as the definitive playwright," she had never performed in any of his works, except as a schoolgirl. Now, her Shakespearean debut was to be made with England's most prestigious repertory company, opposite the actor who was considered the apparent heir to Laurence Olivier's acting throne.

This time she needed no arguments or pep talks and accepted the offer in an instant. When the conductor Don Pippin asked a typical Broadway question, "Why are you doing Shakespeare?" (implying, when you have the chance to keep doing musicals) she replied, "Because I think it's time I worked on my craft instead of my career."

But first, she flew to California to say goodbye to Moyna, for it was clear that she was dying. "The cancer had spread through her body," Angela says, "and it was a hopeless situation." Sitting at the bedside and holding her mother's hand, she had the chance that so few have, or take, to express their feelings toward the end of a parent's life. "I just told her how much I loved her and how much she had given me in her life, and what her encouragement had meant to me.

"She listened, and we both wept in mutual understanding."

Anthony had been working as the assistant stage manager of a production of William Inge's *Bus Stop* that starred Lee Remick, and he had also been understudying Keir Dullea in one of the lead roles. Now he'd taken over for Dullea, and a beaming Angela Lansbury would be able to look at Anthony Shaw's name outside a London theater not far from where her own name had so recently been posted. Stephen Sondheim, still smitten with Remick, saw that production of *Bus Stop* and found Anthony "terrific. He was attractive and sexy and straightforward."

Angela reported for *Hamlet* at the prestigious National Theatre of Great Britain, where her old friend Larry Olivier — now Lord Olivier — was still the artistic director, but his health was failing. She was moved and saddened, for even the canteen where the company ate showed, she thought, the influence of this great actor. "He was bowing out, but his spirit was so much a part of that institution. You felt that this man had created this wonderful kind of homey place where you could go and have roly-poly pudding and steak-and-kidney pie for almost nothing. All of this was created for the actors, the young kids who had no money."

Rehearsals began late in September of 1975, and she immersed herself in that company atmosphere. Peter Hall, who had directed her in the Edward Albee play, was also guiding this production toward its press opening at the Old Vic Theatre. That was set for December 10, and three months later, *Hamlet* was to be transferred to the Lyttelton Theatre, christening the National Theatre's new home at the South Bank Arts Centre.

Angela was as happy as an apprentice, "pretty frightened" but frightened in a good way. She felt "challenged to mind my diction, to modulate my voice, but those are things that are technically part and parcel of what I do. For blank verse, if you have a sense of rhythm and a musical ear, you're very aided, you pick up the meter."

> In the company of actors in a scene, I love to talk about what we as a group are trying to achieve; what I am thinking when I walk through the door, come on stage, and enter the scene with a situation. But I can't discuss that with outsiders. It's only within the company of actors that I'm able to discuss what I'm thinking or feeling about my character and my position in the scene. Those conversations with fellow players or the director — they are sacrosanct. And I love that part — the interpretive, creative work.

The rehearsals were very no-nonsense, a working situation among classical players, and in that context, she wasn't Angela Lansbury, star of Broadway musicals. Nor was she a Hollywood name. She was just, as she liked to say, "a working actress, an old deep-sea monster," and indeed,

> that's what I am. All the time. That's the odd, center thing. That I am just an actor. That is really, really what I am.

Queen Gertrude is one of the most curious roles in the Shakespearean canon. She is considered a major character in *Hamlet,* an extensive literature is devoted to her, especially to the relationship between her and the prince. Yet, in terms of actual scenes and speeches, the part is a small one. Angela argues that "She actually represents the pivot in the piece. She says so little. In a way, everything she says is unsaid. She is a woman who makes a terrible mistake and subsequently pays for it for the rest of her life."

At least, that was the attitude she brought to rehearsals, but as the weeks went by she began to realize that this small part was, in fact, tiny, especially in the midst of a complete and uncut *Hamlet;* one that was four hours long. The role was so minuscule that ultimately she would bring a sewing machine to her dressing room and work on a patchwork quilt while she was offstage. Moreover, she began to fear that she'd been cast as Queen

Gertrude because of all the bitch mothers she had played in her old movies. "It was an obvious casting ploy of Peter Hall's, and I suppose he had every right to assume I could play this role [without direction]. Coming from *The Manchurian Candidate* I would have been right there, too, if it was a production where the queen was madly in love with her son.

"Instead, I found myself as a kind of mewling, puking mother queen who sort of blubbed her way through scenes for lack of anything else to do."

She became increasingly irritable as the opening night approached, realizing that she was never going to get much direction, and to make matters profoundly worse, on November 25, 1975, just weeks before her eightieth birthday, Moyna died. Angela flew home to California for the funeral, turned around, and flew right back to London for more rehearsals.

> Playing the queen in Hamlet, I of course spoke the lovely speech describing Ophelia's death. "There is a willow grows aslant a brook/That shows his hoar leaves in the grassy stream." Moyna had often quoted the speech to me over the years, and I, as a child, would mangle the words and mispronounce them. It was sort of a joke between us. When I returned to London and was rehearsing that speech, I just sat there overcome by tears in front of the company, unable to utter a word.

Two weeks later Albert Finney's father died. It was not the most blessed of productions, and the critics agreed. Nobody fared well in the reviews, and Angela received the worst personal trouncing of her career. Wardle of the *Times,* who had so admired her work in the Albee play, called her Gertrude "an anonymous performance," and Hurren of the *Spectator* wrote that "she gets most things wrong." She had no quarrel with their assessments. "Those reviews were fair and square. There was no drama. It was the most untheatrical production I've ever been a part of."

The *Hamlet* contract committed her to stay with the production until its spring transfer to the new arts complex. She stayed for the agreed-upon amount of time, but not a day more, longingly aware that the big hit in London at the moment was Stephen Sondheim's *A Little Night Music.* In the year since *Anyone Can Whistle,* he had become the reigning genius of Broadway musicals. Now she reached out for any musical to serve as a tonic, and found it in the empty-headed comfort of a Broadway musical at its most superficial — the five-performance *Milliken Breakfast Show* for the Seventh Avenue garment industry. It was certainly possible for such a show, an "industrial," to seem more satisfying than *Hamlet*. Angela thought so. "What a wonderful thing to do. *I can't wait!* I immediately threw the box of sweeties away, lost all the weight I'd put on, came back, had my face lifted, and did the Milliken show — and those shows were great!"

The decision turned out to be a turning point, the end of the Irish chapter. Deirdre and Anthony were in their middle twenties. Deirdre had already gone off to live in Italy, and Anthony, as Angela realized, "in his mind, was already in New York." He told his parents, "I want to leave London and Ireland. I'm an American and I want to live there. It's time for me to go home." Peter and Angela had always known they couldn't cocoon the family forever. They sold the house in Ireland and went home.

Her Milliken show, fun though it was, sat quite some distance from the Stephen Sondheim musicals she so admired. He was already ruminating about his next show. The seed of his idea had been planted while he'd been in London working on Angela's *Gypsy.* The composer-lyricist had gone to see a little play called *Sweeney Todd, the Demon Barber of Fleet Street.* It was an intimate production in an out-of-the-way theater in London's East End, where "nobody went," Sondheim says, "except a couple of artsy-fartsy people."

Sweeney Todd was a cheerfully macabre piece by Christopher Bond, an actor-turned-playwright who wrote it in the modest hope of creating a showy part for himself. His piece was based on a classic "penny dreadful," as the Londoners of 1846 called their pulp horror serials. The original publication of *Sweeney Todd, the Demon Horror of Fleet Street* had been hugely popular, running for thirty-eight chapters (sometimes two an issue) in a weekly one-pence London newspaper. Sondheim thought the play would make a funny-scary musical. He urged a friend and collaborator, producer-director Harold Prince, to see the show.

Prince had reservations. A mere entertainment was not enough to satisfy him; he felt that theater should present ideas. But he agreed to the project and even suggested that the splendid British actress Patricia Routledge play the leading role of Nellie Lovett, the somewhat dotty Cockney shopkeeper who pairs up in an idiotic romance with Todd, the serial killer.

"Nope," Sondheim replied, "not sexy enough."

"Who else would you suggest?" asked Prince.

"I think Angie would be perfect," the composer answered.

CHAPTER 17

THE ACTOR

DESPITE Sondheim's preference for Angela, Patricia Routledge remained Harold Prince's actress of choice to co-star with Len Cariou in *Sweeney Todd, the Demon Barber of Fleet Street.* The director even arranged for Cariou and Routledge to confer by telephone, while he was in Vienna making the movie version of *A Little Night Music* with Elizabeth Taylor. In fact, that was one reason why *Sweeney Todd* wasn't being produced in 1976.

Routledge, a splendid actress and a good singer, was not entirely sold on the show, and in fact, had the creeps just thinking about it. "You don't know what it's like," she told Cariou on the phone. "I was raised on that story. I'm not kidding you, it's scary having anything to do with it. For us, that 'penny dreadful' is like Grimm's Fairy Tales. When we were kids, it was always something to be afraid of. Even my parents would say to me, 'You'd better be careful or we'll get Sweeney Todd after you.'"

The story was scary in another sense, too. It sounded like box-office suicide. Broadway audiences were conditioned to sunny musicals like *My Fair Lady, Hello, Dolly!* and *Mame.* The closest a hit got to being serious was *Fiddler on the Roof.* Producers did not usually undertake musical comedies about serial killers, but then, there was nothing usual about Prince and Sondheim. The composer had become preeminent by doing one "unexpected" (as he put it) musical after another. Prince had emerged as a singularly dynamic director, specializing in concept musicals with brains. As a team, collaborating on such vibrant and intelligent shows as *Company* and *Follies,* they were exploring the more adult possibilities of the genre. Their elegant *A Little Night Music* was as close as they would ever come to commercialism.

As a team, Prince and Sondheim stood for musical theater at its most artistic, but in such highmindedness, their shows also seemed elitist, winning prizes but not mass audiences. And *Sweeney Todd* wasn't even the most offbeat of their notions. At that very moment, the pair had an even unlikelier project in mind, and to delay *Sweeney* still further, Prince (who was producing as well as directing their shows) decided to first present *Pacific Overtures,* a Kabuki musical about the westernization of Japanese culture.

Even as work on that show proceeded, Sondheim continued to argue on behalf of Lansbury for *Sweeney Todd.* Prince agreed that she was "clearly the best for quality," but he feared that she would be too "obvious" a choice to play the middle-aged Cockney who was the show's female lead. He wanted somebody "different, an unusual choice." However, by the time *Pacific Overtures* opened — so unusual a show that audiences wouldn't come — the director changed his mind.

By then, Angela herself was hedging. There was nothing subtle about her concerns. She was simply protecting her position as a star, a position that she was not about to relinquish. Perhaps she was still something short of being a movie star — she hadn't even made a picture in seven years — but on Broadway she played title roles only.

"Listen, Steve," she said, "your show is not called *Nellie Lovett.* It's called *Sweeney Todd.* And I'm the second banana."

"But," he argued, "you carry all the comic weight."

"You're going to have to prove that to me," she warned him. She did want to do a musical, but she didn't have to do this one. She'd read the script, and Nellie Lovett was indeed not yet a funny character. Aside from anything else, Angela had quit playing unlikable women a long time ago. She was not quite thrilled about playing the weird girlfriend of a mad killer. Besides, she loved her house in Ireland, from which it was easy commuting to London to make movies. After a hiatus since *Bedknobs and Broomsticks,* she made two in 1978/79, the all-star (Bette Davis, Mia Farrow, David Niven, Maggie Smith) *Death on the Nile,* which reunited her with Peter Ustinov; and a peculiar, halfheartedly distributed remake of Alfred Hitchcock's *The Lady Vanishes* with Cybill Shepherd and Elliott Gould.

In any case, *Sweeney Todd* had been delayed again, to allow Prince to direct Andrew Lloyd Webber's *Evita,* which would become a huge success.

Those projects were soon completed, however, and Angela was "at liberty," as they put it in the days when entertaining was known as "the show business." She was at such liberty that for two weeks she played Anna in a Broadway revival of *The King and I,* to provide a star attraction while Yul Brynner took a vacation. She also accepted a six-week assignment at a regional theater, the Hartford Stage Company, to do Edward Albee's one-act plays, *Listening* and *Counting the Ways.* It was there in Hartford, during rehearsal, that she had her first experience with atrial fibrillations, or heart flutters. The incident began with a migraine headache that grew so painful she had to practically "knock myself out" on pain killers.

> All the retching upset the vagus nerve that goes from the stomach to the heart, and it threw my heart out of whack. That was a frightening feeling, the heart beating erratically, and *being so loud about it.* Well I didn't know what had happened. All I knew what that I couldn't stand up, I was dizzy and weak, and they called the doctor, and he explained what was going on; that my heart was in fibrillation. Finally it flopped back into sinus rhythm. I'm really a very healthy person, but I had to learn what it is that sets it off, because it can become a rather chronic situation.

She did not let her condition affect her readiness when *Sweeney Todd* was at last getting under way. She was curious to see the added comic weight, and she certainly was attracted by the originality of the show. That is where Angela Lansbury, star of Broadway musicals, separated from the others. It is unimaginable that Ethel Merman, Mary Martin, Barbra Streisand, or Carol Channing would have considered doing *Sweeney Todd.* Channing could have done it, probably quite marvelously, but she wouldn't even have contemplated such a role.

It was the actress in Angela who responded to the fascinating challenge, just as it was the star in Angela who took another step toward accepting that challenge after Prince agreed to give her the final, solo bow. With that, and after the production schedule was set, she and Peter took an apartment near Lincoln Center.

She was fifty-three years old and ready to begin rehearsals for her fifth Broadway musical.

A lot of the show's music had already been written. Sondheim, a notoriously slow composer, was working like a man inspired. He was almost finished with the first act, musicalizing so many scenes in such a complex way that the show was beginning to seem operatic. Yet, being hopelessly in love with Broadway musicals and also something of an anti-intellectual snob, he refused to call it an opera, which he defined as "something that's sung in head voices, in an opera house, for very few performances."

Whichever genre *Sweeney Todd* actually was, it wasn't going to be easy to sing and it certainly wasn't going to be a traditional Broadway musical. There would be no exhilarating overture, no catchy show tunes, no big dance numbers. Angela Lansbury would not come plunging down a staircase in a fabulous dress, to be carried aloft by chorus boys and serenaded by a huge ensemble. Somewhat to the contrary, it would feature harrowing organ music, sudden screeches, slashed throats dripping with blood, and a barber chair with a trapdoor seat to send murder victims plummeting out of sight. Sondheim's notion was a merry Grand Guignol that began with the prologue:

Attend the tale of Sweeney Todd.
His skin was pale and his eye was odd,
He shaved the faces of gentlemen
Who never thereafter were heard of again
He tread a trail that few have trod
The Demon Barber of Fleet Street

The idea was to make it an intimately spooky tale bathed in lamplight and fog, "a show about just two people," as the composer explained to Angela. "I don't know how many songs there are going to be, but *a lot,* and you and Len (Cariou) will be doing the bulk of the singing." And Sondheim says, "She knew I wouldn't lie."

Although *Sweeney Todd* would end up as a big production with a big cast, it was true that there were only two main characters. They are the shopkeeper Nellie Lovett and Benjamin Barker, a barber who takes the alias "Sweeney Todd" when he escapes from a remote prison in 1846, after fifteen years of wrongful incarceration. He had been convicted on a false charge contrived by the evil Judge Turpin, who lusted after Barker's wife, Lucy. Returning to the site of his old shop, Barker finds the addled Nellie selling wretched meat pies (made from cats) in her tacky eating house. When he asks about his wife, Nellie realizes who he is and replies that Lucy poisoned herself, omitting the minor detail that she survived and is the mad old whore Barker has been encountering on the London streets.

He vows to avenge her death, and Nellie responds to his rage as if it were undiluted testosterone. She begins snuggling up to his ghoulishness (chalk makeup, fright wig), for she has found just her kind of man and, in their mutual outlandishness, they do make an appropriate couple. As she hands him his old set of glittering silver razors, which she'd been safeguarding, she sets her sights on the man. But when he is foiled at the very moment he has Judge Turpin in the barber chair, razor at the throat, his mind cracks, and the plot sickens. Todd embarks on a killing spree (even telling the audience "You all deserve to die"), while the resourceful Nellie, not one to waste, comes up with the notion of grinding his victims into meat for her pies.

A perfect idea for a musical? Not everyone would agree, but visions define genius, and Angela grasped this one. When Sondheim told her that the character she was playing was "loony in a British music hall style, that's the kind of funny she's supposed to be," the actress was already rubbing her mental hands at the prospect of attacking the role. However, she also knew that much of this was just pep talk, and that the fun had still not found its way into the script.

She'd told them that they were going to have to prove to her the importance of Nellie Lovett's comedy, and Sondheim was now prepared to do just that. He had written two songs to demonstrate what he meant, "which was unusual for me," he says. "I'd never done that before." Now he sat at the piano on the parlor floor of his East Side town house, explaining the numbers. He began by warning her that this score was going to be harder to sing — in his phrase, "more spreading" — than *Mame* or even *Anyone Can Whistle.* This was elaborate, challenging, rangy music, often dissonant, written in uncommon rhythmic patterns with frequent changes — and clashes — of key. As he describes it, "It's into the realm of operetta, and it would show Angie's versatility. It would let the world know that this lady could do more than swarm around and do Jerry Herman title numbers."

The first piece he sang for Angela was "By the Sea," a very long number of which he'd written a full half. In its own syncopated and dissonant way, it is a traditional music hall piece, sung by Nellie in the absurd hope of becoming, with Sweeney, an ordinary couple taking conventional working-class vacations at the shore, notwithstanding his somewhat unconventional occupation.

"It's a very good idea for a song," even if Sondheim had to say so himself, "because it's about the banality of Mrs. Lovett, and about the horror of Sweeney's life if he were going to be stuck with her. And so, while he's listening to her singing, he's thinking, 'It's better that I should die by the hangman's knot than to have to live 'By the Sea' with Nellie Lovett.' "

Angela was not overly enthusiastic. The song was an inside-out version of the little Cockney number "How'd You Like to Spoon with Me?" that she'd sung in *Till the Clouds Roll By.* Sondheim might have written the piece as mock banal, but it sounded like the real thing to her, and it was hard to sing because there were long stretches with no places for her to breathe. It was obvious, too, that this would not be the showstopper Sondheim wanted, and even he sensed that. He did, however, have another song that would stop the show, and Angela knew it, too, once he began "The Worst Pies in London" in his pretty terrible singing voice.

It was her first number, an all too frank description of the disgusting pies that Nellie makes from cat meat. It introduces her to the audience as she flirts with Sweeney, not yet recognizing him as Benjamin Barker the barber whose shop used to be above hers. Her idea of flirting is to be cheerfully, cozily, and candidly lowbrow, and she sings out with hilarious frankness about the horrible food she serves.

The worst pies in London,
Even that's polite.
The worst pies in London,
If you doubt it take a bite.

As Sondheim sang, he relished his own lyrics' humor and, no doubt about it, the piece was funny.

Is that just revolting?
All greasy and gritty
It looks like it's molting
And tastes like —
Well, pity.

Angela was encouraged. The lyrics were comic, the music was sophisticated, and she could see how this character could be an energetic and perhaps pathetic clown. She was already imagining how the role might be played and agreed with the composer when he reiterated, "I want Mrs. Lovett to have a music hall character. It seems to me that's the right tone for the part."

"Not just *music hall,*" Angela said, "but *dotty music hall.*"

She spun like a top and popped her big eyes, gripping her own elbows and snuggling her shoulders.

"Right," Sondheim said. "Music hall can be a little crazed, which is nothing but a musical number *slightly up.*"

They were on the same wavelength, but she was still wary.

Book rehearsals began with the traditional reading, the cast crowded around a long table. As they went through the script, Prince "could see right away that it was unrelievedly depressing. It seemed so obvious to us all that you've got to laugh a little." But where? If Angela was carrying the comic weight, there was nothing funny for her after she sang "The Worst Pies in London," and by the second act, the director knew "she was just as grim company as Sweeney." He was sure to lose Lansbury if the role wasn't enriched, and moreover, he believed she was right. "If Steve and Hugh Wheeler had left that reading and said, 'It's fine the way it is,' she would have found a very diplomatic way of saying, 'Gentlemen, you don't need me.' "

Her prodding for better material was less, he thought, a matter of wielding star power than of being canny. "How else," he asked, "do you get to be as good an actress as there is alive? As smart with her choices? Get to do everything she's done and yet at the same time never seem to be throwing your weight around?"

The answer was: by investigating a role, analyzing a show, picking it apart to see if it worked and how it worked, not just for her but *with* her, and then developing the character. Prince also realized that "We needed more of a balance," to offset Sweeney's monstrousness. She had to have another comedy number. He glanced at Sondheim, who nodded in agreement. He'd already begun to jot down ideas.

Then Prince showed everyone a wood model of the set and explained that, although it would stand in the middle of a big stage, it would actually be quite compact — a cube-like affair with the basic barber shop upstairs and the pie shop below, the levels connected by a flight of stairs. After everyone left, Angela stayed behind to talk to Prince. "Darling," she asked, peering closely at the model, "how high are the steps of those stairs going to be?"

The surprised director stammered, "Why — I have no idea."

"It's very important," she said. "I'm going to be spending the whole night running up and down those stairs, and if they're too low or too high, I can do serious damage to my knees."

"Just tell me how high you want them," he said. "And," he continued, "Gene [Lee, the set designer] and I had a great idea about the stage around it. We're doing the whole thing in a huge factory, because this is too realistic." As the most pictorial of directors, he envisioned that factory giving the story an otherworldly look, but he also had another reason for it. The show was going to play in the Uris (later renamed Gershwin) Theater, which was the largest on Broadway. He knew that the cavern had to be tamed by a dominating set. To do so, Prince believed, "First, we have to fill the proscenium [and not have a big bare stage], and then we have to pull the audience into the stage."

It is not easy to write funny numbers on demand, but Sondheim came through with exactly the right piece for the moment. "A Little Priest" was to be sung at the end of the first act. Prince was aware of its importance to the show. "For that song to come out of the first meeting, well, you just couldn't ask for a more important meeting."

The composer's rendition was not overwhelming. Paul Gemignani, the show's music director, knew that "it makes Steve crazy to perform, he hates to, and he isn't the greatest performer of his own work, but even if he can't sing the notes he wrote, you learn a lot about where he's coming from with the song by hearing him do it."

"A Little Priest" is a giddy list of the sort of people serving as Mrs. Lovett's pie fillings:

Business needs a little lift.
Think of it as thrift,
If you get my drift.

Set to a bouncy and ultimately madcap waltz tempo, it is playfully macabre, exuberantly murderous, and quite lunatic.

NELLIE

It's priest.
Have a little priest.

SWEENEY

Is it really good?

NELLIE

Sir, it's too good,
At least.

Then again, they don't commit sins of the flesh.
So it's pretty fresh.

SWEENEY

Awful lot of fat.

NELLIE

Only where it sat.

SWEENEY

Haven't you got poet
Or something like that?

NELLIE

No, you see the trouble with poet
Is how do you know it's
Deceased?
Try the priest.

Lansbury loved the song. She was getting excited about the part, for now she knew that

> Mrs. Lovett was going to be an incredible departure for me — an opportunity to do something that really came from my roots, my Cockney London roots, and I am a Cockney, I was born within the sound of Bow bells. I was quite prepared to go to town with it and play the total slattern. I felt there was something beguiling and pathetic about this lost soul who didn't know good from evil and was caught up in the maelstrom, the Dickensian background, of London in those times.

Such acting would have to be tucked into what few spaces the music allowed, and Lansbury would provide character detail by gazing adoringly at Sweeney, or wiping down her hands on her apron, or pulling at her ratty sweater. She could play deadpan irony when her lines gave her the chance. ("If ever there was a maternal heart, it's mine.") And meanwhile, there was the immense musical challenge. This was not the old song and dance. Gone were the rhythms that had driven her while working on *Anyone Can Whistle* and *Mame.* Gone was the good sweat of physical exercise and the electric thrill of dance routines at the Variety Arts rehearsal hall. This show had no choreography, and anyway, Variety Arts had been destroyed in a fire, as if symbolizing the end of the old school of musicals. Too, and very curiously, even though *Sweeney Todd* had much more music than a traditional musical, the rehearsal process was more like that of a play. Since both Angela and her co-star, Len Cariou, were essentially serious actors rather than musical performers, they approached the piece that way.

If Angela hadn't realized it before, she was now reminded that much as she'd loved doing *Mame* — and for an idyllic time, even *becoming* that character offstage — the show had not converted her into a performer. She was still an actor. In a strange way, the unhappy *Hamlet* in London and the experience with her British colleagues had restored for her that certain center of her self.

So she dug into the role of Nellie Lovett, freed by the bizarre story and the unreality of musical theater to enlarge her characterization. She was creating a portrayal so flamboyant that, odd as the comparison might seem, it would be a counterpart to her explosive performance in *Mame.* Just as she had approached the star quality of Mame Dennis as character acting, so she now readied to portray, as an actor, the batty energy and the mindless, almost good-natured evildoing of Nellie Lovett.

In both parts, it was essential that in being outsized, her acting not be freakish or overboard. That would require professional discipline. Her work would have to be judiciously edited, and for that, she wanted the supervision and contribution of a director. She was not getting it. Instead, she and Len Cariou would sit in a corner of the 52nd Street studio where they were rehearsing, and work on their scenes by themselves. "We talked about our characters," Cariou recalls, "in terms of where they were coming from. For instance, there were lots of times when Nellie would be talking and Sweeney's mind would wander. And while this chatterbox was prattling away, maybe she would drop in one of her bons mots, and catch his attention. I'd tell Ange that I was going to play it that way, and she'd say, 'If you're going to do that, then, okay, I know how to support it. So I will do *this,* and set that up.' That is the kind of help actors give each other.

"Listening in character," Cariou says, "is the most difficult thing any actor has to do. You find out in rehearsal how your character listens. Then on stage, it isn't Len listening to Ange, it's Sweeney listening to Mrs. Lovett. You have to understand who your character is and listen with that intent."

But, she asked him, "When is *Hal* going to start directing us? I don't know quite what I'm doing here."

This, Cariou told her, is how Hal Prince operates in the theater. Having worked with the director in *A Little Night Music,* he knew that Prince liked his lead players to be dependable professionals who were sure of what they were doing, and, personally, Cariou preferred it that way.

> In a sense we are a tribe unto ourselves. Sometimes a director will look at us as if we're hopelessly dumb. And then there are directors, lots of them, who don't do anything at all. They haven't a clue, and they're waiting for you to enlighten them. Hal has a pretty good idea of how the scenes should play, but basically, a director is waiting for you to bring stuff to the piece, and create the character. His job is to stand outside and say, "Oh, yeah, that's great, more of that," or else, "Whoa! No, you've gone too far!"

Angela disagreed. "One is hoping for at least a dialogue on the subject of what we are doing. He didn't particularly want to have it."

She wanted a director to direct her, but instead,

> I was dazzled by Hal Prince's ability to stage a scene, but I was disappointed in his lack of input as to how a scene could best be played. There were not that many dialogue scenes, but there were some exchanges and I felt his contribution was pretty sparse.

She told Hugh Wheeler, "I don't know what's happening anymore. Is what we're doing okay here? I'm looking for some direction and I'm not really getting it."

"I don't think Hal is going to give you much more," the librettist replied. "You run with what you've got. What you're doing is great. It's what I had in mind when I wrote it. And Steve's happy."

Prince's attitude was,

> I give what people need. I have to do a shitload of directing with certain people. When you're doing a show, if you're lucky you've got Angela and Len and come good characters in the middle. But somewhere down there, you have somebody who just got out of drama school and has a bit more to do than maybe they should have — and all these people are supposed to look like they came to the show with the same amount of experience. So you spend more time with them. For an actress

> with Angela's amount of talent, the director's editorial role is primary. I can establish parameters and stimulate her, edit her. But do I give line readings? To others, you bet, but who would ever give Angela Lansbury a line reading?

Rather, Prince focused on the overall look of the show, its arc and production concept, and in that regard he had another reason for the factory setting. He wanted to link Sweeney Todd's rage and frustration to the Industrial Revolution.

> The truth about the factory — because I read so many smart pundits who say, why was the factory necessary? — is that I couldn't have directed it without the factory, because I needed some social explanation for why everyone was behaving that way. Otherwise it's a thriller, otherwise it's just Grand Guignol.

Because that factory setting was too cumbersome to move, there were to be no out-of-town tryouts. The set itself was a real steel foundry that was bought intact in Rhode Island, dismantled, and then shipped to New York. As it was reassembled on the stage of the Uris Theater, the cast seemed to take it as a cue for serious-mindedness. Christopher Bond — the British actor who had written the original little play in London — looked upon all this darkness of mood with bemusement. Turning to Angela, his only fellow countryman around, he asked, "Why is everyone so gloomy? What's the funeral about? This is supposed to be a comedy, ya know."

She peered up in her habitual way, from under her eyebrows without raising her face, and said, "Well, I agree with you. I'm sorry you feel it's so grim."

"*You're* doing all right, though," he said cheerfully, because she certainly was providing what comedy there was in the show. Prince thought that her contribution was comedy enough. "If you wanted it any funnier," the director says, "then serve meat pies in the lobby during intermission. That's what they did in that little East End production in London. I wouldn't want any part of that.

"It's a subject I care a lot about — what that period in history did to the soul."

This was the difference between Prince's approach to the theater, which was involved with content and ideas, and Angela's approach, which was involved with character and dramatic interpretation. She was already deep into the process of shaping Nellie Lovett into a kewpie doll conspirator in murder, a figure so giddy and childish she was practically lovable. In short, hers was *creative acting,* a stage rarity. An actor is usually a performing artist, sometimes an interpretive one, occasionally an inventive one, but invariably an artist confined by the role as written and limited by the author's intentions. But as Cariou says, "The cuckoo style of playing Mrs. Lovett was pretty much Ange. She invented that character," and it was a rounded, vivid, and original character who had only a potential existence in the script. In conceiving and then fulfilling this marvelous creature, Angela Lansbury became the actor as artist.

Cariou gives Prince credit for providing her with the freedom and the atmosphere to do that. "Hal let us create, he let us bring things to the piece. We were two experienced, authoritative actors. We know we don't have to prop the other one up. Angela knows exactly what she's doing, and it's great to get into that arena with somebody. It's challenging in the right way. When you're at that level, you look at one another and bang! — you're off.

"Then, the arena where the creativity is going to take place is up on a high level instead of down among the basics."

When the set was fully installed, with the factory looming behind the barber/pie shop, the company prepared to work directly on the Uris Theater's stage. Sondheim suggested that Angela walk out with him and look the auditorium over. This was their third show together, and they considered themselves old friends. The composer was fretting about how uncomfortable she might feel playing a show conceived as intimate in "this big, vast theater." Cariou considered it "a barn," and was worried about its acoustics, but Angela surprised Sondheim. She had been on this stage only recently, when she did *The King and I,* and turning to the sea of empty seats, she stretched her arms out wide. "This," she said, "is the one I love."

Then, she showed Sondheim "how the whole kind of horseshoe-shape theater funnels the focus onto the actor. It makes me feel," she said, "that the auditorium is welcoming me."

"It's funny," he would remember. "Standing on the stage of that immense theater, the whole auditorium seemed to funnel itself like the Boulder Dam into where you were.

"Maybe she fooled me because she said it with such fervor, but I believed her."

"Was Nellie trying to land me?" Cariou thought so, "but I was about as interested as the dirt in the window. She was pretty weird. Then again, they both were pretty weird. Only it's her that comes up with the idea of meat pies."

They were both beginning to identify with their characters, at least while they were working. Cariou sensed it. He also knew when to leave off.

> You can never let a role become so real to you that you are swallowed up in it. You can't ever be out of control. You have to know exactly where you are at all times. I suppose if you're not disciplined, not trained, I guess you could get a little carried away, but we both came out of the same school. She did it in England, I did it in Canada. You just learn — that's part of the process — to get it there, to keep it there, and how to leave it there. And not let it encroach on your life.

Still, he sometimes seemed too much like Sweeney for comfort. "Len would come downstage and glare," Prince says, "and I would shrink from him instinctively. He was dangerous just to start with. And that's why the show was so great with him."

Angela's approach was that, however bizarre a character, the playing must be realistic. She understood Nellie to be "this kind of slovenly, overtly sluttish woman. Yes, the show is supposed to be funny," she says, and that is how she entered as Mrs. Lovett, bouncing on stage like a wind-up doll, flipping a dish towel over a shoulder, blowing the dust off yesterday's pies and pounding the flour for the new ones. But however exaggerated the characterization, she knew that "it's got to be *grounded* in something."

Sweeney Todd came still closer to looking like a show with the introduction of costumes, and both Lansbury and Cariou took acting cues from the makeup and hairstyling created for them by the costume designer, Franne Lee. Angela wore a bright red wig with two wacky buns ("puffs") on top. Cariou's wig was a huge mass of black hair, split in the middle and shooting out on either side — as the actor said, "like yak hair." Prince had that wig replaced with a more moderate version, but Sweeney would still

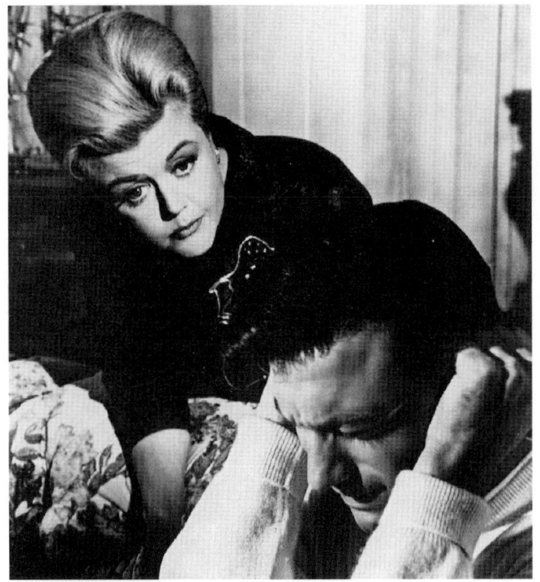

Playing malevolent maternalism in her best picture, *The Manchurian Candidate,* 1962. At thirty-five, Lansbury was only three years older than Laurence Harvey, who was cast as her son.

With director John Frankenheimer on the set of *The Manchurian Candidate.*

The Manchurian Candidate, with James Gregory and Laurence Harvey as Angela's husband and son.

With director Norman Taurog, making *Blue Hawaii,* starring Elvis Presley. "I played a number of roles where I look back and say, 'My God, how could you do that?' Simple. We needed the money."

Hotel Paradiso, 1957. "I got a great education just working with Bert Lahr and some other great farceurs."

With Harry Guardino in *Anyone Can Whistle,* 1964. "She got cold feet," says director Arthur Laurents, "and wanted to pull out after she'd committed. I wrote her a letter and that was the end of that."

Mame, 1966.

"Who else but a bosom buddy/Will tell you how rotten you are?" Stopping the show nightly, Angela and her real-life pal Bea Arthur, who played Mame's "cobra-tongued" friend, Vera Charles, in *Mame.*

With Frankie Michaels as her nephew, Patrick, Mame is toasted by fox huntsman Charles Braswell. The show's title song "is unique," says conductor Don Pippin, "in that it is all about the star and it showcases the star, but she doesn't sing it. We glorify her. It's what you call 'the high kicks.'"

Her closing night as *Mame*.
(*Stephen Paley*)

Many of Lansbury's *Mame* fans were not happy with *Dear World,* which presented her as a bizarre eccentric.

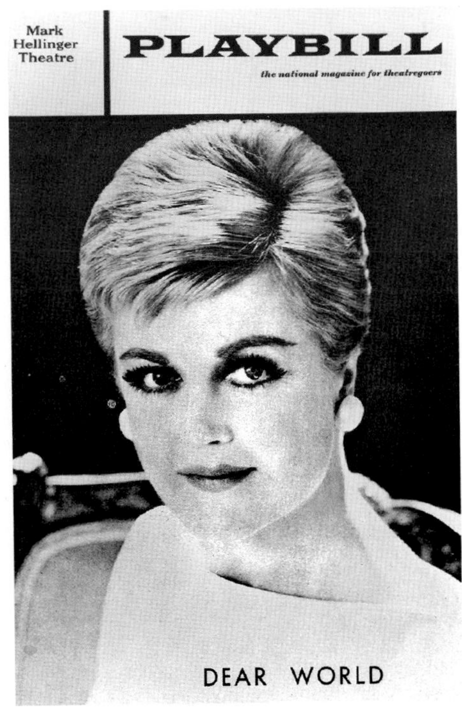

Mark
Hellinger
Theatre
PLAYBILL
the national magazine for theatregoers
DEAR WORLD

In order to attract her *Mame* following, and much to Lansbury's annoyance, a picture of her in that show was used in the *Dear World* advertisements — and even on its program cover.
(*The Brian Gallagher Collection*)

Lansbury in *Sweeney Todd* with Len Cariou. "Making personal, noncharacter eye contact during a performance," he says, "can be distracting to an actor. If I did anything like that to Angela, she bloody well would have said something to me. And rightly so."

With the *Sweeney Todd* creative team (left to right), librettist Hugh Wheeler, director Harold Prince, and composer-lyricist Stephen Sondheim. (*Kennedy Center/Photo: Jack Buxbaum*)

Sweeney Todd, 1979.
(*Martha Swope © Time Inc.*)

"Angie's *Gypsy,*" says director Arthur Laurents, "was infinitely different from Ethel Merman's. Angela could play the romantic aspect [here with Rex Robbins] and she was even convincingly stupid."

Lansbury (with Michael Kermoyan as the King) startled the costume fitter of *The King and I* when she refused to wear the classic horizontally striped dress for "Getting to Know You." The billowing, floor-length, Irene Sharaff design had been made famous by Gertrude Lawrence on Broadway, and then by Deborah Kerr in the movie. Lansbury does not remember the episode, but the fitter suspected her of considering horizontal stripes unflattering to her figure.

In the early seasons of *Murder, She Wrote,* there were hints of a potential romance between Jessica Fletcher and the town doctor, played by William Windom, an actor Angela especially liked. Later, she insisted that Jessica have no love life.
(© *CBS Photo Archives*)

Arthur Hill in a *Murder, She Wrote* episode. The roster of guest stars was a nostalgic roll call, thousands of names long.
(© *CBS Photo Archives*)

Van Johnson. (© *CBS Photo Archives*)

Mickey Rooney. (© *CBS Photo Archives*)

Grandmother Angela on the set of *Murder, She Wrote* with her son, Anthony, and his son, Ian. (© *CBS Photo Archives*)

Angela finally got to act with her friend Laurence Olivier, in *A Talent for Murder,* a 1984 television movie. Although he was in failing health, she found the experience "thrilling, just to sit down at lunch and hear his stories about working with Ralph Richardson and Peggy Ashcroft and all those wonderful people. I have such admiration for their ability to switch, to turn and bob and weave and play so many roles. [But then] I admire anybody who can get up there and entertain an audience. I just love actors."

A particularly proud achievement of Angela's was the 1989 television movie *The Shell Seekers* (with Sam Wanamaker), based on the bestselling novel by Rosamond Pilcher. Director Waris Hussein remarked, "Angela was very anxious to get this character right, but she was also very much aware of what she wouldn't do, so as not to jeopardize the audience perception of her as the lady from *Murder, She Wrote.*" She supported the sponsor and the network in changing the novel's ending to a happier one, but ultimately agreed with Hussein that the revision was regrettable. (*Hallmark Hall of Fame*)

The Love She Sought (1990) was a rare love story for Angela and a chance to play big emotional moments. One of her best and favorite television movies, it is a story of unexpressed love between a priest (Denholm Elliot) and a devout Catholic spinster. (*NBC photo by Sven Arnstein*)

Angela and Omar Sharif played out a delicate, unexpressed suggestion of affection between two people worlds apart in the 1992 television movie *Mrs. 'Arris Goes to Paris.*

With Peter's son David during location filming of *Mrs. 'Arris Goes to Paris.*

Mrs. Santa Claus was filmed in Los Angeles during a steamy August in 1996. Two episodes of heart fibrillations reminded a seemingly inexhaustible Angela Lansbury to take care of herself. (*Randy Marcus*)

The gardener in her element. (*Philip Saltonstall*)

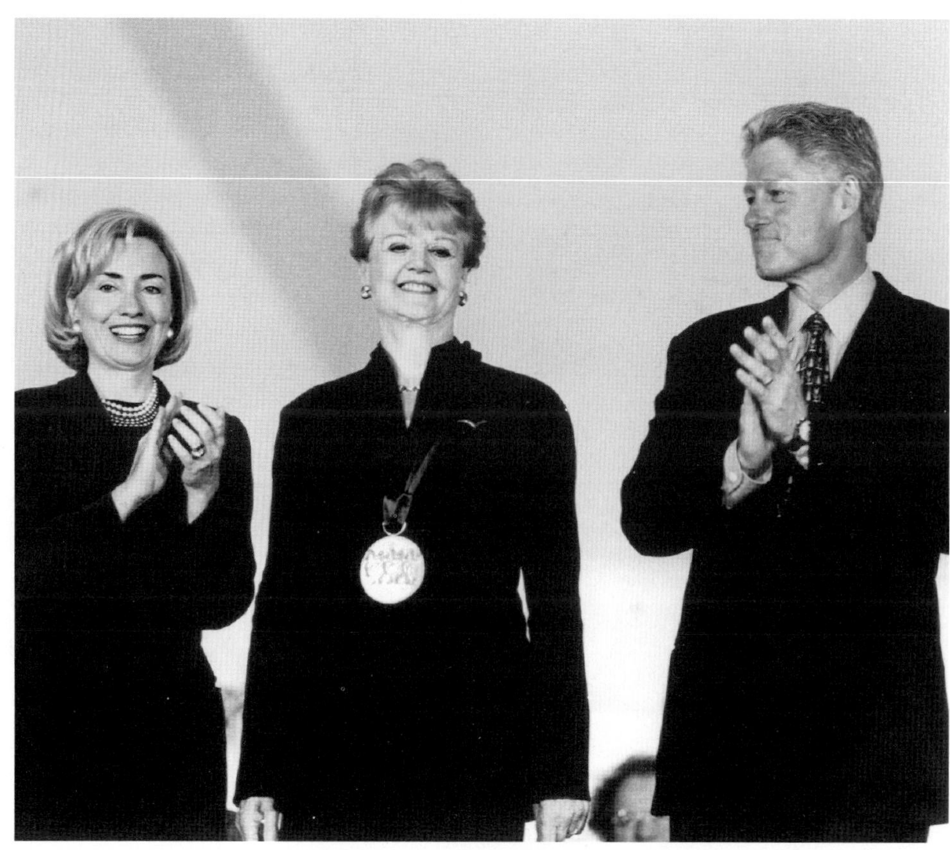

President and Mrs. Clinton applaud as Angela is awarded the National Medal of Arts in 1997. Although she has hundreds of photographs of herself with the world's famous ("I have a couple of cartons in the closet just for president and king pictures"), the only one displayed at home is with the basketball star Michael Jordan. "Well," she shrugs, "meeting him, *that was a thrill.*"
(*Official White House Photograph*)

be a frightening sight, especially when Cariou put on chalky makeup, taking the idea from the lyric "His skin was pale and his eye was odd." Even so, the character sometimes seemed to be coming from outer space, and it was essential, as Cariou kept pointing out, "to walk the fine line between farce and melodrama." Angela occasionally wondered whether she was going too far with the wacky portrayal of Nellie Lovett. "Am I hanging myself?" she asked Peter, "or is this working?"

"Keep at it," her husband told her. "It's terrific."

And so they came down the stretch, toward the start of previews. Scene rehearsals and work on the music turned into run-throughs of the whole piece.

Previews began with a private spattering when Cariou flourished Sweeney's razor ("At last my arm is complete!") in the first act and sprayed stage blood all over conductor Paul Gemignani's white music paper. The music director would let it stay there "for the entire run of the show, because it looked so cool." To Cariou, the blood spots were reminders of how anything can happen at a first preview.

> It was three hours long. We had all sorts of technical problems getting the pie shop on and off the stage. We had to vamp while the thing practically fell apart. And then there was a forty-five-minute intermission while they worked on some other technical problem. So for the audience, that performance was unfair. But they were out there, so we had to do it.

Sondheim, however, was thrilled by that first audience and after the show, he was waiting at Cariou's dressing room door as the actor came offstage. The composer was exultant. "They understood it!" he cried. "They fucking understood it!"

The actor, a tough professional, said, "Yeah! I think they did — those who stayed long enough."

But they didn't love the show, not even after the running time was reduced. Angela feared "the gray-haired and matinee ladies weren't getting it." At one preview, a woman hit producer Marty Richards with her pocketbook and cried, "How could you do a show like this? A musical about eating people up?"

By opening night, Angela had taken her performance to places she'd never before ventured as an actor.

> I just ran with it. The wide-openness of my portrayal had to do with my sink or swim attitude toward it. I just figured, hell, I've done everything else on Broadway, I might as well go with Mrs. Lovett. And I did it, maybe disgracefully at times, but it helped the show, I think. I mean, it gave the audience a chance to laugh. It was a pretty grim subject matter, let's face it, but I had my moments where I was able to run with my piece of material and make it fun and ridiculous. I think the people got that, and they got the deep seriousness that was inside this woman.

The balance between horror show and comedy worked exactly as hoped. "Have a Little Priest" never failed to delight the audience, and Angela was all but carried away with the lunacy of the number and her own twittery rendition. She came to immerse herself in the piece's staging, like a child splashing around in a swimming pool. She would pick up one pie and then another, getting the laughs and keeping the beats. But she wanted even more musical staging, and mentioned it to her husband. "Nobody has choreographed this number for me, Pete. I don't know what to do while I'm singing because it's never been staged."

Shaw said, "Oh, you know, Angie. Just do that old clog dance you always do."

Prince approved, and every time she did it, it brought down the house. She seemed to be having the time of her life, and it was all in character — even in the blackout after the number. At those times, conductor Gemignani sometimes felt little pings, as if he was getting popped with something. He finally realized that Angela was flinging balls of pie dough at him. "She would never actually *fool around* on stage during a performance," he says, "but she is probably one of the most relaxed performers I've ever dealt with."

She was relaxed enough to "cheat," as she puts it in theater jargon. "I'm from the English music hall and I don't look people right in the eye when I talk to them onstage. I look halfway between them and the audience.

"Of course if the audience is bad I'll be right back home with my leading man, face to face."

When the show opened on March 1, 1979, the reviews were generally excellent, but the Lansbury performance did not require a critic's certification. She had transcended mere excellence, rising into the realm of artistry. She had become the ultimate actor, one who could do everything from the classics to musical comedy. If *Mame* had realized her dream of singing and dancing on Broadway and being the glamorous musical comedy star, then *Sweeney Todd* stamped her as an actor of prodigious originality. "I was thrilled," Angela says, "when people told me, 'That's the best thing you ever did.' "

They were right. It was the finest stage work in a career of dazzling variety, the sum of thirty-five years of practicing her profession, and aspiring to its highest standards. Hers was an unparalleled versatility. It was as if she had become all actors, and her work stood in tribute to the heart, the daring, even the nobility of every player who had ever braved a stage.

"We loved doing the show," Angela says, "and I did believe in it, but I could see that audiences were having a tough time swallowing it."

In fact, *Sweeney Todd* would ultimately win a slew of prizes but never be a smash hit. The show simply was not for the mass taste. "It was only because of Angie's humor," producer Marty Richards says, that it ran for a year and a half. Prince put it a different way. "The reason it ran for only a year and a half, and not forever," he says, "was not because audiences didn't like it. It was because you couldn't drag people in there who didn't want to see it. No matter how much you told them, 'It's about cannibalism but it isn't *really* about cannibalism — *you've got to go'* —

"Forget it. They wouldn't go."

Full houses and long runs define the hits, but do they define quality? Is Broadway's common wisdom valid — that a hit is a good show and a flop is a bad one? Is the audience an essential factor in the theatrical equation, and is its approval definitive? Angela Lansbury does not think so.

> They can be dazzled, or taken in by actors' fancy footwork. The audience on occasion will accept second-rate stuff, jumping to their feet and giving standing ovations for sheer shmaltz. Or by *material.* It can carry a piece. The acting is overboard, and not particularly good, but the audience will rise to its feet. There are also tricks an actor can play. They milk the audience. I don't begrudge them. They've been in a show for fifteen months, why not? Do anything in the book to grab the audience.

Although she herself would not do that, she could not bring herself to come down on actors and stay down on them.

> Actors fall into various categories. There are serious and studious actors, and there are those who do it for the money, or are journeyman actors playing a part for its worth for very little notice or kudos — and they can be playing in a regional theater where they have a weekly audience who come back for whatever they're doing — they are out there to entertain. They're not stars. They're actors. And there are actors who only play small parts. And they're happy to do it because they have the work. They never get the accolades and the attention. They go to the theater, do the job, leave, go home and pay bills. So you've got all these different categories of actors.

She loves them all and loves being one of their number. As she had said, "An actor. That is who I really, really am."

CHAPTER 18

A SEVEN-YEAR SENTENCE IN JAIL

FOR TOO many people work is drudgery. For the fortunate it is fulfilling. Angela Lansbury's work as an actress could not have been more enriching. It was a vocation — a calling in the richest sense of the word. Her two years in Ireland had been a partial leave of absence from it, for which *Sweeney Todd* was making up, but in the meantime the children had been growing up. Anthony was already twenty-seven and Deirdre twenty-six.

As *Sweeney Todd* wound down its New York engagement, Angela agreed to stay with the show for a six-month national tour. Between the Broadway closing and the Washington reopening, she flew to England to make a movie called *The Mirror Crack'd,* in which she played Agatha Christie's dowdy detective Miss Marple.

While working on it, she told Rex Reed, "If this film is a success, I've been offered a whole string of Miss Marple movies, but realistically speaking, I think my future is in the theater, so I'm looking for a home in Connecticut for a long-term option."

> Peter used to drive up the Palisades Parkway, miles up in Columbia County, looking for a house. He never found what we wanted. They were always on roads, but being English, we imagined ourselves back from the road, up a long driveway. But

of course the old houses were never built that way because, with snow in the wintertime, people had to have access to their homes. Consequently all the great old early-American houses were right on the roads. Some were nice, quiet country roads. Maybe we should have settled for one of them.

She said to Reed, "We've been getting feelers for a television series, and there's piles of money there, but a seven-year sentence in jail is what it would be if I got chained to one character at this point in my life."

There was a big budget for *A Mirror Crack'd,* but there was also something seedy about the picture. Lansbury's co-stars, Elizabeth Taylor, Rock Hudson, Kim Novak, and Tony Curtis, had all seen better days — in Hudson's case, much better ones, for he was mortally ill and looked it. As for the movie, she would ultimately consider it unwatchable.

George Hearn had replaced Len Cariou during the New York run of *Sweeney Todd,* and it was he who went on tour with Angela. A superb singing actor, Hearn's performance was quite different from Cariou's, for he was a gentle spirit, and his Todd had a tragic dimension. As the conductor, Paul Gemignani, compared the two versions,

> George was just a different kind of psycho in the show. Angela wasn't any different other than in her adjustment to another actor. When you're playing lead roles, you can't play the moments exactly the same because there's a different emotion coming at you, so you have to find out where the electricity is with the new co-actor. Rather than George adjusting to her, she adjusted to him. She made him feel like what they were creating together was happening for the first time. That is very generous.

She was also generous with professional advice, as for instance, when Hearn mentioned that he felt caught between Prince's and Sondheim's preferences in the Sweeney Todd throat-cutting technique. "Hal wants me to cut the judge's throat in a muscular, sweeping way," he said, "but Stephen tells me, 'This is about finesse. I don't like bullies.'" Angela suggested, "When Stephen comes, do it his way. When Hal comes, do it his way. When they're not here, do it your way," and she also gave him a few lessons in professional ease. During one performance, Hearn remembers, "she kicked her foot and one of her slippers went flying off in a high loop. The audience roared. She kind of hobbled around after it happened, and howled.

Just uncontrolled laughter at the silliness of watching this slipper go ass over teakettle. But I never saw her *go out*," meaning that even in such playful moments, she remained in character. It wasn't Lansbury giggling over the looping slipper — it was Nellie Lovett.

And she was relaxed enough to pass wind right in the middle of a show. The young Angela who had been so proper that she would never let a curse word cross her lips was giving way to an earthier, if not exactly saltier, version. "As I was walking across the stage," she remembers, "if I'd eaten something like beans for dinner, I would whisper to George, 'It's happening.' With each step I would let a little out."

The two of them would then share this esoteric experience, for Hearn says, "I was farting my way across the stage, too."

She also sympathized with his straining voice. "This is tough," he said to her, "I'm reaching down in my boots for these high notes."

"Honey," she said, "we're pumping iron," but she could carry the weight.

> Your voice is there only if you feed your body properly. But you have to give your voice and your body rest during that day. Take the nap in the afternoon, get enough sleep at night. If you don't get that sleep you won't have it, forget it, you can't deliver the goods. I learned that on occasion, when I didn't get enough sleep, and it was frightening how reamed out my voice was, how my energy was gone, and my sense of confidence.
>
> I never lost my voice during *Sweeney Todd,* whereas the boys — both Len and George — lost theirs. I learned what tenors learn, which is to pull your buttocks together and pull your stomach in *to support the tone.* You've got to support it with air. When you run out of air and your voice is in your throat, you lose your voice.

While the road company was in San Francisco, Angela and Peter finally got the chance to host a wedding, when Anthony married Lee Speer Webster, a Nebraska artist, on May 30, 1980. The ceremony was held in the chapel of Grace Cathedral. The couple had chosen San Francisco for the occasion so that Angela could take part in the wedding arrangements, which she found "tremendous fun. I got all the flowers from Podesta Boldacci, the great flower shop in San Francisco." Deirdre — who had been living in Italy — came over to be the maid of honor.

As the tour wound down in Los Angeles, *Sweeney Todd* was videotaped for commercial broadcast, ensuring a permanent record of the extraordinary Lansbury performance. George Hearn was hardly surprised by her confidence around a camera, but his own acting was abruptly unsettled. He had not expected that there would be such a difference between theatrical acting and camera work. "Some of the people who were very good in *Sweeney* on the stage are not very good in the videotape. Angela was the only member of the cast who knew how to gauge the performance for the camera and at the same time, still seem as if she were on the stage. She knew *I've got this makeup on. It's not a movie. It's very clearly a photographed stage play. But I can't be quite as big.*

"She knows how to do it big," he says, "but camera-size."

That was the end of *Sweeney Todd* for Angela. She had missed very few performances. ("If somebody else goes on for me," she told Hearn, "I feel as if somebody's sleeping with my man.") A West End production of the show was in the offing, but just as with *Mame,* she declined to repeat a musical triumph in London, this time claiming, "There are a hundred actors in England who can play Mrs. Lovett." Her refusal seems to have been a factor of split nationality. When she was in England, her British identification was dominant, and she could sound positively condescending about musicals, as when she told a London interviewer, "I come back [to London] to get into the theater properly. . . . I don't think a musical is a test of the mettle of an actor. It's a different challenge."

In America, movie work still slow in coming and, eager as ever to work, she found a play to do, *A Little Family Business,* by Jay Presson Allen, who had adapted Muriel Sparks's *The Prime of Miss Jean Brodie* for the stage. Years earlier, Angela had announced that she was going to do *Brodie* on the London stage "before I take it to New York and then I'll do it as a movie." She and Peter had hoped to buy the producing rights, but they lost the play, and she didn't get the part. Vanessa Redgrave played *Jean Brodie* in London, Zoe Caldwell did the play on Broadway, and Maggie Smith starred in the movie version. It was a wonderful role, and all of them were triumphant playing it.

A Little Family Business hadn't a prayer of being another *Prime of Miss Jean Brodie.* It was a farce that Mrs. Allen had adapted from the French original *Potiche,* by Pierre Barillet and Jean-Pierre Gredy. The plan was to test the comedy in Los Angeles. When it was badly received, a new director —

Martin Charnin — was engaged, and changes were made in the cast, but the play fared no better in New York. Angela's only pleasant memory of the experience was working with a handsome young actor named Anthony Shaw, who was making his Broadway debut in the play. She had told Charnin, "If you have any problem with that — *don't.* Just forget that he's my son," but the director thought Anthony "was quite good as an actor."

While the whole family was in New York, Angela got the chance to throw a wedding for her daughter, too. Deirdre was marrying Enzo Battara, a young man she'd met in Italy. His family came over for the ceremony, which was held in the chapel at the United Nations. "We had a reception in a wonderful sky room," Angela remembers, "overlooking Central Park," and although it was an informal affair, the bride got her wish of wearing a full-length, traditional gown.

A Little Family Business opened on Broadway at the end of 1982 and ran just three weeks. Lansbury shrugged it off as "a play-play, a sitcom." She was already interested in the idea that Harold Prince and Hugh Wheeler were proposing, a musicalization of the movie classic *Sunset Boulevard.* Prince had not yet found the composer for it. He'd suggested it to Andrew Lloyd Webber, with whom he had done *Evita,* but Webber was busy writing *Cats.* Prince told Angela that he was going to take it to John Kander and Fred Ebb, or Sondheim. Meanwhile, she agreed to yet another revival of *Mame,* this time for the producer Mitch Leigh.

Leigh was in partnership with Yul Brynner, running a money machine in the perpetually revived *The King and I.* Angela's two-week stint in that show was surely what gave him the idea of doing the same thing with her and *Mame.* The production was to open in Philadelphia, play a Boston engagement, and then come to New York. She had told George Hearn, "I'm not going to do any more musicals. It's too hard — the costume changes alone . . ." and besides, she had developed "a little hip problem." But now the fifty-eight-year-old Lansbury got into the same toned condition, doing the same choreography, that she had mastered at forty-one. Jane Connell was again playing Agnes Gooch, and one night at a cast party in Philadelphia just before previews started, she suggested a parlor game. She passed out pencils and blank sheets of paper, with instructions for everyone to divide their pages into six segments. In each one, Connell instructed them to draw anything that came to mind. "You can put a circle in one," she said, "and a couple of squiggly lines in another. Or you can draw a vertical line, or anything you like. You can even leave one of the spaces blank."

After collecting the pages, she "analyzed" them for the participants.

"It's fascinating and amazing," she thought, "how people reveal themselves in that," because some would fill in every inch of the pages, leaving "jagged marks or some disturbance," while others would make placid little drawings, like circles with smiling faces. "The circle symbolized ego, for instance. Some people would put in bigger circles, which represent big egos and how they feel about themselves."

Angela declined to participate, even though the exercise was just for fun. "I'm not a psychiatrist," Connell said, "I don't want to scare anybody, but Angie just refused until she saw how I did the interpretations." The next night, Lansbury stopped by at Connell's hotel room and handed her a sheet of paper, divided into the six sections. She had done the drawings.

"Would you analyze it?" she asked.

It was a very simple, uncomplicated set of pictures. One was indeed a circle, made into what Connell described as "a little daisy in the breeze. That ego circle was a little blossoming thing in the field, no big deal about her, just sunny and bright." More significantly, it was drawn only after there was foreknowledge of the analytic approach. Which, then, reflected the true Angela Lansbury — the page with the drawings or the blank page the night before? Was one the actress and the other the role? Did this suggest a reluctance to ad-lib her life? Was she insecure, and fearful of self-revelation?

The show's dance captain, Diana Baffa-Brill, another veteran of the original *Mame,* felt, "Whatever her insecurities are, I don't know, but boy, does she have securities."

Connell decided that the reserve and the insecurities were linked. "She waited to risk revealing herself only when she knew how I read the drawings, but that made it very endearing to me. Being controlled and private adds to the mystery of her performances. Because to me, the kids nowadays — telling all, revealing all — there's no mystery any more. The excitement of someone is the mystery to me. I don't mean she's devious or dishonest, in fact just the opposite. But she does reserve a portion of herself for herself, and that makes me respect her even more."

Doing *Mame* again was, like so many of her money-motivated decisions, a poor one. The schedule called for playing the big East Coast cities in midsummer, when middle-class audiences took vacations. The Philadelphia engagement actually began on the Fourth of July weekend. At the first preview, Diana Baffa-Brill looked through the curtain peephole and saw "nothing but oceans of empty seats." The closing notice was put up on opening day, and the engagement was aborted after a week. With virtually no advance sale in Boston, that booking was canceled, and the show came directly to New York, without advance publicity or advertising. Baffa-Brill called it, "Nightmare, nightmare, nightmare. Angela was devastated by the experience."

But she seemed incapable of explosive anger. At the opening night party, all she could say about the producer was, "I just can't sit next to him." When the show closed after only six weeks on Broadway, Baffa-Brill remembers,

> Mr. Leigh took a full-page ad in *Variety* about how much money *The King and I* had made to date, congratulating Yul Brynner and reading, "Now THAT's a star." It was like a kick in the teeth to Angela.

Then the *Sunset Boulevard* project collapsed when Sondheim rejected the idea. He told Harold Prince that years earlier, he'd also thought of musicalizing the movie and had even mentioned the idea to Billy Wilder, who had co-written and directed *Sunset Boulevard.* Wilder's reaction was, "It's got to be an opera. It's about a dethroned queen," and Sondheim agreed. "Angie," he told Prince, "would be a great Norma Desmond. If I wanted to do an opera, this is certainly a possibility.

"But I don't want to do an opera, so this is not a possibility."

Operatic musicals were the style of composer Andrew Lloyd Webber, and when he subsequently musicalized *Sunset Boulevard,* that was how he did it.

So it was that Angela's brother Bruce, who was the head of television programming at Paramount Pictures Television, wrote her a note from California, suggesting that she consider doing a situation comedy series. Since there was no other work on the horizon at all,

> Peter and I decided that I was definitely ready to go into a television series. I'd exhausted my theater chances at that point. Also, I was *of an age,* and I thought, while I've got the strength and the get-up-and-go, I really should get William Morris onto trying to get me a good script.

It is in the nature of the acting profession that one goes where the work is. For Angela, being "chained to one character" no longer loomed "like a seven-year sentence in jail."

* * *

Early in 1984 Harvey Shepard, the head of programming at CBS, contacted William Link and his partner, Richard Levinson. The two men, both about forty-five and friends since childhood, were among the most successful writers of mysteries in network television. They had sold more than a dozen series, including *The Ellery Queen Mystery Theater, Mannix,* and *McCloud.* They were under contract to Universal Television as producers but were already enormously wealthy because of their biggest hit, *Columbo.*

Shepard had come up with what Link considered an "innovative" idea — a mystery with a woman protagonist," and the actress he had in mind for it was Jean Stapleton, who had been free for a few years, ever since *All in the Family* ended its eight-and-a-half-year run. Between that show's enormous success and its popular reruns, Stapleton still had one of the highest *TvQ* ratings. *TvQ*, as one network executive describes it, is "a published rating of television actors according to likability and recognizability. The networks all subscribe to it. It's a number, a ranking." Bruce Lansbury likened it to the McCarthy era's notorious *Red Channels* in the way it affected a performer's employability, and he considered it equally inane. "You get a rating only after you've done something. That's what makes it so useless. Before *All in the Family,* nobody ever heard of Jean Stapleton. Now she was at the top."

Besides her television familiarity quotient, Stapleton offered other attractions for CBS. *All in the Family* had given the network a powerful Sunday night combination, having followed the top-ranked *Sixty Minutes,* but ever since its demise CBS, according to Shepard, "had had an erratic history" on that night. An ABC series called *Love Boat* "was destroying us no matter what we scheduled." Stapleton would be a familiar face in the eight o'clock time slot, even though there was no thought of having her play the central character as Edith Bunker. ("If they'd suggested that," she said, "I wouldn't even have read the script.")

The idea of the series, a lady mystery writer/solver, struck the liberal-minded producer William Link as provocative and progressive. "There were very few women stars of dramatic series on television," he says. "Comedies, yes, and that went for minorities, too. The industry take was that women and minorities were okay for laughing, but not in a dramatic series where you had to take them seriously."

He and Richard Levinson contacted Peter S. Fischer, a writer whom they had employed ever since their business became too big for them to write individual episodes. In any case, they now preferred to write issue-oriented television movies, like *The Execution of Private Slovik.* Fischer was hungrier. "And," he says, "Dick and Bill didn't like to write mysteries as much as I did." They suggested that if the series were to work out, Fischer would become the executive producer and they the consultants. That would mean a great deal of money for him, more than a million dollars a year.

Fischer was a self-described "writerly type," tall, slender, bespectacled, and fond of playing golf and poker. He had come to television relatively late in life. Only ten years earlier, at thirty-five, he had been supporting his wife and young children by editing a sports car magazine out of his Long Island home. "One day," he says, "I sat down at the kitchen table and wrote a movie and actually got it sold." He promptly "sold the house, packed up the kids, and came to California to try my luck."

His luck held. He sold a story idea for *Columbo,* and here he was, tossing ideas back and forth with that show's now legendary creators. (Link and Levinson would eventually join Rod Serling and Paddy Chayefsky as the only writers in the Television Hall of Fame.) They were still trying to refine the concept for the new mystery series.

"To our knowledge," Link says, "there had been only one woman detective in American television, and that had been *Police Woman,* the Angie Dickinson show. But she was like the little woman the males always bailed out. We wanted to do a show with an intelligent woman who solved things in her own right," and with Jean Stapleton's age in mind, their thoughts inevitably gravitated toward Miss Marple, the Agatha Christie detective. But Fischer suggested a variation on that character. "Why don't we do not Miss Marple but the writer Agatha Christie as the solver of mysteries, and then combine the two and put it in America?"

Link and Levinson approved, and joined by CBS's Shepard, they soon met with Jean Stapleton and her agent-manager in the dining room of the luxurious Bel-Air Hotel. The writers described the show they had in mind. Stapleton, a sophisticated and articulate woman and a serious-minded actor, said that she could not form an opinion from just a verbal description; she would have to see a script. Shepard suggested that the fellows write a two-hour television movie as a pilot, "and that's what the three of us did," Link says. "Fischer wrote the teleplay under our tutelage."

Upon reading it, Stapleton's reaction was, "I didn't understand it."

"We were nonplussed," Link remembers. "We thought it was a nice script, but it certainly wasn't quantum physics. What was there not to understand? There were clever clues but not anything that cerebral."

After three sets of revisions and as many meetings at the Link and Levinson offices in the Universal Studios building — the infamous Black

Tower — the actress remained unconvinced. She urged them to be more specific about "Jessica Beatrice Fletcher," as they named the character. She had good reason to feel knowledgeable about television writing. Doing "*All in the Family,*" she says, "was like going to a university for writers. Mr. Levinson and Mr. Link were very clever and very professional, but the pilot script was plot driven, and they didn't seem to comprehend that the thing an actor looks for is *character.*"

Stapleton had found that "the development of Edith Bunker was a fascinating, very stimulating experience. She lived in New York where everybody walks fast — and she had all this pressure from Archie to get the dinner cooked, or other chores — so a run developed for her. Then, I had done that nasal talking when I was in *Damn Yankees,* so I took that on, because it's funny. And with that added, Edith began to evolve. Because of her desire to please Archie, she became less canny. I decided that she had no contact with the world except television or else whoever came into the house. So that was how her mental level developed. And the writers saw these clues, and brought other clues, and it was such a good collaboration. Finally, even while she was getting laughs, she was bursting the bubble of Archie's bigotry and self-importance.

"Now with Jessica, the writers were probably depending on the actor to bring that character, but I have to see some degree of color and characterization on the page. There wasn't enough detail. For instance, Jessica was an English teacher, but there was nothing in the script to show her doing that, or to suggest a delectability on her part, of language. Now Edith Bunker, her character developed through the first thirteen weeks, but it was on the page to begin with. The humor was there, the relationship with Archie was there.

"And," she adds, "intuition comes into the mix, one's instinct in making a decision about taking a role. Intuition and instinct are similar but not identical. The intuition is something we must listen to carefully. So my decision was a matter of following the little voice."

When Jean Stapleton rejected the show, Fischer assumed the deal was dead. Instead, Shepard told them, "We love this damn thing and we're going to do it one way or the other, so let's get another actress."

As they left the meeting, Link, Levinson, and Fischer asked one another, who is intelligent? Who's got some clout? Whom do the networks like? Link knew, "The marketing aspects always come into this. It's not who's best for the role; it's who fits and also has a high *TvQ.*"

They considered the possibilities of various middle-aged movie actresses — June Allyson, for instance, and Rhonda Fleming. As Fischer said,

"We needed an actress in her late fifties with some name recognition." Then it occurred to Link that "a casting agent at Universal had told us that Angela Lansbury was available and looking for a series."

Levinson took to that idea. Like Link, he was a theater buff. In fact, their popular Columbo character originated in a play they had written in 1960, *Prescription: Murder.* They had grown up going to Broadway tryouts in Philadelphia, where they went to college. It was there that they had seen Angela Lansbury in *Anyone Can Whistle.* They thought of her as a stage star — but not as a movie star. "She never made it in a big way," Link said, worrying about her clout with the network.

Fischer had other doubts. "You watch some of her old movies," he said, "like *State of the Union* or *The Manchurian Candidate* and you say, is that really Angela Lansbury? Is she really a cold fish?"

Link replied, "It was just good acting, and sometimes the best actors are the character people, not the ones with the marquee weight. That's what she is, a very fine dramatic actress who is also good at comedy."

As far as he and Levinson were concerned, "When we learned that she was available and interested in a series, we were bedazzled. And then we found out that she really didn't have a *TvQ.* She wasn't even listed. How were we supposed to sell her to Mr. Shepard at CBS? We walked into his office with our heads on the curb. We thought we were going to be kicked out. We said we wanted Angela Lansbury — that if you do a literate show with a lot of dialogue, a lot of actors can't handle it. But she had the English flavor of Miss Marple, and she had an intelligence, and an incisiveness." Even so, "in our minds," a gloomy Link felt, "we had already given up the series for dead."

> At another network, the guy might have started screaming when he heard Angela's name. "Yeah, she's a good actress, but have they heard of her?" You see, there was always that great divide between New York and Hollywood. There was a snobbery that New York had toward Hollywood and then there was the reverse. But this guy, Shepard, he was intoxicated with the idea of Angela.

Now she had to be convinced. Late on a spring Friday afternoon, Lansbury kept an appointment with Shepard, Link, Levinson, and Fischer in the office of Robert Harris, the president of Universal Television. "She was charming," Link says, "and she looked great." She was even more appealing to Fischer. "It was unbelievable. Meeting her for the first time, I thought, 'Oh my God, why haven't they recognized this in this woman?' We all fell in love with her.

"Well, how can you not?"

Harris said to her, "There will be males in the show, but it's going to be *your show.* Jessica Fletcher will be a brilliant mind of detection, and will solve these cases on her own. We aren't going to pander. There aren't going to be any males to the rescue."

Link could see that she was intrigued, "but then she told us that she'd been given a sitcom script by Norman Lear. He was hot as a pistol, and that series would be done with Charlie Durning."

Angela said, "I'm going to read Norman's script over the weekend." Link and Levinson looked at each other in defeat. Then she added, "I'll read your script, too. I'll give you my decision on Monday morning."

As everyone headed for the studio parking lot, the two old friends exchanged doubts. "You usually hear that from a star," Link said. "It's always a lot of bull." Even so, they were "on tenterhooks" for the whole weekend.

The Norman Lear proposal was a husband-and-wife detective series. As a half-hour situation comedy, it would be performed live on a stage, in a theater, before an audience, and with three cameras video-recording it. In contrast, the Link-Levinson pilot was for a one-hour show, an anthology series that was made like a movie, on film with one camera and of course no audience. Reading their script, Angela shared some of Jean Stapleton's doubts. She thought that the plot wasn't very good, and that "there was no hard-driving tension." But she also saw possibilities in the central character.

She called her agent, Jerry Katzman, a top man at William Morris (he would become president of the agency) and asked what he thought of the two proposals.

"In my opinion," he said, "you should do the Lear sitcom. The work is not as exhausting as a one-hour anthology, and it's so much closer to the genre you're used to doing on the Broadway stage. If the network buys it — and let's face it, this is a Norman Lear show — doing it would be easier and more comfortable."

Angela replied, "I'm sure you're right, but this Jessica Fletcher stimulates me."

"If that's what you prefer," Katzman said, "we'll do it, but that's a tough and grueling exercise, and I'm going to say something else that you're not going to like. In the history of television, there hasn't been a dramatic show with a woman lead that has been successful, except for maybe *Police Woman,* and that was only a moderate success. It lasted just a couple of seasons, so this is a real, real long shot."

"But," she argued, "I love it, that it's a long shot."

"Well, when it comes to mysteries, those guys are the best," her agent conceded, "and Peter Fischer is a top-drawer writer."

She spent the weekend weighing the two possibilities. Naturally, she focused on the character she would play in each, and when it came to the mystery series, she reacted differently than had Stapleton. It seemed to her that, although the character of Jessica Fletcher was not yet fleshed out, the writers had done a good job of creating a basis for her. Their purpose in this pilot script, she felt, was for "the audience to see as many sides of her as possible," and she was already beginning to imagine whom Jessica might develop into. "The possibilities," she concluded, "are definitely there."

On Monday morning, she called Levinson and Link and told them that after reading their script, "the actor in me bubbled to the fore." She talked to them about Jessica's potential, and about "refining that." They listened. She perceived an adult woman in this character. The main point, she said, was, "I love this project of yours. It's the one I want to do."

They were "ecstatic," and Link knew that

> we'd gotten exactly the person we wanted. In television, the major thing — even more than the writing, excellent or mediocre — is the star and how well the star fits in that role; how *likable* the person is in that role. This is a major, major element, the personality's likability. I don't care what they say about scripts, about terrific production values. The audience doesn't even notice those things except maybe on a primitive, subconscious level. It's a *people medium.* They buy the people. You're not going to invite somebody you don't particularly like into your home every week, and that's basically what television is.

Coincidentally enough, the script for the series proposed by Norman Lear was eventually made by Bea Arthur. Angela thought that "the fact that Norman could see me and Bea in the same role was interesting. We couldn't be more different." That pilot was televised. The series went unsold.

In April of 1984, even before their pilot was made, Link, Levinson, Fischer, and O'Neill hurriedly filmed a handful of scenes from it and sat Angela down at a typewriter. She chatted into the camera in the character of Jessica Fletcher. She would interrupt herself, saying, "Let me show you something," and that was where several scenes were spliced in. "We sent it to New York," O'Neill says, "and when they showed it to advertisers, everyone wanted to buy in."

With that, CBS not only approved immediate production of the pilot, but ordered a full season's worth of episodes. Angela and Peter settled into Los Angeles for the duration, despite her feeling that "I could never live there again." They would be there for a year at the least, and they rented a house on Highwood Street in Brentwood. Needing a series title, Link, Levinson, and Fischer once again looked to Agatha Christie. She had called one of her mysteries *Murder, She Said*. It wasn't much of a jump to *Murder, She Wrote*. The two-hour pilot script was called *Who Killed Sherlock Holmes?* The director was Corey Allen, and the line producer (who was responsible for budgets, contracts, and generally administering the show) was Robert F. O'Neill, who had been Fischer's regular partner on the *Columbo* series.

Bob O'Neill was a wiry fellow, so homespun that he actually used expressions like "golly," "gosh," "darn," and "God love her." As a group, the makers of television series — the line producers, the writers, the directors — generally seemed, unlike their movie and stage counterparts, closer to the average American than to show business. One of O'Neill's story editors, Robert Van Skoyk, says, "Fellows like us appreciate television because we don't have to go all over the world to work. We can stay home with our families and still have our careers. You're home evenings and eat with the kids."

It made for a sharp personality contrast with the network executives, who tended to be more Hollywood, like the head of CBS Television in Los Angeles, who came to the office in a tennis shirt, tennis shorts, and tennis sneakers. Those businessmen upstairs, O'Neill knew, were still uncertain about casting Angela Lansbury. "There were people who knew she had a long career in film and four Tony Awards, but they felt that the fly-overs really did not know her."

Being one of them himself, he knew all about "fly-overs," which was how the network executives condescendingly viewed the people who made up the greater part of the television audience — CBS's in particular. The "fly-overs" were, in short, the average population, everyone between the smart East and West coasts. O'Neill grimly accepted this attitude as a fact of television life, but Fischer was rankled by such arrogance toward a Middle America for which he had real affection and respect. While he himself was from the New York area, he was not especially fond of the place. For him, the heartlands of the country, home of the "fly-overs," represented a sorely missed way of life. He admired their values, their civility and decency, their preservation of the traditional American ethos. He meant *Murder, She Wrote* to be a show for and about these people, and was "consciously aiming for heartland American values."

Yet, he was not a brand-name conservative. Rather, he was a nostalgist, a New Yorker worn down by crime, urban tensions, crudeness, and street anger. He longed for a considerate and sensible way of living, and in his mind, it would be personified by Jessica Fletcher, a woman who "comes from a Cabot Cove where she could and did always leave the door unlocked."

Cabot Cove, Maine, based on the real Maine town of Castine, was to be the series setting, and it was where the two-hour pilot episode opened — the photographed "Cabot Cove" being the picturesque California town of Mendocino. Jessica Fletcher is established as a substitute English teacher with an interest in mysteries. Her nephew finds a manuscript of one such novel she had written as therapy after her husband, Frank, a real estate agent, died. The nephew brings it to a New York publisher played by Arthur Hill. It promptly becomes a bestseller, and it is soon followed by a second book.

When Jessica visits New York to publicize the new mystery, she finds the city, the media, and even the people on the streets abusive. One of her book interviewers is a supercilious snob who denigrates average Americans and the television they watch: "We know it takes very little to please the folks from Dubuque," he says. "How else do you explain television?"

Such details do create a conservative subtext, and there are other swerves to the right, as for instance, when another interviewer — a stereotypical feminist — is presented as so dumb that she gives away the identity of the murderer in Jessica's novel. But *Who Killed Sherlock Holmes?* is essentially an entertainment, and these themes are just undercurrents. If the pilot film makes any points, they are more societal than political. It is big-city life that is being derogated. Jessica is even mugged, and after three days in New York City, she is muttering that she has been "insulted, browbeaten, and patronized." Hill, her publisher, agrees. "Believe me," he says, "it took years to get used to this town." He invites her for a weekend in his country home to meet "real people." That is where the murder occurs; Jessica finds herself attracted to this publisher of hers and then discovers that he himself is the murderer.

The pilot gave Jessica Fletcher her first and last serious on-screen kiss, and it ended with the traditional, detailed explanation of exactly how she solved the mystery. In the trade, this scene is called the "Gotcha!"

Fischer had already decided that he would implement a policy of guest stars playing the suspects. He had done that on his *Ellery Queen* series and learned that there had to be more than one guest star because, "If you set up six suspects and five of them are played by unknown actors, while the other one is played by Robert De Niro, guess who the killer is?" In addition to Arthur Hill, the two-hour pilot movie was cast with Brian Keith, Ned Beatty, and Bert Convy. As for the script, the clues are clear, and the mystery is properly baffling. Fischer revised the dialogue that had been written with Jean Stapleton in mind, and Bob O'Neill thought he did it well.

> Peter has an excellent ear and he picked up right away on Angela's speech patterns. Because things that Jean Stapleton might state, although the thought was there, would be said in a different way. Angela has a twinkle in her eye. He adjusted the dialogue for her, while the thoughts and the action remained in step.

One of the reasons for Peter Fischer's success as a television writer was his sheer industriousness. Even while *Who Killed Sherlock Holmes?* was in production, he'd been filing away ideas for the episodes ahead. He had to, for the fall season was only three months away. He called Harvey Shepard's assistant, Carla Singer, who, he was certain, had come up with the idea for the show in the first place.

"Let's get going," he said. "Can I send you some story ideas?"

"Well, I'm leaving for vacation," she said. "I'll be away a month."

"But we're in May," Fischer said irritably." I have to start turning the cameras in June or early July if we're going to make a September beginning date." He knew how grueling the schedule ahead was going to be, if the twenty-two episodes ordered by CBS were to be completed by March 1985.

Sensing the shrug at the other end of the line, he hung up. The confident and intelligent Fischer would prove to be an executive producer with little patience for contradiction, or for any frustration of what he thought made sense. In this he and Angela Lansbury were alike, which was all right as long as they agreed.

He called his people at Universal and complained, "How can I produce shows if I have to wait thirty days to get a story approved?"

The answer was, "Just do the stories. We're not going to worry about the network."

And, Fischer says, "We came up with a bunch of stories. By the time we started shooting in July, we had ten scripts ready. That's called breakneck. I wrote three of them myself."

An opening montage was created. It begins with a series of preview clips after which, as the theme music starts, there is a close-up of an old desk typewriter. A sheet of blank paper is rolled into it. The word "Murder" appears to the clacking of the keys. While the music continues, there is a succession of shots of Lansbury, first on a bicycle, waving; then near a harbor, ready to go fishing in a yellow slicker, with a box of bait at her side; then, gardening in jeans, a sun hat, and a flannel shirt. Finally, the typewriter and the sheet of paper are seen again, as "She Wrote" is typed.

The theme music was commissioned from the English film composer John Addison. The intention was to get a British quality to suit Angela, but it was so musically mindless and cartoon cheerful that she "hated it from the start." One of the show's directors, Vincent McVeety, felt, "It's more Jessica's music than the show's. It's for when you see her riding on her bicycle, or you see her in Cabot Cove and how she relates to all the people. Until something dire happens, she could be the woman next door — even if she's not the kind of woman who bakes cookies. It's the music for that woman."

That homey quality, for Lansbury, was precisely the problem. The theme music was so bouncy that it sounded more appropriate for a cooking show. A few years later, her stepson David would suggest adding a few measures of "It's Today!" (from *Mame*), at the end of the show as a musical signature for the Corymore Corporation logotype — Corymore being Angela and Peter's family corporation. David was particularly musical, and the little coda promptly became a private message to theater buffs.

With production rolling on the first episode, she approached the character of Jessica Fletcher much as she did any part — as a character actor dealing with the externals of the role to be played. "First and foremost in my bag of tricks," she says, "is to know exactly what I'm going to wear, what kind of shoes, whether I wear a lift-up bra or a flattening bra — all those things are part of the lady I'm playing. The makeup, hair, everything.

I had a terrible time with the hair on the first script — couldn't get it right at all. I knew what I had in mind but I couldn't find anyone who knew what I was talking about."

She took Fischer aside on the set, and said, "We have to start talking about my wigs and my costumes."

"Wigs?" he laughed. Perhaps she was planning to play Jessica the way she'd played Miss Marple in *A Mirror Crack'd,* but it was time to tell her the facts of television life.

"Angie," he said gently, "you're not going to be wearing wigs on the show. "You're *not* going to be playing a character. There are no character quirks in these scripts."

In fact he intentionally omitted characterization at the start of any series, waiting for the actors themselves to provide the personal details. He told her, "You're going to have to basically play yourself."

She had never done that before, but he explained, "You're going to have to start, because this schedule in episodic television hours is so brutal that if you don't get comfortable with a character who is close to who you are — your personality, with your personality meshing with this character — you are going to be exhausted. You won't be able to stand it."

He was, in short, telling her that acting in the traditional sense was out. She was going to have to deny her calling, but what was that calling? Angela Lansbury is speaking from the depths of her soul when she says, "I am an actor — that is what I really, really am." Because who is that? An actor is always playing someone else.

Fischer was denying her the protection of that somebody else, forcing her to renounce the disguise of a character to be played. Perhaps the little girl in her had felt safe, hiding behind a character as she had once hid behind her mother. She could hide no longer. She was going to have to reveal herself in public.

CHAPTER 19

MURDER, SHE WROTE

WHEN COMPLETED, *Who Killed Sherlock Holmes?* was a smooth and professional two-hour television movie with excellent production values and a cast of experienced actors. Nevertheless, the doubters around CBS were already feasting on Harvey Shepard's rash commitment to twenty-two episodes, a full season of *Murder, She Wrote.* The head of programming was hearing shop talk that warned, "You're going to be thirteen and out." Thirteen shows, including the pilot, were the usual minimum airing of a new series. In doing the full complement, he had gone ahead with the "back nine," as they put it, before the series was even launched. In fact the two-hour pilot/premiere got the show started with, quite literally, a bump when it was delayed by the World Series, and it was not broadcast until the Sunday evening of September 30, 1984.

As Jean Stapleton watched, she thought,

> Angela isn't just a character actress; she's a leading woman. I've never characterized myself that way. There are character parts that fill the leading role but that doesn't make the actress a leading woman. She brought her own persona so tremendously to it, and pulled it off — I think — in that way. But she also has so

much dimension. Yet she's a character actress, too, and I thought, "Boy! She's the one to do this." She made it work. I wasn't right for it and couldn't have pulled it off like that.

The overnight ratings did more than give *Murder, She Wrote* a big send-off. Angela Lansbury, a career actress for forty years, a character actor even when playing the lead in a glamorous Broadway musical like *Mame,* was at last heading toward the one thing she thought she never could be. She was on her way beyond star roles, to being the star herself.

A character actor submerges personal identity to explore the role being played. A leading woman, as Jean Stapleton put it, "brings her own persona," so as to dominate a production in its central role. A star, however, glories in his or her own persona. The play is not the thing, the star is, projecting a unique chemistry of charm and sexuality. That is what the audience comes for, and these (not to mention beauty) were qualities Lansbury never thought that she had. Moreover, even if she discovered a hidden resource of charisma, she could never play to it, for it was precisely from such self-exposure that she shrank, onstage as a matter of professionalism, offstage as a matter of emotionalism.

Or was it, rather, that she had not been mature enough or confident enough at MGM — not *herself* enough — to become the movie star she'd yearned to be? Even as a leading lady of Broadway musicals, she could only come down the stairs by enacting a star coming down the stairs.

Television was offering a different opportunity. The charisma that makes stars of stage actors and the good looks so important to screen stars do not register with equal importance on television. It, like radio, is an intimate medium, reaching into the home. A stage star deals in presence and electricity; a film star plays to an audience community snug in the glow of a movie screen; but the television star performs for people who are alone in their homes. At such close range, the power is in the personality rather than looks, the charisma, the act. This secluded audience can celebrate the hominess of an Arthur Godfrey, the ease of a Perry Como, the good sense of a Walter Cronkite.

In the case of *Murder, She Wrote,* television communicated the decency, the civility, and the maturity of Angela Lansbury through the wisdom and warmth of Jessica Fletcher. It offered the fundamental integrity and fair-mindedness of the amateur detective as filled out, and filled in, by the actress who embodied her. In doing so, the medium made an idol of a character and an actress who blended to present a strong, adult woman. Lansbury did not have to be young, gorgeous, and dazzling, to be a star. A real person was worth celebrating, too.

So she fulfilled her innermost hope of stardom because of the honest, principled, and compassionate person she was. The American public, presumably materialistic and youth-obsessed, somehow gathered up the good sense to find such a person worthy of its admiration, and Peter Fischer appreciated that as he watched his pilot show. Angela Lansbury personally represented the values that he had set out to champion through Jessica Fletcher.

After the exhilarating overnight ratings for *Who Killed Sherlock Holmes?* William Link told her,

> Not only will this series be a hit; this will change your life. You've done movies, you've done the stage, you've done television plays, but you will not believe the popularity that you will have. Once you get out of this rather provincial Hollywood society and go into the rest of the country out there, a television star is *owned* by the people. You just have no idea.

Corymore Corporation was a Subchapter "S" corporation with neither stock nor partners, and Angela was its singular asset. CBS was to pay Universal Television the "licensing fee," which was supposed to cover the production cost of about $1,200,000 per episode, according to producer Bob O'Neill. Of that, Universal would pay Corymore $40,000 per episode for Angela's services. Finally, Corymore would pay Angela a weekly salary. It was a common legal arrangement, hardly unique to actors or show business.

Angela did not have to wait very long to appreciate Peter Fischer's warning about exhaustion. Fundamental to the production of a weekly one-hour series was the requirement to produce twenty-two episodes in the nine months between July and March. That meant finishing a show every eight days. In order to run the required length of fifty-two minutes, a script had to be between fifty-three and sixty pages long, depending on the number of locations. The production schedule for each episode was then a matter of simple and brutal arithmetic, dividing the number of pages in the script by the number of workdays. Therefore, in order to finish a show every eight workdays, each day had to result in finished film covering seven and a half pages of script. That meant fourteen-hour workdays, some of them involving as many as three locations, and since Jessica was in almost every scene of every show, Angela was going to have to be present every one of those days, Mondays through Fridays, from eight o'clock in the morning until ten o'clock at night, ready to be made up at seven o'clock in the morning. In short, the show was being manufactured on an assembly line schedule. Intensifying the pressure, director Walter Grauman explains, was the fact that "if you have eight days for shooting, and the show is on every seven days, you keep losing time, so toward the end of the season you're desperately hustling to keep up."

For a dressing room and retreat, she was given a trailer — actually, a Winnebago-like motor home. It had a mini-kitchen with banquette seating, and that was set immediately behind the driver's seat. Next came an airplane-type bathroom, equipped with a shower, and finally, in the rear, a makeup table and mirror, and a couch for napping. "I lived in that motor home with Dolores," Angela says. "We were right on top of each other, so any kind of mood swings or misunderstandings were very felt. You couldn't be in that small place and not feel them."

"Dolores" was her veteran dresser, Dolores Childers, whom she had requested. She also asked Bob O'Neill if there was anything that her son might do on the show, and the producer started Anthony out watching postproduction. From there the young man progressed to being a dialogue coach.

Peter Fischer had not exaggerated. *Murder, She Wrote* was produced with virtually no rehearsal. There simply was no time for it, except "fifteen or twenty minutes for a scene," he says, throwing the actors a bone. "They can go off with the director and fiddle with a scene while the cameras and lights are being set up." As for his opposition to Lansbury's characterizing — finding a Jessica to play — that would never change. It wasn't only the time constraints; he was looking for Angela Lansbury, not Jessica Fletcher. "We found that some of the quirky things we had given her didn't work or were unnecessary — like fumbling around in her purse, or a couple of catch phrases that she repeated and they were useless, so forget it.

"Then we would watch dailies and we would see things that she would do, and attitudes that she would take, and we would write to those. So we started writing to her strengths, and she started to pick up on our rhythms, and it began to become a blend. The writer learns from the actor, the actor learns from the writer."

Even so, Angela Lansbury could not instantly accept the notion of not characterizing. She had been a character actress too long to change overnight. She started, as always, with the character's appearance.

> What did I want Jessica to look like? Like a woman who was probably forty-eight to fifty years old; who still had a tremendous zest for life; who was energetic, who jogged, who wore sweatsuits, who was totally current in every respect of her life. The clothes I wore on the pilot were kind of *pottschkied* together in a hurry. But I wanted every thread I put on my back to be in character for this woman. I didn't want to just go to the store and buy a bunch of clothes. So I asked my friend Julie Weiss, who is a distinguished designer, and she and I met in New York. We knew we couldn't buy what we were looking for in Los Angeles, so we went to Paul Stuart. We went to Abercrombie and Fitch. We went to Saks Fifth Avenue's sportswear department and we bought shirts, we bought skirts, we bought slacks, we bought blazers. We bought all sorts of rather dowdy, older college girl–look clothes and we had a ball.

An actor could view a continuing role in a television series as the perfect part, one that is constantly evolving in a play that does not end. Every performance includes another development in experience, if not character. Angela started to notice details that Fischer and his little stable of writers were adding to Jessica's background, and as she began identifying herself with the character, she even suggested a few details from her own life. For instance, in one of the earliest episodes, *Sing a Song of Murder,* Jessica's maiden name is revealed as Macgill which, of course, was Moyna's name. That plot involves Jessica's cousin, Emma Macgill, who is a music hall singer in England. Angela not only plays both parts in this charming episode but, as Emma, she sings "Goodbye, Little Yellow Bird," the song she sang in *The Picture of Dorian Gray.* (A few seasons later, Emma Macgill would reappear in another episode, that time singing "How'd You Like to Spoon with Me?" which Angela sang in *Till the Clouds Roll By.*)

By December, the ratings for *Murder, She Wrote* were climbing steadily. The reason for its popularity was not the brilliance of the scripts. Mysteries, after all, are mysteries. "What takes one of them to a higher level," the co-creator of this one, William Link, believes, "is a great character. If you read Conan Doyle, the stories aren't anything special, but the character of Sherlock Holmes is wonderful. The stories are subsumed by the richness, the details of that character — his eccentricities, his relationship with Dr. Watson, who is Everyman, his Sancho Panza."

Was Jessica the "great character" in *Murder, She Wrote,* or was it Angela? For Bill Link, it was Angela.

> What she has, and it's God-given, is she's a very strong person but she doesn't intimidate. You still like her, and the male audience isn't intimidated. Now usually they're unthreatened by weaker women, women who cater. But Angela's not like that. She's a tough act. There's a real tensile strength there.

Unlike Peter Fischer, Link did not identify with heartland Americans. His interests were intellectual, and his Beverly Hills home was palatial. But he knew that Fischer's favorite theme of small-town decency was central to the show's success, and he knew how effectively Lansbury exuded that quality.

> Angela plays her as decent, fair-minded, unbigoted, warm — a role model. She is sunny without being a goody two-shoes. Forgiving of flaws, but not namby-pamby or corny. There's still some steel there. She doesn't suffer fools, she's charming, but there is an innate decency — a decent person from a more decent time.

The American public was beginning to idolize her — Angela as well as Jessica. One episode was being filmed aboard the *Queen Mary,* the old luxury liner that had become a tourist attraction in Long Beach. The cast and crew were having dinner on the vessel when people started to come over with their menus, asking Angela for autographs. She turned to Bob O'Neill and said, "You know, until recently, I could go to the grocery store and nobody would bother me. Now, all of a sudden, this."

O'Neill realized, "She was becoming a full-blown, recognizable star."

The first year's ratings justified the faith that CBS's Harvey Shepard had put in the show. "*Murder* came in at 27," he said. "That's quite high." During that summer's first batch of reruns, Angela says, "We picked up this enormous audience. From then on, we never looked back."

Certain, now, that they would be staying in Los Angeles for a while, she and Peter went hunting for a more permanent house and found a very livable place on Bonhill Road, a quiet, curving lane not unlike Kidderpore Gardens, where she had lived as a girl in the days of Leckie Forbes. Bonhill Road was in a comfortable but hardly ritzy part of Brentwood, and she liked the house's easiness.

> This house is like a condominium on one floor. The architecture is completely bastardized, Southwest Greek. It's about twenty-eight hundred square feet on about a half acre, a small house, three bedrooms. The exterior is stucco, it was a frame house originally. The architect was named Craig Johnson. He was also a very good landscape architect. The whole front of the house is very cleverly done because you never have to touch it. All of the huge desert plants kind of take care of themselves with a little bit of water. Who needs a grand house? It isn't that I don't like grand houses. But circumstances just won't permit me to get them. [Anyhow] we bought this house simply as a stopgap to use while I was doing the series, and we thought the series might be over in two or three years.

As the second season got underway, producer Bob O'Neill says, "We climbed and climbed, reaching the top ten." Television success was familiar enough to him. He'd been with *Columbo* when Peter Falk took it sailing into the ratings stratosphere, but O'Neill felt that he had never experienced anything like *Murder, She Wrote.* "Its success shocked Universal. It rocketed toward the top. Advertisers were standing in line."

With production in high gear, Fischer was relying on a small but top-drawer staff of writers and directors, men who had come through for him in the past. There were virtually no female writers or directors in network television, and the prejudice can be detected in a remark like one director's.

> Somehow female-directed shows don't have the hard edge that the male shows have. They're about relationships and they become soppy. It just is totally against reality. It sounds sort of chauvinistic but it's not.

Such sexism rankled Angela, and what was worse, she felt that because Jessica Fletcher was written by men, the character thought like a man. Fischer asked, "Is there really a difference between how a woman or a man thinks?" Lansbury believes so. "I can tell from the expression on a man's face that he *just doesn't get it.*" She urged Fischer to hire female writers, and "three or four were tried," he says, "but only one wrote well enough to be used."

The mainstay directors were Walter Grauman and Vincent McVeety, and the story editor was Robert Van Skoyk. They were career television professionals, for nothing less would suffice in prime-time network broadcasting. Grauman and McVeety directed two out of every four shows, while Van Skoyk looked for

> character-driven stories that didn't just swirl around Jessica, and mysteries that add to "Who is Jessica?" The plot is the murder and its solution. The formula is for the detective to find out who did it before the audience does. The difference between a male detective and the female detective is her conflicts with the police. She is regarded as not as capable as the male. Our viewers knew that if a chief of detectives sneered at our lady, he was going to get his comeuppance by the end of the show. He couldn't get away with that.

With twenty-two mysteries a season, a certain sameness of plot was inevitable. Then again, William Link believed that "one of the basic principles of television is to give the audience exactly what it is accustomed to, and never surprise them." Bruce Lansbury agreed. He called it "the repetition of the familiar."

Instead, a parade of guess stars lent the series a sense of freshness. There were two and three each week, former major and minor movie players, people on whom Peter Fischer doted, chosen from the ocean of actors who had once made Hollywood *Hollywood* — but who were, as one of them put it, "old, dead, or just forgotten." Dane Clark, Margaret O'Brien, Robert Culp, Gene Nelson, Virginia Mayo, Martin Balsam, Howard Duff, Laraine Day, Tom Ewell, Vince Edwards, Mel Ferrer, John Ireland, Cornel Wilde, Barbara Rush, Terry Moore, Carole Baker, Edd Burns, Cyd Charisse, Capucine, Sheree North, Macdonald Carey — ultimately there would be almost two thousand of them, even Angela's schoolmate in London drama school Patrick Macnee, as well as her co-star from *The Picture of Dorian Gray,* Hurd Hatfield. In one nostalgic episode, Fischer used the device of a beauty parlor in Cabot Cove as an excuse to reunite some of the players from the old MGM musical unit — Kathryn Grayson, Betty Garrett, Gloria DeHaven, June Allyson. Because Angela had made a couple of those musicals, people thought it was her idea. "In fact," she says, "I had problems with that. I complained that Jessica doesn't go to beauty salons. She isn't the type to sit around talking with the women while she has her hair done. But I had to go along with it because it was the only way that kept Peter's scene with all the girls."

She did urge Fischer to use actors from the New York stage — Eli Wallach, Lucie Arnaz, Jerry Orbach, Charles Cioffi, Tammy Grimes, and people she'd worked with like Len Cariou, Harry Guardino, and George Hearn. To some, such assignments were heaven-sent, for stage work is notoriously unsteady, but professional standards were never lowered for sentimentality's sake. Some of the older actors were too rusty to remember even the few lines they had, while others were overcome by nerves. Despite the relentless production schedule, they were replaced.

Too, some of the stage actors were unaccustomed to television work. They still spoke up and out as if they were projecting to a theater audience. They had to tone down their stagey performances. When George Hearn began filming his first episode, he asked Angela, "How does this work? The camera is way over there. There's no proscenium arch. Where do I focus?"

She patted him on the cheek. "Think of it as a cold room, and the camera is the fireplace. With a fire going."

Hearn realized that "it's loving the camera instead of being daunted by it, as most people are and as I was." He ultimately made three episodes.

Lansbury's approach to film acting, as opposed to stage acting, was of course based on decades of experience, and she was specific about the comparative approaches.

> When you rehearse the scene, you don't know where the camera is going to be. But later, you start rehearsing with the camera, and it's terribly important that you do. Indeed, in some instances you have to *cheat* to look to the camera. The person you're talking to may be next to you but you don't look directly at them. In some cases, they will move the camera to bring your look around. It's very technical but it's part of your vocabulary as a film actor.

> Often the actors who come to do *Murder She Wrote* from the theater will say, "Thanks for telling me. I forgot — I was thinking of playing out to the audience, but of course I must keep it close." And they learn how to cheat their look. Then they say, "Oh, isn't this fun? I'm cheating my look!"
>
> In a musical you have to cheat [look slightly toward the audience]; you do it all the time. Because if you're on a line with somebody, if they have very bad manners and they're upstaging you, then you have to look downstage while you're supposed to be looking at them. The audience can't tell the difference. And if you're in one [up front], on stage, you're going to look six inches to a foot toward the audience. Because the audience must see your face. If you're talking across stage, you will do that in a musical.

As the line between Angela and Jessica blurred, the actress settled on her own view of the kind of person she was presenting.

> Jessica was supposed to have a youthful quality of expectancy and excitement in her life. Here she was, a woman who'd been widowed for several years, meeting success on her own terms for the first time in her life. She was getting recognition and she was a wonderful teacher. She loved young people. They usually don't like to interact with old fogeys but with her, they were being taught by somebody who had the ability to raise their sights; to take them by the scruff of the neck and force them to pay attention and to learn. Jessica was able to do that — she was a very good teacher, the kind of teacher you would wish every child to have because she simply inspired them to learn. And she was a wonderful role model — somebody who'd made something of herself!

In *Witness for the Defense,* a young man admits to Jessica that he has been unfaithful to his wife. "I'm not proud of it," he tells her, and she accepts that, being a liberal-minded woman who knows that such things do happen. In *Killer Radio,* Jessica runs into an offensive radio interviewer. While she tries to discuss her novel, he snarls, "Well, maybe you can tell me why mayhem mongers like yourself get such a thrill out of killing men in your books."

"If that is your understanding of 'mayhem mongers,'" retorts Jessica, "and women in general, I must say you are dead wrong. What really astonishes me, however, is that of the many guests who must have put up with the same tacky, pretentious, intellectually impoverished pop psychobabble that I have been putting up with for the past hour, not one of them has had enough of the right stuff to do you in long ago."

That episode was a rare example of social relevance. From Levinson and Link to Fischer and Lansbury, everyone agreed that the purpose of the show was entertainment, not pamphleteering. It was sufficient that Jessica be a role model. Lansbury refused to take credit for that or any other Fletcher virtue. "I'm really not acting Jessica Fletcher, but everyone's loving me for being her. Me, a saint? I'm no angel. I'm a very determined, difficult, stubborn woman. I'll play the cards as I want to play them."

But of course, that was Jessica/Angela, too. George Lansbury's idealism had endured and evolved in his granddaughter. Hers was perhaps a more sophisticated, experienced, wiser, and feminine approach, but his essential morality and hope were its foundation. Taking her own professional route to it, she had ennobled all actors by her shining example. Now that she had found herself, she was publicly playing that self, and it was making her an American institution, the model adult woman for 28 million people every week.

As the show's success grew — and with it, the recognition that she *was* the show — so did her clout, and she began to take a more aggressive approach to shaping the material. In the beginning, there was a local fisherman to provide Jessica with a romantic interest, but Angela didn't think he was the right type. She convinced Peter Fischer that, if there was to be any suggestion of romance, it should be with the more intellectual town physician. That also made sense from Fischer's point of view. "We needed somebody whom we could get into every week's story. The two obvious people that she has to deal with are, one, the sheriff, whom we've always had, and then we brought the doctor in, because if there's a killing, you bring him over, and they can discuss the case and also, they can discuss the personal stuff."

Finally, she decided against any romance at all. "Jessica," Lansbury says, "must never embrace a man. It would seem uncomfortable if she did, which is why she never does. I wouldn't know how to play that scene." It was more important, Angela felt, "to keep her a woman alone," and the identification with this character is clear when she adds, "I'd had this wonderful marriage to Frank and I didn't want to sully that."

Fischer agreed for his own reasons. "A romance would get in the way of the story, and a serious one would spoil the arc of the series."

As for the "Gotcha!" — the explanation at the end — Bill Link loves to mock that convention. "You went there at eight-fifteen and the train left at seven forty-five, and when Dr. Brown came — and he left the suitcase . . ." He laughs at the devices of his own profession. "It's all so contrived, totally unnatural. Whereas in a drama there's some emotional logic — an emotional ping-pong game between people. You don't find that in a mystery show. 'The cigar butt was on the floor and you said you didn't see it, but the maid said . . .' "

The Gotcha! would always present "a severe acting problem for Angela," director Vincent McVeety says. "She didn't learn it. It was the only time she used cue cards instead of learning her lines. And the clues were always so obscure you'd wonder how in the world anybody in the world would pick up on them. The flashbacks that occurred over her dialogue kind of helped because the audience would see the clues and say. 'Oh yeah, I never noticed that.'

"I would only show the scene from her point of view when we got to the comeuppance, and that was certainly a trademark with *Murder, She Wrote,* and I don't think that it was a necessary evil. People are very interested in that aspect of the show. But I know Angela hated playing it because it's four pages of dialogue that she had to learn."

She was hardly embarrassed about reading those lines ("I'm one of the best cue card readers in the business"), although in McVeety's experience, the ultimate cue card reader was Raymond Burr on the *Perry Mason* show. "In those days, we used TelePrompTers instead of cue cards, and Ray would have five prompters. He would have them up in the scaffolding, or in the corner, he had one on the lens and one next to the lens when he wanted to look at the audience. And he never wanted the actor — same with Angela — whom he was talking to to be standing anywhere near the camera — because it would be too distracting. If the actor was there, the tendency would be to look at the actor; but the cue cards or the TeleprompTer became the actor. He would emote and relate to that. Ray was marvelous.

"As for the Gotcha! the only person better was Angela."

Perhaps, but she found that after a few minutes of the explanation, "Your mind starts reeling." She would plead with Fischer, "This is double Dutch — nobody's going to understand it." He tried cutting them down, "but," she realizes, "it was not easy to clarify, and you had to show how you solved the mystery. It was a constant battle. Such a pain in the ass."

* * *

The Barbara Walters Christmas Special in 1985 had a comeback theme. Cybill Shepherd, Michael J. Fox, and Angela were introduced by Ms. Walters as "three people who were down but not out." Angela was scheduled as the last interview, and Walters, as was her specialty, promised televised heartbreak at the outset, declaring, "She almost gave up her career to save her family."

Angela — characteristically reserved, intensely private, and fiercely protective of her family — had never spoken in public about her children's drug problems. For this interview, she agreed to do so. Her segment begins with a series of film clips showing highlights from her Hollywood career, followed by brief excerpts from *Mame* and *Sweeney Todd,* and then the opening sequence of *Murder, She Wrote.* Finally, Angela appears at home in Brentwood, casually dressed in blue slacks and a yellow button-down-collar shirt, with a red sweater over her shoulders. She leads Walters to a sunny corner of the living room, and they sit.

Dramatic tension was inevitable, since emotional reticence was Angela's specialty, and emotional exposure was Walters's. She doesn't wait long to "go for the tears," as Angela puts it. "She always does."

Walters says, "You had one year in which just everything fell apart." It is a prod designed to touch a nerve, and Angela responds accordingly. "In the sixties," she begins, "when Deirdre and Anthony were twelve and thirteen, and we lived in Malibu, they unfortunately got into hard drugs. Most of the kids there did. The next-door neighbor — our son's best friend — died, and Anthony was on his way to doing the same thing. Heroin, acid, you name it, they did it. We were the generation of parents that had to face it first, without any help."

She bites her lip. "We didn't know what to do."

She pauses, swallowing hard, pressing her lips together and struggling to compose herself. Walters looks on with sympathy, and murmurs "They're so well now, think of that."

It is a suspect sympathy. With Angela plainly vulnerable, Walters goes for a kill, asking a question so calculated to upset that it is very nearly ridiculous. "You say a wonderful thing happened, but in the midst of that your house burned down."

The insensitivity is so absurd that it seems to jolt Angela into composure. "That," she says, "oddly enough, turned out to open the door to a solution. Ireland, an oasis, a place where drugs had not reached." Asked what she and Peter learned from the experience, she concludes, "To be there and not fall apart. If the child can beat it, he will know that the family is ready to take him back." Not about to take credit for a rescue, she adds, "But he is the only one who can do it."

She did not want to be shown in such an emotional state, and was embarrassed and furious when she saw the December 2, 1985, broadcast. She had naively "assumed that they would cut that piece out, but that's Barbara Walters's interviewing style. Go for the jugular, find a chink in the armor.

"You didn't have to see me fall apart, but that's what they want."

She wrote a note of complaint to Walters, and received the patronizing reply: "The most important thing is for you to know how genuinely I like you."

It was hardly the most important thing. The show had violated her privacy, and her family's as well, yet there was no great shame in what had been exposed to Barbara Walters's enormous television audience. Throughout the 1960s and 1970s, many American families had groped through the same uncharted drug territory. Any number of Hollywood figures had gone through such crises with their children. In time it would seem to Angela that "being a parent and working in the entertainment business must be the hardest trick to bring off successfully. As a young working mother, I had to hire help on a full-time basis to care for our young children. At the time, I believed I was bringing the right responsible help into our home, however in retrospect, I regret that it was not their mother who gave my kids the hour-to-hour, day-to-day attention and supervision that all kids need from their parents."

She knew that "Pete and I arranged it that one of us was always at home, but when a career dictates that one or the other parent is absent for long periods of time, things can go drastically wrong. I realize that we gave in to our children with permissiveness and with material things in the mistaken belief that we could make up to them for what we had failed to deliver as parents by our presence — continuing guidance, discipline, and, most important, attention and involvement in their education on a day-to-day basis."

She came to believe that "*our* perception of our success-driven lives was not theirs. There *were* feelings of resentment and jealousy — and why wouldn't there be? When so much attention revolved around their mother."

She concluded that "Pete and I have suffered for years with a deep sense of regret and blame, as I'm sure all parents do when their children suffer and become victims of circumstances beyond their control. We tried to comfort ourselves with 'We did the best we knew how at the time,' but looking back, I know in my heart that it wasn't enough. I do know, however, that we loved them and tried to help them in the only ways we knew how, and through it all they loved us. And we were eventually able to talk through the mistakes of the past and go forward with a new respect and understanding of each other."

The relentless schedule of television series production left virtually no time for friendships, or even extended family. It was only during the summer hiatus, when Angela escaped to Ireland, that she could visit with her sister in Brighton, where Isolde had taken a flat. The rest of the year, contact between the "full sisters" was restricted to telephone calls, or the letter writing that was so traditional a part of their family life.

It was during one of the phone conversations that Angela noticed a slurring of her sister's speech and suspected that she might be drinking. She telephoned Isolde's daughter, Tamara Ustinov, who had become a busy actress, living in London. The thirty-two-year-old told her aunt, "Mom is having difficulty with her speech because of a motor neuron problem."

Angela immediately called Isolde's doctor in Brighton. The "shocking news" was that her sister was suffering from ALS — amyotrophic lateral sclerosis, or "Lou Gehrig's disease." It is incurable, degenerative, and ultimately fatal.

Under those circumstances, Angela thought her sister was being "amazingly brave."

During a break in making *Murder, She Wrote,* she took Bob O'Neill aside and said, "Come with me, I want to talk," and led him for a stroll around the Universal lot. "She had her arm around my waist," the producer says, "and we were talking like two friends. This was a mother concerned about her children, talking with a father concerned about his. She suggested that Anthony should be given an opportunity to direct an episode of the show."

O'Neill promised to talk to Peter Fischer about it.

This was a difficult situation for the producer of an important and expensive series, but Fischer agreed to the proposal, reasoning, "If you can find someone who has the confidence of the star, and he knows what he's doing, it's a godsend." The producer assigned "a very good assistant director to work with Anthony so he wouldn't stub his toes."

Bob Van Skoyk, the show's story editor, looked on with understanding. The young man was thrown in with experienced professionals in high-stakes network television. "There was so much to learn," he said, and inevitably, the first episode was a shaky effort. When it was wrapping up, O'Neill tried to make a fair judgment. It was a good start, he said. "At least the mechanics were correct. Anthony had been asking to put the camera in a wrong position — mechanical mistakes like that. But the cinematographer helped, and he wasn't allowed to make a grievous mistake."

Peter Fischer delivered the judgment to Angela. "Anthony is a very likable guy. It isn't that he's not willing to work hard enough. He just doesn't have the experience, he doesn't have the expertise." She certainly understood, for nobody respected professionalism more than Angela Lansbury. With that, "Anthony took a crash course," O'Neill says, "from a professional director. When he came back we gave him a few more assignments," and again, Fischer went along with the plan. "She has a son who's got a background in show business and she wants to give him an opportunity. I don't blame her one bit. If my kids wanted to write a script I would have done what she did. I would have said, 'Okay, show us what you can do. We'll help you learn, but at some point you have to succeed on your merits.' And that's what he did."

After Anthony directed his next episode, Fischer told Angela, "His work has improved remarkably. He's really doing a nice job" and the young man joined the regular rotation of directors.

After three seasons of snowballing success, *Murder, She Wrote* had found its rhythm, and was rolling along under Peter Fischer's smooth and knowing producership. Fischer considered the character of Jessica Fletcher to be fully developed, and he codified her in a "bible" that was distributed to all prospective writers.

> Who is Jessica Fletcher, what makes her tick, and how does she operate? A few guidelines: She is warm and compassionate, intelligent and curious, funny without being sarcastic or hurtful. Her humor is more irony and bemusement. She is strong-willed but once she gets an idea in her head, no amount of bullshit can deter her.

That might well have been Peter Fischer's description of Angela Lansbury herself, although to her, it was a description of Jessica from a man's point of view.

He also described what Jessica was not.

> She isn't a detective or a policeman. She is not judgmental, schoolmarmish, prissy, or old-fashioned. She is contemporary in her thinking, although she rarely uses modern slang to express herself. When Jessica is "investigating" a crime — this is very important — she has no franchise, no business being involved, therefore, she has to behave in such a way that either the suspects *want* to talk to her or they don't realize what she's up to. Also, she is not a hero. When she discovers something, she tells the police. Nor is she naive. Her home is a small town but her blueberry pies do not win blue ribbons — she has been exposed to all strata of society.

As a final note to writers, he adds,

> If you have a scene where Jessica is silent, passive, or a bystander, you usually have a scene that won't work for the show. Put her in the middle, and soften her questions, or conclusions, with self-effacing comments like, "I may be a little confused, but . . ." or, "Is it possible that . . ." or, "Unless I'm mistaken."

And, he concluded,

> Even though she is more intelligent than the people she is dealing with, she avoids letting them know that. If fact, one reason she's as successful as she is is because those about her underestimate her.

Through two years of her terrible, debilitating illness, Isolde had "managed to keep going," Angela says, but then she arranged, with Tamara, to put Isolde in a Brighton nursing home, and that was where she and Peter last saw her, at Christmas in 1986. Isolde died the following May at sixty-seven.

* * *

When *Murder, She Wrote* began, Angela had signed a standard guarantee that, were the show successful, she would remain for five years. It never occurred to her that it might be so successful that she would be held to the guarantee. As *Murder, She Wrote* entered its fifth year, CBS and Universal Television opened negotiations for a contract renewal. The show had hit the top spot in the television ratings at the end of its second season and had remained in first or second place ever since. The people at Universal Television and CBS seemed to look upon it as a product that could be manufactured indefinitely. *Product,* in fact, was what television shows were called, but as director Vincent McVeety realized, "The stories — after you've done a year or two of them — how many more can you come up with?"

Bob O'Neill cheerfully admits, "We used *Macbeth* four times, and *The Treasure of the Sierra Madre* twice."

McVeety realized that the originality or unoriginality of the plots did not determine the popularity of *Murder, She Wrote.* "Ninety percent of its success," he acknowledges, "is Angela's warmth and hominess." In short, there was no *Murder, She Wrote* without Angela Lansbury and everyone knew it.

> I'd always been available — to run to a theater here, a theater there. Suddenly I was unable to do that. Suddenly I was *trapped.* Every time I thought, "Gosh, maybe I can very quietly close the door and creep away on this wonderful success, I realized that I couldn't, because it wasn't just a question of the success of the show. It was a question of really depriving an audience of a tremendous slice of entertainment that they had become used to on a Sunday night. It was like a bedtime story, at this wonderful, kind of precious, special Sunday night time, and every time I said, "I'm not doing this anymore, I can't do it anymore," that is what came to me and I said, "Yes, you are going to continue."

That was hardly the whole story. She was acutely aware of the financial facts of her family's life. "This was a very big business to me and my family and to my company. So those were also reasons why I had to consider [a new contract]. But on the other hand, in my heart of hearts, much as I didn't want to leave that audience, I was oftentimes ready to move on, because I was exhausted.

"And tired of doing the same thing."

However, the stakes were now so very high. *Murder, She Wrote* might have still been the series title, but for the American public it was The Angela Lansbury Show and it was hard to believe that in the beginning, she had not even been given star billing. ("My name was in tiny letters and sometimes, in *TV Guide,* for instance, the blurb wouldn't even mention me.") When her contract was renewed, a changed Angela was at hand, sure of herself and sure of who she was; sure of what she thought, and sure enough to say it, and play it for a national public. And the country was appreciating and loving her, equally sure of who she was and what she believed in.

She was mindful of that, not only when playing Jessica Fletcher but when accepting other roles in television movies that she made during the seasonal hiatuses. She felt "a certain responsibility not to tamper with Jessica's image."

As *Murder, She Wrote* settled into its sixth and seventh years, always in the top or second place in the ratings, it was in harmony with the national mood, and perhaps with the Ronald Reagan presidency as well. It seemed to appeal to a people yearning for times when moral choices were clear and the sense of national character was sure. Those times and that fictive country were the retro-America that Fischer had wished to idealize, and for which he had designed Jessica Fletcher, his "decent person from a more decent time." It was beginning to irritate Angela.

On any series, after the initial five-year contract, renewals come due every May and are sometimes extended to two years. In the Lansbury case, with each renewal, the money increased, passing $100,000 for each episode, and then $200,000. At each renewal time too, there was the suspense of a network dependent on the superstar who was the main attraction of its top-rated show — and for her, the question of "whether or not I was going to go back."

She was not being coy, and was not balking as a negotiating strategy. She had her moments of "tremendous self-recrimination," feeling that she was "stuck in this vise" and telling herself, "you're not being true to yourself, you're a hypocrite." But, she unhappily admits, "the money that was proffered to me was enormous, and in the end, money talked."

She talked, too. She had always expressed her opinion when, in her opinion, scripts were second-rate. Now, more serious matters were troubling her. She began her rebellion slowly. One afternoon, during a break on the set, she handed a note to Peter Fischer.

> I've spent all these years building the character of Jessica into a first-class, highly intelligent, vivacious, energetic, and hopefully lovable woman — and for the sake of one script you reduce her to the lowest common denominator by trying to pair her off to a chauvinistic fat old bore, with whom she has *nothing* in common. Jessica has never wanted for companionship — she is never lonely. Her life as a woman alone is full and productive and if she ever *does* decide to get hitched again, it will undoubtedly be to a younger man (at least young in heart) who will be able to match her enthusiasm and zest for life — and with a real sense of humor.

While perhaps the immediate case — a romantic interest — was trivial, of greater importance was a budding clash over ownership rights. Did Jessica Fletcher primarily represent American values or adult womanhood? Did she belong to Peter Fischer, who was her inventor and author? Or to Angela Lansbury, who was her physical embodiment and living image? The two creators liked each other and they respected each other, but the battle line was being drawn.

As the series moved into the 1990s, its popularity held fast. Fischer "put Jessica on the road, and she would visit anywhere from London to Russia to Atlanta, Georgia. We were trying to see if we could cover every state of the union." However, she would always return to Cabot Cover for five shows a year. "It was always five," Fischer says, "and never more than that, because that was her route." Still, he held to his original concept of who she was and what she stood for.

> She had the small town where everybody knew her as Jessica and not the famous mystery writer. Nobody ever treated her like a celebrity in her hometown. There was something endearing and kind of real American about that. So we had that solid base

> that we could use to paint her as the all-American grandmother, or aunt.

That, in Angela Lansbury's view, reflected "a very old-fashioned view of women. Peter's idea of a woman is Doris Day. A nonperson kind of woman." She points out that he "grew up on Raymond Chandler." His *Ellery Queen* series, she feels, had been in the same genre. "And those are the terms on which he sees men and women." She suspected that, while hardly afraid of strong and independent-minded women, Peter Fischer disliked them. "There's a certain strength which I have myself. I recognize that. I'm an old battle axe, a very tough lady. Well, I hope not tough.

"Strong."

William Link noticed the increasing friction between his show's executive producer and its star.

> Fischer tried to keep Angela away from stories. That's pretty unheard of. When you have a star who's made your show, as a common courtesy you give outlines. If a star is interested and wants input, which I think is important, you involve them. That's the way it works. I'd heard that Fischer did not, and that can be pretty off-putting. So she had little say about the stories.

By 1991, as the show was winding down its seventh year, Angela was all but fed up with quaint Cabot Cove, its quaint people, and a quaint Jessica Fletcher. "As far as I'm concerned," Angela felt, "that's *Little House on the Prairie* time." As if it were her own life, she was restless for Jessica to escape this provincial existence.

> I wanted to show this woman as a participant in sport and the fun side of life. I felt it wasn't right for Jessica to devote her life to this rather confining avocation of solving little murders in a little village when she was becoming an internationally known author.
>
> The other thing was, this was an opportunity for her to go back to teaching. She had been a very good English teacher, so why not give master classes at one of the New York universities? Some people objected . . . they loved the family aspect. But it was another audience that I wanted to attract and they wouldn't

settle for Cabot Cove. I wanted to take her further afield and grab them — make her a much more worldly person, which she wanted to be, because she is a woman of education.

These were notions to drive a stake through Peter Fischer's heart. Doing it would be Peter Shaw's responsibility.

CHAPTER 20

THE DEAL OF DEALS

LINK TOOK Angela and Peter to lunch in the hope of smoothing out the conflict with Peter Fischer, only to find that they were already searching for a new producer, "somebody," they said, "with a good mystery mind." Their decision, it seemed to Link, was already final, and he felt, "You could see their resolve — they were going to be involved." Not only did they feel that they were being "kept at a remove," but they associated him with Fischer ("I was being tarred with the same brush"). So the scene was set for the Shaw-Fischer confrontation.

From experience Peter Fischer had learned, "Angie doesn't strong-arm. She's always courteous, always a lady. Peter Shaw takes the tough role, and he's good at it."

Shaw was so good at it, and Fischer was so good at reading strategy, whether in poker or other male power games, that in their ultimate confrontation the action and reaction were over quickly. Shaw simply told Fischer that Angela felt she should become more involved in the storytelling process, and Fischer's countermove was inevitable.

> There are a lot of things I will discuss with Angela, a lot of input I'll take, a lot of things we'll agree on — at least agree to talk about — but the storytelling is not one of them. Because I

> feel that once a star of the show gets involved with the privileges and responsibilities of the executive producer, it takes away from the energy they spend performing and divides their focus, and very frankly, some of them — I'm not sure about Angela — are not qualified. They can tell you whether a scene works but they can't tell you whether a story works. So I could see the handwriting on the wall, and I'd had such a wonderful relationship with her for seven years that I just didn't want to spend the next season yelling and screaming and having a terrible time and getting approval on stories. I felt that it was best I leave.

He took Bob O'Neill with him, and a $60,000 fee for every show, as long as the series remained on the air. He was replaced as executive producer by a man named David Moessinger, but Angela immediately made it clear that she intended to run the show. The show's co-creator, William Link, was in no mood to quarrel with that. He had been devastated by the recent death of his partner and best friend, Dick Levinson, who was only in his early fifties. They had been pals since high school in suburban Philadelphia. Levinson's death also took a lot out of Peter Fischer ("We were born just three days apart") as well as Bob O'Neill. They had all been friends, with Levinson regularly ribbing both Fischer and O'Neill about having "818 mentalities." (The number was a reference to the area code for the San Fernando Valley and the Hollywood hills — Valley Girl territory. Levinson would say, "When you go 310" — referring to the Beverly Hills area code — "then I'll start listening to you guys.")

Now the original staff of *Murder, She Wrote* was all but dispersed. Even Link was taking a back seat and offered no protest when Angela and Peter decided that, after one season with David Moessinger, she would herself become the executive producer of *Murder, She Wrote.* With that decision, Peter's son David joined Corymore on the business side, and the two of them sat down with Angela's agent for a set of negotiations with CBS that would result in what the family would eventually call "the deal of deals."

It was predicated on the shrewd realization by Jerry Katzman, Angela's agent at William Morris, that while CBS had a contract with Universal Television for *Murder, She Wrote,* it did *not* have a contract with Angela Lansbury. As Katzman describes the deal,

> Universal and CBS couldn't get together. Each one was protecting its own turf. Universal's attitude was they didn't have to make

> the deal because ABC and NBC wanted the show, too. CBS felt cornered because *Murder, She Wrote* was still their number one show out of the Entertainment Division — since *60 Minutes* was from the News Division. So we came up with a scheme that absolutely threw Universal. CBS thought there must be a catch to it because it was so simplistic. That scheme was, make a deal with Angela and her company [Corymore] whereby she is exclusive to CBS. Now Universal has to come to the network. They own *Murder, She Wrote* but CBS has Angela, and Universal can't take it anywhere else. In return, CBS gives Angela various series commitments, and movies-of-the-week commitments for her company. The numbers are all tied up in those commitments. So, what she was paid for *Murder, She Wrote* [now approaching $250,000 for each episode] is insignificant compared to what all these other ancillaries provide her and her family. Plus the penalties.

That deal, Katzman says, "made Angela and Peter secure forever." Not only did it involve prospective series and movies-of-the-week, but she did not even have to star in them, a provision that paved the way for Anthony and David to have projects with CBS not only beyond *Murder, She Wrote* but even after Angela's retirement or death. In addition to Corymore Corporation, a family producing company — Corymore Productions — was formed for all these interests. That, Angela says, was her own idea. "I said, 'I'm this actress, and we should have the company that makes the most of it. This is a business. Forget the mother side of it. This is something we can all be a part of.' "

With Angela as the executive producer of *Murder, She Wrote,* Anthony became its primary director and David the chief executive officer of the production company. As usual, Peter was the behind-the-scenes strategist, and Angela has a special image for that.

> I think of him as my "white stallion." In some of those medieval tapestries, there is this white horse that is sort of looking through the bushes. You see this white horse's head coming through, and one day I said to the children, "You know, Dad is like the white horse that's always in the picture, but not in the forefront of the action." And that's the way he's been for the last twenty-five years, since he retired. He has refused to take an of-

ficial position in the company. He wanted his sons to take over. They are Corymore Productions. He is in fact the power behind the throne. That is the way Peter is.

It seemed to Jerry Katzman that "her family was the whole idea behind all this. She really didn't care if she did more than seven years [of *Murder, She Wrote*]. The only reason she did it was that it was a wonderful opportunity for them to have a family business."

Even her brother Bruce joined the staff—as a chief writer. He was certainly qualified since, aside from his immense success producing and writing *Mission: Impossible,* he knew the real Jessica Fletcher intimately. "I don't write for Jessica," he says, "I write for Angela. I understand her sensitivities, her instincts, and her sense of humor. Everything that she has put into Jessica Fletcher has to be part of what I write. Jessica wouldn't do that, she wouldn't associate with those people, she would do it this way." And should his writing stray beyond those parameters, he says "Angela will find a way for Jessica to do things that will keep that character true. She is the expert on what Jessica is and what the audience expects of her, which is very important to Angie. She doesn't want that audience to be let down."

Her responsibility to that audience was one she felt deeply. "*Murder, She Wrote,* she says, "was never given much credence in Los Angeles [broadcasting]. People in the business don't watch it. Only the public. I have respect for that national audience. Because I am entertaining them in a way that only I, in that role of Jessica Fletcher, can. If they're women *of a certain age,* I give them hope. Men, I believe, find age very attractive."

She could enforce that responsibility, now that she was the executive producer, and, Bruce says, "she was, in the truest sense, the executive producer, deciding story lines, the approach, the wardrobe, the direction, the cutting, every element of the show." Not everything was changing. She still mothered the actors. As director McVeety noticed, "She never liked anyone being on the set ahead of her, particularly on the first day. She wanted to be there to greet them — to make them feel warm and welcome."

As promised, her first decision was to move Jessica out of Cabot Cove and into a New York City apartment. That was accomplished with a part-time teaching assignment, a master class at "Manhattan University" (actually, the Columbia University campus). A new opening montage was filmed showing Jessica aghast while reading a murder story in the *New York Post*; Jessica buying flowers on a New York street; Jessica wearing stylish clothes. And although the old desk typewriter still pounded out the title of the show, she herself was shown writing on a word processor.

One thing did not change, and it was something her audience regularly wrote to ask about — Jessica's inability to drive a car. She didn't get a driver's license because "if she did drive," Angela knew, "we would get into chases," which would make it an action show, a genre that she did not want the series to become. There were other aspects, she declared, that also would not change. As she wrote in a memorandum to the staff,

> I do not want nor did I ever intend that the basic format of the show should be diminuted or weakened by the additives we discussed, that is, strengthening of characters, apartment in New York, etc. *Murder, She Wrote* is the title of our show and that's what the stories and what Jessica's business is *all about*. Everything else is incidental. Jessica must not be represented as being in any way different than she has been in the past. She is a role model for women of her generation. She is a New England Yankee. Does not buckle under stress or reveal her feelings easily. Is fair — compassionate — sometimes blunt. (As you may consider this letter to be!)

Lansbury used her new position to seek out female writers and directors, but she was no more successful than Fischer had been and, she says, "It was to my sorrow. There are women doing sitcoms," but, she finds, "they do not understand the form of *Murder, She Wrote*." That was perhaps obviously a generalization, but she would not let ideological considerations compromise her professionalism. The series' new setting, however, certainly did suggest that contrary to Fischer's original implication, it was possible for somebody representing common decency and civilized behavior to survive in a place like New York without being constantly assaulted physically and verbally. Jessica's good sense and personal integrity could be as triumphant in the cities as in the hinterlands. And while she was at it, Lansbury/Fletcher and *Murder, She Wrote* could also recognize the existence of minority groups. African-Americans, Hispanics, and Asian-Americans began cropping up in major and minor roles on the show, and as she expected, its popularity held.

As for the immense amount of money that was now assured the family, Angela insists, "I did not need it. I say to myself, 'You're not being true to yourself,' and part of me really could turn from it. But because of family circumstances, plus my own difficulty in walking away from huge amounts of money . . ." She leaves the rest of the thought unspoken.

"The money didn't make that much of a difference in our lives," she insists. "It just enabled us to establish Corymore Productions. It didn't change our lifestyle one iota, but it did give us total security. The big splurge was to buy the land in Ireland and build the new house."

Perched on a bluff facing the Atlantic Ocean, "Corymore House" was created from the ground up and set on seventeen acres. Angela designed it herself, with the help of an Irish friend who was not an architect but an artist. She drew the floor plan on the back of a shirt cardboard from a laundry, sketching the layout and figuring the dimensions. "The house is in a place called Ballywilliam," she says, "and it's right on the sea, and the rocks are down below. It's very windswept but we managed to create some sheltered spots. We have a vegetable and salad garden, and a lot of roses, of course."

She had complete freedom in making that new home. "Peter let me have my head in this instance — allowed me to just go ahead and build the house I wanted to build. It was my reward for the many, many years I put in on *Murder, She Wrote*. And it was a dream come true, to build it. I couldn't live in California without knowing that I have the house in Ireland."

It would stand empty for most of the year. They would fly over for the Christmas holidays, when the *Murder, She Wrote* schedule permitted. Otherwise, they would just be there during the summer hiatus, and even then, Angela would usually be making a television movie for much of the time. The summer of 1991, for instance, was largely spent in France and England making *Mrs. 'arris Goes to Paris*.

Just before leaving to make it, she was approached in her trailer by an upset Dolores Childers, who had been noticing that Angela "was saying funny little derogatory things, putting me down." The dresser brought up the subject directly. "I feel as if I haven't been pleasing you. Is something wrong?" Angela looked down at the floor for a moment. "As a matter of fact," she told Dolores, "I wrote you a note over the weekend." It read, in part,

> If what I'm about to tell you seems hurtful, please forgive me, because I'm sure you know that that is the last thing in the world that I would want. . . . [As executive producer] my modus

> operandi is going to be different. . . . your job, as it is, will no longer exist. . . . Our friendship will endure. . . . You wish to announce at some point to the crew that you have decided not to stay on for another season.

Childers was stunned. "If she'd hit me in the stomach, it wouldn't have hurt so much. I didn't cry, not in front of her." Instead, she fled the trailer, and "just fell apart. I always felt like she was my sister and we were so close."

The reason Angela fired her was that

> Dolores wanted me to behave like she thought I should behave; on the set and everywhere else. I once said to her, really mad, "Dolores, whose side are you on? Are you on my side? Are you with me or are you with them? I have a job to do, I have to get out and do it. If you're not for me, and with me; if you're working against me, and you're talking about me to these people on the set — and you're saying, *Oh, she's this and this today* — if you're talking about me as 'she,' you're no friend of mine. I can't work that way."

Paul Gallico's bestselling novel, *Mrs. 'arris Goes to Paris,* is about a London charwoman (a house maid) who is dazzled when she sees a Christian Dior evening gown owned by her aristocratic employer. She decides that if there's nothing else she does in her life, she is going to own a gown like that, and so this frumpy, sixtyish, widowed, lower-class woman saves for two years and then goes to Paris to buy a Dior gown. She has just enough money to get there, buy the dress, and come home the same day.

She is nearly barred from the salon because of her appearance and Cockney mannerisms, but the sales *directrice* is touched by her story and slips her in among the rich and titled, including Princess Margaret. After buying a glamorous evening gown, Mrs. Harris learns that she must stay several days for fittings. When another employee offers her a room, she begins a week-long period of making new friends, who help her triumph over the continuing efforts of the salon manager to bar her from the House of Dior. But she helps them, too — a young man feeling hopelessly inadequate to the beautiful model he loves; a youthful widow hoping for government recognition of her war hero husband; and finally, an elegant, titled gentleman (Omar Sharif) who is estranged from his grown daughter and granddaughter. Brushed by that unspoken suggestion of romance, Mrs. Harris returns to London, taking with her the memory of this adventure and her Dior gown.

It is a slender bit of whimsy, nearly maudlin, yet there is a warmth about it, and ultimately a chill of delight. The central figure throughout is, of course, Mrs. Harris, and in the role, Angela Lansbury gives a controlled and finally glowing performance. One moment seems like actual magic, when the narrow-shouldered, mousy little lady she has been playing with a delicious and flawless Cockney accent is suddenly transformed into a tall, slender, very beautiful woman in her gorgeous new gown.

Even so, it is a dangerous role, traveling as it does through such a sentimental minefield. Lansbury makes her way through it with skill, drawing upon a lifetime of experience to make the one-dimensional woman in the thin conceit into a touching figure in an enchanting fairy tale. Her acting, despite twelve years of what in her mind was relative disuse, is not remotely rusty. She creates a believable figure who is both spunky and intimidated, interested in everyone but not a busybody. Although Anthony Shaw, who directed this Corymore Production, was hardly responsible for his mother's performance, he certainly can be credited with supporting it through mood and tempo, while helping to surround it with a cluster of other solid portrayals. His production is confident and sometimes even radiant, framing a delightful little film, beautifully told and lovingly photographed in London and Paris.

The same year, Angela agreed to play the voice of Mrs. Potts in the animated Disney movie *Beauty and the Beast*. It would be a novel kind of acting for her, voice only, but ultimately, in her own view, it would have as wide and strong a public impact as anything she ever did. Much of that effect came from her singing of the title song, a success that seemed unlikely when she started to prepare for the project. The songwriters, composer Alan Menken and the late lyricist Howard Ashman, had sent her a tape recording that demonstrated how they thought "Beauty and the Beast" should be sung — with soulful inflections and a light rock beat. That was hardly her style, and eager as she was to sing the movie's title song, she told them, "I don't think this is for me, guys."

Ashman said, "Angie, we want you to sing it the way *you* would sing it. How do you want to sing this song?"

In the first place, she replied, she didn't even understand the lyrics.

Barely even friends
Then somebody bends, unexpectedly

She had read the script, but it had been months earlier and "I didn't connect the lyrics with the story." Ashman reminded her of what she called "the root of the song." As Angela put it, "Mrs. Potts was this sweet, warm, lovable, roly-poly lady who, being a mother and the cook/housekeeper in the castle, understood totally the whole story of the prince. And she recognized what a beautiful happenstance it was that this lovely young girl had come into his life. That she might be able to salvage things.

"What would there be in life that Mrs. Potts could imagine more wonderful? So this would be in her voice. It would be in her understanding of what was going on, and she recognized that what was happening could happen to two people anywhere, anytime. It's a universal thing and so, that it should happen between the Beast and Belle, this lovely young woman, was as natural as if she had been a princess and he a young prince. Which of course he turns out to be. And Belle knew it even before he was transformed back into the prince, because his beauty was in his spirit. It was in his ability to be a tender, loving person. And when you saw the two of them dancing, of course all of that came out in the song."

And so, she says, "I worked on it, and worked and worked, and worked it out and did a tape. Reluctantly."

When Ashman and Menken heard it, all questions were answered. She flew to New York to record the song with the New York Philharmonic.

"That was before they ever drew anything," Angela says, "so a lot of what was drawn came from the song. That's the way it went, and getting this wisdom and beauty into the song — that's the work of the actor, and I do know it worked. I know that many, many people wept. Children found it very comforting because Mrs. Potts is a mother, and they loved her singing about the lovers. They felt her warmth, her tenderness, and that's what I went for." Thus acting with the voice.

After the recording session, the orchestra's first violinist told her, "There's nobody who can phrase like you. It is absolutely amazing." She considered that "one of the greatest compliments I've ever received in my life."

When the song was reprised during the run of credits at the end of *Beauty and the Beast,* it was performed by a couple of pop singers in Ashman and Menken's original soulful style, with the light rock beat. It became a hit, but it had none of the beauty and dramatic power that Lansbury poured into the movie's thrillingly romantic finale.

On a spring day in 1994, Angela received a "mysterious" message from the British consul in Los Angeles, who informed her, confidentially, "I'm happy to tell you that you are in the Queen's Honors List." She knew, of course, that this was the Palace's list of titles and other awards, published every year in the *Times* on the Queen's birthday. Angela, the consul said, was to receive a "CBE," which was shorthand for the honorary title of Commander of the Most Excellent Order of the British Empire. American citizens were eligible for this honor although, in fact, both she and Peter had retained dual citizenships.

> Well, I was absolutely blown away. I'd never thought about honors, why would I? I don't live in England anymore. Of course, I know that the Queen doesn't do it herself. It's the government in power. But she has to okay it and, nice lady that she is, she must have put a tick against my name. I did know that *Murder, She Wrote* was enormously popular in England. So it had to do with a former British subject bringing honor to her own country.

She was sworn to secrecy until the official announcement, but already knew that she couldn't attend the investiture at Buckingham Palace to receive the honor from the Queen, because the series would still be in production. A few months later, however, Prince Charles was visiting Los Angeles and a ceremony was arranged at the British consulate. Angela brought the family along and they were all ushered into an informal reception room. Moments later, Prince Charles entered and, glancing at Angela, he beckoned for her to approach.

"Just come over her, dear," the young man said. "I think it's my pleasure to present you with the CBE on behalf of my mother, Her Majesty the Queen."

Approaching Prince Charles, Lansbury curtsied. "My grandfather," she said, "would have been very proud of this moment. If he's around, I share that pride with him."

Everyone stayed for cocktails, and Angela took her award home. "It's a perfectly beautiful medal," she says, "and a very nice recognition from your country. But you can never wear it unless you attend some very hifalutin dinner at which it says on the invitation, 'Decorations Will Be Worn.' "

Early one Los Angeles evening in May of 1995, the telephone rang just after Angela and Peter had finished dinner. She often associates landmark events with household details; the Malibu fire, for instance, was linked to the clicking sound of a clothes dryer. This call came as she was loading the dishwasher, which she and Peter were doing together. She had just begun the series' production hiatus, and it was only days before they were to leave for Ireland. The call was from Peter Tortorici, the head of West Coast television for CBS. He was in New York for the network's summer meetings and at the moment was with Peter Lund, the network president. Tortorici was phoning to tell Angela that the network was seriously considering switching *Murder, She Wrote* to Thursday nights. The rationale, he said, was to "restructure Sunday night to attract a younger audience. That's it in simple terms."

She was stunned; the move didn't make sense to her. The ratings had slipped, that was true, but they were still high. She sputtered, "Why would you do that? We've been in the top ten — or fifteen — all year. Why would you replace us on Sunday nights? We're a Sunday night show."

In fact, CBS had guaranteed a Sunday evening time slot to *Murder, She Wrote*. While the guarantee had never been put in writing, nobody at the network did or ever would deny it. Realistically speaking, however, such an understanding could not be enforced if a network felt that rescheduling was in its best interests.

"We're a family show," she protested, upset and repeating herself. "If you moved us to a school night like Thursday, the youngsters wouldn't be able to watch."

Young people, in fact, were what this was all about. Angela's agent, Jerry Katzman, understood that CBS's proposal was merely a fact of life in television:

> The ratings are an ego thing. The top ten list means more in terms of prestige than in terms of profit. It's impossible to explain that to most any performer but the advertisers pay a lot

> more money for audience demographics in the eighteen to forty-nine range, and they'll pay twice as much money for eighteen through thirty-nine. Even with lower ratings.

The situation, Angela says, "did not become emotional or acrimonious. I never lost my cool or flew into a screaming fit. That's not my style. The situation was very emotional for me, but I wasn't going to let *them* know that. It was a matter of business. I was on the last year of a two-year deal, so that meant that the following fall, after going to Thursday night, the show would go *boom!*"

Even so, she left for Ireland "hoping that there would be a last-minute reprieve" but of course one never came. When she got back, she made a lunch date with Leslie Moonves, who had in the meantime replaced Tortorici as new head of CBS Television for the West Coast. She knew that Moonves hadn't had anything to do with the time switch.

A Thursday night time slot, she pointed out, "puts me in a no-win situation. I can't go head to head with *Friends*." NBC's new hit series was aired the same evening as the country's top show (and Angela's personal favorite), *Seinfeld*, a combination that made Thursday a hugely popular comedy night for the opposing network. Competing was futile.

Moonves, who had come to television from the New York theater, was even more of a Lansbury fan than the rest of the CBS executives, but he knew that the decision was irrevocable. "Angela," he said, "other than moving you back to Sunday, which I cannot do, what *can* we do for you?"

The network did not have the capacity for guilt or gratitude, but it did sweeten Corymore's deal of deals to the extent of adding more television movies to the commitment. In exchange, Angela agreed to continue the show for at least another season, but when the time switch was announced, "the outcry from the viewers," she says, "was gargantuan. Inwardly I was seething but I'd been on the air for eleven years at that point. You get on with it, but I thought, 'I'll play out this last year, and that's it.'"

It was, and so concluded the weekly habit, her rhythmic coexistence with the vast television public.

CHAPTER 21

LIFE AFTER *MURDER, SHE WROTE*

SHE WAS always emotional at the end of a project, whether it was a movie or a stage production, but the end of *Murder, She Wrote* was more than the end of production on a movie, and it followed a longer run than *Mame*. The television series had been her way of life for twelve years.

> I didn't want to work on the final day of production. The emotion was too much. I couldn't have gotten through it. I couldn't have said my lines. It would have been impossible for me to do it. The last day that I did work, I stayed afterward on the set, I remained with the crew. . . . The last scene that I actually did on the series was an insert of the actor Gregg Henry putting a key in my pocket. . . . I wept all through it, but the audience will never know.

Even though there were still going to be *Murder, She Wrote* television movies, she wrote a "Goodbye from Jessica" to her television audience, and it was shown onscreen at the end of the last episode on Thursday, May 8, 1996. She read it as a voice-over. "Tonight on *Murder, She Wrote*, you have watched our last and final *weekly* episode. My gratitude and appreciation to all of you, our last and great family of viewers who along with me have solved two hundred and sixty-four murder mysteries over twelve great years. With love, Jessica Fletcher."

The last program concluded with a still picture of Angela Lansbury, holding the letter in her hand, gazing at it and smiling, and it is hardly surprising that she used the device of a letter to bid farewell to her audience of twelve years. She has been a letter writer all her life.

It had taken a dozen years to shake the fan who had been pestering Angela. She felt partly responsible, having made the mistake of answering the young woman's first letter. She finally screwed up the nerve to write a five-page letter of rejection.

> I'm glad to detect a new note of maturity in your attitude — the fact that you understand that for all these years you have indeed been conducting a virtual one way "fan" relationship by way of letters and attention to me, which is in fact the fan psychology to bring attention to *yourself.* If you truly want to get to Broadway . . . you're going to have to disassociate your theatrical career from me. . . . Most young people in our business who get ahead don't keep talking about what they're doing. They just get on with it. This is the difference between the amateur approach and the professional. I know this is a tough letter, but "Mrs. Shaw" is a tough lady, or I wouldn't be who I am today!

More than once, Angela had felt creepy about this fan, and sometimes a bit frightened. Happily, her letter succeeded and the aspiring actress went away. ("I never heard from her again.")

Whether the letter was to a fan, to her discharged dresser, or to her national *Murder, She Wrote* audience, letter writing was a habitual, an important, even an essential mode of communication for Angela Lansbury. She inherited the habit from her mother and continued to practice it long after personal correspondence had gone out of style. It made no difference to her that in a computer age writing by hand was considered laborious and anachronistic. If typewriters and long-distance telephones had not tempted her to cut back on her handwritten letters, e-mail wasn't likely to succeed, either. Jessica Fletcher might have switched from a typewriter to a word processor, but Jessica Fletcher was not *exactly* the same person as Angela Lansbury.

Angela used to write to her mother and to Isolde and to her children; she still wrote to friends. A lifetime earlier, as a contract player for MGM, she would occasionally enclose notes with autographed pictures. When she was a musical comedy star on Broadway, she would respond to especially touching letters from people who had seen the show. She wrote to fellow cast members in gratitude and in farewell when a play was closing.

Writing a letter always seemed to her the most personal way of expressing feelings and thoughts, and the clearest and most cogent way to say something that was on her mind. Yet, at the same time, there was something *impersonal* about personal correspondence. It made for a detached relationship, a one-at-a-time conversation conducted without interruption, allowing for the preparation of thoughts and fully formed statements. A letter was, in the complete sense of the word, *composed*, and it was also impassive. Its voice was never raised, its writer's expression unseen.

If these were psychological advantages, others were practical. A letter could be revised, rewritten, not mailed, even destroyed. She herself would write first drafts of even her most personal notes. They would be filled with scratch-outs and write-overs, then neatly copied over before being mailed, so that there was no risk of overstatement or misstatement, or accidental self-revelation. The originals were saved for records.

That is the essential Angela Lansbury. Meticulous. Cautious. Self-editing. Deliberate. It is what the British call reserved, what psychologists call inhibited, what diplomats call tactful, what the genteel call discreet, what the conservative call private, what gamblers call poker-faced, and what anyone might consider self-controlled. At best, it is maturity, and all of those qualities apply. They are the same qualities of preparation and deliberation that underlie her acting.

Her personal stationery is likewise revealing in its various guises, reflecting different identities and roles to play. The stationery comes not just in different sizes and colors, but with different letterheads. Some is embossed with a replica of her signature, "Angela Lansbury." Some is engraved with a simple "Angela." Some comes with her complete married initials, "A.L.S.," for Angela Lansbury Shaw. And there is some that is genderless, marked "A. L. Shaw," which is also the way she hand-writes her return address on an envelope, or sends a mail order.

These are the various names by which Angela Lansbury has lived, the roles she has assumed in her own life — as actress, wife, and mother — keeping each of them in balance so that one does not outweigh the other. As for *Murder, She Wrote* having made her into a star personality, she would ultimately come back to seeing herself as a character actress. She realized that her huge television audience identified her with Jessica Fletcher, but being an actress meant more to her. Once the show was over, she became Angela Lansbury, actress, once more, or so she insisted. For twelve years, she said, she'd been playing Jessica Beatrice Fletcher.

But for twelve years, hadn't Jessica Beatrice Fletcher been Angela Lansbury?

Her brother Bruce believes that this conflict goes to her essence, but sees it as an ambiguity. "In Jessica," he says, "she found a character that people loved so much that they made her a star. She played that character, that is what an actress does and it's why she thinks of herself not as a star but as an actress.

"It is a fascinating distinction."

As to her self-editing and reserved nature, it does not qualify the genuineness of her warmth. Angela Lansbury is as concerned, as sensitive, and as sympathetic as anyone might want in a friend. It is just that while she can offer compassion, she cannot readily give of herself. "I don't have a best friend," she says. "I never did," and she adds, genuinely puzzled, "why would I?"

Even though she would explain that many of her friendships foundered because people couldn't grasp exactly how busy her work kept her, the truth was that she gave work — which in her mind meant good, disciplined, well-prepared work — a higher priority than friendship. As for the family unit, that is her private universe. "My husband. My children," she says. "They are my best friends."

Life after *Murder, She Wrote* began with an indulgence of her grandmotherhood. Angela was "Grange" to Lee and Anthony's three children, and she was enjoying it. "I don't get a tremendous number of calls to babysit," she says, "but we do try and involve each other as much as possible."

Anthony says, "My mother and I have a tremendous relationship, one of trust. She's happy for me and my life, my marriage and my kids." He had become a strong family man, a protective and even conservative father. "I find myself parenting in a strict way," he says, "diametrically opposed to the way my parents did. Which is interesting. But I suppose that's what one does."

Deirdre, who had been living in Europe with her husband, Enzo, came home and started a restaurant called "Positano" near Santa Monica. Everyone in the family invested in it, "and," Angela says, "it was charming. [It closed in 1996.] The two of them created this lovely ambience. Deeds decided to have these murals, and there were colored tablecloths from Positano — not just on the tables but hanging overhead, to bring the high ceilings down."

As for her own work, Lansbury had been at it for more than fifty years, sometimes because she had to, but always because she wanted to. She loved her homemaking, her mothering, her gardening, but she was also an actor, and had to do that, too. That she was entering her seventies was irrelevant to her. It didn't matter that her family's financial security was now certain. The will and energy were still there. As her agent, Jerry Katzman of William Morris, said, "It doesn't make a difference to Angela that Corymore [Productions] already has a full plate. She has to get on the other end of that camera."

And so even while *Murder, She Wrote* was still in production during its final season, she began preparations for a television movie to be made immediately afterward, a musical with a Jerry Herman score. It was one of the extras that CBS had agreed to in exchange for the switch to Thursday nights. She wasn't sure that she really wanted to do a television musical, and she told the composer that she was worried about not having sung for such a long time. She was also concerned about the way her *Murder, She Wrote* audience would respond to Jessica Fletcher singing. But now there was a transcending concern: Jerry Herman had for some time been HIV-positive, and there was concern that he might now be suffering from full-blown AIDS. Angela told her stepson, David, "He doesn't think he's going to live much longer. He needs something. He's crying out, and we can help him."

Herman had originally wanted her to do *Mame* for television, believing that she could still carry it off, and her husband agreed, but "she just didn't want to do it," her agent Katzman says. "She felt too old for it," and she told him, "I want to do something for Jerry. It just can't be *Mame*."

The composer revived the idea of *Mrs. Santa Claus*, an original musical for television that she had rejected two years earlier ("There's no character here — nobody at home. It's a piece of fluff"). Even his musical director, Don Pippin, thought "it was a little bit like *Sesame Street*." But the composer pointed out that the script had been rewritten to underline feminist themes and to develop a husband-and-wife relationship between Mr. and Mrs. Claus.

Angela was still not overly impressed, but she found the revised script acceptable. "I knew a lot of my Broadway friends would think it was corny, but that didn't bother me. I've always compartmentalized myself, doing this for one audience and that for another."

As work on the movie was about to start in August of 1996, Jerry Herman celebrated his sixty-fourth birthday with a party at his magnificent home in Bel-Air. Looking frail and frighteningly pale, he went out to the terrace to greet Angela, his old friend from *Mame* and *Dear World*. "She is a legend, now," he thought. "The great lady of television. One of the richest women in the business." She turned from the people who'd surrounded her, and gave him a hug. "Isn't this exciting!" he said. "We're going to be working together again." And they stood together, watching, as Eydie Gormé was urged toward the grand piano that had been moved out of doors. The crowd gathered around as she prepared to sing "If He Walked into My Life," with the desperately ill composer standing before her, and he remembers,

> Before she sang it, she said, "You know, everybody, this wasn't my song. I didn't introduce it. I just made a record of it. The great lady over here, Angela Lansbury, she introduced it in *Mame*." And Eydie held out a hand. Angie came over to the piano and Gormé suggested that they sing it together. Now Eydie Gormé is a great singer and still sings it in her nightclub act, but I bet Angela hadn't done this song in twenty years. I thought, no, she's not going to sing it. She's going to go up there and kind of kibbitz around but she's not going to sing that song. She's going to let Eydie Gormé sing it. But no, and you know what? She outsang Eydie Gormé.

Jerry Herman had just begun taking protease inhibitors, the medical "cocktail" that was a new and seemingly only hope for late-stage AIDS sufferers. "I truly believe," Angela says, "that he felt he had only another year to live, if that."

With this grim foreboding, rehearsals began for a Christmas musical with sleighs and snow, made in the thick of a blistering August hot spell in southern California. The script, by Mark Saltzman and Robert L. Freedman, centers on a frustrated Mrs. Santa Claus, "the invisible wife" of the benevolently sexist husband she calls "Nick" (Charles Durning as a generally offstage Santa). It seems that he expects his wife to serve cocoa rather than participate in the Christmas workload. Needing a breather from solitary Christmas Eves, she takes her husband's legendary sleigh for a joyride, and sets down by chance on the Lower East Side of Manhattan. It is the turn of the century, and the neighborhood is stocked with colorful immigrants.

When she notices that one of the reindeer (Cupid) has injured a leg while landing, she has a reason to stay for a week. It is no vacation. What follows are Irish cops who give precinct Christmas parties, Jewish immigrants who dance the hora, suffragettes who sing as they picket, and children who scamper through factory sweatshops where they labor to make toys of inferior quality. The show, in short, is a blend of *Oliver Twist* and *Annie*, in every way a Hallmark Greeting Card Presentation. At the end of its two hours, Mrs. Claus has not only furthered an interethnic romance, but helped to reform child labor conditions. Even more remarkably, Angela Lansbury has managed to slog through the two hours of theme park kitsch with her talent not only intact but triumphant. If *Mrs. Santa Claus* demonstrates anything positive at all, it is the classic quality and indomitable performing integrity of its leading lady.

Television musicals had long been out of fashion. This one's songs are in the Broadway vernacular, with lyrics that are occasionally embarrassing ("There's a pushcart full of bagels coming your way"). However, some of the melodies have the catchiness and verve of Jerry Herman at his most musically endearing, and one song is quite wonderful, the ballad, "He Needs Me," a reminder of the tunefulness, the unaffectedness, and the open heart that have made this composer the natural successor to Irving Berlin. Lansbury sings the big ballad to a fare-thee-well but, "Someone told me later," she says disappointedly, "Jerry'd written it years ago. They all do that. Everything's in the trunk." She always minded it when composers dug out old material — most performers do.

Herman continued to work throughout the making of the movie and, she says, "he never for one moment revealed to me any of the pain and suffering that I'm sure he must have been going through. He was so bound and determined to keep going, keep producing, to keep up his interest. I felt he would work himself into a terrible emotional state sometimes and that was hard to deal with because we felt so for him. You knew what he was going through, you knew how ill that 'cocktail' made him feel. But he never betrayed, really, at any time, what those physical symptoms were. He covered them. He worked through them. It was so important for him to finish and provide us with the material we needed for the show; and for him to have this wonderful example of his talent at this time."

Mrs. Santa Claus was broadcast in December 1996. "It wasn't so well received out in Los Angeles," Angela says, "but I'm often not well received here. I was very grateful for the good review in the *New York Times.*" More important, the show was a major ratings success, and CBS immediately contracted to run it again the following Christmas.

Best of all, Jerry Herman responded beautifully to the combination of AIDS drugs. He gained weight, his color returned, and his blood cell count soared. "His excitement and relief," Angela says, "that he possibly had the rest of his life to live was so overwhelming to him. He was a man who had been given this incredible bonus."

Angela, very healthy and rarely ill, looks wonderful in the show, but the schedule, her brother Bruce says, had been "crushing." The costumes were heavy, the rehearsals were strenuous, and the heat was unrelenting. As often as possible, she had retreated to her air-conditioned trailer, but immediately after recording the songs, she woke up in the middle of the night in a cold sweat, "with my heart either pounding or running a mile a minute."

She was experiencing a recurrence of the fibrillations that occurred years earlier, and Peter rushed her to the hospital. It was only an overnight stay, and she wrote off the incident as unimportant, but her brother knew better. A month later, she suffered another episode.

"Only when something like that happens," Bruce says, "does she get scared enough to take it easy. We all said to her, 'Who the hell do you think you are? You've got to slow down. You've got a body you've got to take care of.' She's as strong as nails, but I would get scared, too."

She started to indulge in the rare-for-her pleasure of free time. She'd worked since she was seventeen. She now took time out for domestic chores. "I love shopping," she shamelessly admits, whether it is shopping for food at the supermarket or buying toys for the grandchildren. Customers at Toys R Us were startled to see her browsing in the tots section, much like any other grandmother.

"I go to the big hardware stores, the lumber company, the florist." Invariably, there are compliments and requests for autographs, but, she says,

"I refuse to allow my visibility to interfere with my free actions. Occasionally I will say, 'Thank you very much for your interest. Please forgive me. I am here because I have to shop. I have to buy something."

> People are always so well-meaning. They always think they're the only persons who are doing this to you. They don't know that in every supermarket or department store, somebody has done it, so you have to try and deal with them gently. Don't make them feel that you're putting them down or that you don't appreciate their interest. But you always hope that people who do see you around and about, going about the business of shopping, buying socks for your husband or buying sheets, will have the sensitivity to know that that's all you're doing and that you're not *on*. You're not on the stage, you're not there on the screen, and that this is the woman who's there and not the actress.
>
> That's one of the things I've worked hardest at — not allowing such things to intervene in my life. I simply don't encourage any behavior from anybody that smells of dealing with me in a different way because I'm a celebrity. As far as I'm concerned, I'm a person and they're a person and I don't want them to deal with me any differently and I don't want to have to deal with *them* any differently than I would if I were anyone else.

She takes time to savor the slowing down and enjoy domesticity. "I cannot bear having live-in help, people around me all the time. I want the house to ourselves. I want to feel that *our* atmosphere is pervasive, not some maid saying, 'When do you want me to serve the dinner?' because she wants to go home. I don't want that. My sense of home is peace and quiet. Aloneness with the people I love is more important than having somebody serving the meal. I'd rather do it all myself. Looking after the house, cleaning, the laundry, and all those things."

She isn't ready to call the Brentwood house her final home. "I don't want to be living in this house when I'm ninety years old, I want to have a house that has a couple of acres around it. I want to have an orchard and a garden and people to do the work along with me. That is how I think. But Peter doesn't think that way."

Like so many men, he is a creature of habit, comfortable with things staying exactly as they've been. "So," she says, "we have a problem about houses and the way we live, y'know."

She also has a physical reason for moving. It has to do with age, with her flowers, and with the sharp slope of the garden in the back of the house. She has had both hips replaced with artificial ones and finds that "The gardening gets difficult here because it's on a slope and climbing up and down the steps all the time, bent over, is tiring. It would be nice to walk out on the flat. As for the house, I appreciate it," she says, "but from a woman's point of view, it's too small. Do Pete and I fight over that? No, although we do have conversations where I nudge and push. But even if I say, 'Well, why don't we add on a room over there?' he'll say, 'I think it's great just the way it is.' That's very frustrating.

"The days go by," she says with contentment and just a trace of restlessness.

CHAPTER 22

IN HER OWN WORDS

MY TALENT

I have to use it terribly carefully and I've always tried to do that. Never to sort of spread myself thin. I do cherish it and I try to take care of it and I never just splodge it around. I had to use it indiscriminately at one time for the purposes of making money to put food on the table but beyond that, when I finally reached the point where I didn't have to work except for the joy of it, I've been picky about what I do.

It was all gift. Not hard work. You are born with it. Absolutely. Actors are not made, they are born. What they do with it, that's up to them. And you've got to recognize that you have it in the first place and you don't mess around with it. You don't waste it, you don't put it to the wrong tests. You have to understand what you can handle and what you can do. But you build on it, once you know it's there. I had to learn an awful lot of technical things along the way that I didn't have in the beginning. You can add to it, embellish it, learn how to use it.

Having that rock at the center has been my salvation, because even though, to outward appearances, mine has been a life filled with success and happiness and joy and laughter and attainment, what was going on behind the apparent joys and happiness was in fact a war of turmoil; in some instances terrible tragedy of good intentions and having to deal with that in my own private life — *our* private life. The only way I could deal with it was by having this rock which represented stability. The one thing I knew that was right and true and possible. A repeating ability to produce a result which kept me always in the forefront artistically if I was doing something that was meaningful and had substance.

FEMININITY

I've been accused of having balls. There is a difference between tough-minded and a tough woman like an agent or a producer. Women don't in the main find themselves in situations where they can be strong. Society simply doesn't allow them to. Men don't allow them to, and it's a male-driven society. Therefore, women — if they are strong — are always the exception. Whereas, it should be the norm. Because women, I think, as a whole, *are very strong.* Are stronger. And they end up having to hold everything together. And they live longer, too. That's a big difficulty for them, I think. Because they lose their mates, sometimes, before they're ready to go — and then have to sort of devise another life to continue. The women who never learned to take care of themselves — they end up as bag ladies of one kind or another — in retirement homes or in nursing homes.

I often think like a man, but I also think like a women. It means that I think of doing things that men usually do, that other woman would not think of doing. Making things, doing things, picking up hammers. Taking over jobs that men used to do.

ENERGY

I think energy is one of the tremendous adjuncts that was given to me at a very early age. People are tremendously attracted to people who have that energy; who have a light, who have buoyancy and an ebullience about them — an enthusiasm. This is true in my case. Very often people just want to stick close by because they want to kind of bask in that energy and excitement.

I find light extraordinarily exciting. I'm so excited sometimes when I get up in the morning, simply by the light. The brilliance and the energy of the day, whether it's in California or in Ireland or in a garden — it's a moment of absolute exultation that I feel. What it is — is it's a welling of energy, and I can find it at the damnedest moments. It's marvelous if you're fortunate enough to be one of those people — and there are millions upon millions of people who feel the same way as I do. But there are many who don't feel that; who feel that life is just one tremendous problem to be dealt with and overcome.

That isn't their fault. I think a lot of it is just genetic. I think a lot of *my* energy comes from my genes; from my grandfather, George Lansbury, who led an extraordinary life of activity. Talk about energy, this man walked in his early days when he was speaking — he would walk all the way to his house in Bow from the train station because nothing was running. He was tremendously strong. His energy was absolutely boundless.

The energy that actors use. When somebody comes on stage and *takes stage* and says their lines . . . that is energy.

ON LOOKS

I certainly never considered myself beautiful, not to this day. But I know now how to put myself together; I know *how* to be an attractive woman when I want to be. And I do want to be an attractive woman, but I want to do it on my terms. I don't want to be like somebody else, so I found that individual look for myself in *Mame.* And kept it for many years.

I never look at my old movies. When I do, I think, "What a plain woman I was." I suffered from a certain lack of self-regard in the looks department.

TELEVISION

Seinfeld — I love it. It absolutely gives me the best laughs. I laugh out loud. I used to enjoy *Roseanne* — she was really intelligent. Bright. I watch PBS all the time. I used to watch *Masterpiece Theater.* With the reduction of money subsidies, I'm sorry to say they haven't been able to do as much as in the old days.

I think laughter is the greatest tonic in the world. The best drug. It's terribly important for your heart, did you know that? My mother was full of jokes, some of the best dirty stories. I sure do like a good dirty story. Bea [Arthur] is the one who provides me with them. I can't remember them, I'm very, very bad at that.

KEEPING HOUSE

Where men think about cars or stereos or making money, women think about making homes or houses. I am what they call an "earth person." I'm very rooted to the ground as far as my physical being is concerned; my mental being can soar and fly and imagine and I use that, but to enable me to do that, I've found that I need to be very much in touch with the soil, the ground, with growing things, with very basic, rather boring creature comforts: a home, an environment that was warm and encompassing— not just for myself but for all those that I love; my family around me.

I always wanted to create this sort of nest of necessity. Where I've gone, wherever I've been, I've always carried some of that on my back. If I was on tour, I took a whole kitchen.

I love making beds. There's a whole art in that. I have magnificent pure linen sheets from Ireland. I wash them in the machine and iron them on the dining room table, which I cover with a blanket. I love ironing. The only problem with linen is that it's impossible to keep unrumpled. You have to change the sheets every day. I don't, of course. I just lie flat, perfectly still, in a little section of my bed. I don't move.

I try to be organized. I make lists. I'm sort of driven to a certain extent by lack of order; I hate things to be out of order. It still doesn't mean that I can find anything, you understand, but I'm organized to the point of— well, I'm not very good at filing and tabulating, but I make a hell of a stab at it.

ROSES

I love roses. I think I got that from Moyna. I'll talk roses with anyone, and I wish I had the time to learn how to really prune them. They have to be tended, and fed, and pruned once a year. Back in California, it's difficult gardening, because they never really want to go into a dormant state. In the East or in Ireland — in the cold climates — by the time the fall comes, and they've done their whole job all through the summer, when the weather starts to get cold, the roses stop performing. In very severe winters you have to cover them with burlap and chippings to prevent them from getting killed by the frost. The snow doesn't bother them, but the frost does. They can freeze, and if they freeze right down into the roots, down into the ground, then they die. So you have to cover them.

I buy them from catalogs. Red roses, pink roses, yellow, white. I'm all enthusiast and no expert. When I'm away I have a man who maintains the garden in California. I leave instructions about how they're taken care of.

In Ireland, we planted a lot of roses — rambling roses that grow over the top of the stone walls.

WORK COMPULSION

So one of my failings as a human being, in my own estimation, is that I never learned to do anything except work. Really. Keep house and work, that's what I know how to do. Play? I don't know how to play. Never have. Just don't know how to do it. It's a failing, as far as I'm concerned. I feel as if I've missed a hell of a lot. It all goes back, I suppose, to early years of having responsibilities foisted upon me by certain events. My mother's widowhood. I just always had to be a responsible person. Who could be there on time. Who could be relied upon. Who would deliver the goods. Who would be successful. Who would make a lot of money. Who would have a family. And go through all of the motions of living life and being apparently, to all intents and purposes, very very dependable.

I mean my whole life, my whole career has been a mixture of wanting to work and not wanting to work; wanting to go back to the woods; wanting to get back in the mainstream. I'm constantly at odds with myself as to what I really want to do to be happy. And it's fascinating, really. But as I say, as I've matured I've learned to understand and live with this, because it's who I am.

RELATING TO OTHER PEOPLE

It depends on where your focus is at the time; how aware — how *self*-conscious you are. How conscious you are of yourself in relation to the people you're dealing with. How you perceive them, and, let's face it, my perception of something may be totally different from others. Well that's obvious.

I'm very forgiving but at the same time I don't put up with people's weaknesses. I certainly don't put up with their flaws. I try to sieve those people out of my daily life. I don't make it a practice to consort with people who have traits I don't agree with, don't approve of — dishonesty, small-mindedness, etc. I don't like to use the word "approve," but I guess at my age I can.

I tend to be judgmental but keep it to myself. I try to be nonjudgmental and try to see both sides. I'm very encumbered with the ability to see both sides of everything. Which puts me smack in the middle sometimes, and I find it very hard to decide. If I disagree on something, I can see the other person's point of view constantly.

MONEY

It's not a big thing to me. It does represent security. I'm not a great collector. I don't collect paintings. I collect comfort. I like to surround myself with a very kind-of-cozy house. At some times in my life, I've *put on the dog,* as they say, and had a decorator help and do a house. That was the 1950s and I enjoyed doing that. And that was what everybody was about, keeping up with the Joneses. Yes, Peter and I did that along with the rest of our friends. Cars were important. I loved cars. I always had the best. I had a Mark VII Jaguar. I still love them. Because of my gardening, I have a station wagon — a Volvo — but often I would like to have a two-door sports car. I bought the new Volvo sports coupe and then traded it in for the same model in a convertible.

PERSONAL REPUTATION

I'm known as such a goody-goody, just the greatest person. What they don't understand is that I've worked at it. I *have* to get along with people. I cannot work in an atmosphere of friction and misunderstanding. So to make my relationships with the people I work with smooth and wonderful, I go out of my way to try and make them happy. They don't make me happy.

I've got this reputation for being a superwoman. My audience and the press perceive me that way. It has a great deal to do with the roles I've played in the last thirty years. Prior to that, no. And I would think very hard before playing an unpleasant character again. Depending on the role. I don't want to lose a whole audience at this point. I'm very happy the way I am.

Being a role model does get on my nerves. It's a hell of a mantle to support, to be thought of as this terrifically good person. Balanced. Reliable. Moral. Kindly. Dignified. All those things. Those are things that have come upon me without me doing anything about it. I've never changed. I'm just the same person I've always been.

But I'm not that person, Jessica. Of course I understand why I am perceived that way. It would take an extraordinary individual not to feel a sense of responsibility to a given image or conception of how people perceive you. However, there is nothing to take credit for when it is a modus operandi which seemed perfectly normal and natural. One never encouraged people to take this extraordinary attitude toward one. Sometimes, too, it was behavior for rather selfish reasons. Just because I'm an easy person to work with, people think I'm very nice. But I'm doing what I like to do, so it's a quid pro quo.

I do care about people's feelings terribly, I really do. I think it's because I'm so desperately worried about my own. So I go overboard and bend over backward. I have great difficult losing my temper; however, as I'm getting older I lose my cool quicker with ineptness, stupidity, and carelessness, with certain young people that I'm working with, sometimes.

So there's two sides to the coin. On the one hand, people say, "Oh, she's so nice." The minute I demand some kind of performance from people they say, "Oh, she's becoming uppity." Nothing to do with that. I was asking for performance from people in the crafts departments — Hair, Makeup. I'm tough with those people and many of them like it; they're very pleased to learn from somebody, particularly the young ones coming into the business. These days, our standards have lowered so drastically.

DEALING WITH DISAPPROVAL

I've never really been aware that somebody truly disapproves of me. But if somebody gets angry with me, I'll be angry back if I feel the basis for their anger is unjust. Or unqualified. I'm not afraid to fight with anybody, but I very seldom find myself in such situations. I don't give people call to be angry with me. I'm very self-protective. I can't bear not to be liked; for people to think ill of me or less of me. I spend a hell of a lot of time at that. It's a lot of work. I could kick myself sometimes. I have great difficulty saying no because somebody will dislike me if I say no. There's no question in my mind that that's the root of why I bend over backward to be nice, and I think it's a problem for me. To a great extent. However, I've decided at this late age that the plusses make up for the minuses.

MARRIED LIFE

I've had an incredible marriage. I've spent a tremendous amount of my life being a wife. Looking after *stuff*. Domestic things. That is a very big part of my life. And that's the hardest part of the balancing act — to keep one's hand on that part of your existence. Women do — they have to think about — fifty thousand more things in the home than men do. And half the time, because of the difference between men and women, men don't realize how much has to be constantly thought through by women — to do with the domestic side of marriage. And the domestic side of the marriage is terribly important. The trick is to have a career and also be able to think about those things as well. And I think that most working actresses who have families, who have homes, will agree with me — that that's the other side of the coin. I love having a home and family; having a house, buying my husband clothes, all of those things. It isn't a conscious decision, it's just the way I am. That domestic side of me is something I inherited from my mother, my grandmother.

AGE

Everybody's ears get bigger. Yes. Mine are getting bigger and I used to have tiny little shell ears. I don't have little shell ears any more — I have much bigger ears.

I'm beginning now to realize the limitations that years do finally put on one, but in my mind I'm not any older than I've ever been. I still feel like a young woman in my mind. I've never lied about my age, anyway I never could because everybody always knew when I was born. But I guess I would be taken aback if somebody said I looked my age, or could guess it. I don't think that's necessary in this world. If somebody said I looked sixty, I'd be satisfied.

I don't consider that my day is over; there's lots more sunshine there. But I don't go looking for parts just to exercise my talents as an actress. Perhaps if I were a different kind of person, I would, but my interests are not one hundred percent acting. This is not the motor that drives me. The motor that drives me is the participation in life and it has to do with a lot more than just acting.

Birthdays have never been tough for me. Aging simply opens up new pages of possibilities. Age really doesn't have any bearing on my ability to look forward with joy.

REGRETS

I have had a good, varied life. The only thing I regret is that I've never gotten the opportunity to play a really great woman's role in the movies.

Someday, I want to play just one great movie role. And I'd like to one day buy forty acres of absolutely rural land someplace in America, which our family can fly to easily and have total privacy.

RETROSPECT

Looking back over my life, I regret not knowing more about the rest of the world — about not having been to certain places. I regret that I haven't taken time to relax more and enjoy what's out there. I'm very interested, on paper, in an awful lot of things, but I've never had the time — because of my marriage, the demands of the family, I've never been able to just take off and do a lot of things. But I've done a hell of a lot. But when you're lying in bed in the early hours of the morning, and start thinking about your life, you tend to think of the things you wish you had done. Yet, by any standard I've had a very rich life. And every year that you live, you change. Your attitude about your life — past, present, and future — changes. I'm quite sure there comes a time for reasons that you don't necessarily know now, you'll be very pleased to close the curtains and *fuck off.* You will have had enough.

I've had an incredible relationship with my husband, with my family. I know they've had problems of their own, but we have never wavered in our closeness as a family. I've had a hell of a life.

ACKNOWLEDGMENTS

THE RESEARCH for this book began before the research for this book began. The movie part started in my youth, with Angela Lansbury's first pictures, *Gaslight* and *The Picture of Dorian Gray.* The stage research began with her performance in *A Taste of Honey,* which I saw as an enthusiast, and it continued when I became a professional dramatic critic in 1963 and saw her every show. (No, I never gave her a bad review.)

Angela Lansbury herself was, of course, the most important source, and no biographical subject could have been more cooperative. She gave me weeks of concentrated time, spread over a full year. We taped interviews for four and six hours at a stretch, each session filled with useful information, recollections, and observations. Her family cooperated without hesitation or self-censorship. For that I am deeply grateful to her husband, Peter Shaw; her children, Deirdre Shaw Battara and Anthony Shaw; and to Peter's son David. Equally cooperative were Angela's brothers, Bruce and Edgar Lansbury, and the many friends and fellow actors whom she asked to share time with me. As for the dozens of sources I sought out alone, she never asked who they were or what they'd said.

Biographical research is not unlike detective work, and as there were many personal friends and professional colleagues to be interviewed, so each led to several others. Ultimately, about one thousand hours were spent conducting interviews over an eleven-month period. There is not a word of dialogue or any incident in this book that was not directly witnessed by at least one of these sources or another participant whose account appeared in print. I have all of them to thank and I am grateful for their time, their memories, and the pleasure of getting to know them a bit.

They include Arthur Laurents, Sondra Lee, Elaine Steinbeck, Gene Saks, Eli Wallach, Alexander H. Cohen, Nan Pearlman, Frank Military, Jane Connell, Arthur Cantor, Jay Presson Allen, Joseph Harris, Martin Charnin, Don Pippin, Terry Little, Diana Baffa-Brill, Barbara Matera, Dolores Childers, Nancy Hopewell, Jerry Herman, Bea Arthur, Lew Wasserman, Delbert Mann, Sheila Mack, John Bowab, Jack Hutto, Len Cariou, George Hearn, Robert Fryer, William Link, Ron Young, Martin Richards, Stephen Sondheim, Shirley Herz, Walter Grauman, Margaret Williams, Robert Mackintosh, Hurd Hatfield, Paul Gemignani, Freddy Wittop, Betty Comden, Allan Lewis, Ralph Lutrin, Harold Prince, Stephen Paley, Barry Brown, Onna White, Rex Reed, Waris Hussein, Sir Peter Ustinov, Heather Hanbury Brown, Les Moonves, Sir Peter Hall, Ruth Mitchell, Zella Merritt, Leslie Stahl, John Frankenheimer, Robert Van Skoyk, Robert O'Neill, Harvey Shepard, Vincent McVeety, Peter Fischer, Charles Schramm, Esmee Chandler, Jerry Katzman, Jean Stapleton, and acknowledgeable far from least, Katherine Wallace at Corymore Productions.

Once again, I took shameless advantage of the cooperative, knowing, and helpful staff at the Library of the Performing Arts at Lincoln Center. That place is home to a special community, whether we are professionals, writers, students, or mere patrons of the performing arts. We are all in love with show time, and it is very good to feel a part of that family.

My old pal and nemesis Genevieve Young yet again went over the manuscript of a book of mine with her knowing and dependably evil eye. Finally, I was lucky indeed to come back to Little, Brown after making my publishing debut there, some thirty fleeting years ago — and was luckier still to happen upon Rick Kot for my editor. At that critical job, he is the real thing in a time of ersatz, painstaking where others are perfunctory. He is a literary fellow with a love of show business and that was exactly what I needed. His assistant, Michael Liss, repeatedly demonstrated the potential to become an exceptional editor too. Finally, I am particularly grateful to Betty Power for not just the copyediting that helped keep my spelling, commas, grammar, and facts in order but also for her providing a final reaction to the manuscript from the viewpoint of a *Murder, She Wrote* aficionado, an admirer of Angela Lansbury, and, first of all, from the viewpoint of a woman.

CREDITS

THE ANGELA LANSBURY CAREER

MOVIES

1944

Gaslight, with Ingrid Bergman and Charles Boyer. Director, George Cukor, MGM.

National Velvet, with Elizabeth Taylor and Mickey Rooney. Director, Clarence Brown, MGM.

1945

The Picture of Dorian Gray, with Hurd Hatfield and George Sanders. Director, Albert Lewin, MGM.

1946

The Harvey Girls, with Judy Garland. Director, George Sidney, MGM.

The Hoodlum Saint, with Esther Williams and William Powell. Director, Norman Taurog, MGM.

Till the Clouds Roll By, with Judy Garland, Frank Sinatra, and Robert Walker. Director, Richard Whorf, MGM.

1947

The Private Affairs of Bel Ami. With George Sanders. Director, Albert Lewin, United Artists.

1948

Tenth Avenue Angel, with George Murphy and Margaret O'Brien. Director, Roy Rowland, MGM.

If Winter Comes, with Deborah Kerr and Walter Pidgeon. Director, Victor Saville, MGM.

State of the Union, with Katharine Hepburn and Spencer Tracy. Director, Frank Capra, MGM.

The Three Musketeers, with Gene Kelly and Lana Turner. Director, George Sidney, MGM.

1949

The Red Danube, with Walter Pidgeon and Ethel Barrymore. Director, George Sidney, MGM.

Samson and Delilah, with Hedy Lamarr and Victor Mature. Director, Cecil B. DeMille, Paramount.

1951

Kind Lady, with Maurice Evans and Ethel Barrymore. Director, John Struges, MGM.

1952

Mutiny, with Mark Stevens. Director, Edward Dmytryk, United Artists.

1953

Remains to Be Seen, with June Allyson and Van Johnson. Director, Don Weis, MGM.

1955

A Life at Stake, with Keith Andes. Director, Paul Guilfoyle, Filmmakers.

A Lawless Street, with Randolph Scott. Director, Joseph Lewis, Columbia.

The Purple Mask, with Tony Curtis. Director, Bruce Humberstone, Universal International.

1956

Please Murder Me, with Raymond Burr. Director, Peter Godfrey, Distributors Corporation of America.

The Court Jester, with Danny Kaye, Basil Rathbone, and Glynis Johns. Director, Norman Panama, Paramount.

1958

The Long Hot Summer, with Joanne Woodward, Paul Newman, and Orson Welles. Director, Martin Ritt, Twentieth Century–Fox.

The Reluctant Debutante, with Kay Kendall and Rex Harrison. Director, Vincente Minnelli, MGM.

1959

Season of Passion, with Anne Baxter and Ernest Borgnine. Director, Leslie Norman, United Artists.

1960

The Dark at the Top of the Stairs, with Dorothy McGuire and Robert Preston. Director, Delbert Mann, Warner Bros.

A Breath of Scandal, with Sophia Loren and Maurice Chevalier. Director, Michael Curtiz, Paramount.

1961

Blue Hawaii, with Elvis Presley. Director, Norman Taurog, Paramount.

1962

All Fall Down, with Eva Marie Saint and Warren Beatty. Director, John Frankenheimer, MGM.

The Manchurian Candidate, with Frank Sinatra and Laurence Harvey. Director, John Frankenheimer, United Artists.

1963

In the Cool of the Day, with Jane Fonda and Peter Finch. Director, Robert Stevens, MGM.

1964

The World of Henry Orient, with Peter Sellers. Director, George Roy Hill, United Artists.

1965

Dear Heart, with Geraldine Page and Glenn Ford. Director, Delbert Mann, Warner Bros.

The Greatest Story Ever Told, with Charlton Heston and Dorothy McGuire. Director, George Stevens, United Artists.

The Amorous Adventures of Moll Flanders, with Kim Novak. Director, Terence Young, Paramount.

Harlow, with Carroll Baker. Director, Gordon Douglas, Paramount.

1966

Mr. Buddwing, with James Garner and Jean Simmons. Director, Delbert Mann, MGM.

1970

Something for Everyone, with Michael York. Director, Harold S. Prince, National General Pictures.

1971

Bedknobs and Broomsticks, with Roddy McDowell. Director, Robert Stevenson, Buena Vista.

1978

Death on the Nile, with Bette Davis, Mia Farrow, and Peter Ustinov. Director, John Guillermin, EMI/Paramount.

1979

The Lady Vanishes, with Cybill Shepherd and Elliott Gould. Director, Anthony Page, Hammer/Rank.

1980

The Mirror Crack'd, with Elizabeth Taylor, Rock Hudson, Tony Curtis, and Kim Novak. Director, Guy Hamilton, EMI/Associated Film Distribution.

1982

The Last Unicorn (animated). With voices of Jeff Bridges and Mia Farrow. Directors, Arthur Rankin, Jr., and Jules Bass, ITC.

1983

The Pirates of Penzance, with Kevin Kline and Linda Ronstadt. Director, Wilford Leach, Universal.

1984

The Company of Wolves, with David Warner. Director, Neil Jordan, Cannon.

1991

Beauty and the Beast (animated). Buena Vista.

1996

Anastasia (animated). 20th Century-Fox.

TELEVISION DRAMAS AND GUEST APPEARANCES

1950

Robert Montgomery Presents, "The Citadel."
Lux Video Theater, "The Wonderful Night."

1952

Lux Video Theater, "Operation Weekend."
"Stone's Throw."

1953

Robert Montgomery Presents, "Cakes and Ale."
Revlon Mirror Theatre, "Dreams Never Lie."
Ford Television Theater, "The Ming Lama."
Playhouse of Stars, "Storm Swept."

1954

Four Star Playhouse, "A String of Beads."
GE Theater, "The Crime of Daphne Rutledge."
"*The George Gobel Show.*"

1955

Fireside Theater, "The Indiscreet Mrs. Jarvis."
Four Star Playhouse, "Madeira, Madeira."
Stage Seven, "Bully and the Bride."
Rheingold Theater, "The Treasure."

1956

Studio 57, "The Rarest Stamp."
Rheingold Theater, "The Force of Circumstances."
Front Row Center, "The Instant of Truth."
Screen Directors Playhouse, "Claire."
Studio 57, "The Brown Leather Case."

1957

Climax, "The Devil's Brood."

1958

Playhouse 90, "Verdict of Three."

1959

Playhouse 90, "The Grey Nurse Said Nothing."

1963

Eleventh Hour, "Something Crazy's Going on in the Back Room."

1964

The Perry Como Thanksgiving Show.

1965

The Man from U.N.C.L.E., "The Deadly Toys Affair."
Track of O'Brien, "Leave It to Me."
The Perry Como Christmas Show.

1973

The Julie Andrews Hour.

1975

The Story of the First Christmas Snow (animated).

1982

Sweeney Todd, the Demon Barber of Fleet Street.

1986

The Spencer Tracy Legacy.
Magnum, P.I., "Novel Connection."

TELEVISION MOVIES AND MINISERIES

1982

Little Gloria . . . Happy at Last, with Bette Davis and Martin Balsam. Directed by Waris Hussein.

1983

The Gift of Love: A Christmas Story, with Lee Remick. Directed by Delbert Mann.

1984

A Talent for Murder, with Laurence Olivier. Directed by Alvin Rakoff.
Lace, with Brooke Adams and Bess Armstrong. Directed by Billy Hale.

1986

Rage of Angels: The Story Continues, with Ken Howard and Jaclyn Smith. Directed by Paul Wendkos.

1988

Shootdown, with George Coe and John Cullum. Directed by Michael Pressman.

1989

The Shell Seekers, with Sam Wanamaker and Irene Worth. Directed by Waris Hussein.

1990

The Love She Sought, with Denholm Elliott and Robert Prosky. Directed by Joseph Sargent.

1992

Mrs. 'arris Goes to Paris, with Diana Rigg and Omar Sharif. Directed by Anthony Shaw.

1996

Mrs. Santa Claus, with Charles Durning. Directed by Terry Hughes.

1997

South by Southwest (two-hour *Murder, She Wrote*). Directed by Anthony Shaw.

1998

The Unexpected Mrs. Pollifax. Directed by Anthony Shaw.

THE STAGE

1957

Hotel Paradiso, by Georges Feydeau, with Bert Lahr. Directed by Peter Glenville. Opened on April 12 at Henry Miller's Theatre.

1960

A Taste of Honey, by Shelagh Delaney, with Joan Plowright and Billy Dee Williams. Directed by Tony Richardson and George Devine. Opened October 4 at the Lyceum Theatre.

1964

Anyone Can Whistle, music and lyrics by Stephen Sondheim, book by Arthur Laurents. With Lee Remick and Harry Guardino, directed by Mr. Laurents. Opened April 4 at the Majestic Theater.

1966

Mame, music and lyrics by Jerry Herman, book by Jerome Lawrence and Robert E. Lee. With Bea Arthur and Jane Connell, directed by Gene Saks. Opened May 24 at the Winter Garden Theatre.

1969

Dear World, adapted by Maurice Valency from *The Madwoman of Chaillot* by Jean Giradoux. Music and lyrics by Jerry Herman, book by Jerome Lawrence and Robert E. Lee. With Milo O'Shea, Carmen Matthews, and Jane Connell, directed by Joe Layton. Opened February 6 at the Mark Hellinger Theatre.

1971

Prettybelle, music by Jule Styne, book and lyrics by Bob Merrill. With Charlotte Rae and Joe Morton, directed by Gower Champion. Opened in Boston, February 1, at the Shubert Theater.

1972

All Over, by Edward Albee, with Peggy Ashcroft, directed by Peter Hall. Opened January 31 at the Aldwych Theatre in London.

1973

Gypsy, music by Jule Styne, lyrics by Stephen Sondheim, book by Arthur Laurents. With Zan Charisse and Barrie Ingham, directed by Mr. Laurents. Opened May 29 at the Piccadilly Theatre in London.

1974

Gypsy, with Zan Charisse and Rex Robbins, opened September 24 at the Winter Garden Theatre.

1975

Hamlet, with Albert Finney, Susan Fleetwood, and Denis Quilley, directed by Peter Hall. Opened December 9 at the Old Vic in London.

1977

Counting the Ways and *Listening,* by Edward Albee. With William Prince and Maureen Anderman, directed by Mr. Albee. Opened January 28 at the Hartford Stage Company.

1979

Sweeney Todd, the Demon Barber of Fleet Street, music and lyrics by Stephen Sondheim, book by Hugh Wheeler. With Len Cariou and Victor Garber, directed by Harold Prince. Opened March 1 at the Uris Theater.

1982

A Little Family Business, by Jay Presson Allen. With John McMartin, Hallie Foote, and Anthony Shaw, directed by Martin Charnin. Opened December 15 at the Martin Beck Theatre.

INDEX